Teaching Thinking in Social Studies

Using Inquiry in the Classroom

A Revised Edition

Barry K. Beyer
Carnegie-Mellon University

Charles E. Merrill Publishing Company
A Bell & Howell Company
Columbus Toronto London Sydney

Published by
Charles E. Merrill Publishing Company
A Bell & Howell Company
Columbus, Ohio 43216

This book was set in Oracle, Paladium, and Charger.
The production editor was Lynn Copley-Graves.
The cover was prepared by Will Chenoweth.

Library of Congress Catalog Card Number: 79–83954

International Standard Book Number: 0–675–08280–3

1 2 3 4 5 6 7 8 9 10—85 84 83 82 81 80 79

Printed in the United States of America

Preface

This book is a completely rewritten and considerably expanded revision of my earlier book, *Inquiry in the Social Studies Classroom: A Strategy for Teaching*, first published in 1971. That volume began with the question: "What? Not another book on inquiry?" The same question seems as appropriate to ask of this revision as it was to ask of its predecessor. But the answer differs considerably, and in that answer lies the rationale for this new volume.

In the five years preceding the publication of my first book on inquiry, social studies education devoted considerable attention to inquiry and inquiry teaching. Scores of articles and books about these topics had been published during that period; innumerable curriculum projects and publishers had developed or were developing instructional materials and programs based on inquiry. In 1971 it appeared as if little of value could be added to this outpouring of information and material.

However, eight years ago I intended to accomplish what others had not yet done: to explain in detail the nature of inquiry and inquiry teaching (at least as I understood them) and to suggest some practical ways to implement both in social studies. Such an approach seemed especially appropriate because confusion and misunderstanding about inquiry teaching appeared to be limiting awareness of its potential and thus restricting its use in social studies classrooms. Therefore, my 1971 book summarized in part and built on the existing literature on inquiry. I intended to produce a practical book addressed to the needs of classroom teachers as I perceived them. This new volume seeks to provide even more in the way of practical suggestions for using inquiry teaching in the social studies classroom.

My initial book suffered from a number of significant omissions, however, especially in areas related to applying inquiry teaching to common classroom teaching tasks—areas such as values education, basic skills, and evaluation, for example. These omissions reflected, in part, my limited experience with inquiry teaching as well as the "state of the art" at the time. However, in the years since 1971, several social studies educators have explored to some depth how to apply inquiry teaching in these neglected areas. I, too, spent these years refining the use of this strategy relative to concept and skill teaching, for instance, and exploring other dimensions of the strategy, especially evaluation of inquiry learning and the design of inquiry lessons, courses, and curricula. This current volume attempts to close the gaps that existed in the original work.

Furthermore, the professional literature of the past few years has focused relatively little attention on inquiry teaching. Since 1971, the few books published on this teaching strategy have mostly stressed selected aspects of inquiry or inquiry teaching such as evaluating classroom interaction and integrating various teaching techniques with inquiry teaching. We still need to clearly relate inquiry teaching as a classroom strategy both to the nature of inquiry and to the various instructional goals sought by social studies teachers. *Teaching Thinking in Social Studies: Using Inquiry in the Classroom* speaks precisely to these needs.

This volume seeks to accomplish two major goals. For those somewhat familiar, or indeed expert, with a strategy of inquiry teaching, this volume provides the opportunity to review and reappraise what you are doing and hopefully offers insights into how you can use inquiry teaching to accomplish even more in your classrooms. For teachers as yet unfamiliar or unclear about the nature of this teaching strategy, this book provides a basis for understanding the nature of this strategy and its potential for facilitating learning in the social studies classroom.

In my half dozen years of exploring further the ideas expressed in my initial book about inquiry teaching, I spent much time refining and revising the elements of this strategy by repeated classroom application and reflection on this application. In a way, this book illustrates an attempt to practice what one preaches. It represents the product of a continuing inquiry into inquiry teaching. In no way does this book represent a final or definitive "answer," nor does it intend to be prescriptive.

This volume has both a point of view and a message. As the title implies, the point of view is that teaching thinking should be one of the major goals of social studies instruction today. Indeed, educators have long claimed critical thinking as one of the major objectives of the social studies. Unfortunately, however, over the past decades few social studies teachers have systematically taught students the skills of independent, rational thinking. Even those who use inquiry often fail to realize the connections between inquiry and thinking, between inquiry teaching and teaching students the skills of thinking. This book thus seeks to make explicit the relationships between inquiry teaching and thinking in order to more fully realize the classroom potential of inquiry teaching.

Attention to thinking as a skill essential for effective citizenship has never been of greater concern than it is today. Most social studies educators would undoubtedly echo Milton Eisenhower's assertion of a decade ago:

> As never before in our history we now need citizens who can reason objectively, critically and creatively within a moral framework; we need, in other words, a new breed of Americans who will devote as much time and energy to being *wise* democratic citizens as they do to being good physicians, engineers or businessmen.[1]

These remarks underscore the 1961 NEA position that the central purpose of formal education ought to be "development of the ability to think."[2] Since then, many social

---

[1] Milton Eisenhower quoted in "Ike's Brother Delivers Talk," *Columbus Dispatch,* June 9, 1968. (Italics mine)

[2] Educational Policies Commission, *The Central Purpose of American Education* (Washington: National Education Association, 1961), p. 12.

studies educators have endorsed this view, including former President of the National Council for the Social Studies, James P. Shaver, who noted in 1977:

> Thinking and rationality are vital to our society. . . . Analytic thinking is basic to citizenship in a society that assumes the right of all to participate in government. [3]

The message of this book is even more direct. One most effectively way to teach thinking in our classrooms is through inquiry teaching. Of all the teaching strategies used in our schools today, only inquiry teaching enables us to engage in rational thinking *while* we consciously and systematically learn the thinking processes and operations as well as the information we are using.

Since so many assert that learning to think is a viable goal of social studies education, we should be aware that the conventional, expository teaching strategies do not help us accomplish this goal. Expository teaching does not foster the ability to think; it merely teaches students *what* to think—or what to think about. Even requiring students to do things that make them think does not necessarily teach them the skills of thinking. Unless we systematically instruct students how to think within the context of specific subject matter, they simply cannot learn the skills of thinking. Inquiry teaching offers both the opportunity to think and a framework for providing instruction in thinking without interrupting the flow of substantive learning and without contradicting the very instructional approach being used.

The reasoning behind this book can thus be summed up in three premises:

1. Teaching our youth the processes and skills of systematic rational thinking is a major goal of formal education.
2. Teaching our youth the processes and skills of analytical thinking about individual and societal issues, concerns, and phenomena is a major goal of social studies education.
3. Of all the approaches to thinking that we can use to accomplish these goals, inquiry teaching is the most rewarding and most effective.

The preface to this book's predecessor attempted to explain this relationship between inquiry teaching and teaching students how to think:

> No longer is it possible to teach myriads of facts with any assurance they will be applicable, let alone true, in years to come. No longer can teaching concentrate on passing on almanacs-worth of data. Instead, we must prepare our youth to live satisfying lives in a changing world. And this includes helping them learn how to develop new knowledge from what is already known while at the same time coping with change. This, in sum, means helping them learn on their own, helping them inquire.
>
> It is no secret that school-age children spend more time out of school than in school. A considerable portion of this out-of-school time is still spent in learning, however. And students continue to learn even after graduating—or dropping out. A rewarding contributing life in a society such as ours requires that our youth know how to use their intellectual abilities rationally. Indeed, the future of our existence as a society may very well depend on this.

---

[3] James P. Shaver, "A Critical View of the Social Studies Profession," in *Social Education* 41:4 (April 1977), p. 306.

Because there is a wide variety of ideas and activities competing for our attention today, it frequently becomes necessary to make choices. For some, choices are made on faith, for others on the basis of some authority. For still others choices are made at a more basic, gut level. None of these ways, however, is sufficient for intelligent social action. A rational way of solving problems is needed.

Moreover, there is today considerable peddling of what others *think* is true as if it were the absolute truth. The clamor to "tell it like it is" seems incessant. News media report an event the way they think it is—or wish it were. So, too, do public figures. And textbooks. And teachers. How many times, for example, have you heard yourself ask [students], "What was the main cause of the Civil War?" or "What is the major problem facing India today?" or "Why did Jackson attack the Bank?" For each of these questions there is in most classrooms one and only one "right" answer. And the students are queried until they "get it."

Who should decide what is right? Textbooks? Professors? News media? Teachers? Students are usually required—indeed, often willing—to accept without question what so-called authorities say because "They wouldn't go to all that trouble to print it or report it if it weren't true," or because "It's in the book," or because, more practically, those who challenge established authorities usually find that low grades result.

Questions such as those just listed and the belief that anyone can really "tell it like it is" (or was) are naive to say the least. In all frankness we don't know the way it is—or was—or even will be. The best we can do is tell it like we *think* it is. I emphasize the word *think*. Each of us thinks differently. What we think—or know—is, among other things, a product of the questions we ask, our methods of investigation, the quality of the information we use, and our own unique frames of reference. These differ for each one of us.

Apparently we forget that most of what is passed off as knowledge in history and the social sciences is nothing more than interpretation—and someone else's at that. Witness how different scholars examine a major event, such as the Civil War, or major phenomena, such as [Islamic revolts] or [energy crises], and arrive at different conclusions as to their causes. Which interpretation is correct? Which should be taught—and presumably learned—as the truth?

Should it be a function of social studies to stuff children's minds with other people's perceptions of reality? To make them first sponges and then parrots? To make their heads nothing more than data storage bins—bins full of answers to questions they never asked? To teach them to accept unquestionably someone else's perception of "the way it is"—or was? Or should it be a function of social studies to teach youngsters how to establish their own perceptions of reality in more honest, rational, and reliable ways, how to evaluate what others present as the truth, how to find out for themselves?

The answer, it seems to me, is obvious. Our social studies programs must teach children *how to know*—not just what someone else thinks or believes [or] knows. Students must be taught how to learn on their own through rational inquiry. Suggesting a way to help them do this is precisely what this book is all about.

And that is exactly what this present book is all about, too. *Teaching Thinking in Social Studies: Using Inquiry in the Classroom* is intended to serve as a practical guide to using inquiry teaching in intermediate and secondary school social studies. This book specifically seeks to answer these questions: "What is inquiry teaching?; How can inquiry teaching be used to accomplish fundamental social studies goals, especially goals of critical or analytical thinking?; What are the implications of inquiry teaching for the social studies classroom?"

To use inquiry teaching successfully, we must understand what it is all about. To understand inquiry teaching, we must first understand the nature of inquiry, the process of learning from which inquiry teaching is derived and which it is designed to facilitate. This can be accomplished by examining and reflecting on specific examples of both inquiry and inquiry teaching. We must engage in inquiry as learners reflecting systematically on what occurs as inquiry takes place just as we must later engage in inquiry teaching and reflect on how this strategy works in our classrooms.

The structure of this book reflects these assertions. The Prologue presents a sample inquiry lesson through which you can proceed as a learner and then use as a concrete referent throughout the chapters that follow. Part One describes and analyzes the nature of inquiry using not only the initial sample inquiry lesson but also a case study of a person engaged in inquiring. Part Two explains one strategy of inquiry teaching and describes classroom techniques for using it, with continued reference to the inquiry lesson in the Prologue as actually used in fifth- and tenth-grade social studies classrooms. This part concludes by applying this inquiry teaching strategy to content typically taught in American history courses.

The remaining chapters explain how to use inquiry teaching in social studies and the implications of its use for curriculum, teacher, and students alike. Part Three illustrates ways to use the inquiry teaching strategy presented here to teach concepts; basic skills of thinking, reading, and writing; and various affective objectives. Part Four explores ways to use an inquiry teaching strategy to organize whole courses, units, and daily lessons—again using the Prologue lesson as a referent. Additional chapters also explain how to evaluate learning in inquiry teaching and the implications of inquiry teaching for the classroom. An Epilogue suggests follow-up activities for mastering this teaching strategy.

Since inquiry teaching itself is a skill, the sequence of chapters reflects a specific skill-teaching strategy. This strategy, outlined in Chapter 8, involves introducing the skill (the Prologue); explaining, analyzing, and demonstrating the skill (Chapters 1–6); and applying the skill and reflecting on its nature and implications (Chapter 7). The skill is then demonstrated and analyzed in terms of the major cognitive and affective goals sought by most intermediate and secondary school history and social studies teachers and in terms of its curricular and classroom implications (Chapters 8–15). Thus, this volume extends as well as revises the concepts of inquiry teaching presented in its predecessor and seeks to apply it directly to the classroom realities of both experienced and inexperienced teachers.

I should perhaps explain briefly the absence of any attention to decision-making and social action, both important aspects of social studies education today. There are three reasons for not touching on them directly here. First, over the past several years a number of educators have written on both decision-making and social action. Their contributions are quite good. Duplicating their efforts, especially in the limited space available here, makes little sense. Second, a combined treatment of all these processes might tend to confuse inquiry teaching with decision-making and social action. These processes are not synonymous. Decision-making and social action employ the skills and processes that constitute inquiry—indeed, one's success in decision-making or social action may well depend on his or her mastery of inquiry. But there is more to decision-making or social action than thinking. Third, decision-making and social action are but two of the purposes to which inquiry can be put. Inquiry has utility far beyond these processes. This volume thus stresses a strategy for teaching skills and processes of thinking that prove crucial for accomplishing an extremely wide variety of civic, social, personal, and intellectual goals.

Professor Samuel P. Hayes claims that the criterion of a good course is its "imaginative potential"—its potential to free the mind and to stimulate new ways of looking at experience. [4] So, too, can the measure of good teaching be regarded as its imaginative potential. I believe inquiry teaching has the most imaginative potential—creative or generative power—of all the strategies used in our classrooms. I have explored the nature of this potential and suggested ways to use inquiry teaching to accomplish major social studies goals. Again, the ideas presented here should not be considered as absolute or final; indeed, most continue to evolve as they are tested and refined by classroom application. But these ideas have proven workable and productive of learning in history and social studies classrooms and continue to do so. They are presented here for the benefit of those who seek to improve social studies teaching—our ultimate, and hopefully mutual, goal.

Barry K. Beyer

Department of History and Philosophy
Carnegie-Mellon University
Pittsburgh, Pennsylvania

---

[4] Samuel P. Hayes, "History and the Changing University Curriculum," *The History Teacher*, VIII:1 (November 1974), pp. 64–72.

contents

acknowledgments

The ideas expressed in this volume represent the results of considerable study, classroom experimentation, and reflection. They reflect the results of a continuous dialogue among social studies students, teachers, researchers, curriculum developers, and myself in the years since my first book. I am indebted to all these individuals for the challenging and stimulating exchange that has helped create this volume.

I wish especially to acknowledge my indebtedness to my colleagues at Carnegie-Mellon University who have contributed to my interest in and knowledge about inquiry teaching in history and social studies. I am especially grateful to Professor Michael Weber for reviewing this manuscript and for offering his invaluable suggestions and comments. To Professors Ludwig Schaefer and Irving Bartlett and to Professors Jan Cohn, Tony Penna, Roland Smith, and Ted Fenton, too, go my thanks for helping over the years to generate and evaluate some of the ideas and materials presented here.

I also wish to express my appreciation to my colleagues in social studies education throughout the country who reviewed this work in manuscript, including Professors Carole L. Hahn of Emory University, M. Eugene Gilliom of Ohio State University, and Ronald Galbraith, Director of the Peabody Center on Economic and Social Studies Education at the George Peabody College for Teachers. I am indeed grateful for their comments, criticisms, and suggestions. And I owe a special note of appreciation to Dr. Stuart Lazarus of the Social Studies Curriculum Center at Indiana University for the stimulating suggestions and astute insights he contributed to this undertaking.

Many other colleagues have contributed to this effort in one way or another, including Dr. Ben Sauers of Shady Side Academy in Pittsburgh, Dr. Jarrell McCracken of the Denver Public Schools, and Tom Jones of the West Irondequoit (New York) Public Schools. Professors Jack Mallan of Syracuse University, Frank Bloomer of Texas Tech University, George Gregory of the S.U.N.Y. College at Geneseo, and E. Perry Hicks of S.U.N.Y. Buffalo also gave valuable assistance for which I am grateful. Special thanks go to Lee Lintz, Ann Hanushek, and their students in the Peters Township (Pennsylvania) Public Schools for their help in testing some of the materials presented in these pages. And I am also deeply indebted to my friend and neighbor, Bevo Johnson, for his invaluable assistance in securing permission to use various materials in these pages.

Finally, to the scores of teachers who have listened to my thoughts, questioned them, and challenged them, I am most grateful, for without their interest, suggestions, and probing questions, the ideas developed here would not have evolved as they have. To all of these people and others too numerous to mention goes much of the credit for whatever makes sense here.

Preparing this manuscript was no easy task. To my wife Judy and to Genevieve Davidson, Patti Harbulak, and Vicki Sharapin, whose tireless efforts at the typewriter finally turned my miserable handwriting into readable manuscript, I wish to express my deepest thanks. The patient comments and timely suggestions of Lynn Copley-Graves—a tireless editor—have been most helpful in readying the manuscript for publication. Her contributions have been immeasurable. They are deeply appreciated.

Most of all, I wish to acknowledge the support and encouragement in this undertaking of my wife and family. To them go my deepest thanks for their patient understanding of the long hours required to make this book a reality and for the support that has made this whole undertaking an exciting experience.

BKB

For   Gary

Steve

Judy

ProloGue: An Introduction To Inquiry

> *It makes a difference in the development of human intelligence whether children* learn to say that *something is true or whether they* learn that *something is true.*[1]
>
> —*Alan Griffin*

No statement better underscores the importance of the ability and disposition to think—clearly, rationally, systematically—than does Alan Griffin's incisive observation. And no society requires the intelligent use of this ability by all its citizens more than does the participatory democracy which the United States strives to become. Clearly, instruction and experience in thinking constitute, or ought to constitute, two of the most important goals of formal schooling in our nation today.

Over the years, the social studies at all grade levels have made numerous attempts to achieve these goals. Teachers have devised and used a variety of teaching strategies designed to help students think and learn how to think. These strategies take many forms. Yet, as different as they may appear at first glance, these strategies share a common central process—a process best described as *inquiry*. By using this process in the classroom as a teaching strategy as well as a learning goal, teachers can and do help students learn how to think.

What is inquiry? Perhaps the best way to find out is to do it. Let's try.

Imagine, if you wish, that you are a student in a fifth- or tenth-grade social studies class. Respond to the questions that follow as you think such a student might respond. Or, if you prefer, proceed through the following pages as yourself, using whatever knowledge and skills you possess to complete this sample lesson.

1

Some years ago archeologists and other specialists uncovered the remains of a society that existed almost 1,000 years ago. One question that motivated their investigation was, *What was life like in this society?* We can deal with this question here.

1. Before we start, however, we need to be a bit more precise about this question. What does "life" mean when used in this way? What is a "society"? List below three or four questions whose answers will help define these words and thus help answer the larger question of what life was like in this society around A.D. 1000:

— *What occupations did people have?*

—

—

—

—

—

—

—

The pictures on the following pages show some of the objects produced or used by this society.[2] All of these objects were found in the same general area and date from about the same time, around A.D. 1000. Look at them closely to answer the questions you wrote above. *What was life like in this society around one thousand years ago?*

1

2

3

4

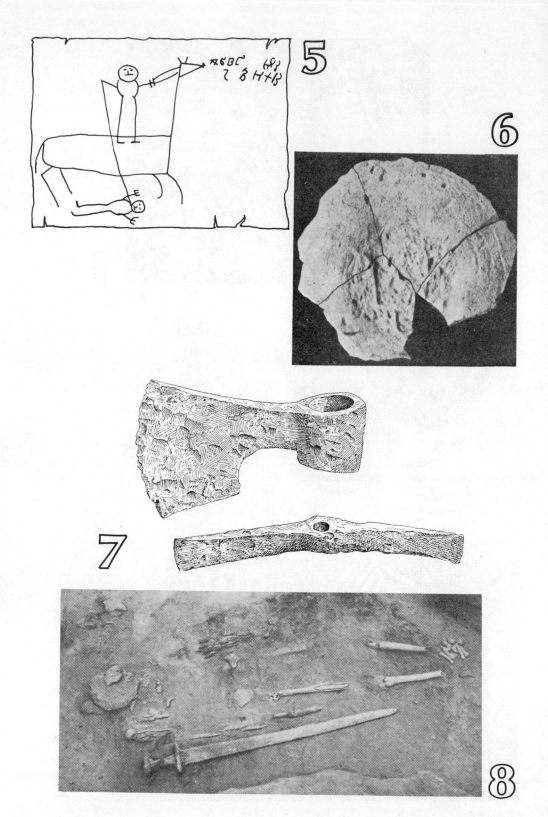

4

2. Did you find some possible answers to the questions you wrote in item 1? List below some of the things you think typified life in the society that made or used the objects shown in the pictures:

   — *lived near a large body of water*

   —

   —

   —

   —

3. How can you be sure the things you listed in item 2 really did characterize this society? What evidence would you want to find to confirm the accuracy of your guesses? For example, if you think this society existed near some body of water, what evidence would you want to find to prove this guess accurate? List some other evidence you want or need to find if each of your guesses is to prove accurate:

   — *remains of large boats*

   —

   —

   —

   —

4. What kinds of sources would most likely provide the evidence you want or need? Perhaps an account written by an individual living at that place at that time would contain such evidence. What other kinds of sources might provide the evidence you seek?

   — *diary or letters written by people of this place*

   —

   —

   —

5. Suppose you could examine some of these sources. What would you look for? For example, among the items found at this site was a record of the laws that governed the lives of the people who lived in this society. *If the features you listed above really typified life in this particular society, what kinds of laws would these people have had?* What would their laws have been about? Pick two of the characteristics you listed in item 2 and list each under *Characteristics* below. Then, under *Evidence Needed or Expected*, list for each characteristic what you would expect these laws to be about or to say if your two guesses about life in this society are accurate:

a. *Characteristics*   b.   *Evidence Needed or Expected*

(1)   —

                                       —

                                       —

                                       —

(2)   —

                                       —

                                       —

                                       —

6. A translation of these laws follows. Read them to find the evidence you expect or need to find if the characteristics you listed above are, indeed, typical of life in this place.

SOME LAWS[3]

These laws refer to amounts of money. The grivna was a coin like a silver dollar. A rezana was 1/50th of a grivna. Think of a rezana as a two-penny piece.

LAWS

1. If anyone kills the prince's steward, he must pay 80 grivna.
2. If anyone kills a free worker on the prince's estate, he must pay 5 grivna.
3. If anyone kills a peasant or a herdsman, he must pay 5 grivna.
4. If anyone kills a slave who is a teacher or a nurse, he must pay 12 grivna.

5. If anyone kills the prince's horse, he must pay 3 grivna; for killing a peasant's horse, 2 grivna.

6. If anyone kidnaps another man's male or female slave, he must pay 12 grivna to the owner.

7. If anyone beats a peasant without the permission of the prince, he must pay him 3 grivna; if anyone beats a sheriff or another assistant to the prince, the fine is 12 grivna.

8. If anyone plows beyond the boundary of his property, the fine is 12 grivna.

9. If anyone steals a boat, he must pay 30 rezana for the boat and a fine of 60 rezana.

10. If a slave runs away from his owner and someone hides him but the owner finds him, the owner receives back his slave and 3 grivna for the offense.

11. If anyone cuts a man's leg and the leg is cut off or the injured man becomes lame, the injured man's son must avenge his father.

12. In time of war all males in the city shall become a part of the army. The peasants of the countryside shall surrender all of their horses and join with the army. The prince shall supply the weapons.

13. If a member of the local guild commits a crime and is not caught, the other members of the guild must pay for the offense.

14. If an indentured laborer runs away from his lord, he becomes the lord's slave. But if he departs openly to complain of an injustice on the part of his lord and goes to the prince or to the judges, they do not make him a slave but give him justice.

15. If a peasant dies without male descendants, his estate goes to the prince. If there are daughters left in the house, each receives a portion of the estate; if they are married, they receive no portion.

16. If a mustache or a beard is forcefully cut off, the offender must pay 12 grivna.

7. What evidence do you find in the laws that you expected or needed to find to support your ideas about life in this society of 1,000 years ago? Check (✔) any of the evidence listed in the second column of item 5 that you found in the laws. Add any additional evidence you found to support your ideas in the remaining space under Column b in item 5.

8. Look over the laws again. In the first column below list any evidence you found that you didn't really want to find because it contradicted your ideas. Perhaps finding this evidence suggests that your ideas might be inaccurate. In the second column list evidence that you wanted to find but didn't.

a. *Evidence Contrary to My Ideas*   b. *Evidence Needed But Not Found*

—   —

—   —

—   —

—   —

—   —

—   —

9. What new ideas about the characteristics of life in this society in A.D. 1000
   did you get from these laws? List two of these new ideas here under *Characteristics* and list in the second column one or two bits of evidence from the
   laws that gave you each idea.

     a. *Characteristics*   b. *Supporting Evidence*

(3)   —

—

(4)   —

—

10. Researchers also found records written by the people who lived in or near
    this society at that time. Excerpts from some of these stories and documents
    follow. If the two characteristics you listed in item 5 accurately describe this
    society, what kinds of evidence should you find in these excerpts? If your
    new ideas (item 9) about this society are accurate, what should you find in
    these excerpts to prove their accuracy? List below the evidence needed to
    support these ideas.

Evidence Needed to Support

(1)   (2)

(3)   (4)

11. Look at the excerpts that follow.[4] What evidence can you find that you need
    or expect to find to support the ideas you have about what this society was
    like about A.D. 1000?

SELECTION 1

Upon his return [the prince] ordered the idols to be cast down, and some to
be cut to pieces, and others to be consumed by fire; but Perun he had tied to
the tail of a horse, and dragged down the hill over the Borichev to the brook,
and placed twelve men to strike him with rods.

SELECTION 2

The people having been baptized, they all went to their homes, and [he] ordered churches to be built, and to place them there where formerly stood the
idols. He sent out men to take the children of noblemen, and to put them out
for book instruction; but the mothers of those children wept for them, for
they were not yet firm in their faith, and they wept for them as for the dead.

SELECTION 3

He invited each beggar and poor man to come to the prince's palace and receive whatever he needed, both food and drink, and money from the treasury. With the thought that the weak and the sick could not easily reach his
palace, he arranged that wagons should be brought in, and after having
them loaded with bread, meat, fish, various vegetables, mead [wine] in
casks, he ordered them driven out through the city. The drivers were under
instruction to call out, "Where is there a poor man or a beggar who cannot
walk?" To such they distributed according to their needs.

SELECTION 4

No mercy was shown to anybody, nor any effort at rescue made from any
quarter while the churches were burning, and Christians were being slaugh-
tered or shackled. Wives were led into captivity and violently separated
from their husbands. Children wept bitterly seeing their mothers thus
treated. A great amount of wealth was carried off, and the churches were
stripped of their pictures, the holy crosses, and their vestments and bells;
and there was in among the whole population sobbing and depression and
great sadness and tears.

What did you find? To what extent does the information in these selections confirm what you thought life in this society was like? To what extent
do these excerpts contradict your initial guesses? What new ideas about this
society do these items suggest? Return to your initial lists (items 2 and 9) and
check or add to these items.

12. Now, *what was life like in this society around* A.D. *1000?* Select your guesses that seem to be confirmed by evidence in the laws and excerpts. At this point what three things can you say *for sure*—or at least almost for sure—about life in this society around A.D. 1000? List these conclusions here:

—

—

—

Which of your ideas were not proven by the information in the laws or in the written excerpts? What new ideas did the laws and written excerpts give you about this society?

Ideas Not Proven	*New Ideas*
—	—
—	—
—	—
—	—

13. Just to double-check, let's look at one last bit of evidence that bears on our initial question. If you could visit the place where this society existed, you could see many structures and other remains which could help you check the conclusions at which you have arrived, however tentatively or reluctantly. But such a visit is not possible, so photographs will have to suffice. The photos on pages 11 and 12[5]—of structures, of paintings and drawings in these structures, and of illustrations from other records—also come from this site and date from this same time. To what extent do they confirm, contradict, or modify the three or four major ideas you had about what life was like in this place almost 1,000 years ago?

St Sophia Cathedral

* Reprinted by permission of the
American Heritage Publishing
Company

Woodcutters

* Reprinted by permission of the
American Heritage Publishing
Company

Sons of the Prince

* Reprinted by permission of the
American Heritage Publishing
Company

4

Peasant
* Reprinted by permission of the American
Heritage Publishing Company

5

Outdoor Baptism
*Reprinted by permission of the American Heritage
Publishing Company and Foto Biblioteca Vaticana

14. Now, in your judgment, what was life *really* like in this place? *What were three features of life in this society around* A.D. *1000?* List these features here:

—

—

—

Finished? At this point you must certainly know something about life in this society—not much perhaps, nor with much certainty, but surely considerably more than when you started. Yet, there may be some more questions to answer before you can state for sure what this society was like. For example:

- How do you know the objects pictured really came from this site?
- How do you know the laws and excerpted documents came from this site? Or are accurately translated?
- How do you know there is such a site in the first place?
- *How do you know?*

Inquiry is one way of knowing. If you became involved in the preceding investigation, if you attempted to work out the answers to the above questions and to any others that may have come to mind as you progressed, you were engaged in inquiry. You were thinking. I was engaged in inquiry teaching—in helping you think. Helping students to think and to learn how to think are the subjects of this book.

INQUIRY LEARNING

Inquiring is thinking. Inquiry teaching is teaching thinking. Reflect for a moment on the preceding investigation. What did you do as you followed the directions? In general, you put the *scientific method* to work to resolve a problem! You took a given question and tried to answer it, not by consulting some authority or other type of answer-giver, but by using a variety of information and your own thinking skills to generate an answer of your own.

Are you satisfied that your "answers" to the initial question are accurate? Do you have some questions of your own for which you would like answers? List some of your questions here:

—

—

—

How do you *feel* about what you did and about what you now "know" about life in this society around A.D. 1000? List some of your feelings here:

—

—

—

—

The steps through which you have proceeded, the knowledge you have used and gained, and the feelings that motivated and arose from this whole process illustrate both the nature of inquiry and the nature of inquiry teaching. But there is much more to these ways of learning and teaching than may be thus far apparent.

In order to help students learn how to think, one can use a strategy of inquiry teaching. However, one cannot expect to understand inquiry teaching without some familiarity with inquiry itself. Anyone who wishes to help students to learn on their own, to go beyond and behind the given data, *to think,* must first have some familiarity with how people learn through inquiring. Part One presents a concept of inquiry, an analysis of which will serve as the basis for understanding the inquiry teaching strategy introduced in this Prologue and developed in subsequent sections of this book.

notes

1. Alan Griffin as paraphrased by Lawrence E. Metcalf in "Research on Teaching in the Social Studies," N.L. Gage, ed., *Handbook of Research on Teaching* (Chicago: Rand-McNally Co., 1963), p. 935.
2. The sources for the visual materials used in this lesson are cited in detail elsewhere in this book in order not to unduly influence the direction of the inquiry being conducted. I am indebted to Dr. Jarrell McCracken of the Denver Public Schools for permission to adapt this sequence of learning activities from his doctoral research.
3. Austin P. Evans, ed., *The Records of Civilization Sources and Studies* (New York: Columbia University Press, 1947), 41. Reprinted with adaptations by permission of Columbia University Press.
4. Sources for the excerpts on page 9 are cited in detail elsewhere in this book.
5. Sources for the illustrations on pages 11–12 are cited in detail elsewhere in this book.

part one

inquiry and thinking

1

A concept of inquiry

Inquiry is one way of learning, of knowing, of making sense out of experience. But what is inquiry? What do you think of when you think of inquiry? For some individuals, the word *inquiry* brings the following words or ideas to mind. To what extent and in what way do you associate these words or ideas with inquiry?

enlightenment   seeking
questioning   participation
interest   curiosity

Other individuals associate the following with the term *inquiry*. To what extent do these words or phrases reflect what inquiry means to you?

observing   research
using evidence   comparing
personal challenge   hypothesizing
having a problem

What other ideas or words do you associate with *inquiry*? What does *inquiry* mean to you? List what you consider to be the four or five most significant aspects of inquiry:

—

—

—

—

Inquiry means different things to different people. To many people inquiry simply means asking questions, any questions. To others inquiry is synonymous with student conducted library research. Inquiry entails much more than either of these activities, however. Inquiry, to paraphrase Dewey, involves the making and testing of assertions in the light of information relative to these assertions.[1] Inquiry is purposeful, systematic thinking. Its goal? To make new meanings out of the given information—to gain new insights, to resolve a problem, or to answer a question. If you worked through the Prologue answering the questions and following the directions as best you could, you engaged in inquiry; you were thinking in a purposeful, systematic way. The following pages present and analyze one way of conceptualizing the nature of the learning in which you engaged—inquiry.

BASIC COMPONENTS
OF INQUIRY

Any way of learning may be divided into several dimensions, or components, for purposes of analysis. Figure 1.1 presents one set of components common to all ways of learning. Any particular way of learning includes, of course, a *process*. But each specific way of learning also consists of certain kinds of *knowledge* as well as certain *feelings, attitudes,* and *values* about learning. The specific attributes, or features of these three components give any way of learning its own distinctive character. The interactions of these components shape the way we go about learning and, to a large extent, shape what we learn as well.

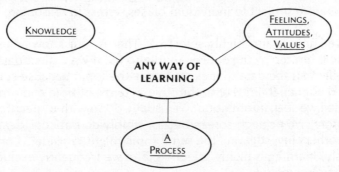

Figure 1.1. Some Basic Components of Learning

Inquiry is but one way of learning. As with any other way of learning, inquiry consists of the three components noted above. But inquiry is distinguished from other approaches to learning by the particular features of the process involved, by the type of knowledge it employs, and by the specific attitudes and feelings upon which it is built and that it engenders. In order to understand the nature of inquiry, we must understand the unique attributes of inquiry learning.

Knowledge

In order to be successful at inquiry, we must possess at least three types of knowledge. First, we must know something about the nature of knowledge itself. Second, we must know the basic tools of inquiry, their functions, and how to use them. Finally, we use our general background knowledge, including our biases, assumptions, and general information.

1. The nature of knowledge. What we know, as individuals or groups, is neither complete nor final. Actually, our so-called knowledge is quite fragmentary and usually highly selective. Our knowledge also constantly changes and is therefore tentative. Moreover, what passes for knowledge actually consists of nothing more than interpretation. To learn by inquiring, one must understand the character of what we call *knowledge* and its implications for trying to determine the "truth" about anything.

The amount of information and knowledge we accumulate reportedly doubles about every ten years. As it does, some currently assumed truths may be substantiated by the new data, while other accepted truths may be challenged or proven invalid. In some instances new knowledge raises new questions. Recognition of this state of flux means that what we accept as true today must be considered at best as only tentative and therefore subject to change in light of future information and investigation.

Knowledge is also fragmentary at best; it is rarely complete. Frequently we cannot secure all the information we should have to make a timelessly valid judgment. This is due in part to the difficulties of locating and collecting all pertinent information. It is also due to knowledge being a product of the human mind and therefore subject to individual biases, errors in reasoning, and hidden assumptions.

What we know is also highly selective. That is, our knowledge about any specific topic is limited by the data available to us. If we collect data ourselves, we rarely collect all the data that exists about the topic because such an act is either beyond our capabilities or prohibitive in terms of time and other costs. In addition, when we seek information, we usually do so with a specific purpose in mind. Therefore, we neglect, screen out, or simply do not consider some information that others investigating the same topic might consider. Consciously or unconsciously, learning is highly selective, and we frequently exclude more information than we include.

When information is collected by others and presented to us, the selective nature of the information itself and what we learn from it become even more strikingly evident. Textbook authors, for example, face the frustrating task of deciding what to exclude from their texts, as well as what to include. Imagine producing a history of the United States in 800 pages or less—think what has been left out! And what remains in the text we too often take as a complete history. Historians know that our records of the accessible past (records, documents, artifacts, and other sources) are considerably less than the total body of past events. Thus, the mere passage of time, the survival of some records and not others, the preferences and goals of authors, and our own perceptions make what we think we know incomplete, very selective, and extremely fragmentary.

In the last analysis, what passes for knowledge primarily represents interpretation, and interpretation of highly selective information at that. What we "know" is the product of individuals dealing with reality within the framework of their own past experiences. As noted earlier, each individual lives a unique experience and, as a result, develops a special set of prejudices, biases, likes, dislikes, inclinations, and ideas. Together these comprise a frame of reference that conditions what we select to perceive, the questions we ask of experience, how we deal with what we notice, and how we report it.

Consequently, what we report as The Truth—the end product of some perception of reality—is not the way things really are, but merely the way we *think* they are, the way we *perceive* them to be. What we think we know is not Absolute Truth, but only our approximation of it! This means that different people can share an identical experience or work with the same data and come up with different, but equally legitimate, answers. There can be many sides to the same question. Thus an inquirer knows that it is important to search for and investigate many aspects of a question, to be aware of how a frame of reference does shape "knowledge," and to make every effort to identify these frames of reference when dealing with what others report as knowledge.

> The investigation you conducted in the Prologue illustrates these aspects of knowing. Obviously, the information presented in it is quite fragmentary and selective—just as are the information on which people base their daily decisions and the data included in the textbooks used in school classrooms. The inferences you made from the data presented in the Prologue reflect your frame of reference and your own background knowledge. These inferences represent your interpretations that hopefully changed as additional data became available to you. And at the end of the investigation, you probably consider your beliefs about life in that society most tentative, quite selective, and fragmentary. To be absolutely sure of what is really true about life in that society 1,000 years ago requires considerably more thorough evaluation and examination of much more information than was provided. Being aware of these limitations on "knowing" can help individuals succeed in inquiry and can also help them keep what they think is true in proper perspective.

Knowing what we do about the nature of knowledge has other implications for inquiry. "Knowledge" can be determined in a variety of ways—by word of some authority, by superstition or by very superficial examination of the data, for instance. Thus, what is reported as true may or may not be an accurate representation of reality. This means, in sum, that the accuracy of what is known and the degree to which it corresponds with reality are ultimately determined by the quality and quantity of the relevant evidence and the way in which this evidence is manipulated. The closest approximation to the way things *really* are or were can only come through honest and sustained intellectual inquiry that takes into account a variety of viewpoints.

It is important, of course, to recognize that some experts spend most of their lives conducting research in their respective fields and may be closer to understanding the realities in those fields than some novices are ever likely to be. Thus, in the search for knowledge it is not always necessary to go through the process of original investigation. Instead, we could examine the qualifications of the experts who have already researched the particular subject and consider the quality of their work. What the experts have learned may then become information for use in our own learning; or flaws in their work may become evident, thus necessitating more research on our part. Successful inquirers realize these facts about knowledge and conduct themselves with these limitations in mind.

2. Tools of inquiry. Although effective inquiry requires the use of data, this does not necessarily mean that we must know all the data prior to the start of our investigation. One important aspect of inquiry is that data can be gathered as the inquiry proceeds rather than accumulated in isolation from or prior to the inquiry itself. In fact, we usually cannot acquire much data without first initiating some inquiry and getting an idea of what data to seek. Knowledge of potentially rich and reliable sources of data and how to use them is more important for effective inquiry than prior accumulation of all relevant information. Command of a wide variety of techniques is also useful in both locating and processing evidence.

To succeed at inquiry we must know where to find reliable, up-to-date sources of a wide variety of information. This may include reports by others of what they believe to be true and accounts of events, experiences, and other useful data. Inquiry also demands an assessment of the reliability and validity of each source and a knowledge of how to work with the data to compensate for any distortions or inaccuracies. Finally, we must know how to use an almanac, index, encyclopedia, statistical abstract, card catalogue, museum, or other commonly available sources of primary and secondary data. Knowledge of existing sources such as these and of ways to use these sources—rather than only detailed knowledge of the precise contents of each source—is essential for conducting effective inquiry.

Knowledge of a wide variety of specific problem-solving techniques also proves to be important for successful inquiry. Brainstorming—rapid fire listing of terms associated with a given topic or problem—can be effective in generating hypotheses and alternatives, as well as in identifying the evidence needed to validate hypotheses. Inventing or seeking analogies and deliberately searching for opposites or the causes, results, and implications of a given topic or event may also be useful techniques at various stages of inquiring. Considering the assumptions underlying related ideas, possible objections to a thought progression, or questions by interested individuals may also prove helpful. All of these techniques can be used at different points in inquiry to resolve a problem or to make and test hypotheses. Knowledge of these techniques constitutes an important base for effective inquiry learning.

3. Background knowledge. The general background knowledge and experience an individual possesses also play a major role in inquiry. Background knowledge consists of fragments of data culled from past experience and stored in one's memory, assumptions, biases, and prejudices accumulated over the years, and concepts evolved through previous experience. Such information and experience, in reality, constitute an individual's frame of reference, the way in which he or she perceives and analyzes the world outside. Such background knowledge shapes what we look for during inquiry and thus may limit, as well as expand, what we can find. At the same time, our vast storehouse of information or experience can create new insights and make possible new connections denied others with limited experience or scantier background information.

Biases, prejudices, and preferences also constitute part of an individual's frame of reference and shape his or her inquiry. Personal likes and dislikes based on misinformation, unwarranted stereotypes, and untested inferences and generalizations unconsciously and consciously influence inquiry. All individuals possess biases and prejudices and make assumptions; no one is bias-free or completely objective. However, an effective inquirer recognizes such biases and assumptions and conducts the inquiry in a way that acknowledges and compensates for these variables in order to conduct as open and objective an inquiry as possible.

Concepts, too, comprise an important element in background knowledge, thus serving as important inquiry tools. Concepts organize disparate information into patterns that suggest or reveal meaningful relationships. In addition, concepts generate questions that may help make experience or data meaningful. By generating and ordering evidence, concepts produce new knowledge. Thus, concepts, too, play a crucial role in inquiry by both initiating and guiding thinking. Although there exists an almost infinite number of concepts that could be used, some prove more useful to inquiry than others. These concepts consist of those that generate useful questions to ask of experience: analytical concepts such as *areal association, status, leadership,* and *scarcity,* for example, or action concepts such as *decision-making, cultural interaction,* and *conflict-resolution.* Such concepts may be applied to the analysis of a wide variety of data in order to make it meaningful.

> You employed, deliberately or intuitively, selected concepts in attempting to answer the questions posed in the inquiry you conducted in the Prologue. If you were familiar with a concept of feudalism, social class, or commerce, you may have asked questions generated by these concepts. And if you did, the inferences you made about life in this place not only would have reflected your version of these concepts but also would have shaped your answers to the initial question.

Concepts are so extremely important to successful inquiry that they deserve separate treatment at a more appropriate place (Chapters 8 and 9). At this point, however, we should remember that concepts rank among the most basic tools of intellectual inquiry. Productive inquiry teaching and learning require knowledge of selected concepts from history, the social sciences, and other disciplines.

> The data used in the Prologue investigation come from many sources. As one step in working with these data (item 4), you were asked to list some types and sources of data that might provide information useful in helping you test your

hypotheses. Your familiarity with potential sources would have been most useful here, especially if you then had actually been asked to locate these sources to complete the investigation.

The fact that you were not asked to find these sources does not mean this step is unimportant. Indeed, if you were to engage in an original inquiry on your own, such an operation would be absolutely necessary. But in this instance, the major goal was to introduce you to inquiry by engaging you in an actual and complete example of this way of learning. So the data sources were provided for you. Had the lesson required you to find sources related to the subject of your inquiry, and if you had been unable to locate such sources, the lesson would have come to an abrupt end right there; this introduction to inquiry would have failed.

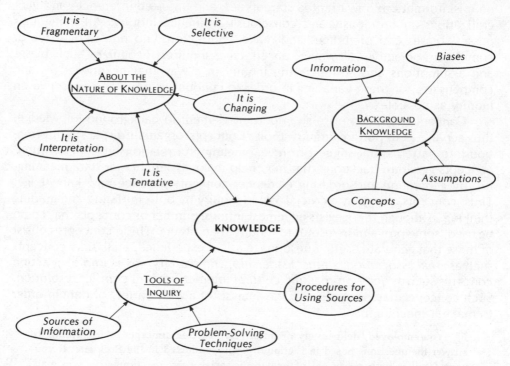

Figure 1.2. The Knowledge Component of Inquiry

In sum, we must possess and/or acquire certain kinds of knowledge in order to be successful inquirers. In general, this knowledge differs considerably from what we must know to learn in other ways. And it is this knowledge, summarized in Figure 1.2, that helps make inquiry unique as a way of learning.

Feelings, Attitudes, and Values

Inquiry consists of affective as well as cognitive components. In most instances these feelings, attitudes, and values derive from, or are at least associated with, the three kinds of knowledge just described. Moreover, this affective dimension does not usually characterize other ways of learning. Successful inquirers, for example, value objectivity and the use of rational thinking to resolve problems. They respect evidence as the test for accuracy; they express willingness to suspend judgment and, to a point, to be tolerant of ambiguity. Above all, good inquirers value curiosity and imagination. Each of these feelings, attitudes, or values plays an important part in inquiry by helping to initiate and sustain inquiry after making it possible in the first place.

1. Skepticism. The keystone of inquiry is skepticism, a kind of questioning attitude that doubts simplistic answers or single-factor causes and solutions. Skepticism generally manifests itself in a reluctance to accept unsupported assertions or the assertions of so-called authorities as the final truth. Conversely, it inspires a desire to find out for oneself. Skepticism is a doubting feeling that leads to a reluctance to accept things as they are reported by others, and to a willingness to suspend judgment while the search for truth goes on. Skepticism not only helps initiate inquiry, but also stimulates and guides it.

2. Curiosity. Skepticism implies curiosity, for even though one doubts something, inquiry will not occur until there exists curiosity enough to want to know more or better. Curiosity is a "wanting to know." It closely relates to and derives from imagination, that realm of fanciful thinking that enables one to go beyond the way things appear to be in order to postulate new ways of viewing things, create hypothetical alternatives, or invent new ways of dealing with tasks. Like skepticism, curiosity and imagination initiate and nurture inquiry. Without them, inquiry simply could not occur.

3. Respect for the use of reason. Individuals are not likely to inquire unless they value the use of rational investigation as the most effective way to learn. Rational processes have much more value as determinants of knowledge than appeals to emotions, superstitition, and authority. Given a choice between consulting an authority to answer a fundamental question or problem (such as, How can one account for high rates of inflation and unemployment at the same time?, or, What is a citizen's legal relationship to the government?) or finding out on their own by inquiry, people who value rational methods select the latter. Of course, such individuals also consult reliable sources of specific information, for they would be as foolish not to take advantage of other valid inquiries as they would be to try to resolve all problems themselves. However, on problems of major import, those committed to inquiry use authorities essentially as resources for information rather than accept, without evaluation, what the authorities themselves assert to be true.

4. Respect for evidence as a test for accuracy. There exist many tests for truth. One essential to inquiry involves the quality and quantity of the evidence relative to the question, problem, or task at hand. The successful inquirer regards validated evidence as the final determinant of the accuracy of opinions, hypotheses, or data. He or she will disregard, unless validated, the assertions of anyone who shouts the loudest, flaunts a college degree or a title, claims a prestigious record, writes a popular textbook, or appeals essentially to the emotions.

5. Objectivity. We know that what people report as true represents only their perception of what they think is true. Because we all perceive things differently due to our individual frames of reference, successful inquirers realize that there are more than two sides to every question. Consequently, inquiry requires that we dispassionately search out and examine all possibilities in as unbiased a way as possible. We must, then, deliberately search for evidence contrary to what we might expect or seek. If such evidence does turn up, we must then evaluate it as objectively as possible rather than merely dismiss it as worthless. As inquirers, we must remain aware of our own biases and prejudices and strive to avoid allowing them to distort our data or our handling and working with the data. Even though we may very well be subjective about the kind of questions into which we elect to inquire, we must be as objective as possible in *how* we inquire.

6. Willingness to suspend judgment. This is very closely related to a respect for objectivity. A willingness to suspend judgment involves realizing that it takes time to locate sufficient evidence to prove a point beyond reasonable doubt. In fact, a person experienced in inquiry realizes that reaching a position "beyond reasonable doubt" rarely, if ever, occurs. Although one cannot often wait to make a decision or judgment until all the evidence is in—because it rarely, if ever, is possible to secure *all* the relevant data on any point of inquiry—one must still hesitate to jump to conclusions before sufficient data has been examined. To study one or two major wars and then generalize about the causes of all wars would certainly be inappropriate and invalid. Instead, data about a larger number of wars must be analyzed before pronouncing any generalization regarding the causation of war with any degree of credibility. For this reason the inquirer must be most hesitant to jump to final, irreversible conclusions on the basis of very limited evidence.

7. Tolerance for ambiguity. A desire for certainty—for closure—seems to typify humanity. People exhibit varying degrees of tolerance for uncertain, ambiguous, open-ended situations. Some can stand considerable ambiguity without frustration, while others can stand only very little. One's degree of tolerance for ambiguity plays a key role in inquiry.

The degree to which one can tolerate uncertainty may be viewed as a continuum running from a high degree of tolerance on one end to almost complete intolerance, or a demand for immediate closure, at the other. Many people can tolerate a certain amount of ambiguity; open-ended or unsettled situations do not bother them. This makes it possible for them to accept what appears to be an answer and to act on it, even though all the evidence may not yet be in. Sometimes it even makes people willing to accept the unsettled nature of a task, to tolerate the absence of an answer, and to resist almost indefinitely a demand for closure. The degree of uncertainty for them remains so minor that it just doesn't bother them at all.

At a certain point, however, one that seems to vary for each individual, people seek an end to ambiguity. At some point people want certainty, an answer, and they will move actively to seek it. A growing intolerance for any more ambiguity motivates them to seek a solution, to tie up loose ends, to bring some degree of certainty out of uncertainty. This pursuit of certainty leads to learning and sustains inquiry. The learner's desire for an answer, not to satisfy the teacher but to satisfy himself or herself, provides motivation for inquiry.

At a further point on this continuum the existence of continued ambiguity inhibits inquiry. At this point one may no longer tolerate any more uncertainty and may become so frustrated that, instead of continuing the attempt to seek closure, may simply turn away from the effort altogether. He or she "turns off" and becomes divorced completely from the learning situation.

A person's attitude toward uncertainty or ambiguity thus plays an important role in resolving problems by rational inquiry because inquiry actually builds on the natural human desire to close the gap between uncertainty and certainty. There must be some degree of ambiguity for inquiry to occur. On the other hand, too much uncertainty causes people to turn away from the problem altogether. The willingness to tolerate uncertainty to a point serves to motivate inquiry. But too much ambiguity can end inquiry. A good inquirer has a low "turn-on" point and a high "turn-off" point as far as tolerance for ambiguity is concerned.

The way in which you conducted your investigation of the problem in the Prologue evidenced some of the feelings, attitudes, and values so crucial to successful inquiry. If you did complete the investigation, you certainly evidenced a curiosity that served to motivate your inquiry—to keep you going.

Your willingness, or desire, to do this also reflects the degree to which you can tolerate ambiguity. If you can tolerate some uncertainty, perhaps you are satisfied with the conclusions you made at the end of the investigation. If you cannot tolerate much ambiguity, perhaps you stopped in the middle of the investigation, or did not do it at all, or felt very frustrated after having completed it, without knowing whether you were correct or not. The extent to which you modified your interpretations of the data in the light of new data reflects the value you place on evidence (as well as your skill at analyzing evidence), your willingness to suspend judgment, and the degree of objectivity with which you conducted this investigation. And the feelings that this investigation engendered—perhaps frustration, excitement, enthusiasm, boredom,

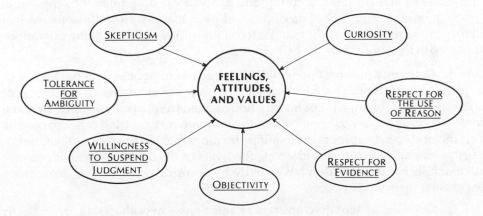

Figure 1.3. The Affective Component of Inquiry

a desire for a quick answer—all reflect attitudes and values that either inhibit or facilitate effective inquiry.

The feelings, values, and attitudes outlined here form an integral component of inquiry. Together they motivate and guide the way in which one inquires. They grow, in general, out of what one knows about knowledge and the tools of inquiry and out of his or her previous learning. Figure 1.3 summarizes this affective dimension of inquiry.

A Process

Inquiry consists not only of knowledge about the nature, sources, and tools of knowledge and the possession of attitudes and values supportive of this way of learning, but it also consists of a unique procedure for processing data or experience. This procedure is best described as a process of inquiring.

The process of inquiring grows out of and also reinforces the feelings, attitudes, values, and knowledge already described. Although an intellectual operation, this process does not involve just a single act. Rather, inquiring consists of a number of related acts, each of which includes a number of unique cognitive operations. This process requires the individual first to define a question or problem about which to inquire and then to guess at tentative answers or alternative solutions—to hypothesize. The resulting hypotheses must then be tested (evaluated) against relevant data. Next, one must conclude about the validity of the hypotheses being tested. In time, as additional evidence becomes available, the conclusion may be reevaluated as new evidence is applied to it, or as the conclusion itself is used to make sense out of this new evidence.

The process of inquiring is continuous. It is neither a "one shot" activity, nor does it produce an irrefutable conclusion that is never rethought or retested. Inquiring as an ongoing process generates new insights. These insights in turn often then become the subjects of further inquiry as the quest for a tested answer continues to involve the search for, and analysis of, data related to the initial problem or question. A brief description of each major step in this process will clarify the sequence, purposes, and interrelationships of the thinking operations included in the overall process of inquiring.

1. Defining a purpose for inquiring. Inquiry commences with the feeling of a need to know something. This "something" may be an answer to a question or solution to a problem, a bit of information needed to satisfy a curiosity, or some information necessary to bring closure to an otherwise unsettled experience. The first major step in the process of inquiring includes making the task explicit, defining it in manageable terms, and setting the limits of the quest. Individuals cannot successfully inquire until they have a fairly accurate idea of what they are looking for or what they need to know.

2. Guessing at tentative answers or solutions—hypothesizing. Hypothesis means a tentative answer to a question or an alternative solution to a problem. Once a purpose (perhaps a question or problem) for inquiry has been delimited, such as "What causes war?," one can guess at a possible answer as perhaps, in this case, "War is caused by greed." The guess, or hypothesis, emerges from whatever data can be found immediately, combined with the existing knowledge of the inquirer as conditioned by his or her own particular frame of reference and goal. This guess then determines the nature of the ensuing inquiry.

3. Testing the hypothesis. Once formulated, a hypothesis or series of hypotheses must be tested (evaluated) to see how well the relevant information or evidence supports the hypotheses. This often long and involved operation includes gathering data, evaluating it, and analyzing it in terms of the hypotheses being tested. Even the process termed *analysis* is quite complicated, for it involves taking information apart as well as identifying the relationships between the bits and pieces of this information. Patterns among these data may even become evident during the process. Finally, this step requires evaluation of the data to determine the extent to which it supports or refutes the hypothesis.

4. Drawing a conclusion. A conclusion reflects a decision about the validity of the hypothesized answer or alternative solution being tested. In this stage, the inquirer states the degree to which the hypothesis seems valid or invalid in terms of the evidence examined. If the evidence supports the initial guess, then it can be accepted as a much more definite answer or explanation. In such an instance, the conclusion may merely be a restatement of the original hypothesis. If the investigation suggests the hypothesis is only partially correct, the conclusion may be a revision of the hypothesis incorporating the new conditions suggested by the evidence. On the other hand, if the evidence refutes the hypothesis, the conclusion may simply be that the hypothesis is incorrect, in which case the inquirer must rehypothesize and submit the new hypotheses to the test of additional evidence. Making a conclusion about the validity of a hypothesis often serves as a culminating step in inquiring. But since most conclusions are based on limited evidence, even a conclusion must remain somewhat tentative in nature awaiting further corroboration as new evidence emerges in the future.

5. Applying the conclusion to new data and generalizing. The quest for meaning usually leads an inquirer to go beyond a simple conclusion. Future experience often provides repeated opportunities to test earlier conclusions against new information not readily available at the time of the initial inquiry. In such instances, what was once a conclusion may thus be treated as a hypothesis to determine if it stands up in the face of the new data; resulting conclusions may then be broadened to explain the new data. Sometimes, however, such application results in modifying the original conclusion. Usually the conclusion becomes more general and less tied to specifics. Concepts emerge in this way. So, too, do generalizations, i.e., broad statements about the relationships between several classes of data or several concepts.

One can also check the validity of a tentative conclusion by using it to make sense out of new data. In other words, a conclusion can be used to determine whether data that purport to relate to the same topic do, in fact, bear any such relationship. Or a conclusion can be used to identify among a variety of data all the data that do relate to the topic of the conclusion. Thus a conclusion, whether in concept form or as a generalization, can actually be used to organize and make sense out of new data and to generate additional knowledge at some future time. Regardless of what we label the final statement or how we use it, using the conclusion to organize additional data or as a hypothesis against which to test additional data represents a final step in the continuing process of making experience meaningful.

The investigation that launched this book required you to go through the basic steps in inquiry described above. It started with a question or problem: "What was life like in this society about A.D.1000?" Your responses to this question constituted hypotheses, educated guesses based on limited data provided here (in the form of photographs of artifacts), your own frame of reference, and any inferences you may have made resulting from connections between the two. You then tested your hypotheses and generated new ones by analyzing evidence you pulled from a list of laws and excerpts from documents. At the same time you simultaneously judged how well this evidence supported or refuted your hypotheses. Then you stated your conclusion by listing three characteristics that seemed, beyond doubt, to typify life in this society. And finally, given some new data in the form of photographs taken at this site, you had an opportunity to check further the accuracy of your conclusions, to revise them, add to them, or merely reaffirm them. Thus, in this investigation you engaged in the process of inquiring as you were given a question to answer and then hypothesized some answers, tested these hypotheses, stated some conclusions, and applied your conclusions to new data.

Essentially, then, the process of inquiring consists of five major cognitive operations. These operations are generally sequential: defining a purpose for inquiry initiates the process; hypothesizing can occur only after a problem has been identified but must occur before meaningful analysis and evaluation can be undertaken; and so on. This process may be outlined as in Figure 1.4.

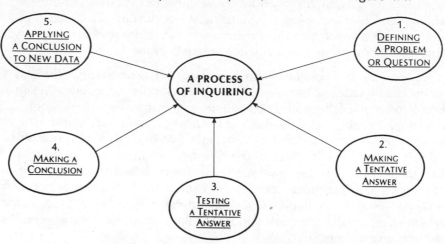

Figure 1.4. The Process Component of Inquiry

THE NATURE OF INQUIRY

Inquiry offers *one* way of making sense out of what we see, hear, read, or otherwise experience. It is *one* way to make things mean something to us. The way this

Figure 1.5. A Concept of Inquiry

process operates is obviously much more complex than outlined here. But this description will do for a start. It is sufficient at this point to note that the process of inquiring is the key to inquiry. This process of making meaning distinguishes inquiry as a way of learning from other ways of learning and gives uniqueness to such variations of inquiry learning as reflective thinking, problem-solving, inductive-deductive learning, and discovery.

As Figure 1.5 indicates, however, inquiry itself is more than a process. It consists of at least three major components: certain feelings, attitudes, and values; certain types of knowledge; and a specific thinking process. Although these elements have been separated from one another here for purposes of analysis, they are in practice virtually indistinguishable. No one part operates with complete independence from the others. Inquiry is, indeed, a very complex method of learning.

One may undoubtedly conceptualize inquiry in a number of ways. Whatever the final conceptualization, it ought to include at least the three components described here. Without understanding that inquiry is more than process, the development and use of practical teaching strategies based on inquiry will prove extremely difficult if not impossible.

notes

1. John Dewey, *How We Think* (Boston: D.C. Heath and Company, 1933), rev. ed., p. 9.

2

Inquiry in Action

Inquiry is more than an abstract concept. It is a very real type of learning behavior. The Prologue provided you an opportunity to engage in this type of behavior. Reference to that study throughout the preceding description of inquiry may have generally clarified the essential elements of inquiry as a way of learning. However, a significant question still remains: Exactly how does inquiry work?

Recall, if you will, what you did in the Prologue. First you used some limited data, pictures of artifacts from a given site, to make your guesses in response to a question about the nature of life in that society about 1,000 years ago. You then checked the accuracy of your guesses against additional information about this society. As you did so, you drew from the information specific bits and pieces that your own past experience and knowledge suggested were relevant to your guesses. You connected what you already knew to the evidence you saw in the information provided on the one hand, and to your first guesses on the other. Occasionally new ideas or guesses about life in the society may have popped up as your manipulation of the information generated new insights.

In other words, you used data to check the accuracy, to evaluate, your initial guesses. Eventually you came to some conclusion, however tentative it may have been. As directed, you decided on three features that seemed to best characterize life in this society, at least in terms of the available evidence. You could have stopped there. But additional information in the form of photographs of structures and other remains located at the site provided further opportunity to apply new evidence to your conclusions to see if, in fact, your conclusions were warranted. Finally, you ended with some of your original guesses confirmed by the evidence or challenged by it—or perhaps even new ideas suggested in their stead. In sum, you

1. Started with a question or problem;
2. Guessed at some possible answers or solutions;

31

3. Tested the accuracy of your guesses against some evidence that you decided ought to exist and that you drew out of available information and your own background of experience;
4. Judged how well this evidence corroborated your guesses;
5. Stated some guesses you believed to be accurate, at least in terms of the available information; and
6. Applied new information as it became available to your conclusions.

As you worked through the investigation in the Prologue, you employed some of the knowledge, the specific thinking skills, and the process that constitute inquiry. The way you conducted your study also reflected the attitudes, values, and feelings typical of a successful inquirer. Reflecting upon what you did in completing that lesson may clarify the concept of inquiry described in Chapter 1.

However, as long as we deal with inquiry only in general terms, this learning method will likely remain rather vague and elusive if not actually confusing. To make inquiry more understandable, we can also analyze a sample of behavior that purports to exemplify inquiry. By so doing, the skeletal outline described in the preceding chapter may be fleshed out and also made considerably more precise. This chapter seeks to accomplish both of these goals.

IT WAS
OBVIOUS

Professional literature abounds with many examples of inquiry. Most of these consist of transcripts of classroom dialogues. The example that follows here, however, differs. This example consists of a brief folktale about a scholar who is an expert Jewish theologian. Marmaresch, the community referred to, was a typical shtetl, an area inhabited by Jews in the late nineteenth and early twentieth centuries in southeastern Europe. The scholar, native to this region, seems well acquainted with its inhabitants and quite familiar with the people and customs of the surrounding areas. Thus, he can make the assumptions he does in the story.

This particular tale is worth reading twice. First, read it as a story. What is the community of Marmaresch like? What is the scholar like? What might it feel like to live in this community?

A Talmudic Scholar from Marmaresch was on his way home from a visit to Budapest. Opposite him in the railway carriage sat another Jew, dressed in modern fashion and smoking a cigar. When the conductor came around to collect the tickets the scholar noticed that his neighbor opposite was also on his way to Marmaresch.

This seemed very odd to him.

"Who can it be, and why is he going to Marmaresch?" he wondered.

As it would not be polite to ask outright he tried to figure it out for himself. "Now let me see," he mused. "He is a modern Jew, well dressed, and he smokes a cigar. Whom could a man of this type be visiting in Marmaresch? Possibly he's on his way to our town doctor's wedding. But no, that can't be! That's two weeks off. Certainly this kind of man wouldn't twiddle his thumbs in our town for two weeks!

"Why then is he on his way to Marmaresch? Perhaps he's courting a woman there. But who could it be? Now let me see. Moses Goldman's daughter Esther? Yes definitely, it's she and nobody else . . . ! But now that I think of it—that couldn't be! She's too old—he wouldn't have her, under any circumstances! Maybe it's Haikeh Wasservogel? Phooey! She's so ugly! Who then? Could it be Leah, the money-lender's daughter? N—no! What a match for such a nice man! Who then? There aren't any more marriageable girls in Marmaresch. That's settled then, he's not going courting.

"What then brings him?

"Wait, I've got it! It's about Mottel Kohn's bankruptcy case! But what connection can he have with that? Could it be that he is one of his creditors? Hardly! Just look at him sitting there so calmly, reading his newspaper and smiling to himself. Anybody can see nothing worries him! No, he's not a creditor. But I'll bet he has something to do with the bankruptcy! Now what could it be?

"Wait a minute, I think I've got it. Mottel Kohn must have corresponded with a lawyer from Budapest about his bankruptcy. But that swindler Mottel certainly wouldn't confide his business secrets to a stranger! So it stands to reason that the lawyer must be a member of the family.

"Now who could it be? Could it be his sister Shprinzah's son? No, that's impossible. She got married twenty-six years ago—I remember it very well because the wedding took place in the green synagogue. And this man here looks at least thirty-five.

"A funny thing! Who could it be, after all . . . ? Wait a minute! It's as clear as day! This is his nephew, his brother Hayyim's son, because Hayyim Kohn got married thirty-seven years and two months ago in the stone synagogue near the market place. Yes, that's who he is!

"In a nutshell—he is Lawyer Kohn from Budapest. But a lawyer from Budapest surely must have the title 'Doctor'! So, he is Doctor Kohn from Budapest, no? But wait a minute! A lawyer from Budapest who calls himself 'Doctor' won't call himself 'Kohn'! Anybody knows that. It's certain that he has changed his name into Hungarian. Now, what kind of a name could he have made out of Kohn? Kovacs! Yes, that's it—Kovacs! In short, this is Doctor Kovacs from Budapest!

Eager to start a conversation the scholar turned to his travelling companion and asked, "Doctor Kovacs, do you mind if I open the window?"

"Not at all," answered the other. "But tell me, how do you know that I am Doctor Kovacs?"

"It was obvious," replied the scholar.*

What is the community of Marmaresch like? Why would an individual as obviously well-to-do as the stranger on the train go to a community like that? Is it obvious to you that the stranger was Dr. Kovacs?

Now, reread the folktale. This time concentrate on the process the scholar goes through as he seeks to answer the question he asks at the beginning of the story. As you do this, write in the *left margin* a(n)

---

* Reprinted by permission of Schocken Books Inc., from *L'Chayim*, by Immanuel Olsvanger. Copyright © 1949, 1977 by Schocken Books Inc. and taken from *A Treasury of Jewish Folklore* edited by Nathan Ausubel. Copyright, 1948, 1976, by Crown Publishers, Inc. Used by permission of Crown Publishers, Inc.

1. *P* next to each line where the scholar states a *problem* or asks a question;
2. *H* next to each line where he states a *hypothesis;*
3. *T* next to each line where he states and/or analyzes information to *test* a hypothesis or tentative solution;
4. *C* next to each line where he states a *conclusion* about the accuracy of the hypothesis he is testing, and a *CC* next to the line where he states the conclusion to the major question he first set out to answer; and
5. *A* next to the line where he *applies* his major conclusion to new data.

In addition, look also for evidence of the knowledge and affective attributes of inquiry. Note in the *right margin* any behavior or examples that illustrate these attributes. What elements of inquiry can you find illustrated in the story?

THE PROCESS
OF INQUIRING

The preceding story vividly illustrates inquiry in action. After sensing a problem that almost demands solving, our scholar begins hypothesizing and then testing his hypotheses until he comes up with an answer. What happens as he engages in these operations?

Defining the Problem

Our scholar is apparently en route to the town of Marmaresch. He boards a train, perhaps in Budapest, and seats himself with other passengers in one of the coaches. Suddenly he becomes aware of a situation that puzzles him:

> . . . Opposite him in the railway carriage sat another Jew, dressed in modern fashion and smoking a cigar. When the conductor came around to collect the tickets the scholar noticed that his neighbor opposite was also on his way to Marmaresch.
> This seemed very odd to him. . . .

To our scholar, the facts just don't seem to fit or to make sense. He senses a gap between what he knows about Marmaresch and what he knows about people dressed like the stranger. Why would a person like *this* be going to a place like *that*? (What image do you have of Marmaresch as a result of reading the tale?) Certainly such a well-dressed, obviously well-to-do man has no business going to Marmaresch, or so our scholar thinks anyway. He seems to know enough about this little town to assume that only some very special occasion could be calling this gentleman there. The scholar is curious—"Who can it be. . . . ?" His statement of the problem is simple and direct. He starts to mentally inquire.

Our scholar doesn't jump to any hasty conclusions. Nor does he tackle the entire problem all at once. Although he seeks primarily to determine the identity of the stranger, he breaks his problem into a number of subordinate problems to make it more manageable. The answer to each sub-problem will, he hopes, lead him to an answer to his major question. He elects first to figure out *why* this man is going to Marmaresch, thinking perhaps that if he can determine this he will have some clues to the man's identity. So the immediate problem becomes ". . . why is he going to Marmaresch?"

Hypothesizing and Testing the Hypotheses

Our scholar again studies the subject of his curiosity and notices that the man is well-dressed and modern. From the stranger's behavior and appearance, he infers the man is reasonably wealthy. The scholar then attempts to recall information about the town that might suggest something important enough to bring a man like this to Marmaresch. As he does, he suddenly comes up with a possible reason: the *town doctor's wedding*. However, examination of information about the date of the wedding and the apparently sleepy, dull nature of the community itself suggests that this hypothesis is unacceptable. A successful businessman such as this stranger would not waste his time for two weeks waiting for a wedding! So the scholar concludes by rejecting this "answer" and returns to the problem once again.

"Why then is he on his way to Marmaresch?"

Courtship! A second hypothesis. So he dredges up some more information relevant to this guess:

". . . Moses Goldman's daughter Esther? Yes definitely, it's she and nobody else . . . ! But now that I think of it—that couldn't be! She's too old—he wouldn't have her, under any circumstances! Maybe it's Haikeh Wasservogel? Phooey! She's so ugly! Who then? Could it be Leah, the money-lender's daughter? N—no! What a match for such a nice man! Who then? There aren't any more marriageable girls. . . . "

Again, analysis of the evidence fails to yield anything that would lead one to believe this gentleman could be courting a girl from the town, so our scholar concludes that this hypothesis, too, is inaccurate and discards it.

"What, then brings him?"

Our scholar states the problem for a third time! Suddenly he recalls more information about events in the town that appears to offer a reasonable explanation. *Bankruptcy!* This becomes his third hypothesis:

. . . "Wait, I've got it! It's about Mottel Kohn's bankruptcy case!"

Concluding

At this point the inquiry into his first sub-problem comes to a close. Our scholar does not discard the idea of bankruptcy, but accepts it as the reason for this man's trip to Marmaresch. He does so because all other reasonable explanations simply do not make sense in terms of all the information available to him. As the last remaining "big event" in the community that he can recall, Mottel Kohn's bankruptcy seems to be the only thing important enough to bring an individual like this to Marmaresch. So for our scholar at least part of the original problem is now solved, even if only tentatively. The stranger is going to Marmaresch because of Kohn's bankruptcy!

Defining a New Problem

The main problem still remains, however. "Who can it be. . . ?" Having decided why the stranger is on his way to Marmaresch, our scholar now attempts to determine the man's possible connection with the bankruptcy case. He asks himself " . . . What connection can he have with that?" A new problem! If our scholar can figure out this connection he will be another step closer to his companion's identity!

Hypothesizing and Testing the Hypothesis

Once again the scholar guesses at an answer:

> ". . . Could it be that he is one of his creditors? Hardly! Just look at him sitting there so calmly, reading his newspaper and smiling to himself. Anybody can see nothing worries him! No, he's not a creditor. . . ."

Creditors would not be too happy or calm about the prospects of receiving only part instead of all of what Kohn might owe them. So our scholar discards that hypothesis and posits a new line of inquiry. What other kinds of people are usually involved in bankruptcy cases?

> "Wait a minute, I think I've got it. Mottel Kohn must have corresponded with a lawyer from Budapest about his bankruptcy. . . ."

Concluding

This makes sense! Now our scholar thinks he is on the right track. His traveling companion must be a lawyer. He is another step closer to answering his original question, "Who can it be. . . ?"

Problem-Hypothesis-Test-Conclusion

Our scholar now turns to another sub-problem. His perception of human nature apparently leads him to believe that people, if possible, do not expose their personal affairs to strangers or to the public in general. He also seems to know Mottel Kohn quite well, or at least he thinks he knows him. Hence, he immediately discards the possibility of this individual being a total stranger. Now the alternative appears to be relatively easy:

> ". . . But that swindler Mottel certainly wouldn't confide his business secrets to a stranger! So it stands to reason that the lawyer must be a member of the family. . . ."

All the scholar needs to do now is figure out which relative it could be. An answer is not long in coming. First, he states the problem again. Then he hypothesizes. He rejects his initial hypothesis because the available data (the date of the marriage and the apparent age of the man in question) do not support it. But then, suddenly, everything seems to fall into place:

> "Now who could it be? Could it be his sister Shprinzah's son? No, that's impossible. She got married twenty-six years ago—I remember it very well because the wedding took place in the green synagogue. And this man here looks at least thirty-five.
>
> "A funny thing! Who could it be, after all. . . .? Wait a minute! It's as clear as day! This is his nephew, his brother Hayyim's son, because Hayyim Kohn got marmaried thirty-seven years and two months ago in the stone synagogue near the market place. Yes, that's who he is!
>
> "In a nutshell—he is Lawyer Kohn from Budapest. . . ."

And so the scholar arrives at an answer to the problem regarding the stranger's relationship to Kohn. Thus, he has stated and answered, to his satisfaction, three questions, each of which has been designed to help him determine the answer to the initial problem "Who can it be. . . ?" Now he has a conclusion.

Stating a Conclusion

A conclusion? Possibly, but not quite, for even though the scholar now knows or thinks he knows the man's identity, several other minor problems remain to be dealt with:

> ". . . But a lawyer from Budapest surely must have the title 'Doctor'! So, he is Doctor Kohn from Budapest, no? But wait a minute! A lawyer from Budapest who calls himself 'Doctor' won't call himself 'Kohn'! Anybody knows that. It's certain that he has changed him name into Hungarian. Now what kind of a name could he have made out of Kohn? Kovacs! Yes, that's it—Kovacs! *In short, this is Doctor Kovacs from Budapest!*"

Finally, a conclusion, an answer to the original problem, "Who can it be. . .?" Of course, this man must be Dr. Kovacs! Our scholar has gone as far as he can on his own. He has stated the conclusion to the question that launched his inquiry.

Applying the Conclusion to New Data

Because our scholar is human, because he, too, can tolerate only so much ambiguity, he wants to know if he is correct. He could ask the man "Are you Dr. Kovacs?" but he does not. Instead, he assumes the man is Dr. Kovacs, that his own conclusion is correct, and applies this conclusion to the situation. Turning to his traveling companion he asks:

> "Doctor Kovacs, do you mind if I open the window?"
>
> "Not at all," answered the other. "But tell me, how do you know that I am Doctor Kovacs?"
>
> "It was obvious," replied the scholar.

Such is the process of inquiring in action. This process is the core of inquiry as a way of learning. As revealed by this folktale, inquiring consists of a

MAIN PROBLEM—WHO CAN IT BE?

1. *Sub-problem #1*   *...why is he going to Marmaresch?*

   *Hypothesize   he's on his way to the . . . wedding . . . .
   Test
   Conclude   No . . . .

   *Hypothesize   . . .he's courting . . . .
   Test
   Conclude   No . . . .

   *Hypothesize.   it's about . . . bankruptcy . . . .
   Test
   Conclude   Yes . . . .

   2. *Sub-problem #2*   *. . . something to do with bankruptcy?*

      *Hypothesize   . . . a creditor . . . .
      Test
      Conclude   No . . . .

      *Hypothesize   . . . a lawyer . . . .
      Test
      Conclude   Yes . . . .

      3. *Sub-problem #3*   *. . .which relative could it be?*

         *Hypothesize   . . . sister Shprinzah's son . . . .
         Test
         Conclude   No . . . .

         *Hypothesize   . . . brother Hayyim's son . . . .
         Test
         Conclude   Yes . . . .

         4. *Sub-problem #4*   *What is his exact name?*

            *Hypothesize . . . must have the title Doctor . . . .
            Test
            Conclude   Yes . . . .

            *Hypothesize . . . changed his name to Kovacs . . . .
            Test
            Conclude   Yes . . . .

CONCLUSION

In short, this is Dr. Kovacs from Budapest!

Then this conclusion is applied to new data to help make sense out
of the situation — and to satisfy the scholar that his inquiry really is
accurate!

Figure 2.1. Steps in a Scholar's Method of Inquiring

number of mental operations. The outline in Figure 2.1 displays the basic steps of inquiring that our scholar went through.

THE NATURE
OF INQUIRY

Inquiry is a self-directed, rational strategy for making sense out of experience. It represents a way of thinking that requires the systematic manipulation of information to find a supportable answer or solution to a question or problem. Reduced to its simplest terms, the process of inquiring consists of the five basic steps shown in Figure 2.2.

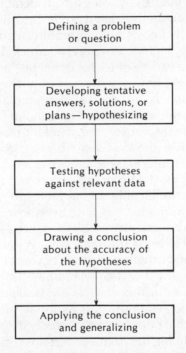

Figure 2.2. Steps in a Process of Inquiring

The process by which one inquires is, of course, central to inquiry as a way to learn. However, as we noted earlier, inquiry is more than a process. Inquiry consists also of certain knowledge, attitudes, and values that guide the use of this process and direct its actions. The folktale example also illustrates these aspects of inquiry.

What other elements of inquiry could you identify in the folktale? The scholar finds himself in a problematic situation that he could solve by asking his traveling companion for his name. But neither custom nor his own inclinations permit him to do so. Instead, he proceeds to work out the answer for himself, to think—to inquire. He obviously values reasoning as a way to solve problems and to learn.

Many attitudes supportive of inquiry are evident in this example. The scholar is certainly curious! A situation that would undoubtedly bother few, if any other, people on this train puzzles him. One reason for his curiosity is the spatial, temporal, and cultural proximity of the problem, making it relevant to him. Furthermore, what the scholar perceives does not make sense. He seems to be a keen observer and to have a wide background of experience. He also seems to have a low tolerance for ambiguity. His interest is quickly triggered: "Who can it be. . . ?" Nor does he give up easily in his quest for an acceptable answer. In spite of several dead ends, he pursues the evidence until he arrives at a conclusion that proves valid, at least to his satisfaction. He reveals a willingness to suspend a final judgment until examining all available evidence; he examines as many sides of the problem as possible; and, finally, he respects evidence as a test for the validity of his guesses by using a considerable amount of information in testing his hypotheses about the identity of his traveling companion.

This scholar obviously knows how to inquire. Perhaps that is what makes him a scholar! At any rate, he has command—knowledge—of the basic tools of inquiry: sources of data, a variety of useful concepts, and a process of inquiring itself. Interestingly enough, however, he has only two major sources of data. One source of information is, of course, the scholar's traveling companion himself, the object of his initial curiosity. Our scholar secures information from this source by observation. Moreover, the scholar's memory serves as a second source of information. Over the past years he has stored away, just as do all people, bits and pieces of information and experiences. He has acquired and stored information about Mottel Kohn, his affairs and family, about an upcoming wedding, and about the eligible young ladies in the small town. Why or when he acquired this information has long been lost, but now, suddenly, this data becomes relevant to a particular problem of interest.

All of us conduct ourselves in this same way. We accumulate data for many purposes over the years and often retain it far beyond the time when it was collected or after the reason why it was collected has disappeared. Students, as do all human beings, function in this way; every student possesses a vast storehouse of information collected in the past that may suddenly become germane to a problem or concern that pops up unexpectedly in the future.

In addition, this scholar has formed certain concepts—of courtship, of bankruptcy, of Budapest lawyers—that lead him to ask questions whose answers guide his search for and analysis of all the information he collects. As does any efficient inquirer, our scholar makes use of all he can recall or find out as he moves to answer the puzzling question that initiated his inquiry.

This scholar also makes a number of assumptions based on his previous knowledge, his observations of the stranger, and the inferences he makes about each. For example, he first assumes that only a major event could bring a gentleman such as the stranger to Marmaresch. He can think of only three such events, a wedding, courtship, and the bankruptcy case. Although the stranger could be going there for other reasons, a family visit perhaps or a business deal, the scholar seems to know enough about Marmaresch to discount these as logical reasons, and thus can make the assumptions he does.

The scholar also makes at least two other assumptions crucial to this inquiry. He assumes that an individual dressed like the stranger must have a certain temperament and type of background, as well as certain personal tastes. Such an individual, he infers, is wealthy and, he assumes, did not get that wealth or keep it by twiddling his thumbs for two weeks in quiet places like Marmaresch! He also assumes that the stranger would seek a certain type of marriage partner. None of the eligible women he can think of match these assumed tastes.

Finally, the scholar assumes that, with human nature as it is, Mottel Kohn or any other individual for that matter might not wish to publicize his personal affairs like bankruptcy if he could avoid it. Thus, the inquiring scholar infers that the stranger, if he is connected with the bankruptcy case, must be Kohn's relative. He bases much of his inquiry on similar reasoned assumptions. All who engage in inquiry base their reasoning on certain assumptions derived from their knowledge and experience over the years, often testing these assumptions implicitly by experience and reasoning but never really submitting them to a rigorous, explicit analysis.

Inquiry is a form of systematic, purposeful thinking. As such, no particular discipline monopolizes this way of learning. Inquiry is, rather, an approach to learning in which all rational thinkers, problem-solvers, or reflective thinkers engage. Inquiry has as much use in resolving everyday personal problems (such as how to retrieve your car keys from inside your locked car or how to go about reducing heat loss in your home over a cold winter) as it has for resolving public policy issues or for learning in a classroom setting.

Inquiry differs considerably from exposition—telling—as a guide to learning. Once mastered, this method of learning becomes self-initiated and self-directed for it involves the systematic use of reason to learn on one's own. Such learning does *not* require constant direction from some outside authority as does exposition. Yet, as illustrated in the folktale analyzed here, the nature of inquiry is complex. At its core, inquiry consists of a process comprising a number of complex steps undertaken in sequence to accomplish a predetermined goal. The more detailed analysis of this process presented in Chapter 3 will clarify the basic elements of this process and the precise nature of each when applied to classroom learning.

3

The
Process
of
Inquiring

The process of inquiring lies at the very heart of inquiry and purposeful thinking. However, this process does not always proceed in a linear fashion from problem statement directly to conclusion. Instead, some of the specific operations involved frequently double back on each other, sometimes occur simultaneously, and occasionally are skipped altogether. At times this process consists of many mini-versions of the overall process linked together into a larger whole. Yet each step in the entire process is important to successful inquiry and, therefore, to learning. Careful analysis of the basic steps provides the groundwork upon which to build a teaching strategy that can facilitate the development and use of thinking in the classroom.

THE PROCESS
OF INQUIRING

As described in Chapter 2, the process of inquiring involves five basic operations. Not so simple as suggested there, each of the operations, in turn, involves a number of subordinate steps or procedures. When considered in its entirety, the process of inquiring consists generally of the procedures outlined in Figure 3.1. This figure indicates the five major operations in inquiring down the center of the diagram. Each operation also includes the procedures designated along the right or left side of the diagram. If this diagram suggests that the process of inquiry is rather complex, such is indeed the case. However, a step-by-step analysis of the process and its components, with reference to the folktale presented in the preceding chapter, can reduce this complexity and make clear the exact nature of this process.

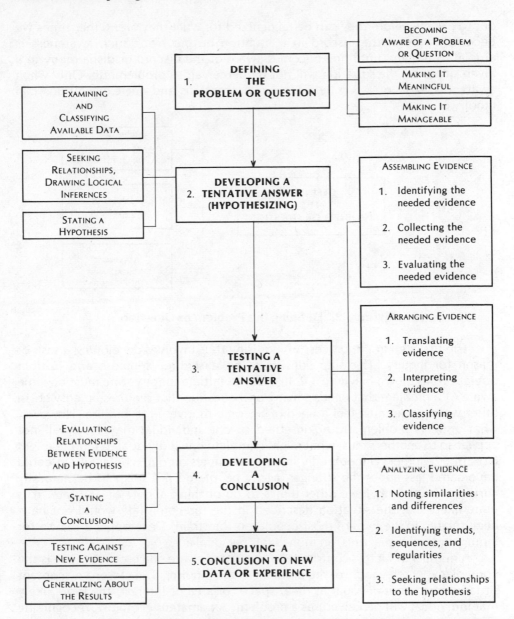

Figure 3.1. A Process of Inquiring

Defining the Problem or Question

Inquiry starts with an unsettled, discordant, or problematic situation that demands some kind of closure, whether in the form of an answer to a question, a solution to a problem, or a bit of missing information. Many such situations exist all around us every day. Others are contrived for a variety of purposes, including teaching and learning. Sometimes these situations have to be pointed out to people before they can be recognized for what they are. Other times we become aware of the discord in a situation on our own. Such awareness is crucial to inquiry; until one becomes aware of the discord or disharmony in a given situation, the situation will not be perceived as problematic. Only when awareness exists of a gap between our perceptions and our expectations can inquiry occur.

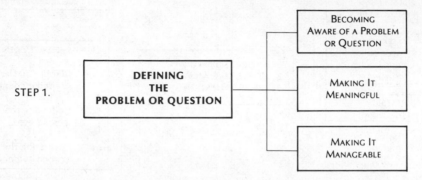

Figure 3.2. Defining the Problem or Question

The first step in the process of inquiring thus involves developing a task or reason for inquiry. This step consists of at least three separate and distinct operations as shown in Figure 3.2. In order to initiate inquiry, one must become aware of a problem that needs solving or a question that requires an answer. In other words, one must feel a need or become motivated to inquire. However, what appears problematic or unsettled to one individual may very well not appear so to another; thus, what might stimulate one individual to inquire might not affect another. Undoubtedly, many passengers on our scholar's train could have cared less about the stranger. Many people do not seem to be naturally curious. Others may have other things to do or think about. At any rate, it is quite likely that the situation described in the foregoing tale would not have been related to the lives of most people on that train. Developing a reason for inquiry or thinking is, thus, an individual, personal act.

A number of factors contribute to becoming aware of a problem. One is the immediacy, or relevancy, of the problem to the inquirer. The closer a discordant situation is to an individual in time, space, or area of interest, the more likely that individual will perceive it as a problem. An amateur geologist, recognizing a piece of basalt in a stream bed, may ask, "How did this get here?" Yet to a nongeologist, the presence of the same rock may simply mean another stone in the stream and suggest no problem at all. What appears relevant to one person may by no means appear relevant to another. Relevancy is not inherent in a situation; it is made by the individual interacting with the elements of a situation.

The degree of apparent cognitive dissonance in a situation constitutes a second problem-making factor. Such dissonance results from becoming aware of an unexplained gap or difference between what one knows or believes to be true on the one hand and what one sees, hears, or otherwise experiences on the other. Cognitive dissonance resulting from such a gap or unexplained difference stems largely from an individual's previous experience and his or her perception of a given situation. If one does not know the difference between basalt or other rock and does not know that basalt is uncommon to an area, then its perceived presence in that area would not be puzzling. One must know something about a situation in order to become aware of an element in it that doesn't make sense. Our scholar, for example, knows enough about Marmaresch to believe that apparently no modern, well-to-do, city-dweller would, under normal circumstances, spend much time there. Yet he sees a modern city-dweller seemingly bent on doing just that. To our scholar, this discrepancy just doesn't make sense. So his inquiry begins because of a sense of discord or cognitive dissonance that results from his awareness of a discrepancy in the data before him.

Thus, the relevance of and dissonance perceived within a situation help make one aware of a problem. Both of these factors depend on the individual's frame of reference. What appears out of order to one individual may be perfectly harmonious to another. A person's knowledge, attitudes, and perceptual set or frame of reference shape how he or she perceives any given situation.[1] Until one becomes aware of a problem by feeling a sense of cognitive disequilibrium or perplexity, the chances of any purposeful inquiry, or thinking, are nil. Moreover, as Dewey noted, the demand for the solution to a perplexity serves to steady and guide the entire process of inquiry.[2]

Becoming aware of a problematic situation doesn't mean that one will automatically proceed to solve it, however. To evoke interest and motivate an individual to inquire, a problem must also be perceived as worthy of further investigation. In order to generate a willingness to inquire on the part of the learner, the problem must not be so complex or remote as to discourage or defy attempts at resolution. Whether or not a specific nation should be admitted to the United Nations may be widely perceived as a problem; yet few individuals seriously grapple with it. Most ignore it: some because it appears irrelevant to them; others because it seems too difficult to resolve. Moreover, most individuals find problematic situations worth attending to only when they perceive that the solution seems to lie within their power. The possibility of being able to resolve a problem plays an important role in encouraging individuals to engage in inquiry.

Once one has become aware of a problem and decides to deal with it, the problem, question, or task must be made meaningful and manageable. Whether a question, mystery, problem, or some other type of puzzle, the initiating task must be cast in terms that have meaning for the inquirer. Ambiguous terms must be defined. The nature of missing or disjunctive data must be made explicit, as must the assumptions implied by the problem and brought to the situation by the individual.

The task to be undertaken must also be made manageable. For example, our scholar notes discrepancies in a situation that confronts him, and he believes he can resolve the problem that creates the resulting dissonance. The basic question facing him becomes: "Who can it be?" This question is too large to answer all at once, so he breaks it down into a number of more manageable subordinate problems or questions: "why is he going to Marmaresch?" and, when that is solved, "what connection can he have with [bankruptcy]?", and so on. By dealing with each subproblem in turn, the scholar resolves his main problem of identifying the traveller. Failing to separate a major problem into several smaller ones capable of easier handling may well hinder effective resolution of a problematic situation.

Initiating inquiry thus requires defining the problem or question to be investigated. This in turn means doing at least three things: become aware of a problematic situation; cast it in meaningful terms; and make it manageable. Once the initial question or problem becomes clear and manageable, inquiry becomes possible and potentially productive.

Developing Tentative Answers—Hypothesizing

Hypothesizing constitutes the second major step in inquiring. *Hypothesis* denotes an educated guess—a statement of a possible answer, solution, or alternative derived from the learner's past experience, frequently a quick, sometimes almost intuitive, analysis of the present, available data. Hypothesizing is generally inductive, for it involves working with separate, often disparate bits of information (data) and coming up with, or inferring, a general statement that asserts a possible relationship between all the data and the initial problem itself. A hypothesis goes beyond the evidence from which it is derived. Its validation serves both as a goal toward which an inquiry is directed and as a tool for directing that inquiry.

In the folktale presented in Chapter 2, bits of apparently unrelated information (a dull, sleepy little town, a number of significant events underway or about to start there, a well-dressed, professional-appearing stranger en route to this town) confront our scholar. Once he clarifies the problem, he begins to search for some way the data might be interrelated to fill in the gap that perplexes him. His resulting explanations serve as his hypotheses.

A hypothesis may result from either intuitive or analytical thinking. Intuition produces that flash in the dark, the light bulb over the head, the sudden big idea! It is generally assumed to just pop into our minds. But it does not. An intuitive guess results from some rapid-fire connections between our perception of the elements of a problematic situation and something we know. An intuitive guess is nothing more than a discovery, and as Bruner has stated, discovery is favored by the well-prepared mind. It doesn't happen in a vacuum. [3]

Thus, in some instances hypotheses may arise without any deliberate or systematic thought at all. Our scholar intuits a hypothesis to explain why his companion is traveling to Marmaresch: "Wait, I've got it! It's about Mottel Kohn's bankruptcy case!" Yet, this hypothesis is no inspiration pulled out of thin air. In actuality, it is based on the results of two previous hypotheses that have been discarded and on the scholar's knowledge that a bankruptcy case is, indeed, in progress in the community.

Intuitive thinking is simply unsystematic thinking. It may not follow the same conscious or deliberate procedures as analytical thinking, but it does involve making connections between observed data and one's previous experiences and present knowledge. Hypothesizing may be facilitated by brainstorming seemingly wild and unrelated ideas, but making these ideas relate to the problem or question at hand requires a deliberate effort on the part of the individual engaged in making the hypothesis.

Analytical thinking, on the other hand, involves a very conscious, step-by-step mental manipulation of information. In hypothesizing, one may systematically attempt to take apart the elements of the problematic situation perceived and then attempt to match the various pieces with relevant knowledge stored in one's memory. When a piece or two matches what we already know, a hypothesis, or tentative explanation, results. Our scholar does this. His companion appears well-dressed, and there is going to be a wedding in the town; therefore, perhaps the stranger is going to the wedding—a perfectly reasonable connection. Or, maybe the stranger is going courting; there are a few eligible girls in the town, and the man seems to be dressed for such an occasion. Not drawn out of thin air, the scholar's hypotheses result from deliberate, yet simple, efforts to make connections between what he perceives and what he knows.

Thus hypothesizing, whether intuitive or systematic, involves a number of discrete cognitive operations as illustrated in Figure 3.3. Of course, this process does not proceed at the same rate of speed for everyone. For some it may require considerable intellectual effort and time; for others it may be a lightning-quick operation. The rate at which one hypothesizes may also vary from problem to problem. But hypothesizing is a crucial step in inquiry, for without it effective learning cannot proceed.

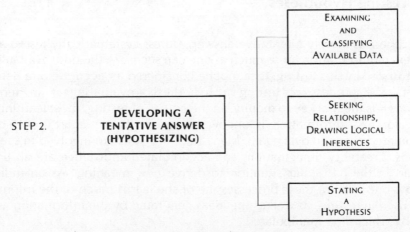

Figure 3.3. Hypothesizing

Hypotheses play two major roles in inquiring. First, a hypothesis serves as a goal or target of inquiry; when the initial hypothesis has been validated or invalidated, the inquiry ends. If, as in the folklore example, further examination of the information about courtship suggests that this guess is not reasonable, the hypothesis must be discarded as inaccurate. Our scholar abandons that particular line of inquiry. He knows that the evidence does not substantiate his guess, and he need not flounder around in a great deal of other related information to test it out. Instead, he must make another guess and test it against the data.

Secondly, a hypothesis serves as a guide for selecting data relevant to the problem. It tells which of all the available data to examine and which to ignore. For example, our scholar's hypothesis that courtship is the reason for the stranger's trip suggests a need to examine information about the eligible girls in the community. There is no need to consider information about job opportunities or vacation spots.

A hypothesis, it must be remembered, is a guess and only a guess. It is not the result or end point of inquiry but a starting point. A hypothesis represents an inference based on examination of only limited information. When we hypothesize we look at whatever data confronts us, just as our scholar has done, and then infer something about the data and its relation to what we know in terms of the problem or question at hand. Our inference may follow from the data but, because our data are so fragmentary, the hypothesized inference does not necessarily have to follow. It may be accurate, but the data from which we have derived it are not sufficient to guarantee its absolute validity.

Hypothesizing thus serves a most useful purpose in inquiring. A hypothesis makes learning efficient by directing our inquiry to the kinds of evidence we need, and it delimits such learning by setting goals. Hypothesizing is, indeed, an absolutely crucial step in inquiry. But it is neither the first nor the final step.

Testing Hypotheses

A hypothesis is merely a tentative answer. Unless systematically tested against all relevant information (or as much as one can secure in the time available) and substantiated by this testing, it cannot be considered an accurate or a definitive answer. The process of testing a hypothesis—evaluating it in terms of evidence—is the real key to inquiry. In the course of testing, most learning takes place, for new information is uncovered, used, pulled apart, refitted, and manipulated over and over again. Many thinking skills are involved in these operations. Creativity, imagination, and accumulated knowledge are all brought to bear on the particular situation to derive new meaning. As an individual employs one or all of these processes, he or she learns much of the information being used in testing, as well as the ideas generated by the information and the skills by which it is manipulated.

Hypothesis testing involves many tasks. Some educators describe these tasks by the terms *analysis* or *analyzing data*. However, the vagueness of such terms obscures the essence of what one does when testing a hypothesis. In reality, these operations may be classified and arranged as in Figure 3.4 into three major steps: assembling evidence, arranging the evidence for analysis, and analyzing the evidence in terms of the problems and hypotheses under consideration.

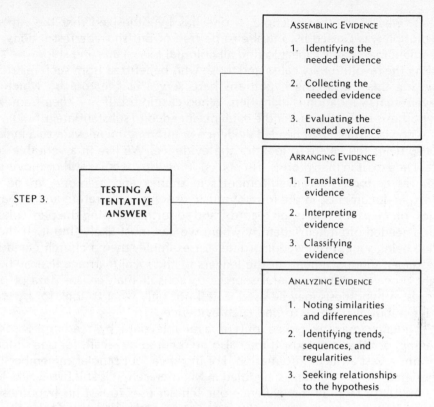

Figure 3.4. Testing Hypotheses

Assembling evidence. Testing a hypothesis first requires assembling the appropriate evidence. This necessitates determining which of all the obtainable data appear relevant to the hypothesis under investigation. In other words, one of the first tasks facing anyone engaged in inquiry involves sifting through all the available information about a subject or topic to identify the items that bear in one way or another on the hypothesis being tested. This identified information becomes evidence. By pulling from all the information available only that which may affect the hypothesis, we reduce the amount of investigation necessary to determine the accuracy of our hypothesis. Thus, in order to start testing a hypothesis, we must assemble the information that relates to it—we must collect *evidence*. Before such evidence can be ferreted out, we must decide what it is. The hypothesis we choose to test actually helps us make this decision.

A hypothesis actually implies or predicts the kind of specific evidence that should exist if the hypothesis itself is valid. Thus, this step of testing commences by drawing out the logical implications or predictions of the hypothesis. Regardless of the nature of the hypothesis, *if* it is true, *then* certain data supportive of it will exist. And, by the same token, *if* the hypothesis is accurate, *then* certain evidence that might refute it will not exist. *If*, in the case of our scholar, the reason that the individual on the train is going to Marmaresch is to attend a wedding, *then* there must be someone who is getting married relatively soon. Finding such evidence will lend credence to the hypothesis; failure to find such evidence may invalidate the hypothesis.

By way of another example, if one has hypothesized that the American Revolution was caused by a desire to be free of British trade restrictions, then one might reasonably expect to find all colonial merchants and shipowners supporting the revolutionary cause and those who benefitted from such restrictions opposing this cause. The hypothesis here serves as the tool by which data relevant to its validation is identified. When cast in this *if . . . then* framework, a hypothesis tells the inquirer the evidence needed to substantiate it.[4]

Knowing the kind of needed evidence or information relevant to a hypothesis also helps tell where to look for the evidence. We live in a veritable sea of data. Data exist in many forms—in books, in newspapers, as still or moving pictures, as cartoons, in advertisements, in diaries and memoirs, in personal letters, in documents, in the form of music or song, in literature and art, as statistics, on maps, on charts, on records, and so forth. Knowing the particular evidence needed often helps identify where we can most likely find it. If the evidence being sought is a wedding date, for example, then a church calendar, a newspaper announcement, or the ledgers of the local marriage license bureau might prove much more useful sources to consult than census data or police records. A hypothesis may be used to tell not only what to look for by way of evidence but also where to find such evidence.

Evidence may be pulled out of available data by reading, observing, listening, or other methods. It may also be secured by recall, for one's memory contains a vast array of information. For instance, our scholar remembers that, although there is a wedding scheduled in Marmaresch, it is still two weeks away. As a matter of fact, all the evidence our scholar uses to test his hypotheses he collects from his own memory or by observation of the elements of the situation confronting him. He could just as easily collect additional evidence from friends and acquaintances or pertinent documents if they were available and if he had the time. Regardless of the source or method of collection, assembling evidence serves as the first step in testing a hypothesis.

Once appropriate evidence has been collected, or more usually as it is being collected, it must be evaluated. The inquirer must determine not only the relevancy of data to the hypothesis being tested (i.e., whether it will be evidence or not) but also the authenticity of this evidence. Each piece of evidence must be examined to determine if it truly is what it purports to be. If it is a diary, did its supposed author really write it? If it is a newspaper description of an event, is its author writing from personal observation or from interviews with those who witnessed the event? If it is a song about work in the coal mines, did the mine workers themselves actually create it or was it written by a folk singer based on his or her impressions of what it must have been like to work in the mines? If the information is in the form of statistics, what were the sources of the statistics, who collected them, when, and why? Most evidence contains clues to the answers to these and similar questions. Yet often one must go beyond the specific piece of evidence under examination to additional sources in order to answer these questions.

Evaluation at this stage of inquiry also requires us to determine the accuracy of the information contained in a source. Does the content of the material accurately portray what it claims to portray? Do the contents of the diary give dates for events that we already know from other sources to be accurate? Does the newspaper account of the event coincide with other accounts in its basic facts? Does the song accurately reflect conditions in the mine as evidenced, perhaps, by a transcript of a government inquiry? Or do the statistics on a chart check out with those found in a reputable statistical abstract or almanac?

Other factors also affect the accuracy of evidence, and these too must be evaluated. An inquirer must identify the assumptions upon which the evidence is based and label and distinguish statements of subjective opinion from statements of objective fact. The biases and prejudices of the authors or sources of the evidence must be made explicit by noting emotionally charged words, omissions, and distortions and their effect on the meaning of the evidence. Information left unevaluated as to accuracy and authenticity makes suspect any conclusion derived from that information.

The evidence used to test a hypothesis must be sufficient as well as accurate. It must also be significant, not trivial, and include enough cases to make the conclusion almost certainly true. This means that we must deliberately search for evidence that, if found, might well prove our hypotheses invalid as well as valid. If none can be found after an honest, thorough search, then a hypothesis stands a greater chance of being valid than it would if we ignored or never searched for such evidence. We cannot validate a guess on skimpy evidence or by ignoring contrary evidence.

Assembling evidence thus constitutes the initial step in hypothesis testing. It consists primarily of three operations: identifying the evidence needed, collecting available information on the topic, and evaluating this information. Our scholar engages in each operation, even if only briefly or by implication, following the generation of each hypothesis. Sometimes these operations go on almost simultaneously; at other times they are very deliberately carried out one at a time. Regardless of the order or method of execution, however, these tasks must be undertaken before the data collected can be analyzed to see how it bears on the hypothesis being tested.

Arranging evidence for analysis. A second set of operations must also be undertaken prior to any attempt to determine how the information collected affects the hypothesis. These operations involve arranging evidence for analysis by means of translating, interpreting, and classifying that evidence. Of course, these operations do not necessarily occur in this sequence. However, it is essential that they do occur, because they help to arrange the information for systematic analysis and evaluation.

Translating evidence means exactly that—changing it from one form into another without changing its meaning. This may involve preparing a written statement of the contents of a map, photograph, or bar graph, for example. This step involves no interpretation—just a literal report of what is seen, heard, read, or experienced.

Interpretation involves another completely different operation. Here one infers the apparent meaning of a piece of information. Interpretation normally follows translation, but it sometimes occurs almost simultaneously with translation. However, the two should not be confused. At one point our scholar hypothesizes that his companion may be a creditor in a bankruptcy case. But in collecting his information he notes that the traveler is smiling, relaxed, and enjoying a newspaper. He interprets his translation of this observed information, his evidence, to mean that the man is inwardly calm. He then infers that he could hardly be a creditor!

Sometimes at this stage of hypothesis testing it is useful to categorize evidence into classes, the elements of each class having certain features in common. Data may be classified in many ways depending on the concept or frame of reference that generates the organizing principles. A biologist might classify data as animal, vegetable, or mineral, or vertebrate and nonvertebrate. A historian might classify data in terms of cause and effect and then classify information in the category of causes as immediate or long-range, necessary or sufficient, and so on. When a large mass of information needs to be examined, classifying compatible information into several different sets of categories makes perceiving meaningful relationships easier. Thus, for example, classifying the original thirteen English colonies in America according to their type of government (royal, charter, or proprietary) yields several insights about the colonies and the Crown's view of colonization on the American continent. Reclassifying these same colonies according to location (southern, middle, or New England) leads to additional insights into their size, economic features, and political power. Multiple classification of data proves extremely useful for determining (1) whether such information bears on a hypothesis and thus may be considered as evidence, and (2) what this evidence may say in terms of the hypothesis being tested.

Analyzing the evidence. Making meaning is the goal of the final stage in hypothesis testing, analyzing the evidence. By now, all the information seemingly related to a hypothesis under consideration has been searched out and evaluated; it has been translated, if necessary, interpreted, and classified. What remains is to find relationships among the bits and pieces of information, to identify trends, sequences, or regularities within the information, and to find relationships between this information and the hypothesis being tested. These challenging cognitive operations form the very heart of hypothesis testing.

Our scholar repeatedly engages in these analytical operations. After he arranges, translates, and interprets the evidence bearing on his hypothesis that the man in question might be a creditor, he seeks a relationship between the man's apparent behavior and the way he should act if he were a creditor. This is a weaker part of the scholar's analysis. But rightly or wrongly he seems to assume that if the traveller were a creditor and stood to lose some money, then he would be somewhat apprehensive, if not downright nervous, during the trip to Marmaresch. But apparently he is not. Therefore, at least to our scholar's way of thinking, the necessary relationship between the observed information and hypothesis is lacking. Similar examples of such analyses may be found throughout the description of our scholar's mind at work. They represent the final stage of hypothesis testing.

Developing a Conclusion

Two additional major steps of inquiring remain. No inquiry would be complete without a conclusion, for this is the target toward which curiosity and a desire to bring closure to an unsettled situation motivate anyone who inquires. A conclusion, in part, represents that closure.

Developing a conclusion basically involves the two operations illustrated in Figure 3.5. First, one must decide the extent to which the evidence and the patterns found therein support and/or fail to support the hypothesis being tested. The resulting decision constitutes a conclusion. Stating the conclusion is the second part of this step of inquiring.

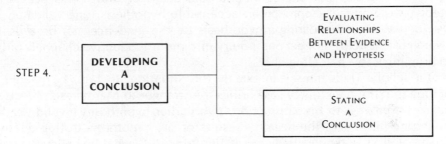

Figure 3.5. Developing a Conclusion

Determining the extent to which the available evidence supports or refutes a hypothesis involves a judgment or evaluation. Here one must first judge against given criteria, whether already established or established by the inquirer, to determine if the evidence supports the hypothesis. One must also judge the degree to which the evidence supports the hypothesis: whether the hypothesis is accurate beyond all doubt because the evidence overwhelmingly supports it and no evidence to the contrary can be found; or whether the hypothesis is merely probable because only a minimum of supporting evidence seems to exist.

In many instances, the process of evaluation occurs throughout the testing stage of inquiry concurrently with the analysis of information. Evaluation involves sifting through data to find just what information relates to the hypothesis being tested. Furthermore, a person engaged in other aspects of hypothesis testing cannot help but make informal judgments about the validity of the hypothesis under consideration as new evidence comes to light. As evaluation unfolds, one often begins to find the hypothesis more or less convincing, depending on the evidence unearthed. Yet, there remains a point where all the evidence must be reviewed to weigh it objectively. The step of evaluating relationships between the evidence and the hypothesis will offer just this opportunity.

If the evidence supports or validates the hypothesis, the concluding statement will probably just restate the hypothesis. But if the evidence fails to support the hypothesis, one must conclude that the hypothesis is invalid—often as important a result of inquiring as validating a hypothesis. The hypothesis must then be either discarded or modified. In the latter instance, a conclusion might bring about a revised statement of the original hypothesis taking into account the evidence that required the revision, or it might be an almost completely new statement.

We should note here that finding a hypothesis invalid in terms of the evidence—getting, in effect, a "no" for an answer—is most useful in inquiry. Such an outcome should not be considered a failure or waste of time. Finding a hypothesis unsubstantiated by the evidence actually serves a positive purpose by moving us one step further toward a valid conclusion. When a hypothesis is invalidated, we know that a particular line of inquiry need be pursued no longer. This narrows our choice of potential answers. And if this occurs repeatedly, we gradually approach an acceptable hypothesis, one validated by the evidence. So, invalidating a hypothesis by the evidence can be a useful answer in that it helps redirect our inquiry into more productive channels rather than bringing it to a halt altogether.

Our scholar finds himself in exactly this situation. In fact, he is able to conclude that the bankruptcy case brings the stranger to Marmaresch precisely because he proves, to his satisfaction, two earlier hypotheses invalid. Rather than setting him back, the negative results of his hypothesis testing about a courtship and a wedding actually move him forward to what he believes a valid hypothesis. This same situation also occurs at other points in his inquiry.

Regardless of the outcome, while testing the hypothesis against the evidence we perceive relationship patterns that support, modify, or negate the hypothesis. When these have been stated, we have a conclusion.

Our scholar, for example, concludes each phase of hypothesis testing with a brief statement of the fate of his hypothesis: "But no, that can't be!"; "(The wedding is) two weeks off."; ". . . he's not going courting."; "No, he's not a creditor."; "So it stands to reason that the lawyer must be a member of the family." And so on. Finally, he states the conclusion of his entire inquiry: "In short, this is Dr. Kovacs from Budapest." This answers the initial question, "Who can it be. . . ?" Closure has been achieved. Almost.

Applying a Conclusion to New Data

No conclusion may be considered completely accurate or final until it has been checked against all the relevant data. The amount and quality of the evidence accumulated and used in the process of testing hypotheses determine the certainty of the conclusion that follows. A conclusion derived from an incomplete sample of evidence must by necessity be considered more tentative than one tested against all the relevant data. The goal of inquiring is to use all the evidence possible so that the resulting conclusion will be as "conclusive" as possible!

Ideal as this goal may be, however, we rarely arrive at an absolutely valid conclusion. Consequently, inquiry often results in a conclusion that, although more valid than the initial hypothesis, may still not be absolutely accurate because all the supportive evidence is simply not available. Such a situation often compels us to go a step beyond merely developing our own conclusions. We may have to consider our own conclusion tentative until a future opportunity arises to test it further against new data. Or we can take more immediate steps to see if we are right by checking our conclusion against the findings of others considered authorities on the subject under investigation.

The final step of inquiring is thus crucial in bringing closure to an inquiry, for it restores the psychological as well as intellectual equilibrium that, having been upset, initiated the inquiry in the first place. The almost innate desire for certainty usually impels us to check out our conclusion to be sure of its accuracy; we need assurance that we are right. Thus, when new evidence turns up, we reexamine the conclusion in light of this evidence and reaffirm, modify, or perhaps discard it. Yet, when the original evidence consists basically of primary data, many inquirers still may consider their conclusions somewhat tentative because they are unwilling to accept their own inquiry as final. And so, as a final step in inquiry, many inquirers turn to established authorities to corroborate the results of their own inquiring.

When individuals thus test their conclusions against expert opinions, usually their goal is not to learn if what the experts say is true, but rather to check the accuracy of their own conclusions. Again, these individuals use their own conclusions as hypotheses to be tested by data consisting of the opinions of others. Checking a conclusion against what others say is, in fact, a common way to validate an inquiry even when one is unfamiliar with how others arrived at their conclusions. Individuals want the satisfaction of knowing they are correct. They seek the psychological security of finding others whose investigations substantiate theirs. Only then do they feel comfortable with the results of their inquiry.

Such reliance on authority, however, may suggest a flaw in this approach to inquiry. Reference to authority for corroborating a conclusion makes suspect one's commitment to learning by inquiry on one's own and reveals a subtle distrust of inquiry as a way of learning. Yet this approach also reveals the essential human element of inquiry, the desire to want to be right that often initiates and motivates inquiry in the first place.

In an effort to compensate for this inclination, some individuals carry out this final step of inquiring in another way. This approach involves using an expert's conclusions as another hypothesis to test against the conclusion and evidence they themselves developed rather than using the expert's statements as an answer against which they should check themselves. Thus, they do not accept the word of a so-called authority as final, but instead subject the authority to the test of the results of their own inquiry. In so doing, they use their conclusions as yardsticks or as devices to organize the expert's data, thus evaluating the accuracy of both the expert's inquiry and their own; this yields further learning about the topic under investigation. The expert becomes a sounding board as well as a source of additional data; inquirers can put the expert on the spot, rather than put themselves on the defensive. Such an approach reflects much more accurately the essential nature of inquiry than does the approach of going through the motions of inquiring only to read what some authority says "to see if I am right."

Regardless of how one chooses to carry out this final step, applying a conclusion to new data reflects a basic human desire to know "for sure." We all want certainty. Furthermore, we seem much more prone to accept as valid conclusions with which we agree than those with which we disagree; we also seem much more prone to criticize or submit to more careful scrutiny conclusions with which we disagree rather than those with which we agree. We not only want to know that what we found out is right, we want to know *that* we are right! Thus, applying a conclusion to new data, either heretofore missing or provided by the work of a supposed authority, serves a psychological need as well as a rational final step in inquiring.

Even our scholar feels a need to substantiate the results of his inquiry. Although he has carefully figured out the answer to his problem, or so he thinks, he still does not know for certain if he is correct, and he wants to be certain. Imagine our scholar's frustration if his companion had disappeared before he had an opportunity to substantiate his conclusion! So he accomplishes in a round-about way what he could have done right at the start, by asking his companion his name. Yet, the scholar doesn't ask directly. Instead, he asks: "Dr. Kovacs, do you mind if I open the window?" He applies what he thinks is true to the authority before him to check the accuracy of his conclusion, as well as perhaps to obtain new information relative to his inquiry. And the authority confirms his conclusion. His inquiry has been successful. Now he can relax for he has achieved closure, his goal.

Sometimes we cannot achieve closure, however. In many instances there is neither an authority to consult nor additional data that turns up. In these instances a conclusion will be little more than tentative. The conclusion will remain somewhat unsettled, and psychologically unsettling, until we can test it further at a later date.

Such would have been the situation, for instance, had our scholar been unable to talk with his traveling companion or to otherwise check his identity. His conclusion in that case would have been at best only a theory and quite tentative. Such a situation is hard for many people to live with. Nonetheless it frequently occurs. Inquiry does not always move directly to a hard-and-fast, definite answer. Learning to tolerate this situation is sometimes most difficult, but unwillingness to tolerate it forever eventually leads to this final stage of inquiring.

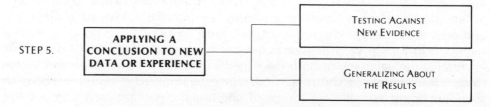

Figure 3.6. Applying a Conclusion to New Data

Applying a conclusion to new data, then, consists of two operations as described in Figure 3.6. Unless one completes this final step in inquiring, the conclusions reached earlier must be regarded as relatively tentative. Only when satisfactorily used to explain new but similar data or checked for accuracy against new evidence can conclusions be accepted as somewhat definitive. Some conclusions will emerge intact, verified as they stand. Some may be completely negated. However, most will probably be somewhat altered in this process. In many instances they will become more general and less restricted to one particular set of data. They thus become generalizations. As such, they become especially useful because they can then serve as tools to make sense of any range of similar experience or data much broader than that which may have initiated the original inquiry.

INQUIRY
AND THINKING

At this point, we must clarify the relationship between inquiry and thinking. Inquiry is thinking. In fact, the process of inquiring consists of two distinct levels of thinking. While inquiring itself is a specific cognitive strategy of processing information, this strategy consists of a variety of other very precise thinking procedures. This distinction between the two types of thinking that constitute inquiry is crucial to understanding the nature of inquiry as a way of thinking and learning.

First, as noted in the preceding pages, the process of inquiry is an overall strategy of thinking, of systematically and sequentially manipulating information obtained from the senses to produce some reasoned product. As a form of thinking, inquiry thus consists of a number of large scale, distinct mental operations ordered in a sequence moving from problem identification through hypothesis formation, testing, and evaluation, to formulating conclusions and applying these conclusions to new data. In this sense, inquiry consists of thinking in large, well-ordered steps, or macrocognitive operations, that form a structure unique to themselves.

Inquiring also consists of thinking at a second level. At this level the process of inquiring consists of very specific thinking procedures and skills, such as inference-making, classifying, and evaluating. These three operations, in fact, are probably the most frequently employed microthinking procedures and command considerable importance in inquiring. Inference-making, for instance, is used at virtually every step in inquiring for it involves going beyond the data to postulate meaning for that data by making connections between the given data and other known or imagined data. The scholar makes inference after inference as he struggles to resolve the question, "Who is it?" Like our scholar, Sherlock Holmes also employed inferencing in answering questions that interested him:

> A lady dressed in black and heavily veiled, who had been sitting in the window, rose as we entered. . . .

1. *Knowledge*—What is known. Evidence of knowledge is given by recall or recognition from memory of previous learning. The previous learning is relatively unaltered in the process.

   1.1 Of *specifics:* definitions, symbols, and specific facts (names, dates, etc.)
   1.2 Of ways of *organizing,* studying, judging ideas; of ways of treating ideas, trends and sequences, classifications; of criteria by which facts are judged, methodology
   1.3 Of *universals*—principles, generalizations, theories, concepts

2. *Comprehension*—understanding the message of a communication.

   2.1 *Translation*—putting communication into other form
   2.2 *Interpretation*—reordering of ideas into *new* meaning in the mind of the learner
   2.3 *Extrapolation*—extension of what is given, i.e.: predicting on basis of given data, inferring consequences

3. *Application*—applying an appropriate abstraction to a new situation to give it meaning; using a previously learned concept or generalization to organize new data. Applying previously learned information to a new situation.

4. *Analysis*—breaking material into its components—and detecting the way in which these parts are related.

   4.1 Recognizing the parts of a communication—i.e.: hypotheses, facts, opinions, assumptions, biases, value statements, conclusions, examples, evidence
   4.2 Determining relationships among elements—between hypothesis and evidence, conclusions-evidence-hypothesis, consistency of part to part, relevance of parts to central idea
   4.3 Recognizing organizational principles—frame of reference, point of view, patterns (form, structure)

5. *Synthesis*—putting together elements or parts to form a new whole or a pattern not clearly existing before; product is drawn from many sources and is more than what originally existed.

   5.1 Producing a *unique communication*
   5.2 Producing a *plan* or set of operations
   5.3 Producing a set of *abstract relations*—a classification scheme

6. *Evaluation*—making judgments for some purpose using given or invented criteria.

   6.1 Judging in terms of internal criteria—internal consistency, logical accuracy, citations
   6.2 Judging in terms of external criteria—compared to other sources, rules of history, sources used **

Figure 3.7. The Cognitive Domain in a Hierarchy of Thinking Skills

*From *TAXONOMY OF EDUCATIONAL OBJECTIVES: The Classification of Educational Goals: HANDBOOK 1: Cognitive Domain,* by Benjamin S. Bloom et al. Copyright © 1956 by Longman Inc. Previously published by David McKay Company, Inc. Reprinted by permission of Longman Inc.

1. *Receiving* (or attending)—Having become sensitized to the existence of something.

   1.1 *Awareness*—being conscious (perhaps only vaguely aware) of some phenomenon but without feeling toward it.
   1.2 *Willingness to receive*—neutral tolerance of something to the point of at least not trying to avoid it
   1.3 *Selected attention*—controlled focussing on a specific phenomenon in the midst of many phenomena

2. *Responding*—actively attending to or showing an internalized selective interest in something.

   2.1 *Aquiescence*—a willingness to attend that is not self-initiated
   2.2 *Willingness*—voluntary attention to or interest in some phenomenon
   2.3 *Satisfaction*—responding that promotes a zest or positive internal emotional reaction

3. *Valuing*—giving worth (value) to something to the point of consistently holding to it.

   3.1 *Acceptance of a value*—tentative but consistent attribution of worth to something
   3.2 *Preference for a value*—commitment expressed in terms of actively seeking or pursuing something
   3.3 *Commitment to a value*—conviction as to the worth of something to the point of action

4. *Organization*—structuring of many values into a system of interrelated super and subordinate values.

   4.1 *Conceptualizing a value*—abstracting the nature of a phenomenon given worth
   4.2 *Organization of a value system*—establishing an ordered relationship among values held

5. *Characterization of a value or value complex*—consistent and stable response in generally all situations reflecting an ordered hierarchy of internalized values.

   5.1 *Generalized set*—a generalized predisposition to act in accord with an internalized, ordered system of values
   5.2 *Characterization*—an internally consistent integration of one's value system to include a wide range of phenomena, a philosophy of life**

**Figure 3.8. The Affective Domain in a Hierarchy of
Thinking Skills**

*From *TAXONOMY OF EDUCATIONAL OBJECTIVES: The Classification of Educational Goals: HANDBOOK 2: Affective Domain*, by David R. Krathwohl et al. Copyright © 1964 by Longman Inc. Previously published by David McKay Company, Inc. Reprinted by permission of Longman Inc.

**The behaviors summarized on these pages are described in considerable detail, analyzed, and illustrated with sample questions designed to elicit these behaviors in the Bloom and Krathwohl taxonomies cited here.

"You must not fear," said [Holmes] soothingly, bending forward and patting her forearm. "We shall soon set matters right, I have no doubt. You have come in by train this morning, I see."

"You know me, then?"

"No, but I observe the second half of a return ticket in the palm of your left glove. You must have started early, and yet you had a good drive in a dog-cart, along heavy roads, before you reached the station."

The lady gave a violent start, and stared in bewilderment at my companion.

"There is no mystery, my dear madam," said he, smiling. "The left arm of your jacket is spattered with mud in no less than seven places. The marks are perfectly fresh. There is no vehicle save a dog-cart which throws up mud in that way, and then only when you sit on the left-hand side of the driver."

"Whatever your reasons may be, you are perfectly correct," said she.*

Inference-making is used repeatedly in inquiring. So, too, are the processes of classifying or categorizing (grouping items according to perceived similarities) and evaluating (measuring against standards or criteria). These more specific microthinking skills constitute the very basis of the larger, macroprocess of inquiring.

Probably the most useful description of microthinking skills was developed some years ago by psychologists Benjamin Bloom, David Krathwohl, and some colleagues who catalogued their interpretations of the essential elements of these behaviors and their interrelationships. These researchers arranged these elements in the form of taxonomies, or hierarchies, each consisting of a series of increasingly complex and sophisticated operations. Figures 3.7 and 3.8 outline briefly the content and structure of these hierarchies.

These hierarchies exhibit two basic features. First, they have been divided into two distinct domains, the cognitive and the affective. Although this division was originally made to facilitate analysis of learning behavior, the behaviors included in these two domains seem to be closely related in practice. An examination of the elements placed at corresponding levels in each hierarchy reveals this relationship. For example, one can hardly know something at even the lowest level of comprehension as outlined in the cognitive hierarchy (Figure 3.7) without also evidencing the behaviors catalogued under the category of receiving in the affective domain (Figure 3.8). One cannot interpret something without being willing to attend to it; nor does one make judgments without some commitment to a value structure or set of value criteria, however implicit or ill-defined those criteria may be. Many psychologists today believe that the behaviors described in the cognitive and affective domains interact in various ways as thinking occurs.

Furthermore, within each hierarchy each level includes and builds on all the preceding levels. Thus, comprehension builds on knowledge. Within the element labeled *comprehension* (Figure 3.7), extrapolation includes and pre-

---

*Arthur Conan Doyle, "The Adventure of the Speckled Band" in William S. Baring-Gould, ed., *The Annotated Sherlock Holmes* (New York: C.N. Potter, 1967), Vol. 1, p. 244. By permission of Baskervilles Investments Ltd. and John Murray (Publishers) Ltd./Jonathan Cape Ltd., Doubleday and Company, Inc.

supposes exercise of the skills of interpretation and translation, all of which again presuppose some level of knowledge, the preceding level in the hierarchy. One could hardly give worth to something (level 3 of the affective taxonomy, Figure 3.8) without first receiving and responding to it. Compare this with our scholar who could not sense a problem without first attending to the stranger and responding to the incongruous situation surrounding his presence on the train.

In point of fact the behaviors outlined by Bloom and his colleagues may well represent two sides of the same coin. While the cognitive domain refers to information processing, the affective domain refers primarily to feelings or attitudes toward that information and to valuing. Yet both domains involve the processing of sensory experience and seem to be interrelated at corresponding levels across domains as well as within domains. In effect, these two taxonomies outline the very specific operations that constitute thinking. And the process of inquiring uses these thinking skills to carry forth the procedure that it constitutes.

Inquiring uses the thinking behaviors outlined by Bloom and Krathwohl at various steps and in varying combinations. Thus, any inquiry involves selective attending and responding to specific data; analyzing, interpreting, and evaluating that data; and synthesizing bits and pieces of information into meaningful wholes. These operations are performed over and over again at almost every stage of inquiring. In the hypothesizing stage, an inference drawn from a quick survey of the immediately available data may be quickly interpreted, analyzed, and judged to resolve the problem, and then synthesized into a hypothesis. In the testing stage, data is pulled apart, interpretations are made from or about this data, and patterns or relationships are synthesized, always in reference to the hypothesis being tested. As in the case of our scholar, this same process may be repeated numerous times before reaching any acceptable conclusion. Finally, these same cognitive operations are repeated when one treats the conclusion as a hypothesis to test against additional data before finally accepting it, as our scholar did in speaking to Dr. Kovacs.

These cognitive operations form the core of the inquiring process, but they are not synonymous with it. One may perform these operations, for example, in other instances without using inquiry. Inquiring involves these procedures for different purposes and at different places in order to carry the inquirer beyond merely learning the data to generating new insights and meanings about that data.

The relationship of Bloom and Krathwohl's specific thinking procedures to the overall strategy of inquiry presented in this chapter may best be illustrated by the following taxonomy of inquiring. Although this taxonomy is described in terms of the cognitive domain, each step obviously assumes the existence of the receiving and responding aspects of the affective domain, and at appropriate places of other aspects of this domain as well. Each major operation in inquiring includes the thinking skills specified below it; the numbers in parentheses refer to the position given the specific skill in Bloom's hierarchy of cognitive skills, Figure 3.7.

A Taxonomy of Inquiry [5]

1. Defining a Problem or Question
    1.1 Translating given information into familiar, briefer, or more general terms (2.1)
    1.2 Interpreting given information in summary form (2.2)
    1.3 Analyzing the elements of data to recognize the parts of a problem (4.1)
    1.4 Producing a (unique) statement of the problem (5.1)

2. Developing a Hypothesis or Tentative Solution
    2.1 Analyzing of elements of data to identify interrelationships between them—such as cause-effect, sequential, or structural relationships (4.2)
    2.2* Extrapolating from given information to predict possible implications, patterns, outcomes, or consequences (2.3)
    2.3* Deriving a set of abstract relations based on given and known information (5.3)

3. Testing Hypotheses
    3.1* Applying the tentative solution to hypothetical situations in order to predict types of data needed for proof (3.0)
    3.2* Collecting additional data—separating relevant from irrelevant information (4.2)**
    3.3* Evaluating authenticity and accuracy of data on the basis of its logical consistency and other internal criteria (6.1)
    3.4 Evaluating authenticity and accuracy of data on the basis of the degree to which it conforms to the characteristics of the class(es) of which it is a part (6.2)
    3.5 Translating information expressed in documentary, graphic, map, or visual form into familiar, briefer, or useful terms (2.1)
    3.6 Interpreting the major idea and interrelationships of these from the data (2.2)
    3.7* Applying the principles and concepts of the social sciences to organize and analyze data (3.0)
    3.8 Analyzing the elements of the data to
        — select relevant data
        — recognize unstated assumptions
        — distinguish fact from opinion
        — distinguish conclusions from facts that support them (4.1)
    3.9* Analyzing the elements of data to
        — identify their interrelationships

— determine those relevant to the hypothesis

— distinguish causal, sequential, structural relationships

— detect logical fallacies in arguments

— identify data essential to the hypothesis (4.2)

3.10 Analyzing the elements of the data to
— detect author's bias, purpose, and point of view
— recognize patterns, categories, and commonalities (4.3)

3.11 Analyzing data to check the consistency of the hypothesis with the analyzed information and assumptions (4.2)

3.12 Evaluating the hypothesis in terms of the analyzed data (6.2)

3.13 Analyzing the results of the analysis in order to recognize basic principles (4.3)

4. Developing a Conclusion

4.1 Evaluating the hypothesis in terms of selected criteria (6.0)

4.2 Integrating the results of the inquiry into a reasonable conclusion, set of basic principles, or solution (5.2)

4.3 Developing an abstract statement that accounts for both the specifics and the principles embodied in the data and hypothesis (5.3)

4.4 Evaluating the tentative solution in the light of this synthesis (6.2)

5. Applying the Conclusion to New Data

5.1 Using previously learned information to act in a new situation or context (3.0)

5.2 Using a previously learned concept or abstraction to organize new data (3.0)

5.3 Using a previously learned concept or abstraction to develop a meaning for new data (3.0)

5.4 Combining previously learned data or abstractions with similar but new data to reorganize or give broader meaning to all data used (3.0)

5.5 Producing a unique statement that takes into account the specifics and principles embodied in the new and/or original data (5.3)

*At these points intuitive thinking, hunching, and divergent thinking also come into play.

**Collecting additional data is not an intellectual skill. It is, rather, an operation based on a knowledge of the process (methodology) of inquiry (1.25) and of sources (1.12) for dealing with a particular problem or subject as well as a knowledge of conventions used in communicating data (symbols on maps, formulas, etc.) (1.21)

The process of inquiring incorporates certain types of knowledge in addition to a knowledge of the process and techniques of inquiring (1.25). This knowledge is assumed by the very fact that the skills being used all subsume this knowledge since they are all ranked at a level higher than knowledge; yet, itemizing these specific types of knowledge once again may be most useful here. This knowledge includes, as indicated earlier, knowledge of sources of data appropriate to the subject and problem or question (1.12); of conventions used in communicating information (1.21); of sequences and patterns in a field of knowledge (1.22); of classifications and categories (1.23); and of criteria by which specific data can be evaluated and judged (1.24). All skills have a knowledge dimension as well as a "doing" dimension.

The strategy of inquiring outlined here uses systematic, step-by-step, analytical and intuitive thinking—guessing, hunching, jumping to conclusions. Inquiring also uses *inductive reasoning* (moving from bits and pieces of data to all-encompassing explanatory statements) and *deductive reasoning* (moving from general overall assertions to specific supporting assertions). Both types of reasoning are used repeatedly and often interchangeably. As a way of thinking, inquiry employs a wide variety of intellectual operations to close a gap in a situation perceived as demanding such closure.

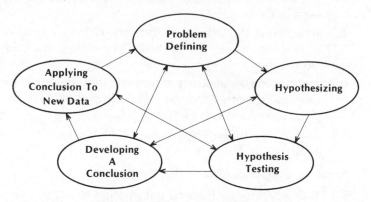

Figure 3.9. A Process of Inquiring

As shown again in Figure 3.9, inquiring thus involves a complex series of interrelated acts, some conscious and systematic, others apparently spontaneous and almost automatic. The process of inquiring is not a neat, linear progression of steps from one simple operation to another a bit more complex. Rather, inquiring feeds on itself. The various steps that constitute this process support and receive support from each other as one engages in inquiry. An inquirer may frequently go through this process a number of times before resolving the initiating problem. Nevertheless, inquiring is a dynamic, self-generative process that starts with a problem or question of some sort and moves at varying rates of speed to some type of a resolution or conclusion. It is one way of making meaning from experience on one's own. And inquiry teaching consists of guiding students through or of providing learning experiences designed to help them do just that. Part Two describes such a strategy.

notes

1. Earl C. Kelley, *Education for What Is Real* (New York: Harper & Row Publishers, 1947), pp. 24–54.
2. John Dewey, *How We Think* (New York: D.C. Heath and Company, 1910), pp. iii and 11.
3. Jerome Bruner, *The Process of Education* (Cambridge: Harvard University Press, 1963), pp. 56, 58, 60, 62.
4. Maurice P. Hunt and Lawrence E. Metcalf, *Teaching High School Social Studies* (New York: Harper & Row Publishers, 1968), second edition, pp. 68, 108–109.
5. This tentative taxonomy was developed with the assistance of Professor E. Perry Hicks of S.U.N.Y. Buffalo.

Part TWO

A Strategy For Inquiry Teaching

4

Learning, Knowing, and Teaching

Inquiry requires, and is, thinking. Learning by inquiring involves perceiving, selecting, and processing sensory experience of all kinds—feelings, verbal data, impressions, sensations, and the like. More specifically, inquiry involves manipulating data input by taking it apart, arranging it, and rearranging it into new patterns; intuiting or reasoning meaningful relationships among these patterns, sensations, and data, on the one hand and, on the other, among these patterns and previous experience and existing knowledge; evaluating the insights that emerge against a variety of criteria; and making assertions about the meanings that we finally discover or invent. Inquiry is a learner-centered process requiring the active cognitive and affective involvement of each individual learner.

Inquiry teaching, on the other hand, consists of putting learners into situations where they can engage in the cognitive operations described above. This type of teaching consists of creating and directing learning experiences that enable students to make and test assertions in the light of the information relative to these assertions and of other assertions to which they may lead; in this way students may make their own meanings or at least develop new meanings out of what they experience.[1] Neither inquiry learning nor inquiry teaching are easy. But they are productive—and fun!

Inquiry teaching itself is not new; it has been written and talked about for decades. Yet, rarely has inquiry teaching been used to its fullest potential in most social studies classrooms, whether elementary, secondary, or post-secondary. In spite of considerable attention to it in the professional literature, especially over the past decade, inquiry teaching has seldom been defined clearly enough to be easily understood or mastered. Inquiry teaching still remains rather elusive.

One reason for this elusiveness stems from the rather obscure nature of inquiry itself. To many people, inquiry consists merely of asking questions—any questions. To others, it involves primarily analyzing information, although just what *analyzing* means is rarely defined precisely. To still others, inquiry remains synonymous with critical thinking, whatever that means. The description and analysis of inquiry in Part One represents an attempt to clarify at least one conception of inquiry, for we cannot develop an effective strategy for inquiry teaching until the nature of inquiry has been clearly defined.

Inquiry teaching, even as a term, remains rather confusing. One confusion stems from the multiplicity of terms educators commonly use to label inquiry teaching. They sometimes refer to it as an approach, sometimes a method, and more frequently, a strategy. Specialists often use terms such as reflective thinking, problem solving, critical thinking, inductive teaching, discovery, and guided discovery almost interchangeably to describe this type of teaching. Obviously, all of these terms do not mean exactly the same. Some refer to ways of thinking. Others refer to ways of teaching. Each has its own subtle, but distinctive, nuances. Yet all these teaching or learning approaches share one common feature: they refer essentially to a specific way in which people manipulate data and sensory experience as they engage in learning. These approaches all involve essentially what we have described as *inquiry*.

A third reason for the general vagueness surrounding inquiry teaching grows out of a tendency to equate teaching with learning. Experienced teachers know these are not the same, however. Teaching and learning are entirely different. Teaching is what teachers do. Learning is what learners do. Unfortunately, there seldom seems to be any meaningful, let alone noticeable, relationship between the two.

Yet there should Be, for the most effective teaching builds directly on what we know about learning. Unless we understand how individuals learn, we cannot design materials or experiences or choose materials that will lead to meaningful learning. This is as true of inquiry teaching as it is of any other style of teaching, for effective inquiry teaching is based directly on how psychologists think inquiry as a way of learning occurs.

LEARNING—
KNOWING—TEACHING

Having explored how one inquires, we now need to clarify several basic notions about learning, knowing, and teaching. We need to remind ourselves of the very fundamental relationships that exist between *how* we learn and *what* we learn, as well as how teaching itself relates to both.

Knowledge as used here connotes a product of learning or experience, processed, abstracted, and with appropriate cues, stored in the mind. Learning is a process—the process by which one develops knowledge from experience. And teaching, too, is a process—one whereby some outside individual or agent deliberately intervenes in a person's life to guide, direct, shape, or otherwise facilitate learning in a purposeful way. Each of these has cognitive, affective, and even psychomotor dimensions. All three relate closely one to another while they also exist as distinct parts of an integrated whole.

Learning and Knowing

Perhaps it is unnecessary to point out here that knowledge and learning are intimately related. However, it cannot be repeated too often: *What we know and how well we know it are the products of how we go about learning.* The reverse is also true: *How we go about learning is conditioned by what we know (and want to know) and how well we know it (and want to know it).*

First, let's look at learning. We learn in many ways and for many purposes. Sometimes we learn simply by drill, by memorizing, while at other times we learn by imitating or copying. Still other times learning results essentially from trial and error. Sometimes we learn by reflecting on or thinking about what we see or experience. Each of these ways of learning differs from the others, and so does the product of each, the knowledge that results.

For example, one way we learn merely requires recording what we see, hear, or otherwise experience by etching it on our memory. We do nothing else with what we thus record. We don't think about it. We don't take it apart to see how it came to be or how it relates to anything else. We just drill it into our memory. We *memorize,* or store it.

We often learn telephone numbers, street addresses, reigns of kings, and names of capital cities in this manner, as well as concept labels and generalizations. Yet, we never really know anything learned in this way in all its complexity or depth. We may be acquainted with it, but we don't understand it. Instead, our knowledge remains a rather superficial, but perhaps still useful, bit of information. This way of learning is suited neither to building new knowledge nor to functioning in new or different situations, but it does prove useful if we wish to learn or absorb what we or someone else thinks is true.

On the other hand when we *use* what we see, hear, or otherwise experience (i.e., when we mentally process this data, think about it, reflect upon it, take it apart, and reassemble it in new ways in order to make sense out of it), we employ a different way of learning, one that essentially involves inquiry. In using this approach to learning, we learn more than just the information we have at hand. We make this information mean something new to us. In this way the whole becomes greater than the sum of its parts. The new meaning, as well as the information we have used to derive this meaning, becomes the knowledge that we have learned. And we go beyond the acquaintance stage with what we have used and learned to understanding it. This way of learning enables us to build new knowledge for ourselves as we simultaneously come to know the ingredients from which we built this new knowledge.

Second, let's look at a product of learning, knowing. Whatever we know, we know in varying degrees of complexity. This merely acknowledges that there are different levels of knowledge. Sometimes we know only in the simple sense of *being aware of.* We may, for example, know about the presidency of Abraham Lincoln in the sense that we are aware of the fact that such a person was once President. At another level, knowing may mean a rather superficial *acquaintance with.* Knowing of Lincoln's Presidency in this sense means knowing a little about this President in relation to other facts that can be properly associated with him in a recall situation.

Sometimes, however, we know much more completely; we understand. We are completely familiar with the major elements of the subject, with their complexities and interrelationships, and with the ramifications of these on each other and on other things properly associated with the subject. This is the highest level of knowing; it goes beyond simple awareness, beyond superficial acquaintance. Knowing about Lincoln's Presidency in this sense means possessing a depth of insight into Lincoln's personality, background, actions, and beliefs, as well as insight into the milieu in which he operated as President and as a person. Indeed, *knowing* in this sense of the term really means understanding. And, according to psychologist Jerome Bruner,

> The opposite of understanding is not ignorance or simply "not knowing." To understand something is first, to give up some other way of conceiving it. Confusion all too often lies between one way of conceiving and another better way. [2]

Knowing in the sense of understanding is rare, yet understanding serves as a major objective of classroom learning and instruction.

How thoroughly we know something relates directly to how we learn it. Understanding does not result merely from recording and storing. *Understanding*—in the sense of possessing new meaning—is not something that can be given intact to anyone. Learners themselves bring about understanding. People may become familiar with the fruits of another's learning as information, but unless they go through the mental processes of establishing that same knowledge, they will not really understand it in all its depth, complexities, and various implications. They may be able later to parrot what someone else thinks is true, but they will lack the insights that constitute true understanding. Meaning in the sense of understanding is built by the individual learner; it does not exist on its own.

To paraphrase an old adage, we get out of learning exactly what we put into it. If we, the learners, put nothing in, if we do nothing with the information with which we are dealing, then all we get out is the information that was there to begin with. But if we work with this information, that is, if we use it to make it mean something, then we have command not only of the information used but also of something new: what it means to us. We understand, and understanding, meaning-making, is the essence of real learning. It requires the learner's deliberate cognitive and affective interaction with information to produce something beyond that information. Such learning does not always come easily. At times it requires considerable effort in the form of thinking; often it requires considerable affect in the form of feeling and sensing. Meaning-making essentially involves finding out for oneself. This is the goal, and essence, of inquiry—of thinking.

Teaching and Learning

The ultimate purpose of teaching is to bring about learning—to stimulate it, guide it, direct it, make it easier, and generally to ensure that it occurs. How we teach reflects and shapes the kind of learning we wish students to employ and the kind of knowledge we—and they—seek to develop. Conversely, whatever type of learning we seek or whatever type of knowledge we wish to develop, whether factual recall or understanding, determines the kind of teaching techniques, strategies, materials, and environments we ought to use.

We use many teaching techniques to facilitate learning, such as asking questions; giving reading assignments; conducting class discussions; lecturing; engaging students in copying, role playing, drilling, analyzing maps, reporting, making bulletin boards, writing essays, and so on. The list is practically endless.

Regardless of the number or nature of teaching techniques available for classroom use, we need to be aware of two important aspects of these techniques. First, each teaching technique has its own special assets and liabilities. Although each may serve a variety of purposes, none can serve all purposes nor get the job done alone. Some techniques seem better suited than others for facilitating different types of learning. For example, if we want students to remember a list of dates or laws or kings or capital cities or other similar data, the most useful teaching techniques to employ would be those that lead to efficient student memorization; they would undoutedly include oral drill, recitation, copying, or perhaps even repeated quizzing. Teaching in this instance amounts essentially to lesson-hearing. The learning that occurs results primarily from listening, repeating, and memorizing. What one thus learns consists essentially of specific facts, words, names, dates, and other similar information.

Furthermore, individual teaching techniques are rarely, if ever, used alone or independently of each other. We arrange them in a sequence to help students achieve a learning objective as efficiently and effectively as possible. This is a key to effective teaching. Such teaching consists essentially of selecting and sequencing a number of specific instructional techniques to accomplish certain established objectives. By arranging teaching techniques in a specific sequence we create a teaching strategy.

Teaching Strategies

Inquiry teaching represents one type of teaching strategy or one way to arrange selected instructional techniques in a specific sequence for specific purposes. But this is not the only one. Many different ways exist to arrange these techniques to bring about learning. Some of these arrangements, or strategies essentially tell or are expository in nature; others stress primarily finding-out-for-oneself or inquiry. As shown in Figure 4.1, Edwin Fenton suggests representing these strategies as the extremes of a continuum on which we can place any type of teaching strategy. [3]

Expository teaching strategies usually aim to help students memorize what someone or something asserts is true. The strategies used to accomplish this goal employ techniques of exposition or telling; they require students to learn by memorizing, repeating, and/or imitating. Expository strategies strive essentially to put existing information into the student's head, information that can later be recalled intact. Exposition relies heavily on sources usually considered authoritative: experts, textbooks, television programs, sound films, and of

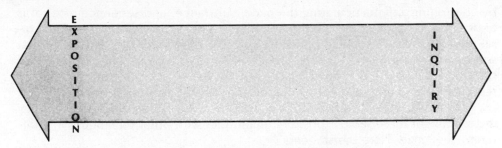

Figure 4.1. Types of Teaching Strategies

course teachers. One such strategy traditionally used in this kind of teaching re-quires students to

1. READ
to accumulate information from a text, film, filmstrip, or a lecture.

2. RECITE
in class what has been learned (*recall*, that is, what has been accumulated) to see if all the essentials have been absorbed; if not, then the teacher conducts a brief

3. MONOLOGUE
to clear up any confusion or add details which explain or supplement the initial material studied. Then, there is a

4. TEST
to see how much the students can recall from what was to have been stored, or "learned."

This type of strategy may be exemplified best by a learning experience in which students read an account of the economic development of the British colonies in America to.1763 (Step 1, above) and then (Step 2) respond in class to teacher questions about the basic features of the plantation, small farm, and commercial trading economies typical of the major sections into which the text divides these colonies. If students overlook or state incorrectly what the teacher or text considers the important points to remember, the teacher may explain these points for emphasis or present a short monologue (Step 3) to clarify what they were and why they were important in the colonial economy. Finally, the teacher administers a test (Step 4) that is usually objective to determine if the students can recall who produced indigo, what the people of the middle colonies did for a living, and what type of trade pattern characterized the com-merce carried on by the merchants of New England.

This type of strategy serves best to transmit a specific body of information. It is highly teacher-centered, for it requires considerable activity, both physical and intellectual, on the part of the teacher. It does not require much activity on the part of students. Indeed, while the teacher makes all the learning decisions by controlling and manipulating the pace, substance, and sequence of what is to be learned, students remain rather passive, absorbing what is offered and retaining it (hopefully) for recall when triggered by the proper cue on the test that surely will follow. Such a strategy proves extremely useful in *telling* students all they have to know and in covering the text. However, such expository teaching requires little, if any, active thinking on the part of students themselves.

Another strategy involves students more actively in learning. This strategy mixes some of these same expository techniques with other techniques in a different sequence. Here the students

1. READ
to accumulate information, probably from a text, a film, a filmstrip, cassette, or lecture.

2. EXPLAIN
to the teacher in class what they read and listen in turn to the teacher explain any corrections or additional information. This latter explanation offers the teacher an opportunity to

3. DEMONSTRATE
what is being studied (perhaps by diagramming on the board or actually performing a skill so the students may observe how it is done). Then the students are given an opportunity to

4. APPLY
what is to be learned by using it to make sense of new data or develop expertise at using this new learning themselves. After this, the teacher and/or students may

5. SUMMARIZE
what has been read, explained, demonstrated, applied (and presumably learned) so that a

6. TEST
may be administered to find out how much the students can recall about the topic under consideration or how well they can apply what they have learned to a new situation or to new data.

This second strategy proves ideally suited for teaching skills such as reading comprehension skills, or map reading skills, or especially ways to use inquiry teaching in the classroom. It can also be used to teach for mastery of subject matter. A lesson on the triangle trade illustrates the use of this instructional strategy to achieve content goals. Students might, for example, start (Step 1) by reading textbook accounts of the triangle trade between the New England colonies, the Iberian peninsula, the plantation colonies in the New World, and back to the Northern colonies again, or the more famous triangle trade between the New England colonies, the African coast, the plantation colonies of the Caribbean and the North American coast, and then northward to the New England colonies. They would then explain (Step 2) the nature of these trading patterns (the items carried, the people involved, and the purposes served by each) and listen to the teacher clarify any significant omissions on their part.

At this point the teacher might also diagram (Step 3) on the board an example of one such trading pattern, labeling each link in the triangle with the goods carried, the direction of the flow of trade, and its goal or target. Here, too, the teacher might introduce another type of colonial triangular trade involving different goods, directions of flow, and trade centers. Then (in Step 4) the students might reproduce these diagrams in their notes and draw new diagrams of still other triangular trades conducted by the colonies, such as the New England-England-plantation colonies-New England trade. After summarizing (Step 5) what they can infer about these trade patterns, the students can finally be tested (Step 6) to determine how much they remember about the content studied and, perhaps, even asked to apply their understanding of the principles of triangular trade patterns to new data about a triangle trade they did not study, such as the Pittsburgh-New Orleans-Philadelphia-Pittsburgh trade that typified much of the interior trade of colonial America during the later years of this period.

This strategy certainly provides more student involvement than does the preceding strategy. Students become involved by practicing or applying what they learn and by actually generating new insights about the information they are using. Here students have the opportunity to go beyond the initial data to generate new learning. However, this teaching strategy also retains some of the *telling* aspects of the preceding more expository strategy. The teacher still determines and controls much of the pace, sequence, and substance of what the students learn. Hence, this strategy falls somewhere toward the midpoint of a continuum of teaching strategies as shown in Figure 4.2, although it is still somewhat in the area of exposition.

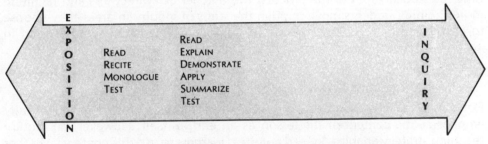

Figure 4.2. Two Expository Teaching Strategies

The two teaching strategies described thus far exemplify only two of the many ways that we may sequence the wide array of available instructional techniques to help students learn. Neither of these strategies requires a great deal of active mental involvement on the part of students. Neither requires students to accept much responsibility for generating new ideas out of given information. In sum, neither strategy is student-centered. An inquiry teaching strategy, however, is student-centered in every respect.

As the strategy depicted in Figure 4.3 indicates, inquiry teaching puts learners into situations where they must actively process or manipulate information to make meanings that did not exist initially or that were not readily apparent on first glance. Inquiry teaching requires much more of students than merely listening or applying something learned from another source; in this type of teaching the students, as well as the teacher, can control not only the scope but also the sequence and substance of what is learned.

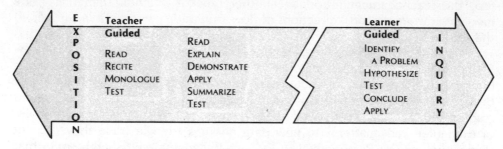

Figure 4.3. A Range of Teaching Strategies

An inquiry teaching strategy, simply described, involves students in moving through the steps you used to answer the question that began this book: identifying a problem to be resolved or question to be answered; proposing possible answers or alternative solutions; testing these against available evidence and one's own knowledge about similar evidence; judging and stating the extent to which some or all of original possible answers or alternatives are warranted by the evidence used; and later, perhaps, applying these conclusions to new data and generalizing or extending these conclusions even further. In first using this strategy, a teacher may provide considerable direction and control over the process of inquiring without necessarily restricting what the students learn. In time, as students master the process, the teacher can direct less and facilitate more, helping students move through the steps of inquiry in areas they choose to probe and in ways they choose to approach their inquiry, rather than in accord with strictly laid down teacher requirements.

Teaching and Knowing

Expository teaching strategies rely on the techniques of telling and usually emphasize the content of the lesson as an end in itself. However, an inquiry teaching strategy enables, indeed requires, learners to *use* this content, whether teacher or text-given or student-generated, to develop broader and more meaningful knowledge, skills, or values. Expository teaching appears best suited for covering a broad area of given information in short amounts of time in order to develop some simple awareness of or familiarity with that information.

But exposition can do little more than help develop familiarity with the data or information being covered. At times it fails to do even that. The verb *to cover*, dictionaries tell us, generally means to hide or screen from view. Unfortunately, that is precisely what results from reliance on exposition or telling as a major teaching strategy; such a strategy obscures or covers up what students can or are supposed to learn from the data rather than ordering it, clarifying it, or helping students generate new meaning from it.

Inquiry teaching, on the other hand, permits the use of different kinds of learning and the development of different kinds of knowledge. Inquiry teaching seems best suited for *uncovering*—for developing new insights into or meanings about large amounts of data, for learning beyond the level of simple recognition, for developing understanding in the true sense of the word—while simultaneously helping students to become familiar with the data being used. Inquiry teaching goes beyond the data, while exposition merely passes the data on as information.

Many variations of exposition and inquiry teaching could be placed in appropriate places on the teaching continuum described above. The particular strategies outlined here describe three basic types of instruction commonly found in all classrooms today. These strategies are quite distinct and lead to distinctive types of knowledge as well as to different types of knowing. An oft-quoted ancient Chinese proverb underscores these distinctions quite clearly:

> *Tell me,*
> *I forget.*   Strategy 1: Exposition
>
> *Show me,*
> *I remember.*   Strategy 2: Demonstration
>
> *Involve me,*
> *I understand.*   Strategy 3: Inquiry Teaching

Inquiry teaching, the third sample strategy, *involves*. More than any other teaching strategy, inquiry teaching helps students engage in an active intellectual search in which they can process data gathered from their own or others experience, observations, or reflections in order *to make sense out of it—to give it meaning—to understand*. Consequently, what individuals learn (knowledge) and how they are taught are closely interrelated. The implications of these interrelationships must be understood clearly in order to comprehend the nature of inquiry and its potential for learning and teaching.

KNOWING—
LEARNING—TEACHING

One final point remains to be made about the relationships that exist between knowing, learning, and teaching: individuals perceive what they expect to perceive (what they are prepared by their past experience, biases, or previous knowledge to perceive) and also what they want to perceive. The same can be said for learning in general. Individuals learn best what they have been or are prepared to learn or expect to learn. Our past experiences, biases, assumptions, knowledge, and beliefs, all wrapped up as our own individual frames of reference, lead us each to look for very specific items in a set of data, lead us to give different weight to the different data we choose to scrutinize, and provide us different questions to ask of that data, different ways to organize it, and different ways to connect it to whatever we now know or believe to be true. [4]

This phenomenon has both positive and negative implications. First, since each person is the product of a different set of life experiences, each of us possesses a different frame of reference or background of experiences. We can each look at the same data or share the same experience and learn different things from it because, as a result of possessing different frames of reference, we ask different questions of the same data or organize that data or experience in different ways. All our answers could be accurate. Thus a frame of reference guides learning, but it can lead to different learning for different individuals. Every classroom contains a great variety of different frames of reference (students) that often do not correspond to teacher or text expectations and that shape what is learned, often regardless of what is presented to be learned.

Secondly, the questions or organizational structures generated by any specific frame of reference circumscribe as well as facilitate learning. Any question can lead to the learning of new knowledge but at the same time preclude learning other knowledge. For example, a question asking, "Where did the Iroquois migrate from?" may well focus a learning or teaching experience on migrations of early Americans; however, this question precludes considering the possibility that such people might have evolved right where they now exist. The question assumes migration and, while the assumption might be accurate, it might also be inaccurate and misleading. Many questions have to be asked on all sides of a topic to establish accurate knowledge about the topic, but our frames of reference often either inhibit such questions or lead us to doubt or fail to consider fully all the answers derived from questions that run counter to it. We learn only what our questions permit us to learn. They, in turn, come from a frame of reference that grows only as our experiences and the questions we ask of them grow and broaden.

Finally, an individual's frame of reference can actually get in the way of new learning. Individuals confronted by data or a phenomenon which their past experience or frame of reference has not prepared them to consider or acknowledge often respond in one of several negative ways. They may force this newly observed data to fit their own biases or concepts, or they may ignore the new data as irrelevant altogether. Such responses, for example, often typify responses to the new data such as that illustrated in Figure 4.4.

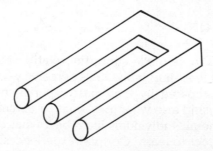

Figure 4.4. A Whatsit?

Some individuals, unprepared to cope with what their eyes report about Figure 4.4, may simply turn off, ignore it, and go on as if it did not exist. Others might try to figure out what it is but do not have an existing conceptual background that can make sense of it. Still other individuals with a broader frame of reference or experiential background might be able to cope with such data by devising a new conceptual apparatus to accommodate or give meaning to what they see. What we now know or believe can help or inhibit what we learn and thus add to or limit our present storehouse of knowledge.

At this point teaching, especially inquiry teaching, becomes crucial. One function of teaching is to facilitate learning so that students can be prepared to cope with an unpredictable, changing future. Teachers cannot use expository teaching to confront a class of students having widely varying frames of reference with a single set of data and expect a common response except at the lowest level of recall where the answer is *impressed on* (rather than becoming a part of) individual minds. Nor can teachers rely on expository teaching to help students learn to think or learn how to think on their own.

However, by using inquiry teaching teachers can use the multiplicity of their students' backgrounds to generate different but legitimate insights into a single set of data. These shared insights, as manipulated by the students, can then become part of the students' ever-enlarging background of experience. Teachers can use inquiry teaching to help students think and learn how to think. The way we teach directly relates to how students learn, as well as to the kinds of knowledge we and they seek and learn. Inquiry teaching recognizes and builds on these relationships as they affect the future needs of our students in a way unmatched by other teaching strategies.

GOALS FOR INQUIRY TEACHING

Any teaching strategy implies a specific set of instructional goals as well as specific assumptions about learning and knowing. Inquiry teaching is no exception, for it may be effectively used to accomplish educational goals in three general areas: skills, knowledge, and affect. These three types of goals typify most social studies and history curricula and courses at virtually all levels of instruction.

Skills, Knowledge, and Affect: Inquiry Teaching Goals

Skill goals. Inquiry teaching facilitates the development of three types of skills: thinking skills, study skills, and social or interpersonal skills. Those that involve the mental manipulation of information or sensory experience fall into the category of thinking skills. Such skills include comprehension, application, analysis, synthesis, and evaluation as outlined in detail by Benjamin Bloom and his colleagues and described in Chapter 3. Furthermore, thinking skill objectives also include the broader cognitive processes or strategies that use these specific thinking skills—processes such as inquiring, decision-making, and problem-solving.

Study and social skills also appropriately serve as goals of most subjects, including social studies. Study skills incorporate techniques for using a text-book, card catalogue, or encyclopedia; preparing a research paper; conducting interviews; and note-taking. Although the procedures students use to complete these tasks also involve thinking to some degree, each of these study skills consists of methods unique to itself. Social or interpersonal skills include such skills as group participation, leadership, and discussion. Again, while many of these skills involve aspects of thinking and aspects of valuing, they also consist of specific techniques that distinguish them clearly from thinking and study skills. Inquiry teaching develops all three types of skills.

Knowledge goals. Social studies instruction by means of inquiry teaching can help achieve a second major goal, in the area called knowledge. As commonly stated, knowledge goals consist of two basic types: learning of specific facts on the one hand and the development of more generalized knowledge on the other. Fact learning consists essentially of taking in and storing in the mind information as it is given in its original form. Dates of specific events, the names of kings, laws, or social classes, and the specific features exhibited by given events or phenomena exemplify the kinds of information usually learned as facts in social studies and history. In many instances conclusions about or interpretations of historical, economic, sociological, and other similar phenomena may also be acquired and stored as facts. In learning these latter types of information as facts, one usually learns to say they are true, as Griffin argues, without learning whether or not they really are true.

Social studies teachers also seek to help students develop a higher, more generalized level of knowledge that results from the processing of various bits and pieces of specific information. Such knowledge consists of ways and means of handling data and of concepts or generalizations. After considerable and sustained mental processing of information about historical, social science, or humanistic phenomena, students can learn that something is true or accurate. They can also invent and develop a concept or generalization of their own and possess it as a piece of knowledge, a substantive product of their learning.

Affective goals. In the affective domain, social studies goals are commonly classified into a number of basic categories including (1) self-concept, (2) values clarification, and (3) commitment to certain specific values themselves. Without going into the complex interrelationships of these three aspects of affect at this point, suffice it to note that each reflects a different type of affective goal of teaching.

Enhancing student self-concept serves as one important goal for much social studies instruction. Because of failure in the classroom or other negative school experiences, many students do not possess positive self-images in the sense that they can say: "I am successful. I can contribute useful ideas. My comments are valued. I am a worthy and respected individual." Teachers of all subjects frequently strive (or should strive) to help students experience legitimate success in the classroom, for self-concept is closely related to classroom achievement. [5]

It should be pointed out, however, that helping improve student self-esteem does *not* mean that students should succeed all the time or that failure is bad. Studies in motivation indicate that students who have only successful experiences in the classroom often prove to be unprepared to cope positively with failures in the future. But students who experience failure and then receive guidance in overcoming this failure—in devising and employing strategies to overcome obstacles and move forward—do develop greater self-esteem and self-confidence.[6] And this is precisely what inquiry teaching can help accomplish, for this teaching strategy allows, indeed requires, students to retest ideas that appear invalid. In inquiry, a negative answer to a hypothesis is an invitation to further learning as well as a piece of information useful in further learning, instead of a put-down or termination of learning.

Values clarification means to identify, delimit, and arrange in some type of integrated hierarchy those things one prizes. As such, it has come to serve increasingly as a second type of affective objective in education, especially in social studies teaching. While a variety of approaches have been developed to accomplish this goal (see Chapter 12), the general result strives for the learner to understand clearly what he or she prizes and how much these things are valued in relationship to each other.

Finally, many teachers and curricula, rightly or wrongly, seek to inculcate in their students certain prescribed values such as patriotism, self-reliance, initiative, respect for other individuals, social responsibility, and allegiance to certain principles (such as justice and freedom). In fact, whether or not teachers seek to do so deliberately or even recognize that they are so doing, our schools and classrooms model and "teach" certain values; the reward system of grades, praise, and awards reinforces specific value related behaviors and punishes others.

Inquiry Teaching and Learning Goals

Recognizing the relationship between a teaching strategy and its intended goals is necessary for a fuller understanding of the nature and value of that teaching strategy. Most teaching strategies, whether expository or inquiry in nature, facilitate accomplishing a variety of cognitive and affective goals. But few strategies offer as many opportunities as does inquiry teaching to achieve the goals commonly sought by social studies and history teachers at all grade levels.

Inquiry teaching deeply involves students both cognitively and affectively in learning. It responds to their own interests and allows them ample self-direction toward the kind of learning they wish to achieve. Thus, inquiry teaching contains a built-in motivation for learning lacking in many other teaching strategies. Furthermore, inquiry teaching helps avoid many of the pitfalls of a disastrous dichotomy between the common undemocratic, authority-centered, hidden classroom curriculum and the content or substantive learning that serves as one goal of classroom instruction. In other words, inquiry teaching practices what it preaches, whereas many other instructional strategies do not.

In addition, inquiry teaching enables students to achieve many learning goals simultaneously rather than seeking to achieve them one at a time in serial fashion. This attribute of inquiry teaching is perhaps one of its most attractive assets. Classroom teaching time is short, much shorter than the 180 classroom periods allotted to a major subject by the typical school calendar each year. Even if this time were completely available for learning, it would hardly be enough to accomplish all the goals many teachers set for themselves or have set for them. Moreover, clerical or administrative duties, special programs that eliminate classes, and unscheduled events such as fire drills or crises of other sorts reduce the time available for teaching. Meanwhile, the intended goals still remain in number and complexity. A teacher who seeks to accomplish a variety of goals in a very limited time must thus strive to achieve several types of goals simultaneously in a single lesson or series of lessons.

For example, an inquiry teaching lesson requiring students to work in groups with texts and discussions can help students to (1) acquire specific content or information while they use selected thinking skills to (2) refine these skills and to (3) begin to develop a specific concept; the group work with this content enables them at the same time to (4) develop further skills of social interaction as well as, perhaps, to (5) develop attitudes of tolerance and respect for others. Inquiry teaching enables teachers to accomplish simultaneously a number of the objectives in the areas of knowledge, skills, and affect outlined above. This strategy permits the most efficient use of instructional time and capitalizes on the relationship between content, skills, and affect inherent in any effective teaching/learning situation.

A Strategy for Inquiry Teaching

Inquiry teaching, in effect, aims to help students develop understanding in the fullest sense of that term.[7] A strategy for inquiry teaching must be based essentially on two foundations: an understanding of inquiry itself as a way of learning and an understanding of the interrelationships between learning, knowing, and teaching in general. With these twin bases of inquiry teaching clarified, the specific components of a strategy for inquiry teaching may now be delineated.

notes

1. Maurice P. Hunt and Lawrence E. Metcalf, *Teaching High School Social Studies* (New York: Harper & Row Publishers, 1968), second edition, p. 65.
2. Jerome Bruner, "After John Dewey, What?" in *On Knowing* (New York: Atheneum Publishers, 1965), pp. 122–123.
3. Edwin Fenton, *The New Social Studies* (New York: Holt, Rinehart & Winston, 1967), p. 33.
4. Earl C. Kelley, *Education For What Is Real* (New York: Harper & Row Publishers, 1947), pp. 24–55.

5. William W. Purkey, *Self-Concept and School Achievement* (Englewood Cliffs: Prentice-Hall, Inc., 1970).

6. See, for example, Carol S. Dweck, "The Role of Expectations and Attributions in the Alleviation of Learned Helplessness," *Journal of Personality and Social Psychology,* April 1975, 31:4, pp. 674–685; Carol S. Dweck and N. Dickson Reppucci, "Learned Helplessness and Reinforcement Responsibility in Children," *Journal of Personality and Social Psychology,* January 1973, 25:1, pp. 109–116; Richard Schulz and Barbara H. Hanusa, "Attributional Mediators of Information Seeking After Helplessness Training," unpublished paper, Carnegie-Mellon University, Pittsburgh, 1978.

7. Peter H. Martorella, "Research on Social Studies Learning and Instruction: Cognition," in Francis P. Hunkins et al., *Review of Research in Social Studies Education: 1970–1975.* Washington, D.C.: National Council for Social Studies, and Boulder, Colo.: Social Science Education Consortium and ERIC Clearinghouse for Social Studies/Social Science Education, 1977, pp. 26–29, 36–37.

5

A strategy of Inquiry Teaching: Part 1

Ideally, inquiry is self-initiated and self-directed. However, few elementary and secondary school students initially have either the conceptual framework or the skills required for purposeful, self-directed inquiry. Their education and training, in school and out, often has tended to minimize the development of independent thinking by concentrating instead, via exposition and memorization, on the acquisition and storing of substantive information and the development of recording and retrieval skills. Inquiry teaching, however, goes far beyond this approach by requiring students to think on their own. In fact, one very important goal of inquiry teaching is to help students develop the skills, attitudes, and knowledge that will enable them to make their own reasoned meaning out of information and experience rather than merely accept without question the meaning attributed to that same experience or data by others.

Inquiry teaching and inquiry are not identical. *Inquiry* is a way of learning. *Inquiry teaching* consists of teaching by using inquiry as a teaching strategy. Inquiry teaching involves creating, conducting, and evaluating learning experiences that require students to go through the same processes and develop or employ the same knowledge and attitudes they would use if engaged in independent rational inquiry. *Inquiry teaching involves students in learning situations in which they must make hypothetical assertions and test these assertions against a variety of evidence.*

A STRATEGY
FOR INQUIRY TEACHING

Inquiry teaching, as indicated in Chapter 4, is just one among a number of instructional strategies that teachers can employ in the classroom. A teaching strategy, remember, is a set of techniques (such as text reading, presenting oral reports, or writing a paper) arranged in a purposeful sequence to facilitate the attainment of selected goals or objectives. Most strategies are usually described in terms of the observable activities in which students and teachers engage. What is supposed to occur in the minds of the students, however, is at best only implied in such descriptions and often gets lost in the actual execution of such teaching.

A strategy for inquiry teaching, on the other hand, can best be described in terms of the cognitive operations students engage in as they strive to achieve their learning goals by inquiring. One does not plan inquiry teaching by first deciding which pages in a text students should read, or what lecture or film ought to be used, or when to assign a paper. Rather, planning and carrying out inquiry teaching requires continuous and explicit reference to what the students should be doing in their minds as they seek to accomplish specific objectives. Since inquiry teaching attempts to facilitate learning by inquiring, this teaching strategy works best when based explicitly on the intellectual operations, knowledge, attitudes, and feelings customarily exhibited by purposeful inquirers.

An effective strategy of inquiry teaching tries to help students accomplish in the classroom or other formal learning situations what the scholar (in Chapter 2) did on the train enroute to Marmaresch. A strategy designed to guide this type of learning could be described in a number of ways; however, its essential elements are outlined in Figure 5.1. Note that Figure 5.1 makes no reference to the instructional techniques or materials that make inquiry operational in the classroom. Every single item in our repertoire of teaching techniques and materials may be used to facilitate inquiry. Textbooks, lectures, sound films, oral reports, class discussions, research papers, slides, and other techniques and materials certainly find their use in inquiry teaching, but never as ends in themselves. It is how we use these techniques and materials to stimulate student thinking that determines the degree to which they comprise inquiry teaching.

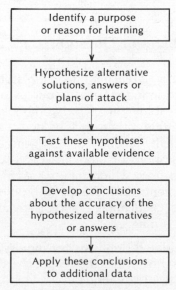

Figure 5.1. A Basic Strategy for Inquiry Teaching

To make decisions as to why, how, and when certain techniques should be employed to promote inquiry, we must know precisely what the students are supposed to be doing in their minds as the lesson unfolds. Knowledge of and reference to a strategy such as that outlined in Figure 5.1 is thus essential to planning and conducting effective inquiry teaching. By deciding to use inquiry teaching in our classrooms, we acknowledge that one of our major goals is to facilitate student-directed thinking and learning rather than to tell students what they are supposed to think or learn.

INITIATING INQUIRY: THE FIRST STEPS IN INQUIRY TEACHING

Inquiry grows out of a felt need to know something. Such a need may arise from a question that requires an answer, a problem that demands a solution, a per-plexing situation that begs to be unraveled, or a curiosity that demands satisfaction. Meeting the need aroused by any of these or similar stimuli involves purposeful, systematic thinking—inquiry. Such thinking can be initiated first by becoming aware of and defining a problem or question to answer or resolve, and secondly by inventing some possible answers or solutions to try out on the available data. The purpose of inquiry thus becomes one of "seeing if I'm right," of bringing closure to a situation that demands closure, of resolving an initial perplexity in a way that restores psychological disequilibrium and makes meaning of the situation that initiated the inquiry in the first place. Problem identification and hypothesizing represent two sides of the same coin. If properly carried out, these activities together initiate inquiry by providing a specific purpose for learning that guides and sustains or motivates that learn-ing. Without a purpose, little inquiry and little learning takes place. Conse-quently, the initial task in inquiry teaching consists of helping students develop a purpose for inquiring.

Identifying a Problem or Question

To initiate purposeful inquiry, a teacher must help students identify a problem or question about which to inquire. Several sources of problems or questions exist. First, teachers, texts, study guides, or workbooks can pose questions or present data that imply certain rather obvious questions or problems needing resolution. Secondly, student, teacher, or text-generated hypotheses can be treated or rephrased as questions or problems for testing against new data or even against the evidence from which they were originally generated. Also, students themselves have plenty of questions or problems that seem worthy of resolution. Each source has its advantages and disadvantages as a starting place for inquiry teaching and learning.

Teacher or student initiated problems for inquiry. Problems or questions for inquiry may be provided by either the teacher or the students themselves. For example, many teachers initiate inquiry by giving their students a question or problem to resolve that they—the teachers—consider will help students accomplish desirable learning goals. This approach seems to be a very practical way to initiate student inquiry along lines that teachers can plan in detail and control. However, it may not lead to much real learning, or even to thinking.

Teacher-given problems frequently consist of little more than traditional textbook topics cast in the form of a question. Yet, how many students are motivated or enthused by questions such as, "Was Louis XIV a divine-right monarch?" or "Why did Jackson veto The Bank?" These are teachers' problems, not students' problems; they rarely interest students and they appear to lack relevance for many. Of course, given these questions, most students will try to resolve them even though they really don't care about them, if for no other reasons than to please a teacher, to live up to what is expected of them, to avoid a tongue-lashing, or even to avoid a failing grade.

Student involvement in learning initiated in this manner may be quite half-hearted to say the least. Many students would rather not resolve such problems because these topics really don't bother them. Pleasing the teacher may be their problem—not Louis XIV or Jackson. Any motivation to resolve the problem will likely be more external than internal. Consequently, student commitment to achieving rational closure is likely to be minimal and the resultant learning superficial.

As a second source of problems or questions to launch inquiry teaching, students can generate their own queries to investigate. The most productive learning, psychologists tell us, starts with problems or questions that reflect student interests and concerns.[1] This often means problems or questions thought up by the students themselves. Individuals with the opportunity to raise and deal with their own questions appear more likely to *feel* that these questions require satisfactory answers; they therefore tend to be more highly motivated to find or devise appropriate answers. Students, in dealing with their own questions or problems (in effect, self-generated goals or purposes for inquiry), demonstrate much greater involvement in and commitment toward achieving closure than they do when trying to resolve problems given them by teachers or texts. Consequently, more and better thinking and learning occur.

This second approach often seems more suited to evaluating how well students can inquire than to teaching them how to inquire. Although letting students inquire into questions they invent out of their own interests may lead to more effective learning than the approach previously described, this approach is in many ways impractical. Inquiry teaching requires extensive use of data. Allowing students to select their own problems means that teachers must have quick access to sufficient audio, visual, and written materials to make inquiry possible for any topic that students might select. Most of us do not have unlimited resources. Instead, we must anticipate the kinds of data that students will need so that we can assure its availability; if it is unavailable even to student research, we must then steer the students into an area of inquiry where we know sufficient resources exist and are readily available. To do this, we must know the kinds of hypotheses most likely to be offered for testing; this means knowing in advance the problems that will give rise to the hypotheses.

In addition, many teachers are required or feel obligated to teach according to a specific syllabus. This generally means teaching a certain body of content in a given number of weeks. However, some teachers feel they cannot do this well if they permit students to choose the subject of study because, given such an opportunity, they fear that students might select frivolous topics or problems—or none at all! Many educators believe that, in order to conduct a worthwhile inquiry teaching experience, to fulfill our responsibilities to the school and students, and to capitalize on what we know about effective learning, we, as teachers, ought to control or determine the subjects and content of study. These teachers believe that the best way to fulfill this responsibility involves guiding the students by shaping their purposes for inquiry.

Regardless of where teachers turn for sources to initiate inquiry activities, they face two basic challenges in attempting to launch and facilitate inquiry teaching. First, they must somehow identify a problem that the students feel worthy of investigation. Secondly, they must ensure that whatever problem is chosen for study involves a body of content or information in which (1) sufficient data are or will be readily accessible to the students and (2) the teacher or school authorities believe students ought to study or learn. Neither of the approaches to initiating inquiry described so far enables a teacher to accomplish both of these goals.

Student and teacher-generated problems. A third source of problems or questions for launching inquiry combines the essential advantages of both teacher-provided and student-generated problems or questions. Teachers can allow or encourage students to generate their own questions for study within a body of teacher selected content. Three techniques may be used to facilitate this approach. The first consists of starting the unit or lesson with a general, teacher-made question and then having the students invent subordinate questions of their own that will help them answer the initial question. The second technique consists of providing students with data or situations structured by the teacher to suggest questions without explicitly stating these questions for the students.

Finally, a teacher might provide a topic (rather than a question or problem) for study and ask students to generate questions of their own around which they can build a study of the topic. Each of these techniques permits the teacher to select the body of content to investigate while allowing students some freedom to determine exactly what they wish to learn within the limits of the content under study.

In using the first technique, a teacher may start by simply posing a general question to the students. By launching inquiry teaching in this way, the teacher delimits the body of data or content to be studied and at the same time sets a general focus for the study. But the teacher should not stop there. To permit the students to define areas of interest in the given topic, the teacher should then ask them to state more precise questions, whose answers will help develop an answer to the main question.

The lesson presented in the Prologue illustrates this introductory technique. Here the text (teacher) poses a question: "What was life like in this society around A.D. 1000?" The students then invent questions of their own that may help them answer the initial question. By raising their own questions at this point, students can direct learning into areas that interest them. Having their own questions to answer instead of just the teacher's question provides intrinsic motivation for the students and stimulates the enthusiasm that often lacks when students seek merely to answer a teacher-given question.

The second technique for initiating inquiry is much more indirect and appears at first sight to be less teacher dominated than the approach just described. Here the initiating problem can be given by a teacher or text *indirectly* to the student, not in the form of a specific question but rather in the form of a situation calculated to create a question or perplexity in the minds of the students. In this way the teacher may delimit the nature of the topic to be investigated. By knowing in advance the kinds of data most likely needed, the teacher can plan accordingly. And the students can have the satisfaction of articulating their own problem or question. The learning experience that follows is more likely to be motivated by the students' desire to solve what they perceive as their problem, not the teacher's problem.

Any one of several different kinds of problem situations may be used to stimulate such student-generated problems. Teachers may present students with

1. an unpopular argument about a topic in which they are known to be quite interested;
2. several conflicting opinions on the same subject (or several solutions to a given problem);
3. material that contradicts the biases or stereotypes held by the students;
4. an incomplete, mystery-type situation that fairly begs for a solution.

A combination of any of these four techniques may also be used to launch inquiry teaching. An example of each of these techniques follows:

1. AN UNPOPULAR ARGUMENT

Let us assume that we wish our students to develop or refine a concept of justice while at the same time they practice their skills of intellectual inquiry. Let us also assume that we want to use content about the role of government in American history. Finally, let us assume that we know that our students, especially those about to qualify for driver's licenses, are quite concerned about or at least interested in the energy situation, particularly as it relates to gasoline usage. To initiate our study we could present, without comment, a quotation, newspaper article, or recorded statement in favor of immediate federal gasoline rationing by raising the federal gasoline tax. Such action will thus drive the price considerably higher than it now is. Some students, especially those who drive or are about to become drivers, to say nothing of those who enjoy the recreational uses of a classmate's automobile, will react adversely to the statement, while others might well agree with it. Responses such as the following might be anticipated: "That's the stupidest thing I ever heard!"; "I agree!"; "Who said that?"; "How could anyone be in favor of that?"; "That's unfair!"; "Is this guy for real?"; "What right does the government have to control my life by taxing gasoline?"—and so on.

Once the students have responded to the statement, the teacher or class can then single out several comments or questions and elaborate on them. Student reaction to these explanations may well generate a question or questions that can serve to initiate an inquiry into the role of government as it affects individuals or into the nature of individual desires versus societal concerns or needs. Investigation of either of these topics can, in turn, lead to an investigation of past examples of the American federal government's intervention in the lives of its citizens or of case studies from American history about conflicts between individual desires and societal needs. These can then lead into a discussion of the nature of justice in terms of the individual and society.

In launching a unit or study in this fashion, we deliberately play on something we know is relevant to the students; we also give students a piece of material that leads them into a specific body of content so that we can have the appropriate data ready for them to use; and, finally, the students, by reacting to this piece of material, will articulate something of concern to them that can serve as the initiatory problem for the entire study. Giving students a statement designed to evoke student-initiated lines of inquiry that lead into a conceptual study using predetermined content may be used to initiate inquiry teaching in any number of content areas; this method may also demonstrate the relevance of studying a particular body of content.

2. Conflicting Data

Another way teachers may create a problematic situation involves presenting students with two or more conflicting views or pieces of data about the same subject. For example, to initiate a study of decision-making by examining the careers of a number of world political leaders, we might present to the students two conflicting statements about the abilities of a generally well-known leader:

I	II
Abraham Lincoln was a man of high ideals. He believed in the equality of all men. He saw the Civil War as an opportunity to free the Negroes from human bondage. His Emancipaction Proclamation was the most humane act of any American president.	There was no greater political opportunist in 19th-century America than Abraham Lincoln. His entire public career was one of making deals and playing politics. When it was convenient for him, he favored slavery. When it was not, he opposed it. Freeing the slaves was purely a political move. Lincoln had no real feeling for Blacks as human beings.

"Which statement is correct?" "Who wrote these statements?" "When were these statements written?" These and similar questions will likely be raised as students read these statements. By asking such questions, students can launch their own inquiry.

Data other than opinions or interpretations can be used for this same purpose. For example, students may be presented the following factual claims or assertions:

1. Europeans created, staffed, and financed schools throughout their African colonies.
2. Europeans financed and constructed bridges, roads, ports, and hospitals in their African colonies.

3. European colonial administrations brought order, stability, and security to Africa.
4. Europeans employed Africans on plantations and in mines for more wages than Africans had ever before received.
5. By the middle of the 20th century, Africans were demanding independence from European control and reinforcing this demand by strikes, riots, and guerrilla warfare.

At first glance, there seems to be a contradiction within this set of assertions similar to the contradiction between the two opinions about Lincoln. The final statement simply doesn't seem to follow logically from the preceding assertions or even to be compatible with them.

Students could raise at least three different types of questions about these assertions; any one could initiate an exciting inquiry unit or lesson. At the simplest level they might raise a most obvious historical question, by asking, in effect, "If Europeans did all these things for the Africans, why did the Africans want to be independent?" At a second level of inquiry, one that generally follows this initial question, students might raise questions about the accuracy of each claim made in this set of assertions, arguing that the final statement suggests the preceding claims might be inaccurate. Student inquiry could then focus on testing the historical accuracy of each of the claims made here. Finally, students might infer that each claim asserted here is a half-truth, that there is another side to each claim that is not evident here but that contributed to the rising African demands for independence; therefore, the final statement is not a contradiction at all but a logical outcome of the situation as described by the preceding claims. By using sets of factual claims similar to the assertions presented here, teachers can help students raise questions about given bodies of content that can lead to further student-generated inquiry of a variety of levels dealing with the logic of claims, their accuracy, and the implications of such claims.

The same technique may be used with pictures in the form of drawings, paintings, slides, photographs, or movies. If we wish to initiate a study of social class by studying Latin America, we might display a montage of magazine pictures or advertisements of the colorful night life, crowded beaches, beautiful buildings, and busy streets of Rio de Janeiro along with another montage of pictures of the shanty slums, lines of unemployed, beggars, and ill-clothed children of that same city. Students will almost immediately identify a problem *they* perceive and the class inquiry will be underway. By providing students with sets of apparently contradictory information in whatever form, we can stimulate questions for further study germane to a preselected topic and thus launch inquiry teaching.

A point should be made here about using statements, statistical data, pictures, or recordings in this manner. If the main objective of the lesson is to start inquiring about the content represented by the initial material, its author or source need not be indicated. Written statements might not even be authentic; that is, a teacher may contrive them in order to sharpen the points of conflict to be raised. On the other hand, if the major objective of the lesson involves something other than a study of certain content (such as to analyze how a frame of reference may affect one's interpretation of reality), then the author's name or source of the quotes, pictures, or recording must be available.

This particular technique serves very well in launching an inquiry teaching experience. The use of written statements, such as the preceding statements about Lincoln, is perhaps best suited to average or above-average secondary school students. The use of pictures or recordings may serve the same purpose with below-average secondary school students or students in the elementary grades. The point here is that the substance of this initial material is not to be remembered or learned; the content serves only as a vehicle to help students perceive a problem that they would like, or at least be willing, to resolve, a problem that is related to the content, concepts, or generalizations that the teacher believes necessary for students to learn. This procedure can lead to achieving the learning objectives set by the teacher, the curriculum, or other authority.

3. Contradicting Student Beliefs, Stereotypes, or Assumptions

Another type of problematic situation may be created by presenting the students with material that dramatically contradicts their biased or stereotyped view of the topic to be studied. Most students, for example, have a Tarzan-like image of Africa south of the Sahara. To them it is full of jungles, wild animals, grass huts, diamonds, and black, naked people who are either under four feet or over seven feet tall! One way to start an inquiry study of Africa would be to present the students a series of two kinds of photographs: pictures of what they think is typically African (the stereotyped image) and pictures of things students do *not* associate with Africa but that really are African (large cities, factories, jet airliners, railroad trains, sidewalk cafes, department stores, night clubs, football stadiums, apartment houses, reapers in wheat fields, and the like). If challenged to pick out the photographs taken in Africa, the students will tend to select those that conform to their stereotyped views. When confronted with the fact that *all* have been taken in Africa, they will most likely protest: "I don't believe it, Africa doesn't have modern cities!"; "These are exceptions." As the students go on to articulate their views and to search for data to support them, inquiry teaching can be launched. Again, teachers can delimit the area of study, but the students themselves can come up with a reason in the form of a question or problem for studying a particular subject.

4. A Mystery Situation

Inquiry teaching can be initiated in another way by presenting students with a mystery-type situation that is open-ended enough to bother them into seeking a solution. An unfinished case study may be very useful as an introduction. Here the students read about or see a specific situation but do not find out how it is or was resolved. To introduce a unit on the political process in which the objectives relate to leadership or decision-making, we might, for example, show a film that traces the events and campaigns of two contenders for a Congressional seat but stops just after the votes have been cast before the winner is known. This is comparable to cutting off Perry Mason or Sherlock Holmes just before they announce "who done it" and explain why. If the topic of the case has some relevance to student interests, the students will be motivated by their own natural desire for closure—to know the answer—to bring certainty out of uncertainty; they will thus ask the kind of questions needed to launch a productive inquiry oriented learning experience.

We can carry such an approach one step further to develop an even better motivation for inquiry. Students can guess or decide what a central character in a dilemma or case study *should* do or how a particular case turned out and then read or see or hear the way the situation actually was resolved. When the actual results differ considerably from their own suggestions or extrapolations, the question "Why?" naturally arises and student-centered inquiry can be launched.

Discovery exercises may also be used in this way. Students can be presented with some uninterpreted information, such as several paintings, or some graphs showing different aspects of the same subject, or a list of words, or some statistics, or even several newspaper headlines and dates. If the material is on a familiar topic but does not quite make sense, the students may want to know, "What is this?" Such a question really represents a problem statement. When the teacher responds with, "What do you think it is?", inquiry may begin. Or, students may imply a problem by offering guesses about the material. Again, inquiry can be launched at this point.

If students do not invent questions spontaneously when confronted with incomplete or mystery type materials, a teacher can ask students directly to invent questions about the material presented. Use of a partially complete document illustrates this approach well. In introducing a unit on the Civil War, for example, students might be presented with the following letter and be asked to list three or four questions that they need to have answered in order to make sense of what it says:

As I write, the heat is oppressive and the air is damp as a result of the past evening's storm. In front of me are long fields of wheat, oak and maple forests, and a spring where we have been getting our water. But this lovely scene is spoiled by a terrible smell which floats over the hills. It is the smell of ▓▓▓▓▓ h burning or ▓▓▓▓▓ p ▓ se help a ▓ a n ▓ how ▓ in ▓ t ▓ com ▓ y ▓ he did th ▓ m ▓

In spite of having left Washington but two weeks ago, all of us are tired, and many horses have died from exhaustion.

It seems hard to believe in this trying time that the anniversary of our independence is but a scant 24 hours away, and that there are thousands of other men in the same position as I.

Now a sound like 1000 hammers hitting the blacksmith's anvil at one time echoes from hill to hill, and the earth seems to be leaping in the air all around me. I see your face before me and I remember that it has been 2 long years since I have seen you and the clear blue bay dotted with numerous sails.

Pray God that in this wretched hole at the edge of this sleepy town, 700 miles from home, I will be protected from all danger and that this message will reach you before August.

Captain Dandee has returned with news and instructions. The outcome is now up to us, and as I watch the long gray line coming toward me, I wonder if the men at the Alamo had the same feeling as do I.[2]

Questions commonly raised by students using this particular piece of material include: "When was this written? What's burning? What's going on? Who needs help?" By raising these or similar questions students can launch an inquiry into the Civil War. Attempts to answer their questions can move the process into the hypothesizing stage and the inquiry learning experience can get underway. Or, student-generated questions can be ranked in order of class interest, potential productivity of historical insight, or any other criteria, then refined by the development of subordinate questions, and finally be used as a focus for further study.

Regardless of what follow-up procedure is used to expand or refine questions thus developed, the mystery-type material can be most useful in helping students to generate questions of interest to them that can provide a purpose and focus for class inquiry into a topic or content selected by the teacher. Documents with phrases or portions deleted, maps with sections missing or torn off, or similar materials can also be used for this purpose. Whatever the type of material used, the key is that something important be missing, something that, if present, would complete the material and make it meaningful to the students. The existence of gaps in the material, however, can lead students to generate questions, and these questions can then set up the individual, group, or class inquiry that can follow.

5. Combinations of the Above Techniques

Several of the techniques described above may be combined to start an inquiry teaching lesson. It would be possible, for example, to confront students with a mystery-type situation consisting of bits of information that don't seem to fit together. This could have been done with the inquiry lesson in the Prologue had we elected to include only two photographs of obviously "primitive" or warlike tools (spears and iron hatchets, for example) and two photos of "civilized" artifacts (paintings of religious figures). Once told these were all found at the same site and date from approximately the same time, readers or students may become perplexed because, when combined, the data in the photos simply doesn't make sense. Yet, because these artifacts were supposedly found in the same place, they ought to fit—or so one usually assumes. Thus questions arise, as do hypotheses implying such questions: "How could people who painted like that make such primitive tools?"; "Why did people who seemed to be very religious have weapons?"; "Did two different people live in this place?"; "Did one group conquer another?" Again, contradictory questions or statements can get inquiry teaching and learning off to a flying start.

Another technique for identifying a problem or question for inquiry allows even more student control of the inquiry, while at the same time it permits a teacher to determine or guide the content to be used in the study. This technique involves two simple steps. First, the teacher selects a topic or body of content for study. Then the teacher asks the students individually, as a class, or in groups to indicate their answers to these questions:

1. What is the one thing you want to know about this topic?
2. What is the one thing you think anyone who claims to know anything about this topic *should* know?
3. What, in your opinion, is the most important thing about this that we ought to know?

Listing and classifying answers to these questions can provide both a focus for study and motivation for that study.

Moreover, the process of generating questions can also be used to help students learn how to invent questions and determine which of the questions they generate will be most useful in helping them achieve worthwhile insights and learning. As Francis Hunkins has suggested[3], students can use various types of teacher-led activities or teacher-prepared questioning guides to help them practice these skills.

Teachers can thus employ a variety of techniques to generate or allow students to generate questions or problems to initiate inquiry teaching. The techniques described here are especially useful because they allow the teacher to guide the selection of content into which the investigation will be made, thus satisfying perhaps local curriculum demands while still permitting students to identify areas of interest to investigate.

Any of these approaches and all their variations may be used to initiate inquiry teaching in almost any social science, history, or humanities content area for any combination of knowledge, skill, or affective objectives. Each approach is designed to tantalize the mind, to tempt further inquiry. These approaches are built on the fact that most individuals have more motivation to learn about what interests them than they have to learn about an area of concern selected by someone else. These approaches also capitalize on the fact that most people have a low tolerance for ambiguity and uncertainty and thus desire closure. Inquiry teaching starts with an effort to delimit a problem or question that requires closure.

Incidentally, following procedures such as these does not mean that the teacher must know the specific answer(s) toward which the student selected problems or questions may lead. Investigation of problems unfamiliar to teachers leads to an important learning experience for teachers and students alike. In fact, the most genuine inquiries involve joint student-teacher research into questions that neither can answer without investigation!

The major goal of the first step of inquiry teaching is to get students to raise questions to identify problems into which they can make meaningful inquiry. Many students, especially those in the secondary grades or those unfamiliar with inquiry teaching, often balk at doing this and may need, at least at first, considerable guidance and direction. This guidance may be provided initially by teacher-created opportunities for students to identify problems for study that relate to one or more of their own concerns or interests. Some ways to do this have been suggested here. Students' responses to these situations ("What is this?"; "Which is correct?"; "Who said that?"; "This can't be true!") all state or imply student-generated questions that merit attention in further classroom study.

Defining and Delimiting a Problem or Question

Identifying a problem or question of concern is only the first step in inquiry teaching. Before students can go about solving a problem effectively, the problem itself must be clear. Thus, as a problem, question, or statement is articulated, the students should clarify the essential nature of the task it implies. They must make the problem or question meaningful and manageable. For the teacher, this means helping students to state the central problem or question they see as simply and precisely as possible and in their own words.

Asking students to devise their own questions helps them define ambiguous terms and delimit the major problem or question at hand. Thus, in the lesson presented in the Prologue, students defined the rather general words *life* and *society* by asking questions that would help them determine what these two features were like at the particular place in question some 1,000 years ago. For example, the tenth graders' questions, including those reprinted on page 99, prove immeasurably important in accomplishing this goal because, in reality, they get at the essence of a social system:

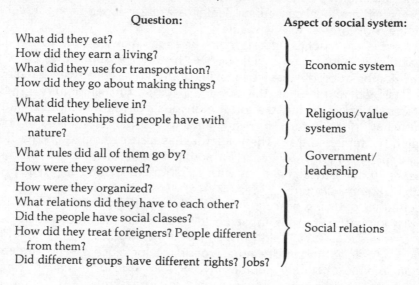

Question:	Aspect of social system:
What did they eat? How did they earn a living? What did they use for transportation? How did they go about making things?	Economic system
What did they believe in? What relationships did people have with nature?	Religious/value systems
What rules did all of them go by? How were they governed?	Government/ leadership
How were they organized? What relations did they have to each other? Did the people have social classes? How did they treat foreigners? People different from them? Did different groups have different rights? Jobs?	Social relations

The answers to this combination of questions go far toward describing the social system into which the students are inquiring.

The processes of defining ambiguous or new terms and of developing more precise questions for investigation often proceed simultaneously, and each reinforces the other. By asking more specific, subordinate questions about a part of the topic we reduce the ambiguity of the search. We also reduce the original question to more manageable size by creating less comprehensive questions; their answers provide portions of the answer to the original general question. It is absolutely essential to purposeful inquiry that unclear or ambiguous words or phrases be identified and defined in the context of the subject being investigated and that the initial problem or question be restated in the words of the students themselves.

As you recall, the scholar on the train to Marmaresch dealt with his inquiry in this same fashion. He, too, reduced his major question to a series of subordinate questions; their answers led him to the answer, as far as he was concerned, to his major question. Regardless of the specific questions devised for this purpose, the point is that the more specific the questions, the more easily they may be answered. The clarity with which these questions are stated also makes devising a valid answer easier. The students must make the problems or questions, once identified, specific and clear, but they may require some teacher guidance to do so. However, teachers provide guidance best by asking questions, not answering them!

It is tempting and sometimes necessary, especially when first using inquiry teaching in the classroom, to give students a question when presenting them with a problematic situation. Teachers often give the students two conflicting statements about the same thing and then ask, "Which is correct?" Or when we show contrasting pictures of the same place, we may ask, "Which are the most accurate?" But by asking these questions and not requiring or permitting students to ask their own, we really give the students our problems to solve rather than help them articulate questions of interest to them. The most productive learning requires establishing student goals; student-initiated questions help meet this requirement. The first step in inquiry teaching involves facilitating, not stifling, the articulation of such questions.

Once a problem or question has been clearly defined and stated in manageable terms, inquiry teaching may proceed. The second major step in this strategy consists of having the students identify or suggest alternative solutions to the problem(s) or question(s) selected for study. Such hypotheses combine with the problem to provide a purpose for further inquiry.

Developing Hypotheses for Study

A hypothesis is a tentative answer to a question or problem. Hypotheses are invaluable tools for thinking and learning because they provide direction and purpose as well as motivation. Developing hypotheses is thus the second major step in inquiry teaching.

Teachers may use at least two different techniques to develop hypotheses, and thus goals, for classroom study. In one very direct approach, the teacher may select and present students with an assertion that they can consider hypothetical and then test against available data. Such assertions may be real or contrived opinions, judgments, or statements that relate to a problem or question selected for classroom study. Even previously tested generalizations or judgments can be treated as hypotheses to be submitted to the test of additional evidence or resubmitted by students to a test against the evidence from which they were generated or that a textbook author gives in support of them. Thus, for example, either or both of the two evaluations of Lincoln as a President (cited earlier in this chapter, p. 90) could be selected for use as hypotheses.

This technique has both advantages and disadvantages. It may not require students to engage in much, if any, serious thinking even when they have the opportunity to select several assertions from a list or to find an assertion they would like to test. However, the technique does permit a teacher to direct student inquiry into a given topic and to focus on other specific skills as well. It is neither productive nor wise to start every inquiry unit with a problem or question. Starting with already given hypotheses can provide useful variety. Moreover, when alternated with activities that require students to invent their own hypotheses, this approach provides some students an often welcome respite from the hard work of thinking involved in the repeated use of the more complete inquiry teaching strategy. At the same time it enables a teacher to focus instead on those skills of thinking used in subsequent steps, such as testing or evaluating hypotheses.

─────────── FOR EXAMPLE . . . ───────────

The lesson presented in the Prologue of this book exemplifies inquiry teaching. This lesson has been taught to fourth and fifth graders, as well as to high school sophomores and juniors, college undergraduates, and experienced teachers. Essentially the same materials and key questions were used in each instance. Only the reading level and wording of some questions differed in order to accommodate the reading levels, experiential background, and levels of cognitive development of the particular student audience involved in each lesson. We are going to use excerpts from these lessons here.

You may wish to review the Prologue prior to continuing with this chapter. This review will enable you to refresh your memory about the questions and directions provided in the lesson, as well as the answers and ideas you came up with in responding to them. Throughout the remainder of this chapter and the next, pages like this will present specific questions and directions used in teaching this same lesson to average fifth-grade and tenth-grade students. These pages will also present a sampling of their responses to these questions, as well as comments, questions, or assertions they initiated as they proceeded through the lesson. These teacher and student moves will illustrate and clarify the various steps in the inquiry teaching strategy described here.

You should note that the student responses that will be cited were taken from actual fifth- and tenth-grade classes. In both classes the students had *no* prior knowledge or study of either the teaching procedure or the subject of the lesson.

As you examine or refer to these student responses, questions, or statements, you might especially seek to identify how the nature of inquiry and the various factors that shape learning (presented in Chapters 1–4) come into play in inquiry teaching. You might also study these excerpts with the following questions in mind:

1. What are the major directions given by the teacher? What are the key questions asked by the teacher?
2. What do you or the student have to do to respond as directed to answer each question asked? What kind of thinking, if any, is required to make each response or complete each activity as directed?
3. In what way does each step in this lesson relate to the preceding step and the step that follows?

A second technique for developing hypotheses seems to be aligned more with the spirit of open inquiry. Here students invent or think up hypothetical solutions or answers to given or self-defined problems or questions. Such a technique may vary in terms of the amount of teacher direction and student involvement. At the very least, however, it requires students to create from bits and pieces of data (often from their own previously acquired knowledge) a more general statement that seems to explain a relationship among and between the data and the problem or question at hand. Devising activities that enable students to engage in the thinking required to do this involves particular attention to the nature of hypothesizing, to data and the way it is used, and to student-centered learning activities.

FOR EXAMPLE . . .
DEFINING A PROBLEM

Some years ago some archaeologists dug up the remains of a place where people lived about 1,000 years ago. These scientists wanted to find out what life was like for the people who lived in this place around A.D. 1000. We can examine some pictures of the items uncovered by these scientists to answer this question:

1.* What was life like for the people living in this place around A.D. 1000? But first we need to be sure we understand the question. What do we mean by *life*? What are some questions you could ask to learn about what *life* was like for a people living someplace?

Fifth graders' responses:

> What tools did they use?
> What kind of homes did they have?
> What did they make tools out of?
> Where did they live?
> What did they do for a living? What jobs did they do?
> How advanced were they? Did they use simple tools or more modern (better made, more complicated) ones?
> Did they go to church? What church?

Tenth graders' responses:

> What did they eat?
> How did they earn a living?
> What did they believe in?
> How did they move around? What did they use for transportation?
> What relationships did the people have with nature? With each other?
> How were they governed?
> How did they go about making things?

What are some questions we could ask to learn what this *society* was like?

Fifth graders' responses:

> Who were their leaders?
> What kinds of people lived there?
> Were the people rich or poor?
> How did the people treat each other?

Tenth graders' responses:

> Did the people have social classes?
> How were they governed?
> How did they treat foreigners? people different from them?
> Did different groups have different rights? jobs?
> What rules did all of them go by?
> How were they organized?

*This number and numbers in subsequent examples of this lesson refer to similar questions in the Prologue to this book.

The nature of hypothesizing. A hypothesis is essentially an educated guess or an untested assertion. It is frequently viewed as a product of *inductive reasoning*—generating a broad statement of relationships from limited and often fragmentary data. At times hypothesizing requires deliberate step-by-step analysis and considerable intellectual effort. At other times hypotheses just seem to pop up suddenly as a result of an intuitive hunch sparked by the consideration of some appropriate data. Sometimes a hypothesis even precedes or develops simultaneously with a clearly defined statement of the problem or question being investigated. Regardless of which method generates a hypothesis, however, hypothesizing usually involves a combination of analytical *and* intuitive thinking.

The role of data in hypothesizing. Data plays a crucial role in hypothesizing. Students cannot speculate about reasonable or logical solutions or answers unless they have some information upon which to base their speculations. However, hypothesis formation does not require much data; in fact, data used for this purpose ought to be limited in amount and complexity. This data may come from either or both of two sources, from the students themselves or from someplace outside the students.

First, students generally bring a certain amount of data or information to most learning situations. This data consists of previous learning in the form of specific facts, generalizations, concepts, assumptions, biases, or prejudices that they feel may relate to the topic under consideration. Such data may be reflected by general mind sets or frames of reference that shape how students perceive a given problem or learning situation.

Students, especially secondary school students, do not approach many social studies topics, questions, or problems in a void, in spite of frequent appearances to the contrary. For example, there are few students who don't have some ideas about why wars, in general, occur; these ideas may help them guess at why a specific war occurred even though they may possess little accurate information about that particular war itself. Or, by way of another example, few students come to school today without some impressions about Latin America or cowboys or England that would be useful in generating hypotheses about related topics such as Argentina or gauchos or an island kingdom like Japan. Almost all student past experiences provide some knowledge that they may draw upon to form hypotheses about a given topic. Indeed, such student-held information is almost invariably used in hypothesizing whether or not the teacher realizes it. This explains why different students can consider the same problem and come up with different but quite legitimate and reasonable hypotheses! Remember, the information used by our scholar in trying to identify his traveling companion came from his own background of experience, not from any library or text or other authority.

Sources outside the students may also provide data useful for generating hypotheses. Such data may be contained in the problematic situation that initiates an inquiry teaching lesson, or it may be presented by the teacher or collected by the students as soon as a problem or question has been defined for investigation.

Many times the data that students use to generate a problem for inquiry also contain data that can help students hypothesize answers to the very problems they invent. For example, the mystery letter presented above can be used to develop hypotheses as well as questions. In examining this letter, students often offer hypotheses without even stating questions; it is not uncommon for students to assert, "This is Gettysburg!" rather than state a problem as directed. The questions of "Where is this?" or "What's going on here?" remain implicit as they jump to the next step in inquiring. Students can make this leap because the letter actually contains clues to the answers to these questions: the distance from Washington, the reference to a "long gray line," the date, and the presence of a wheat field all suggest Pickett's charge on that fateful July 3rd. If a teacher treats assertions like this one as what they in effect are, hypotheses, and not as authoritative conclusions, inquiry can proceed.

Data provided for hypothesizing may also differ from that which students use to develop a problem or question for investigation. Many types of data may be used for this purpose. A single photograph of a village may be used to generate hypotheses about the habitat, social structure, or level of technology of the people living in that village. A site map of an ancient city can serve a similar purpose. A brief, one-page excerpt from a colonial American diary can be used to hypothesize about the values held by some colonial Americans. Even lists of words may be used as the basis for hypothesizing activities.

Word lists, in fact, prove especially useful in generating hypotheses because they stimulate, without confining, the imagination. For instance, in order to initiate hypothesizing about life in colonial America, a list of words that might have been commonly spoken by inhabitants of an early Massachusetts colony could be developed. Such a list might include the following words:

alien	corn	keg	sabbath
apprentice	court	kettle	saint
ax	covenant	leather	sandy
ball	damp	line	saw
banish	discipline	loft	shingles
baptism	exile	maple	shovel
barrel	faith	meditation	skin
bedstead	fall	meeting	sow
bench	father	musket	squash
cannon	flint	muskrat	stranger
chimney	float	net	summer
clapboard	freeman	oak	thatch
clay	goodness	orders	trap
cloak	harvest	outside	truth
clog	heresy	pelt	wheelbarrow
cold	hill	pewter	whipping
community	hoe	pot	will
compact	household	powder	wind
congregation	husband	pray	writ
conversion	husbandry	purity	

Analysis of a list of words like these can develop considerable student involvement in learning and can help students generate innumerable and often insightful inferences about the topic at hand. This list, for example, leads to the development of hypotheses about the climate, values, religious orientation, concern for group unity, and technology of the early Massachusetts settlers.

Preparing a list of words or phrases for hypothesizing activities is not difficult. Sometimes appropriate word lists already exist as in the "Key Words to Know" that typify many textbook end-of-chapter exercises. Sometime they can be pulled from the text itself, as illustrated by the list of words used in Chapter 7. And sometimes word lists must be created by the teacher. This can be accomplished by identifying through reading or other research the key characteristics or features of a topic to be investigated and then selecting words that may lead students to infer these characteristics or features. Thus, if a temperate climate characterized colonial Massachusetts, words such as *cold, summer, damp, cloak, wind, fall,* and so on can be incorporated into the list. If trapping is an important economic activity, then words such as *pelt, trap, skin, muskrat,* and *leather* can be included. And so on. All the words selected can then be listed in alphabetical order, as above, in order to permit students to make their own groupings and thus their own inferences, or these words can be pregrouped by the teacher, as follows, to encourage students to make specific predetermined hypotheses:

clay	covenant	freeman	barrel
sandy	will	husbandry	saw
hill	meeting		maple
	compact		clapboard
cold	writ	purity	oak
summer		faith	shingles
damp	exile	goodness	keg
cloak	banish	truth	bench
wind	court		bedstead
fall	whipping	pray	
		baptism	kettle
father	loft	meditation	clog
household	chimney	sabbath	shovel
husband	thatch	heresy	pot
apprentice		conversion	pewter
	flint	saint	wheelbarrow
stranger	powder		ax
alien	cannon	pelt	
outside	musket	trap	hoe
community	ball	skin	corn
congregation		muskrat	sow
	net	leather	squash
discipline	line		harvest
orders	float		

Word lists like these, if not over used, can prove most useful in launching an inquiry study. These lists may include single sets of words as in the above lists, or they may include additional data in order to make possible even more sophisticated inferences. For example, a list of words for colonial America could include the national origin of each word in order to suggest the idea that colonial America consisted of a mix of peoples from a specific region of the world as well as inferences about the relative influence within this mix of specific national or cultural groups. When studying a culture foreign (whether in time or place) to the students, words can be listed in the original language followed by the current English translation thereof. Students can then use both sets of words to generate hypotheses. Such a list is frequently used to infer statements about family structure based solely on the analysis of endings of foreign words, and also to make other inferences about a culture and habitat based on the English meaning of the foreign words. Word lists can be as simple or complex as one chooses to make them, and they can provide powerful bases for generating hypotheses.

Teachers may provide data for students to use in hypothesizing for any number of reasons. They may do so, for instance, to help motivate student study. Teachers may provide such data to save time so students can get right into a study rather than search through a library, text, or other sources for some rather elusive data. Teacher-supplied data may also be most useful when teachers wish to focus student inquiry on a specific area of content or conduct the subsequent investigation as a class activity with all students testing the same hypotheses.

In this latter instance, a teacher might provide limited and very carefully selected data to the students. While such an approach still permits a variety of student guesses, it also tends to focus attention in a very definite channel and can lead most students in the class to formulate hypotheses about the same general topics.

This approach requires, of course, considerable teacher direction. Teachers can best supply direction by questions or comments that require students to focus on certain parts of the data or that challenge hastily made student inferences. Combining a teacher-directed experience with highly selective data may lead most of the students to come up with the same general kinds of hypotheses. Such an approach may also be used to teach students how to develop hypotheses analytically by helping them move step-by-step through the process of examining available data, identifying trends and similarities, seeking relationships, drawing significant inferences, and preparing a statement that gives meaning to all the data examined.

Perhaps the techniques of teacher-directed hypothesizing can be best illustrated by briefly examining how one piece of instructional material is designed to be used. This visual aid consists of a transparency with multiple overlays on the subject of late nineteenth-century imperialism.[4] It was intended to serve as the basis for a teacher-controlled, one period inquiry teaching lesson.

In conducting this lesson, the teacher first confronts the students with a number of statements that give reasons for securing colonies around the world in the late nineteenth century. The teaching instructions direct the teacher to have the students identify the key words in each statement and then to formulate these into an all-encompassing statement. However, the reasons are highly selective, for they each reflect some kind of economic factor. And it is the economic terms in each statement that the students must identify and explain. Thus, the only possible statement students can reasonably come up with by way of synthesis is an economic explanation for imperialism. This statement becomes their hypothesis. The lesson then continues as students test this hypothesis against highly selective economic and other data that casts serious doubt on their economic interpretation as a valid hypothesis. To conclude, the materials suggest another, possibly more viable hypothesis to test further against other data available in texts or other sources.

Because this lesson focuses on such a narrow field of data, it may seem very limiting and restrictive. Given its stated objectives, however, it is most useful. The material and approach can be used to teach students a very precise process of hypothesizing. This material also introduces students to nineteenth-century imperialism without overwhelming them with data. At the same time it provides an opportunity to practice the skills associated with hypothesis formation. In fact, this approach offers one useful way to go about creating hypothesizing experiences in inquiry teaching. It would be quite appropriate for use in early efforts at inquiry teaching, but it might be less appropriate after the students had become familiar with some essential steps in this process.

Teacher-provided data seems even more useful in hypothesis-making when the students seem unlikely to have any information that might relate to the topic being studied or when the teacher does not wish to call up hypotheses by providing give away name-date-place clues that might unduly bias the student guesses. For example, rather than telling the site of the society studied in the Prologue, the lesson merely provides data from the unnamed site in the form of pictures of artifacts that students can use to generate hypotheses. In many instances, specific clues (such as the location of this site) might prove helpful to only a few students. Moreover, such a clue might result in convergent thinking, rather than the divergent thinking that leads to the development of a wide range of hypotheses. In other words, sometimes brief facts such as name-location-date clues may choke off inquiry rather than stimulate it. On the other hand, by providing easily recognizable data that accurately represents the topic, a teacher can make it possible for virtually all students to help generate a wide variety of meaningful hypotheses.

Data supplied by teachers, school librarians, or local historical societies may vary in type and may be presented in many forms. Replicas of artifacts or real artifacts (if available), an excerpt or two from documents, a list of words, a photograph of an object, one or two slides, a brief selection of music, a portion of a speech, a painting or sculpture, a poem, a map or chart or table—all can serve as starting points for hypothesizing alternative solutions or answers to problems or questions into which a class has decided to inquire. Such data may be presented via transparencies or other visuals, handouts, displays, or any form of media suitable to the classroom.

Thus, data plays an important role in hypothesizing, whether called up from student memories or past experience or provided by teacher or student research. Whatever the source, data used in hypothesizing should be limited in amount, just enough to suggest some possible answers but not enough to completely validate any single answer. In addition, the data used in hypothesizing ought to be readily understood or recognized by a majority of students, because a major purpose of this step in inquiry teaching is to maximize student involvement in the learning process.

Using data in hypothesizing. How data is used determines its usefulness at this stage of inquiry teaching. If students are directed to learn the data, to memorize it or copy it down, learning the data becomes an end in itself. Such an activity is not hypothesizing. Rather, hypothesizing requires students to use data available to them to generate ideas about what it means in terms of the problem they are investigating. Of course, in so doing students may learn the data, but at this point learning the data has less importance than using it as a springboard for further learning.

Teachers can have students employ a variety of techniques to invent hypotheses. For example, students can brainstorm a given topic by listing (from their own memories or from given data such as pictures of artifacts) ideas in rapid-fire fashion without evaluating the validity of each idea. To stimulate or supplement such brainstorming, teachers may ask students to think of analogous cases, or examples of the same type of phenomenon studied previously, or related incidents in their own personal experiences. In hypothesizing about a society with walled cities, for example, students might brainstorm why any city might have walls or merely about all the uses of walls in general; they might also reflect on the walled cities of Rome or medieval Europe or China if they have studied these previously.

Students may engage in brainstorming individually or in groups. On occasion the class as a whole might brainstorm a topic or analyze a given chart or set of quotations. At other times student analysis and brainstorming may be more productive when undertaken in small groups, in triads, or in pairs. The latter activity gives all students an opportunity to take part; group hypothesizing permits several groups to come up with similar statements and talk them over without the "they already said my idea" thinking-stopper. Small group hypothesizing furthermore requires a follow-up report to the entire class that can generate discussion because group hypotheses often contradict one another and are challenged.

In general, the more hypotheses offered, the better. Too large a number may be unworkable, of course, but having students classify similar hypotheses together can reduce a long list to a more manageable number. The ideal number of hypotheses depends, in part, on whether the hypotheses are to be tested by the class as a whole (in this case perhaps only two or three hypotheses may be a suitable number), by groups (with each group testing a different category of hypotheses), or by individuals. Other factors affecting the number of hypotheses include the number and scope of materials that exist for testing the hypotheses and how well the hypotheses contribute to the long range learning goals of the course.

Developing multiple hypotheses recognizes an important factor about human nature in general and about elementary and secondary school students in particular. Students, as do most people, often tend to cling to a single hypothesis, especially if they invented it, in spite of masses of evidence and even logic to the contrary. Most individuals, in testing ideas, not only want to see *if* they are right, but they want whatever they hypothesize *to be* right. They thus overlook all kinds of evidence that may invalidate their claim to find the one, isolated, relatively insignificant piece of evidence that will support an otherwise fallacious hypothesis. To avoid this situation and to keep students from learning or developing flawed generalizations as a result of their inquiry, students should be encouraged or required to generate or adopt for testing several hypotheses. If students develop multiple hypotheses or a variety of alternative solutions, they feel freer to drop one or two if found invalid and switch allegiance to the other(s) that, even if mollified, may seem more valid. The goal of inquiry teaching is not so much to come up with *the* answer as it is to develop a number of possible answers.

To be most effective, therefore, a hypothesizing activity requires students to use limited and fragmentary data relevant to the problem at hand. Such an activity also requires

1. the involvement of as many students as possible.
2. the use by the students of creative, inventive thinking as they seek possible explanations or alternatives.
3. the generation of multiple rather than single hypotheses to test.

The example on the next page presents sample student responses to the hypothesizing step of the lesson you went through in the Prologue. Their responses illustrate how a limited amount of data can be used to invent a number of hypotheses that can serve as the basis for further class inquiry.

Guiding hypothesis formation. In planning and guiding hypothesis generating activities, teachers should be aware of a number of situations that may arise and require their attention. Although these may represent rather fine points, a teacher just beginning to use inquiry teaching should be alert to ways to handle these situations in order to promote as meaningful inquiry as possible.

First, it is neither necessary nor desirable for teachers to strictly direct all hypothesizing activities. The immediate task in introducing inquiry teaching is to teach students the value of hypothesizing and to provide opportunities to generate hypotheses. It is not necessary to teach a step-by-step process for hypothesizing, for this is the same process one uses in testing a hypothesis, and it may be better taught there. Hypothesizing ought to be a creative endeavor of postulating reasonable connections between the initiatory problem and some available data. In making these connections, students should be free to use their imaginations and to engage in as much divergent thinking as possible.

FOR EXAMPLE . . .
HYPOTHESIZING

Question:

2. Look at the pictures of the objects found at this place. All these objects date from A.D. 1000. Make a list of some things that describe life in this place at this time, or list some answers to the questions you wrote (that are now on the chalkboard).

Fifth graders' responses:

they had a written language—there is writing on the coins
they had education—some did, they had to learn to write
lived by the water—seashells
they hunted (with spears)
they had artists—to make the jewelry
people had skills—they made pottery, weapons
they were warriors—there was fighting
they were very religious—maybe Christian

Tenth graders' responses:

there were different classes of people
one group was over the other
they were Christians
they traded with other people—they used shells and coins as money
they had to fight—they had castles, swords
there were hunters, farmers, fishermen, and artisans
they traveled by boat, foot, and horses
they believed in an afterlife—they buried things with the dead
they were warlike—or maybe they just had to defend themselves

---

Secondly, in introducing inquiry teaching and learning, it may be necessary to openly encourage students to guess at possible answers rather than wait for the class genius to come up with the right answer or hypothesis. To stimulate guessing a teacher might ask such questions as, "How would you account for this?" or "What might be a reason for this?" or "What might help explain this?" It might be necessary sometimes to push students into opening their minds.

Reluctant hypothesizers can sometimes be encouraged to "open up" by having them pose and test statements about what something *is not*, rather than what something most likely *is*. Students seem much more willing to guess at negative possibilities than to hypothesize about positive possibilities. By testing negative possibilities, that is by trying to prove that something is not what they think it is not, students can in the process determine what it really may be. This approach affords students considerably less chance of embarrassing themselves since they need not put their knowledge or reputations for accuracy directly on the line for teachers and peers to see. And, at the same time, they can also learn a very valuable research technique.

Teachers may also find it necessary to remind students that their assertions at this step of inquiring are nothing more than guesses, that they cannot be accepted as "correct" without further testing or corroboration. Students must be prevented from treating a hypothesis as *the* answer. "How do you know?" is one question that can be used to point out this danger, just as can, "What makes you say that?" The ideal hypothesizing experience is student-directed, where the students generate a number of hypotheses and where they know that what they have done is to guess, that their guesses represent only tentative answers and that these guesses could change. In too many classrooms, what passes for inquiry is merely hypothesizing, but hypothesizing is only the starting point of inquiry, not the end point.

Keep in mind also that the widely held fear that students, if left to themselves, may come up with a "wrong" hypothesis is really unwarranted. Wrong hypotheses do not exist. A hypothesis may be irrelevant to the problem or inappropriate in the sense that we don't have the data needed to test it, but it cannot be wrong. A hypothesis is not the answer — it is a *guess* at an answer. It is not an end product of inquiry, but a launching pad for inquiry. Rightness or wrongness is determined by the test of the evidence. A "wrong" hypothesis is simply an impossibility, a contradiction in terms.

Sometimes student hypotheses do appear to be wild guesses. Students normally react by staring down such a guess, ignoring it, or perhaps even ridiculing it. Yet the inappropriate guess may very well serve to initiate useful inquiry. It is not uncommon for some students to answer the question, "Who was the general who won the battle of Waterloo?" with the inspired cry, "Charlemagne!" Rather than belittling such hasty guessing, we could instead proceed as one teacher did:

Teacher: "What makes you say that?"
Student: "I dunno. . . . He's a famous general. . . . "
Teacher: "How can we determine if you are correct?"
Student: "Look it up in the textbook!"
Teacher: "How?"
Student: "Find 'Waterloo', I guess, and see who it says won."

A quick pass through the index will enable students to check and discover that Charlemagne did not win that battle. At the same time it will give a good hint as to who did. Thus, a student who always proposes wild guesses can begin to get some insights into the skills of hypothesizing, of using a text, and of drawing inferences from data to avoid being ridiculed out of the entire learning situation. Moreover, the data rather than a statement by the teacher or hoots from the class will disprove the hypothesis, and it will be the student who uncovers that data. Although sometimes wild guesses, hypotheses are never "wrong."

The same caution must be kept in mind when considering what to do if a bright student offers the correct answer as a hypothesis. At first, such a response might seem to mean that the whole planned experience has been ruined before it begins. However, offering what we know to be a correct answer as a hypothesis does not invalidate the planned inquiry, nor does it require that the inquiry be abandoned. For the student who already believes he or she is correct, testing a hypothesis can provide an opportunity to learn new skills, to work with new information, to help others inquire, and to develop or refine additional knowledge. Students may know or think they know something when, in fact, what they believe accurate is actually inaccurate. Even though a student suspects a specific hypothesis is the only one that will stand the test of the data, it is important to treat this hypothesis just as any other hypotheses and submit it to testing. In the process of verifying guesses, real substantive learning occurs; this, after all, is one object of inquiry teaching.

Furthermore, whatever students offer as hypotheses ought to be recorded in their own words, whether on the chalkboard, on a ditto master for distribution at the next meeting of the class, or in the students' notebooks. Teachers should never translate student thoughts into their own words for recording. That practice devalues the students' contributions and usually results in teachers correcting an incorrect or partially correct response. Most students know well that only "right" answers are recorded! But hypothesizing, as has been noted, requires only *probable* correct answers; any response might turn out to be correct when tested. Therefore, student hypotheses should be recorded in their own words as offered, even if follow-up student definition or explanation of the terms they use may be required. This procedure, in effect, gives value to the students by recognizing their contributions, and it encourages participation in subsequent learning activities. It also helps keep the entire learning experience learner-centered.

INITIATING INQUIRY—
A SUMMARY

Inquiry teaching starts by developing problems to solve or questions to answer and follows by posing hypothetical solutions or answers. The specific operations that teachers must guide students to perform in order to proceed through these two steps are shown in Figure 5.2.

Inquiry teaching does not start by tricking students into inquiring. It does not mean using gimmicks (in the pejorative sense of the term) to get students to study about things that have little apparent interest to them. Worthwhile learning occurs only when students feel that the learning experience warrants their attention. They must believe that the experience is relevant to their needs or interests, or else they will not be "tricked" into a similar situation another time. The techniques outlined above ask students for their ideas and build on their ideas rather than turn to something else of interest only to the teacher.

A most productive way to initiate inquiry teaching involves building on the students' own experiences and their own psychological sets to motivate them to want to inquire. The data used to initiate such inquiry must have a legitimate and direct relationship to the content and objectives of the planned study. It must be a natural lead-in. The initiating material or activity must be such that whatever problems, questions, and hypotheses arise out of it lead into the areas

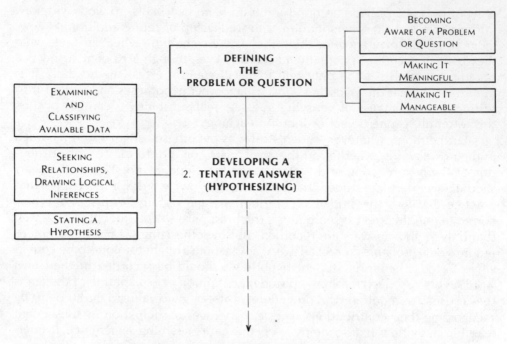

Figure 5.2. Initial Steps in Inquiry Teaching

of content the teacher and/or students desire to study. They must also be such that they permit the students to invent questions and hypotheses of their own, for whatever the students come up with in these first two steps of inquiry teaching becomes the very basis of the steps that follow.

notes

1. David P. Ausubel, *Educational Psychology: A Cognitive View* (New York: Holt, Rinehart & Winston, Inc., 1968), pp. 363–393, 446–448, 495; Sylvia Farnham-Diggory, *Cognitive Processes in Education* (New York: Harper & Row, Publishers, 1972), pp. 168–339, esp. 335–338.
2. This letter was devised by Dr. Alan G. Sheffer, a social studies teacher at North Allegheny High School in Pittsburgh, Pennsylvania. Reprinted with permission.
3. Francis P. Hunkins, *Involving Students in Questioning* (Boston: Allyn and Bacon, Inc., 1976), pp. 100–229.
4. *European Imperialism in Africa 1871–1914*. 12 overhead transparencies—#30051 (Chicago: Encyclopedia Britannica Films, Inc., 1964).

6

A strategy of inquiry teaching: Part 2

Inquiry teaching consists essentially of guiding students through two types of learning activities. In the first type, students develop a purpose for learning by defining a question or problem and then generating alternative solutions or hypotheses for further study. The second type of activity involves validating these hypotheses or alternative solutions. This latter stage of inquiry teaching consists of three basic steps: testing hypotheses, developing conclusions, and applying conclusions to new data. Of all these operations, hypothesis-testing is probably the most complicated and certainly the most crucial.

TESTING HYPOTHESES

Testing—analyzing and evaluating—hypotheses and alternative solutions constitutes the third of the five major steps in inquiring and hence in a strategy of inquiry teaching. It is here that new learning takes place, for as students engage in this activity they come in contact with new information and manipulate it, dissecting it, rearranging it, and evaluating it over and over again. Here creativity, imagination, and intuition intermingle with deliberate step-by-step analysis to develop new meaning. Here also previous knowledge interacts with new data to produce even newer knowledge. The mental processing involved in these activities leads not only to familiarity with the information being used but also to the development of the skills, attitudes, and higher levels of generalized knowledge that can serve as the major goals of inquiry teaching.

In guiding or directing hypothesis testing, a teacher must ensure that students engage in three distinct operations: assembling evidence, arranging evi-

111

dence, and analyzing evidence. Each of these activities, as indicated in Figure 6.1, consists of a number of other subordinate cognitive operations. Of course, these operations do not always proceed in a straight line sequence as shown in Figure 6.1. Nor does one operation necessarily wait on the completion of all those preceding it. Far from it, for as we collect information to analyze, we also frequently make judgments about its validity and authenticity. We may even translate and interpret it simultaneously. We might arrange and analyze a small amount of data before assembling more. Hypothesis-testing is not necessarily a one-at-a-time series of steps. It is very complex. Nevertheless, separation of hypothesis-testing into the three basic operations shown here is useful for a better understanding of this step of inquiry teaching and thus for more effective use of this strategy in the classroom.

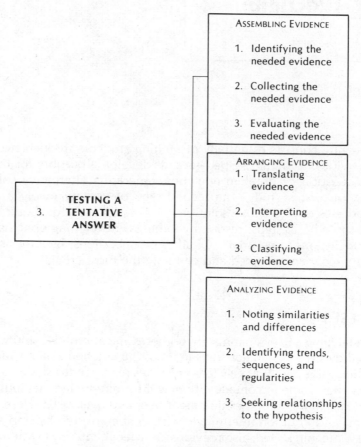

Figure 6.1. Testing Hypotheses

Assembling Evidence

The first step in hypothesis-testing requires assembling information related to each hypothesis being investigated. To accomplish this task, students must decide what evidence they need to validate or prove their hypotheses. They must also decide on the best sources for the evidence. Teachers can help the students use their hypotheses to accomplish both of these tasks.

Hypotheses, or alternative solutions, play the same dual roles in inquiry teaching as they play in inquiry. The validation of a hypothesis serves first as the target towards which the testing proceeds. At the same time, the hypothesis helps determine which of all the information or data available may be used as evidence. The term *evidence* implies much more than data supportive of the hypothesis. Evidence is information that in some way has a bearing on the hypothesis. It may be data that tend to support the hypothesis, or it may be data that invalidate it. Both kinds of information must be sought out and analyzed if a hypothesis is to be thoroughly tested.

The hypothesis itself directs the search for the evidence needed to validate or invalidate it. Once students have formulated a clearly defined hypothesis, they should proceed to identify its logical implications in terms of the kinds of evidence that ought to exist if the hypothesis is valid. This identification may be managed by constructing an "if . . . then . . . " statement.[1] If the hypothesis is accurate, then certain evidence will exist to prove it accurate. If the hypothesis is true, then also certain evidence that might invalidate it—that is opposite to the supportive evidence—will *not* exist. At this step of inquiry teaching, teachers must guide or direct students through learning activities in which they can search out both supportive and negating evidence.

For example, in the lesson presented in the Prologue, students who hypothesized that *if* life in the society under study involved trade with other people might indicate that they would *then* expect to find the following evidence:

—coins or some other money
—records about trade receipts
—things from other places in the world
—trade organizations
—some method of long range transportation—ships

Having made such inferences, the students now have some idea of the kinds of evidence to look for that will validate their hypothesis. But an "if . . . then . . . " statement also suggests evidence that, if found, will invalidate the hypothesis. Thus, in the case of the above hypothesis about trade, such evidence might include the following:

—eating only locally grown food
—wearing only clothes they made themselves
—possessing nothing from another place
—no words for foreign objects or goods

If we expect to find things from other places in the society being studied, we do not want to find evidence of only a subsistence economy. If we expect to find evidence of trade via sea or over land, we do not want to find instead only evidence of a hunting and gathering society. Should only the remains of simple farming or hunting tools be found by our search, then the hypothesis about trade might well be in doubt. But if we find the evidence expected, the hypothe-

---FOR EXAMPLE . . .---

IDENTIFYING NEEDED EVIDENCE AND SOURCES

Questions:

3. What evidence would you expect to find if life in this place around A.D. 1000 was as you think it was? *If* your guesses are accurate, *then* what would you expect to find?

Fifth graders' responses:

a. *If* this place was near the water, *then* we would find

    people using boats
    sea shells
    things from other countries
    fishing equipment—nets and so on

b. *If* there was much fighting, *then* we would find

    forts or castles
    armies
    stories of heroes in battle
    people who made swords and shields
    rules about fighting

c. *If* they had education, *then* we would find:

    books or other things in writing
    something about teachers
    schools

Tenth graders' responses:

d. *If* these people were Christians, *then* we would expect to find

    belief in one God
    monasteries
    religious people—priests, bishops
    crosses and things like baptism
    concern for justice in their rules
    no killing was permitted

  . . . and we would *not* expect to find

    idols
    other kinds of churches
    worship of many different gods
    cutting off hands to punish those who steal

e. *If* these people had different social classes, *then* we would expect to find

    different titles for different people
    unequal property—some rich and some poor
    little houses and big stone castles
    rules on how people inherited things
    different kinds of taxes

  . . . and we would *not* expect to find

    everyone wearing the same kind of clothes
    all people with the same kinds of jobs
    people doing whatever they wanted
    all houses alike in size

4. Where could you find things like this—evidence for what you have listed?

Fifth graders' responses	*Tenth graders' responses*
in our books . . .	in encyclopedias
a movie?	maybe in our history book
go there and look!	someone can tell us—someone who has been there
	a book on coins
	a history book about these people

sis might be valid. Thus, helping students use the "if . . . then . . ." statement is crucial. Using a hypothesis in this way helps students infer what kinds of evidence should exist if the hypothesis is accurate, as well as some evidence that might prove the hypothesis inaccurate just as the excerpt from the classes that used the lesson in the Prologue demonstrates.

Identifying possible sources of data serves as the second step in assembling evidence. Data may be communicated in a variety of forms. It may be pictorial, statistical, audio, or written. If written, it may be recorded on maps, charts, in newspapers, letters, diaries, novels, documents, monographs, and even in textbooks. It may be contained in speeches, lectures, interviews, folk stories, and casual conversation. It may be in the form of physical remains or objects. There are many possible media for students to turn to when seeking evidence. And there are many sources where such media can be found: textbooks, encyclopedias, museums, films, and almanacs, to name but a few.

It is important for students to become familiar with and use these media and sources, not for memorizing their contents but for knowing what kinds of information each source specializes in and how to use that source appropriately in the future. In searching for data relevant to whether or not a certain people engaged in trade, students may want to find written records in source books about trade as, for example: receipts or bills of lading; stories of caravans; coins from many nations; or perhaps even laws establishing tariffs. They may want to examine books containing pictures of coins to see if they can find coins like those from which they derived their hypothesis. They may wish to find historical accounts of a Christian people who fought frequently, lived in walled cities near the sea, and exhibited other hypothesized characteristics of the society being studied. In order to test hypotheses, students must identify the evidence they need and the sources where it could probably be found, and they must be able to use these sources to find their evidence.

Generally, the most meaningful identification of evidence occurs when students think in terms of the kinds of sources they could examine in their search. While students can speculate about what evidence they would hope to find if the society described in the Prologue consisted of well-defined social classes, they could infer this evidence even more precisely if they did so in terms of the specific source to be examined. Thus, if students were asked to state what a society's laws might say if that society had a class structure, they might infer it would have laws

—about the obligations of one class to another
—that use different titles for different classes

FOR EXAMPLE . . .
IDENTIFYING NEEDED EVIDENCE

Questions 5, 10, and 13:

If the society from which these artifacts came was Christian, *then* what would you expect to find in their . . .

	Fifth graders' responses:	*Tenth graders' responses:*
5) Laws?	(What would their laws be about?)	

	religious days—Sunday
	no killing
	can't hurt priests
	maybe the Ten Commandments
	fines for sins
		murder would be punished
		no stealing would be allowed
		church holidays would be
		   stated
		would require people to pay
		   part of income to church

10) Writings?	(What would they write about?)	
	church celebrations saints church leaders	religious wars popes, bishops and priests compassion for the poor education for religious jobs events on religious holidays
13) Buildings?	(What kinds of buildings would they have?)	

	churches—with steeples and
	   crosses
	places for priests or leaders
	   to live
	buildings with paintings of
	   religious things
		churches—large building with
		   domes or steeples
		buildings with stained glass
		   windows, crosses
		monasteries
		schools for priests or monks
		decorations like paintings of
		   religious events—the
		   crucifixion

—that indicate a class difference in taxes
—about who can own property and who can't

As indicated in the example above, once students have identified the general kinds of evidence they would like to find (and not to find) and some sources of it, they should then attempt to specify exactly what evidence they would expect to find in each specific source of information to be used in testing the hypotheses under examination. In inquiry teaching this activity should precede the use of each piece of information or source employed in hypothesis testing.

Once students have identified the kinds of evidence needed and the sources where it can most likely be found, they should begin collecting it. This may involve two separate operations: locating the source of the data and finding the appropriate evidence in that source. Teaching students how and where to locate useful, reliable sources may be accomplished by sending them to the library or study center to seek, without direction, pictures, magazine or newspaper clippings, reference works, textbooks, films, or any other media that might contain pertinent evidence. However, for students who have had no training in how to use the *Readers' Guide,* an audiovisual catalog, or the library in general, such a discovery exercise could become rather time-consuming and frustrating. In this case, carefully guided instruction in the use of library resources should precede assigning activities that require students to use these resources on their own. This sequence of learning activities would then make it possible to create additional activities that require students to apply their abilities to locate information, to separate relevant information from the irrelevant, and to use source materials effectively—skills important to independent learning.

Here, a word of caution may be in order. *Inquiry* is too often considered synonymous with *library research.* That is, many teachers often think their students are engaging in inquiry when they are busy looking for information in library reference books and other sources. Inquiry and library research are not the same, however. Searching for sources and data comprise only two of the many steps that constitute inquiry. Overemphasis on any one of these skills could inhibit mastery of the other skills and steps of inquiry and completely subvert efforts to learn the entire process of inquiry as a way of learning.

Instead of having students flounder around in a library or devote excessive time to developing the skills of library research to the exclusion of other skills, teachers can assemble useful data themselves and present it to students via lecture, film, handouts, or some other media. Use of such media will thus enable students to practice other skills, such as listening, viewing, reading, and asking questions. Or students might use some of the techniques that social scientists use to collect evidence, including conducting surveys, making field studies, developing and administering questionnaires, and interviewing. Engaging in these kinds of evidence-assembling activities will not only help students learn how to collect information but also suggest the attributes and limitations of these techniques. Such tasks ought to be special objectives of social studies instruction.

Finding and assembling evidence constitute only two of the skills important to hypothesis testing. Many other skills must also be used and taught. Unless we deliberately wish to teach the skill of locating appropriate sources, we can provide the students with the required sources and devise learning experiences that have students draw the needed evidence from these sources. These experiences should involve a host of special skills because evidence is collected in a wide variety of ways: by reading or skimming written materials; by selective listening to audio presentations such as lectures, speeches, news broadcasts, conversations, debates, and the like; by reading maps, graphs, and pictures; and by observing personal experiences or real-life events. Evidence-collecting might also involve designing and conducting surveys, interviews, and questionnaires. Students should have the opportunity to practice all these techniques.

It is therefore important for teachers to select information contained over a wide variety of media. If, for example, students were to continue their inquiry into the nature of life at the place described in the Prologue, we might supply them with excerpts from a traveler's diary, recordings of their folklore, and perhaps reproductions of their art or sculpture. We could even present in a lecture about the history of the region some data that might be otherwise unobtainable by them. In collecting data from these sources, the students will be able to practice or refine a larger number of skills than they could if working with only a single source.

Evaluation also plays an important role in assembling evidence. As students find data, they must determine what of their findings should be treated as evidence. Part of this decision is based on how closely the data relate to the hypothesis under consideration. It is also based on the authenticity and accuracy of the data. Just because a piece of data appears relevant to a hypothesis, it will not necessarily be useful in validating the hypothesis because it may be highly inaccurate, outdated, one-sided, or even fraudulent. Consequently, students must learn to evaluate their evidence to determine its validity as well as its relevance to a hypothesis.

In inquiry teaching, the teacher must employ learning experiences in which students examine data to distinguish statements of accepted fact from statements of opinion and to identify unstated assumptions, evidence of bias, and examples of faulty logic. Students must determine the internal and external validity of the source itself: who created it, when, and why, and the author's sources, biases, and purposes. Students must also search for internal inconsistencies, for conclusions unsubstantiated by the evidence cited, and for card-stacking or emphasis on just one point of view. Such evaluation is as pertinent to work with maps, photographs, records, and filmstrips as it is to monographs, selections from diaries, newspapers, and documents.

Students should, for example, study the kinds of words used in a source, whether written or spoken. Emotionally charged words or words that connote value judgments reveal a great deal about authors. They can give clues to the quality of scholarship, biases, assumptions, and even intent. For instance, the following excerpt was purportedly written by a university professor:

> Before the arrival of Europeans, southeast Asia was a cultural wasteland. It had no history, no tradition of art or music, no civilization. Education, government, and religion were frustrated by the trivia of village life. Civilization could hardly thrive in crude thatched huts or behind the menacing masks of savage witch doctors. But the Europeans changed all this. Their guns brought law and order, the first requirement of civilization. Missionaries brought the blessings of Christianity and education and began the task of stamping out such barbarous practices as polygamy and semi-nudity. Traders introduced modern goods and acquainted the natives with the importance of money. Slothful natives were taught the virtues of hard work on European-owned plantations and railroad lines. Colonial governments instructed all people about democracy and how it works. In short, Europe shouldered the white man's burden and brought civilization to the primitive inhabitants of the jungles of southeast Asia.

Notice the evaluative words used by this author: *trivia, crude, modern, savage, blessings,* and so on. Notice, too, the emotionally charged words such as *menacing, barbaro*, *slothful,* and *frustrated.* These words give important clues to the frame of reference, the biases, and the assumptions of the author. There are also obvious statements of error: "it had no history" and of opinion posing as fact: "law and order, the first requirements of civilization." The way an author writes and the words he or she chooses to use often reveal his or her point of view. Identifying the point of view helps students evaluate the accuracy of an account. Such an analysis may also give more insight into the society that produced the author of the material than into the subject discussed. Practice in analyzing newspaper articles, pictorial and audio materials, textbooks, and primary sources in this fashion should be an integral part of hypothesis testing.

Of course, students must also be given opportunities to evaluate the content of the data they use. Does this content accurately portray what it purports to portray? Is it a primary or a secondary account? If the former, what are the author's frame of reference and purpose? If the latter, on what is it based? These and other similar questions need to be answered, and their answers come from comparing sources of data. Students can, for example, examine paragraphs on the same subject from a number of standard history texts, or they can be asked to evaluate excerpts on the same topic from the works of a variety of scholars or to examine and evaluate newspaper accounts, recollections of participants, and a newsreel film of the same event.

A number of opportunities exist to evaluate the accuracy and authenticity of the sources and information used in the lesson that launched this book. If the students knew the location of the site from which this data came, they could, of course, check the data against any possible number of other sources such as encyclopedia accounts, monographs, or scholarly studies about this place. Because they do not know that the site is Kiev, Russia, however, they must evaluate their data by making internal comparisons and analyses. Is the data presented in the photos consistent with that presented in the excerpts from documents? Does the writing in the drawing on page 4 resemble that on the coins or in the photo of the individuals on page 11? Although such an evaluation hardly produces conclusive results, it temporarily serves to authenticate data until additional corroborative sources can be identified and examined.

The fact that no such evaluation was called for in the Prologue sample lesson does not mean that this step should be ignored; the step was omitted merely to keep the lesson simple and direct. Students need not execute every single step in inquiry with equal emphasis in every unit. Care should be taken, however, to see that periodically, when data are available and evaluation can be stressed as an integral part of a unit, students undertake evaluations.

Arranging Evidence

Meaningful analysis of evidence depends as much on how the evidence is organized and displayed as it does on the quality of the data itself and on the frame of reference of the student. Hence, the next major step in testing a hypothesis involves preparing the assembled evidence for analysis. This preparation involves at least three distinct operations: translation, interpretation, and classification.

Before any information can be clearly comprehended, it must be in a form easily understood by the learner. This frequently necessitates translating a piece of evidence into more familiar terms. Obviously translation would be required if the original evidence were written in the idiom of sixteenth-century English or mid-twentieth-century Brooklynese. These, too, must be cast into the language of the student.

Translating evidence from one form into another is also important. Pounds sterling need to be translated into dollars and cents when comparing them to dollars, for example. Kilometers need to be translated into miles, or vice versa, to make the units of measurement comparable. Moreover, evidence should often be translated into several different forms. The data for analyzing presidential election returns, for instance, might best be translated from a list of how the states voted for each candidate to a political map that reveals spatial relationships obscured by a mere alphabetical listing. If the same data were then displayed in another form, perhaps further relationships could be more easily discerned.

Translating evidence from one form into another makes interpretation easier. Translation, however, is not the same as interpretation. Caution must be exercised to prevent interpretation from coloring the results of the translation. Translation involves essentially displaying in a new form information originally presented in another form. It requires students to "read" a graph or photograph for what it says and then to display this information in a new form. What the material literally "says" must not be tampered with, but must be made absolutely clear before the data is examined for significant meaning.

To help students develop or use the skill of translating, a teacher might have students report in writing what they see in a slide, draw a map of a landscape pictured in a photograph, or write in their own words the content of a historic document. Such activities would be useful not only in preparing data for analysis but also in illustrating how translation can change the substance of something, or how different people, because of their unique frames of reference, may translate the same items differently.

Suppose, for example, students view a photograph showing many people moving among tables and counters that overflow with a variety of goods. Some people are handling some of the goods; others are exchanging something with persons stationed behind the tables; some of those people are, in turn, exchanging bundles or goods with those in the crowd, and so on. This is a translation into words of what a particular picture says.

We might just as easily describe this picture as a market scene. However, that description would be interpretation, not translation. Interpretation involves a skill quite distinct from that of reporting the literal contents of something. Interpretation involves making connections between what we see and what we already know from our own unique frame of reference and store of knowledge. Interpretation involves recasting or summarizing our perceptions in terms that describe or explain the meaning we perceive in them. Thus, interpreting this picture as a market scene neatly sums up its contents by giving them a meaning.

By way of another example, study the climograph in Figure 6.2. What does it say? What does it mean?

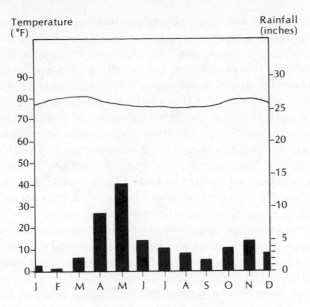

Figure 6.2. A Climograph

This graph literally says that the average rainfall for May for this particular place is about 13 inches, for September just under two inches, and for November almost five inches. It says further than the annual rainfall here averages about 49 inches. In addition, the graph says that the average daily temperature in April is 80°F. These statements represent a literal translation of these data. However, the graph might be interpreted to mean that there seem to be two rainy periods (in April-May and again in October-November), that the coolest period coincides with a period of decreasing rainfall, and that the periods of highest average temperature coincide with the periods of greatest rainfall. What this graph literally says and the meanings it communicates differ considerably—and its meaning depends on our perception of what it says. Indeed, it may mean nothing to us, if we can't even figure out what it says!

Students must learn the essential difference between translation and interpretation, since both are important steps in arranging evidence. Simply put, translation involves answering the question, "What does the data (author, source, etc.) say?" Interpreting on the other hand goes one step further to answer the question, "What does this data (author, source, etc.) mean?" In analyzing any data, students must first ask or be asked, "What does the evidence say?" or, "What is going on here?" They must report literally what the picture shows, the document says, the graph illustrates, and so on. Then and only then should they deal with the question, "What does it mean?" Only then should they suggest the significance of what is going on or what the data means. Every effort must be made to help students realize when they are or should be translating and when they are or should be interpreting; it is essential to avoid the confusion that will surely result when these steps are unconsciously interchanged. One may expect general agreement on the translation of a particular item; however, interpretations of it may vary considerably.

One way to prepare evidence for analysis involves arranging it in categories or classes. Classifying data is especially important when dealing with large masses of information. Categorizing individual pieces of information according to common characteristics facilitates the handling of considerable amounts of data and also makes possible detecting or inferring a wide variety of interrelationships, trends, and sequences that might otherwise go unnoticed.

Students must be taught the value of categorizing the same data in a variety of ways. They should learn to group items according to ways of arranging time, such as by centuries, by sequence, by cause and effect. They should learn to group data in terms of space, such as by relative position, by distance, by location, and by association with other features. They should also learn to arrange data according to other factors that affect human life into economic, political, social, intellectual, geographic, or religious categories.

Arranging data by rank often involves personal opinions or preferences. Ranking certain events or features according to how good or useful or right they may be for a certain person or group helps students to clarify their own values and attitudes; the way they rank the items may provide a good clue as to what they value, or at least to the nature of the criteria implied by the ranking. Discussing the reasons for a certain rank is important to this approach, but ranking or classifying must take place first.

Again, the teacher must help students learn to classify or rank data. At first such help may entail devising specific activities that require the classification of given data. Such activities could consist of giving students certain items to place in prescribed categories, giving them lists of data to categorize however they wish, giving them data already categorized and having them describe the nature of the individual groups by developing appropriate descriptive titles for each category, or having them search out their own data and group it as they see fit. Or, as in the sample lesson in the Prologue, students may classify their evidence in terms of the hypothesis being tested (by answering the question, Which evidence supports the hypothesis that these people were Christians?) and even in terms of the positive or negative relationship of the data to their hypotheses. Arranging data for analysis may be a class, small group, or individual activity. Regardless of how it is carried out, however, this skill should be mastered as part of inquiry teaching, for the ways the evidence is arranged may facilitate or hinder its analysis.

Analyzing Evidence

Analysis is a very broad term. In fact, the term is deceptively vague. *Analysis* refers specifically to those mental operations involved in pulling evidence apart and refitting it in the search for new meaning. It involves the intellectual manipulation of data to identify similarities and differences, trends and sequences, regularities, and patterns of significance. Analysis cannot be done well until the data has been assembled and carefully arranged or displayed. It must be considered an entirely separate operation, a very sophisticated one at that.

What one looks for in analyzing any specific body of evidence depends, of course, on the nature of the evidence and the hypothesis under consideration.

In general, an inquirer ought to seek out items that repeat themselves, cause and/or effect relationships, trends, sequences, patterns, regularities, and other kinds of interrelationships of significance. Knowing what to look for can be most helpful in suggesting where and how to look.

Analyzing data can be difficult. It is made easier, however, by careful but imaginative assembling and displaying of the evidence. An analysis of voting behavior will be facilitated, for instance, by displaying election returns, per capita income, and allotments for public works projects on maps of election districts and by using statistics showing registration and voting percentages, graphs of voting trends, and so on. Grouping this data according to political parties, nature of the elections, major campaign issues, contemporary events, or other categories may also be useful here. But drawing inferences from this evidence, identifying its constituent parts, and positing relationships between these parts represent the more complex steps of analysis. Such operations occur in the minds of the students themselves. The results of another's analysis may be communicated to students as information, but this is no substitute for their own analyses. Finding meaning in data is the essence of learning, and analysis is where it occurs.

This phase of inquiring may be built around a host of questions, including,

- What does this evidence mean?
- How is it related to another piece of evidence?
- Which piece of evidence came first?
- What is the relationship between this evidence and the hypothesis?

Regardless of who asks the questions, teacher or students, in this phase of inquiring one must refer periodically to the hypotheses being tested in order to avoid being sidetracked. Periodic reviews or summaries of how well the evidence thus far examined supports or refutes the hypothesis should be made. Important, too, is recognition of the tentative nature of the hypothesis and of the very real possibility that it might be invalidated by analysis. These are student-centered tasks, but teachers can guide them via oral questioning or written study guides, or even by the way in which they structure the materials used in the learning activities.

Data and Questioning in Hypothesis Testing

The role and use of data. Inquiry uses several important tools: one is information or data; the other consists of the questions asked of this information or data. While inquiry teaching requires the use of both data and questioning throughout the entire teaching process, nowhere are these two tools more important than in testing hypotheses.

Data provides the substance for inquiry learning and teaching; from the data available we extract what specifically serves as evidence for our hypotheses. Thus, data may be used in at least three ways by the teacher to facilitate student inquiry. When first using inquiry teaching, teachers may find it desirable to provide for the students only the data (the actual evidence already preselected) relevant to the hypotheses being tested. This procedure maximizes the time available for learning how to work with evidence, but it does not help students learn how to identify such evidence from the more general store of information available about a topic, also an important aspect of inquiry learning. A second way to use data at this stage of inquiry is to provide students with information about the general topic being discussed and then require the students themselves to extract from it only the information that relates to their hypotheses, only the data that they need as evidence to support or refute the hypotheses being tested.

Finally, teachers could *not* provide any data at all for hypothesis testing. Instead, they can make sources of potential data available or require students to find their own sources by library or other types of research. This third approach requires students to learn and practice procedures for collecting data, another important skill in inquiry. Teachers should provide students at first with only the evidence they need and then later employ inquiry lessons where students extract from given data the needed evidence and even later use lessons wherein students find both data and evidence. This helps students develop and practice slowly and in sequence the basic data using the skills involved in hypothesis testing so that they do not have to learn and use all these skills at once.

However, as important as data are in hypothesis testing, we should note two cautions about its use. First, examining all known data relevant to particular hypothesis, although desirable, is not usually possible or practical. Students, therefore, must become accustomed to arriving at conclusions on the basis of incomplete or suspect evidence. At the same time, they must know that because their evidence is incomplete, their conclusions must still be considered somewhat tentative until confirmed or modified in the light of later analysis of additional data.

Second, under no circumstances should the data made available for hypothesis testing be biased one way only. Nor should evidence contradictory to the hypothesis be suppressed or ignored. As professionals and presumed experts in the subject matter of their courses, teachers are responsible for ensuring that data representative of all views on a hypothesis are examined.

Questioning strategies. Questions also play an important role in guiding students through hypothesis testing. Whether student- or teacher-initiated, written or oral, these questions can be either precise and specific or more general in nature. For example, in testing hypotheses students need essentially to direct their attention to two tasks: (1) to cull evidence from the mass of data available to them, and then (2) to determine the meaning of that evidence as it relates to the hypothesis being tested. To accomplish the former, students can use the following questions:

1. What can you find in the data that you expect or need to find if your hypothesis is accurate?
2. What can't you find that you expected to find if your hypothesis is accurate?
3. What do you find in your data that you don't want or expect to find if your hypothesis is accurate?
4. What new things did you find in your data that you had not thought of or expected?

To determine the meaning of evidence thus selected, students can then use the following questions:

5. What does the evidence say?	Translation
6. What does this evidence mean?	Interpretation
7. What does this evidence mean to you in the light of what you already know? How will it be useful in explaining what you are trying to explain?	Application

Consideration of two factors make these seven questions most useful in testing any hypothesis. First, as noted earlier, most students not only want to be right, but they want to prove the accuracy of their guesses immediately. So we start where they are, with question 1, and help them do what they want to do. By asking the remaining questions, we extend the students' willingness and abilities to search for contrary evidence and to consider the possibilities of being wrong in their hunches. Questions 2 and 3 help move us toward these goals. These questions and the final question also help students generate new ideas that they can claim as their own — as substitutes for hypotheses negated by their investigation or as additional hypotheses to test later.

Secondly, these seven questions keep student inquiry purposeful and efficient. By continuously calling attention to the hypothesis being tested, these questions keep the nature and goal of the inquiry in focus while still (question 4) permitting exploration into other areas of the subject. Thus, the first four questions provide focus, permit students to follow their natural inclination and desire to prove themselves "right," and require them to extend themselves beyond their own inclinations and present knowledge. Questions 5–7 then help them make this evidence meaningful in terms of the hypotheses being studied.

Although questions 1–7 are rather general, they subsume more specific questions that call for more precise handling of the data. One cannot answer any of these general questions without recalling, translating, interpreting, analyzing, and evaluating the evidence. Yet by using these general questions as the key questions to guide hypothesis testing, we eliminate the necessity of having to ask a long series of very specific questions, a situation that often takes on the aura of an interrogation rather than inquiry. Use of specific questions seems necessary only when students need to clarify, justify, or explain statements or responses. Organizing a hypothesis testing activity around general questions such as 1–7 keeps student inquiry as open as possible; at the same time it provides overall teacher direction of the process involved.

The general questions cited here do not function in isolation from each other. Instead they proceed almost simultaneously. As students seek evidence supportive of other hypotheses (question 1) they do so, in part, by answering questions 5–7. They use the same procedure in searching for all types of evidence relevant to their hypotheses. Both sets of questions can be combined in a matrix to teach students how to test hypotheses, as well as to guide them in their analysis. The guide on page 126 illustrates such a matrix. Students can use this matrix as a worksheet in testing any hypothesis once they have identified the evidence they hope to find, and *not* to find, relative to their hypotheses. Use of this two-dimensional approach to questioning focuses student attention simultaneously on the data and on their hypotheses. It also helps students make abstract relationships, a skill important to the development of the abstract reasoning that characterizes what Piaget describes as the stage of formal operational or abstract thinking.

EVIDENCE ANALYSIS GUIDE

If it is true that (hypothesis):_____ _____ _____ _____ _____ _____	A. What does this evidence say?	B. What does this evidence mean?	C. How does this evidence affect the hypothesis?
1. What did you find that you expected to find?_____ _____ _____ _____ _____ _____			
2. What couldn't you find that you expected or needed to find?_____ _____ _____ _____			
3. What did you find that you didn't want to find if your hypothesis were accurate?_____ _____ _____ _____			
4. What new information did you find? What new ideas?_____ _____ _____ _____ _____			

Inquiry teaching serves as one way to help students reach—and develop further—the highest stages of thinking. Hypothesis testing provides one point in this teaching strategy where such development can occur.

Items 3–11 in the sample lesson in the Prologue illustrate the basic operations in hypothesis testing as described here. These items also illustrate how the data can be used and how the general questions described above can be used for guiding analysis. The two types of data comprising this segment of the lesson, a list of laws and several edited excerpts from documents of the period being studied, were selected for their accuracy in describing life in the society at the time as far as experts today can determine, the extent to which selected aspects of life there are illustrated or exemplified, and their relevance to hypotheses that might be generated by using the pictures of artifacts that initiated the lesson.

Although it is impossible to predict with certainty the specific hypotheses one might advance in looking at the photographs in the Prologue, it is possible to anticipate statements about trade, religion, government, warfare, and occupations in the society under study. Indeed, artifacts were included that might stimulate formulation of hypotheses about these topics. Thus, the data provided at this step of inquiry teaching had to contain some information that could have been relevant to such hypotheses in case they were made. But drawing evidence from the available data constitutes the inquirer's task, and different inquirers infer different hypotheses or identify different evidence even for the same hypothesis while using the same data base.

The lesson in the Prologue, as illustrated in the following classroom example, asked general rather than specific questions to guide the testing of hypotheses. This was done to provide considerable latitude for individual inquiry and because the exact hypotheses to be derived could neither be predicted nor followed up in detail. Thus, much of the data in the laws may be irrelevant to hypotheses about war or military events, but there is at least one law that could be cited as evidence in testing a hypothesis about the prevalence of warfare or need for protection.

Even more data in the written excerpts bear on such a hypothesis. The general questions that guided analysis of these data attempted to help you find the evidence you needed or expected as well as to find new data that might have been relevant to these hypotheses but which you had not yet identified. Finally, these questions enabled you to identify new features of the society, in effect to list additional hypotheses for subsequent testing if you wished to do so. Testing hypotheses not only helps one confirm or refute previously made hypotheses but also leads to new insights and new hypotheses about the topic or question under study. Analysis of the accompanying example of how students proceeded through this step of the Prologue lesson further illustrates how hypothesis-testing can be guided using the general questions outlined on pages 124–125.

Hypothesis testing may also be guided by even more specific questions. Any number of questioning strategies may be devised to this end. For example, the following sequence of questions provides a more specific set of questions for guiding students through the various thinking operations that constitute hypothesis testing:

--- FOR EXAMPLE . . . ---
ASSEMBLING EVIDENCE AND EVALUATING HYPOTHESES

Questions:

6-7. What did you find in the laws that you expected to find, if your idea that these people are Christian is true?

Fifth graders' responses:	*Tenth graders' responses:*
killing was punished	murder, hurting people, and
so was stealing	stealing were against the law
people can get justice	the workers could have a fair trial—if they were honest about it
	new . . . Christianity was new to them

8. What evidence did you find that you didn't want to find, if you thought these people were Christians?

Fifth graders' responses:	*Tenth graders' responses:*
things weren't equal for everyone	they allowed revenge—"an eye for an eye" thing
they had slaves	not everyone was treated equal
	property was more important than people

What evidence that you wanted to find, couldn't you find—if they were Christians?

Fifth graders' responses:	*Tenth graders' responses:*
anything about religious days	no dues to church required
anything about priests	nothing about church holidays

9. What new ideas did you get about life in this place from these laws?

Fifth graders' responses:	*Tenth graders' responses:*
they had police—or someone to catch lawbreakers—a sheriff!	they had private ownership of land and things—
they were civilized—they had laws—and justice	they used fences
they had schools and teachers—education	they owned things like slaves
there were farmers—they plowed and had fences	they had a system of education because
	—had written laws
	—were some teachers
	it was male dominated
	—men inherited the most
	—it's all "he" and "him"

11. What evidence did you find in the excerpts to prove correct your idea that these people were Christians?

Fifth graders' responses:	
Prince was against idols	they had churches—once anyway
they baptized people	they used the word "Christian"

Tenth graders' responses:

the leader believed in charity—
   he helped the poor
they destroyed idols
they built churches—and these
   churches had crosses

some people were called
   "Christians"
they had baptism

---

1. If your hypothesis is true, then what kinds of evidence do you expect to find? If your hypothesis is true, then what kinds of evidence do you *not* expect to find?	**Identifying Needed Evidence**
2. Where will you find it? How?	**Identifying Sources and Collecting Evidence**
3. Is the evidence authentic? Is it valid? Is it reliable? Is it significant?	**Evaluating Evidence**
4. What does the evidence say?	**Translating Evidence**
5. What does it mean?	**Interpreting Evidence**
6. In what ways can this evidence be classified?	**Classifying Evidence**
7. What does the evidence mean when classified in these ways?	**Interpreting Evidence**
8. In what ways does this evidence relate to other evidence and/or the hypothesis being tested?	**Seeking Relationships**
9. How is this similar to other evidence? How do they differ?	**Noting Similarities and Differences**
10. Which comes first? Which is nearest? Which repeat?	**Identifying Trends, Sequences, and Regularities**
11. How does this evidence affect the hypothesis?	**Evaluating Hypotheses**

Of course, the final, crucial question follows immediately from both these lines of questioning, for both series of questions lead to and actually evolve from our major concern in testing any hypothesis: What does our hypothesis mean in light of or in terms of the evidence we have examined? Hypothesis-testing ultimately seeks to evaluate the accuracy of a hypothesis or series of hypotheses. Yet careful analysis of the evidence related to the hypothesis must precede this judgment.

Still another type of questioning strategy proves useful in guiding students through hypothesis testing. This strategy is derived directly from the taxonomy of cognitive objectives developed by Bloom and his colleagues, and it seeks to move students from lower to higher levels of thinking as they engage in analysis of the data before them. The following sequence of questions illustrates this strategy:

Translation	What does this information say?
	What are the details?
Comprehension	What does this information mean?
	What is likely to happen if . . . ?
Application	How does this information change what you learned in . . . ?
	How can you use this information to make sense of . . . ?
Analysis	What is the author's purpose?
	What are his/her assumptions, biases, etc.?
	What are the cause-effect relationships suggested?
Synthesis	What is the main idea of all this information?
	What assertion can you m ake that accounts for or explains this data?
Evaluation	How accurate is this information according to what we already know? To our criteria? To other criteria?

The questions a teacher uses to guide, direct, or facilitate hypothesis testing, indeed, to guide the entire inquiry process, may be very specific at times and quite general at other times. The point is that teachers should employ a wide variety of questioning strategies to facilitate inquiry learning. Such variety is useful for purposes other than motivation, because different questioning strategies serve different purposes. Sometimes we might use a series of questions that focus student learning on only two or three selected steps in the hypothesis-testing process, rather than trying to give equal weight to all steps in the process by using the longer lists of questions outlined above. At other times a few general questions may be more useful than many specific ones.

Testing hypotheses is a very important and by far the most time consuming step in inquiry teaching. At this point students must assemble, arrange, and analyze evidence pertaining to the hypotheses selected for investigation. Here, too, students become deeply involved in the content and information selected for study and thus receive an opportunity to practice the skills, develop and use the kinds of knowledge, and exhibit the behaviors indicative of the attitudes and values that constitute inquiry. Hypothesis testing contributes to new learning in a way matched by few if any other learning procedures in terms of retention, thoroughness, and depth of understanding.

DEVELOPING A CONCLUSION

The outcome or result of testing a hypothesis or series of hypotheses can be best described as a conclusion. An inquiry conclusion consists of a statement about the accuracy of a hypothesis judged in terms of the evidence against which the hypothesis has been tested and in terms of other assertions on which it may be based or to which it may lead. Developing and stating a conclusion comprise the fourth step of inquiry teaching.

In order to produce a conclusion, students must judge the match between the evidence they have examined and the hypotheses being tested. This involves (1) knowing some set of criteria for use as standards in measuring this match, (2) judging or evaluating, and finally, (3) synthesizing information into a new or revised form. Such operations duplicate—albeit much more deliberately —the way hypotheses are formulated. But hypotheses represent only very tentative assertions because they are derived from limited data and are often arrived at without any systematic analysis of the data. A conclusion, on the other hand, is much less tentative than a hypothesis precisely because it results from careful and deliberate identification, collection, and analysis of as much relevant data as possible.

In reality, a conclusion expresses a judgment about the extent to which a hypothesis appears correct or incorrect in terms of the evidence studied. The judgment may merely result in a reaffirmation of the original hypothesis. More often than not, however, a conclusion may consist of an elaboration or substantial modification of the original hypothesis, or perhaps even an outright rejection of the hypothesis altogether. Regardless of the form it takes, a conclusion serves to bring a line of inquiry to a close after careful deliberation. Although not the final step in either inquiring or inquiry teaching, developing a conclusion serves as the target for inquiry learning and teaching from its very inception.

In guiding students to develop conclusions, the teacher must direct or provide learning experiences that require students to combine identified relationships among the evidence and between the evidence and hypothesis into statements that bear on the initial problem. Students must then be asked to judge explicitly the relationship between this rearranged evidence and the hypothesis being investigated in order to determine the degree to which the evidence warrants or validates the hypothesis. If, in their judgment, this evaluation negates the hypothesis, the students must return to the original problem or question, develop other hypotheses, and proceed to test them. In fact, most problems are resolved in precisely this way, by the repeated making and testing of multiple hypotheses. When one's informed judgment suggests that a hypothesis is indeed accurate in terms of the evidence, a conclusion may affirm the validity of the hypothesis. In such a case, the hypothesis itself may become the conclusion.

Such is the case regarding the study of life in old Kiev as shown in the excerpts on page 132 that have been used as a point of reference throughout these pages. By making and testing multiple hypotheses concurrently or serially one after the other, you, as well as the students represented in the accompanying example can make some conclusions about the validity of the initial hypotheses or of those generated in the process of testing the original hypotheses. These conclusions answer the initial question, "What was life like in this society around A.D. 1000?" to some degree of certainity (at least with more certainty than the earlier answers based only on the photographs of artifacts). Whatever

───── FOR EXAMPLE . . . ─────
STATING CONCLUSIONS

Questions:

12a. What ideas did you have about life in this place that seem true? Which of your guesses seem to be proved by the laws and excerpts?

Fifth graders' responses:	*Tenth graders' responses:*

they had Christianity—
  churches
  baptism
  used the word
they had writing
  laws were written
  it was on the coins and
    pictures
  they wrote stories
they lived by water
  seashells
  had boats
	Some were Christians
	  they used the cross, had
	  churches, baptism and even
	  called people Christian
	people were in different classes—
	  there were titles, punishments
	  differed for each class for
	  the same crime, some were
	  slaves
	it was a military oriented
	  society—there were wars,
	  they had a draft law, they had
	  swords

b. Which of your ideas were not proved by the information in the laws or excerpts?

Fifth graders' responses:	*Tenth graders' responses:*

maybe they didn't live by the
  ocean—but they did live
  near some water like a river
  or something
nothing about hunting
	not too much on trade—we
	  need more
	perhaps they didn't fish but
	  traded farm things for fish
	  and shells
	who ruled who?

c. What new ideas does this study give you about life in this place around A.D. 1000?

Fifth graders' responses:	*Tenth graders' responses:*

they had police
they were civilized—they
  had writing, schools, laws
  and justice
people had different skills
  some were teachers
  and some made things
	they had large cities
	they had a powerful ruler or
	  prince—maybe a king—who
	  ran the army and courts and
	  punished people
	there was a sense of
	  group responsibility (in the
	  guilds)

What three things can you say for sure about life in this place almost 1,000 years ago?

Fifth graders' responses:	*Tenth graders' responses:*

they were Christian
they fought a lot
they were civilized
	It was military or war oriented
	  or violent
	They had a strict system of
	  classes—including slaves
	Some people—some time—were
	  Christians, including the
	  prince or king.

> It was a feudal society—like
> France at this time. Where
> was this place?

these conclusions, they constitute temporarily acceptable answers to the question that launched this inquiry, and they comprise a learner- or self-derived answer rather than one secured from some outside authority.

The usefulness and validity of the conclusions drawn from the inquiry process depend, of course, on the amount and validity of the evidence on which they are based. Any hypothesis is suspect because it is based on limited evidence. A conclusion built on a test against more evidence may be only slightly more substantial, for it cannot be accepted as absolutely final or true until it is tested against all relevant data. In many cases, securing such evidence is impossible. Yet, such continued testing may well be the ultimate objective of inquiry teaching—especially where concept development or the development of high level principles, generalizations, or generalized skills serve as major learning goals. Thus, inquiry teaching usually involves one more step: helping students to apply a conclusion to new data.

APPLYING A CONCLUSION
TO NEW DATA

At first glance, drawing a conclusion may represent a perfectly logical final step in inquiry, for the problem has been resolved or the question answered. This may be so. However, making one's own conclusion does not always represent a psychologically satisfying final step. For most people, one question still remains: "How do I know that the conclusion I have drawn is really correct?" This nagging question often compels us to go one step further, to apply our conclusion to new data to see if what we think is true really is true. Hence the final step in inquiry and inquiry teaching consists of applying the conclusion to new data.

As noted earlier, this final step serves several purposes. It brings psychological as well as substantive closure to an otherwise still unsettled situation. It permits learners to find out if their own independent inquiries are indeed substantiated by other sources. This step also frequently expands the original conclusion. Applying a conclusion to new but related evidence may well make that conclusion less specific, more applicable to or explanatory of the class of data it relates to without being tied to any specific set of that data. The resulting finding can be even more general, more conceptual. Generalizing and conceptualizing represent for many the final, most advanced stage of thinking and the highest level of knowing. Making such general knowledge must be considered as the culminating step in any strategy of inquiry teaching.

Testing or validating conclusions. Applying a conclusion to new data may ground that conclusion in more evidence, thus giving the original conclusion greater validity and reliability. However, continued inquiring may just as easily turn up evidence that requires modifying the conclusion to account for factors of a more diverse nature; this makes the conclusion applicable to a more general class of phenomena and less content specific. Moreover, applying a conclusion to new data may even uncover evidence that completely invalidates the conclusion—a result not easily accepted by most learners, but a distinct possibility nonetheless. More happily, applying the conclusion to new data may turn up entirely new insights relative to the conclusion or the topic to which it is related. It could even suggest entirely new avenues of inquiry.

Applying a conclusion to new data involves applying the conclusion against data relating to it but as yet unused by the inquirer. This data may be the findings of recognized experts who have made inquiries into the same or different but related evidence. It may be the concluding essay that generally sums up the major established points relating to the problem at hand (but which all too often serves only to tell the inquirer what he should have discovered through his own inquiry). The new data may even be the opinions or conclusions reached by one's peers who have also gone through the same inquiry.

Teachers use these types of data quite commonly in inquiry teaching. But as useful or timesaving as they may be, they have serious drawbacks. For one, checking what the others in class think about something can easily degenerate into voting on the accuracy of knowledge ("How many agree with Susan? Only ten out of twenty-five? Well, Susan, I guess you're wrong!"), an indefensible approach to learning and teaching. Moreover, checking one's conclusion against what the experts say or against what the textbook authors wrote in their chapter summary might be considered indefensible. Inquiring is hard work. As soon as students find that expert opinions are available for use or that chapter summaries do exist, they are likely to feel that further inquiry on their own would be a waste of time. "Why should I go through all that work to solve a problem or discover something when I can find the answer at the end of the chapter?" As invalid as this reasoning may be from the teacher's point of view, it is a very real factor in the attitudes of many students toward thinking in the classroom.

If students must use what the experts say to check their conclusions (and this can sometimes be done very effectively), they should not treat the experts' opinion as necessarily being the answer but as being nothing more than additional sources of data—and sometimes fallible at that. Students should treat their own conclusions as valid and use them to check the accuracy of the opinions of the experts and the evidence they cite in support of these opinions. A chapter summary ought to be treated merely as more data, not as answers but as opinions. Then the students can check the accuracy of the statements in the summary against what they have already found out. By so doing, all kinds of new questions arise, and the student conclusions arrived at earlier can be modified and treated with some suspicion. The opinions of the experts and textbook author should also be viewed with skepticism. Students should question what the so-called expert and the chapter summary say rather than their own conclusion if theirs is based on reasoned inquiry.

The most effective, but also most time-consuming, data against which to apply a conclusion are data relevant to the conclusion but not used in

---

—FOR EXAMPLE . . . —
APPLYING CONCLUSIONS

Questions:

13a. Look at the pictures of the buildings and items in these buildings that can still be found in the place where this society once existed. What can you find that supports, for example, your idea that these people—or at least some of them—were Christian?

Fifth graders' responses:	*Tenth graders' responses:*
a church	a church
people with halos, robes, crosses	religious figures—with halos, robes
a priest	crosses
	a priest baptizing someone

b. What can you find to support—or refute—your conclusion that this society was warlike or violent?

Fifth graders' responses:	*Tenth graders' responses:*
spears and shields	a military leader
man wearing armor	military equipment— sword, shields, armor, bows and arrows, helmets

14. Once again, what are three things you are willing to say for sure (or to stake your grade on!) that really characterized life in this society around A.D. 1000?

Fifth graders' responses:	*Tenth graders' responses:*
Many people were Christians.	Some people who lived in this society were Christians (probably the leaders and upper classes).
There was a lot of war and fighting.	This was a militaristic oriented society based on land ownership (like feudalism in France).
Some people were well educated.	People were divided into social classes, each with different rights and jobs.

---

developing it. An inquirer can use his or her conclusion to make sense of this new evidence. If the conclusion enables one to do this satisfactorily, then the chances of its being valid are greater than they were before this stage of inquiring. If the conclusion does not account for or make sense of this new data, then it will surely require some modification.

This latter procedure was used in the lesson on old Kiev in the Prologue as shown by the example above. An account by an archeologist or historian could have been used as expert testimony against which you or the students in the experimental classes cited in the examples could test their ideas. That approach was not used for the reasons stated above. The intent of this lesson was to create knowledge not only for the sake of learning it and some related data, but also to develop further those skills and attitudes (especially the willingness to accept the results of independent, reasoned inquiry) useful in creating knowledge for oneself. These skills are of crucial import to our society today. Checking one's views against an authority's does not help accomplish this goal nearly as well as using a conclusion to make sense of new data.

Developing generalized knowledge. When extended, the approach used in the Kiev lesson also proves particularly useful where developing generalized knowledge is a major instructional goal. If this lesson were part of a unit or course that focused on various cultures in the world as they were around 1,000 years ago or that aimed to develop a concept of feudalism, this Kiev study could lead to the development of generalizations or concepts that would have value far beyond any specific facts students might learn about old Kiev.

For example, suppose that students conclude after studying the data presented here that life in old Kiev was characterized by a very rigid and sharply defined class structure, close church-state relations, an economy based primarily on private land ownership and agriculture but with developing trade and commerce, military conflict, and so on. They could then use this conclusion (limited at this point in its applicability to old Kiev only) to examine other societies of that period, perhaps in France, China, India, the West African Sudan, Peru, Yucatan, or Mexico. By using their conclusions to organize data about these societies, students could not only learn about these specific societies but also generalize about the characteristics of these societies at the same time. They could perhaps even develop general ideas about the nature of feudalism as a way of life throughout the world. By so doing, students can, in effect, develop generalizations that have considerable explanatory—and even predictive—power.

Applying a conclusion, whether in the form of a generalization, concept, or other type of knowledge, to new data is the final step in inquiry teaching. This step enables students to complete their inquiry by giving it added meaning; it also helps to satisfy a natural desire to know if one is correct. Since most students do not know how to engage effectively in this step of inquiring, they need extensive teacher guidance at first. In time, however, they can be expected to apply their conclusions to new data on their own, in independent learning situations. Regardless of how this fifth step is organized, it provides effective closure in inquiry teaching.

A STRATEGY
FOR INQUIRY TEACHING

The most effective strategy for inquiry teaching is based directly on how we learn by inquiring. As Figure 6.3 indicates, the process of inquiring itself may serve as a strategy for inquiry teaching. This strategy requires teachers to create learning experiences in which students must identify problems for investigation, invent hypotheses relative to these problems, test these hypotheses against

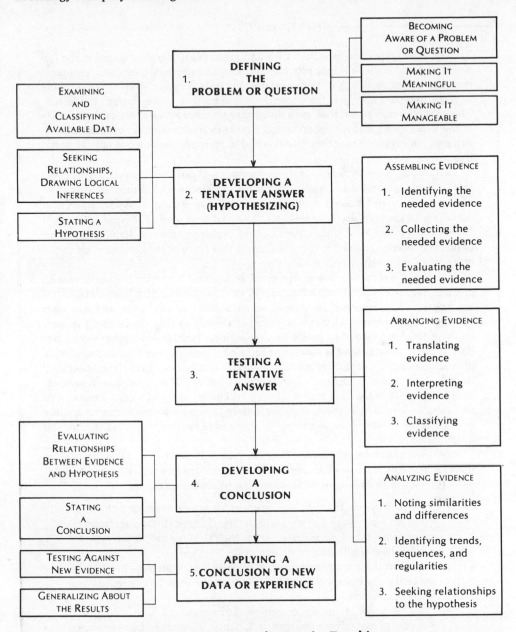

Figure 6.3. A Strategy for Inquiry Teaching

evidence, draw conclusions about the validity of these hypotheses, and finally, either devise new hypotheses for testing or apply their conclusions to new data. This teaching strategy can serve as the basis of daily lessons, weekly units of instruction, one-year courses, and even sequences of courses. When used to teach daily lessons or a series of lessons extending over several days or weeks, this strategy may be teacher or student directed depending on the established learning objectives and the degree to which students can engage in self-directed inquiry. Questions serve as one basic way to provide such direction, and these

─────────FOR EXAMPLE . . . ─────────

The responses excerpted here from fifth and tenth grade classes engaged in the lesson introduced in the Prologue provide only a small sample of their total responses, remarks, and questions. Yet, these excerpts illustrate the basic steps of the teaching strategy used and also how the students used inquiry to move through the lesson. These excerpts also reveal that, even though the students had no idea of the location of this place under study, they possessed a great deal of residual knowledge and experiential information that they found useful in trying to make sense of data about this place.

Of course, these students—like you, perhaps—occasionally asked, "Where was this?", thinking, probably rightly, that such knowledge would help them in their answer. If they had known anything about Kievian Russia, it would have. But revealing the site may also have prevented free and open inquiry. Besides, one might have wanted to test what the students learned in this sequence of activities in terms of both knowledge and skills. Identification of this place might have interfered with creating an extremely useful test for them.

As a final test for this lesson, for example, we could provide the students with pictures, narrative history accounts, poems, or other similar data from three different places and/or time periods (one of which is Kiev in A.D. 1000) and ask them to select the one set of data that best describes the site as they developed it in their study of this lesson—and to justify their selection. Such an evaluation would not only provide insight into the success or failure of the lesson and its strategy while providing a measure of student learning, it would also help students tie up what they have learned and even extend their learning further. This procedure represents another example of the final step of inquiry teaching, applying one's conclusion to new data. It does so by enabling students to treat their conclusions as correct and the new data, no matter how seemingly authoritative, as open for evaluation and questioning.

As you reflect on this lesson, both in terms of what you did as you went through it and in terms of what these fifth and tenth graders did, you might find it most productive to discuss or think about the following questions:

1. In what ways do the fifth and tenth graders' responses resemble each other? In what ways do they seem to differ? In what ways are your responses similar to or different from theirs? What might account for any of these similarities or differences?
2. What did these students know or seem to know already in order to make the statements they did? Where could they have secured this knowledge? How?
3. What level of thinking operation (according to the Bloom and Krathwohl taxonomies outlined in Chapter 3) seem to be represented by the student responses?

Discussion of your answers to these questions and your completion of this chapter can provide you with the kinds of insight into inquiry teaching and inquiry learning that are the prerequisite for effective inquiry teaching in a classroom. One more example of inquiry teaching in action should clinch this knowledge for you. This example introduces Chapter 7.

questions may be teacher- or student-generated; so, too, may they be structured in a variety of ways depending on the instructional objectives and student experience with inquiry. Whatever approaches you finally use in teaching, if students are to learn how to engage in purposeful inquiry, they must go through at least the five basic steps outlined in Figure 6.3.

In guiding students through these activities and operations, it is neither necessary nor desirable to give equal attention to each step in every lesson or unit, for this would be stifling to say the least. Instead, different inquiry lessons or units might emphasize in depth several of the basic operations that comprise hypothesis testing while still engaging students to some degree in all of the activities. By following this approach over a period of time, students will gain enough practice in each skill that constitutes hypothesis-testing to eventually conduct the entire process on their own. At the same time classes will also have the variety and spontaneity needed for motivation. Furthermore, such an approach permits study of as much content as possible in the limited time available for teachers.

Obviously, one can use any number of specific questions or learning activities to engage students in inquiring. However, to meet the criteria of inquiry as identified in this text, the teaching strategy must help students move through the five basic steps shown in Figure 6.3. This inquiry teaching strategy provides a conceptual structure for teaching and learning that develops knowledge, attitudes and values, and thinking skills with their associated cognitive and affective dimensions, all to their fullest potentials. Accomplishing these objectives should be considered a primary task of social studies teaching today.

notes

1. The role of this operation in inquiry has been carefully delimited, especially in its theoretical import, by a number of scholars, foremost among whom are Maurice P. Hunt and Lawrence Metcalf, *Teaching High School Social Studies* (New York: Harper & Row, 1955), pp. 79–87. See also 2nd ed., pp. 221–236.
2. Several different ways of classifying questions have been devised. See, for example: Ronald Lippitt et al., *The Teacher's Role in Social Science Investigation* (Chicago: Science Research Associates, 1969), p. 19; and Norris M. Sanders, *Classroom Questions: What Kinds?* (New York: Harper & Row, 1966). Although published over a decade ago, this latter volume remains the most valuable source of model questions for use in stimulating all types of intellectual acitivity and should be referred to frequently in planning inquiry teaching.
3. The materials used in the Prologue are taken from the following: artifacts, pp. 3–4, from M.K. Karger, *Ancient Kiev* (Leningrad, 1958), Vol. 1. Appendix; p. 6, "Medieval Russian Laws," George Vernadsky, trans., in Vol. XLI of *The Records of Civilization Sources and Studies* (New York: Columbia University Press, 1947), Austin P. Evans, ed., by permission of Columbia University Press; pp. 9–10: Selections 1 and 2

from Leo Wiener, ed., *Anthology of Russian Literature* (New York: G.P. Putnam's Sons, 1902), pp. 70, 71; Selection 3 reprinted by permission of the publishers from *The Russian Primary Chronicle,* Samuel Cross, trans., in *Studies and Notes in Philology and Literature,* Volume XII (Cambridge, Mass.: Harvard University Press, 1930); and Selection 4 from Henryk Paszkiewicz, *The Origin of Russia* (London: George Allen & Unwin Ltd., 1954), p. 286; photos pp. 11–12 from Ian Grey, *History of Russia* (New York: American Heritage Publishing Co., 1970); photos 1, 2, 3 and 4 on pp. 28, 31, 27, 92, respectively; and photo 5 from *The History of Russia,* p. 26, reprinted by permission of the Biblioteca Apostolica Vaticana.

7

Inquiry Teaching
in
Action

Inquiry teaching seems suitable for use in a wide variety of classroom settings, with a wide variety of instructional materials, and with students of varying ability and grade levels. But how does inquiry teaching actually work in practice? The short investigation of Kiev presented in the Prologue illustrates an inquiry teaching strategy in action. The chapters you have just completed refer repeatedly to that lesson—actually a series of lessons—to clarify the nature of inquiry and the basic steps that comprise the inquiry teaching strategy presented in this book. If you proceeded through that lesson and used your experience with it as a referent in reading Chapters 5 and 6, you may now have more of a feeling for and understanding of the essential elements of inquiry teaching. Applying this strategy now to a new body of content may well help pull together the basic elements of this teaching strategy and, in the process, generate or refine insights essential for using this strategy with any historical or social science materials in any social studies or history classroom.

AN INQUIRY
TEACHING LESSON

Another lesson follows here that uses the same strategy employed earlier to study Kiev. As you proceed through this lesson, keep in mind the five basic steps in the strategy of inquiry teaching presented in the preceding pages and the subordinate operations that constitute the steps. This lesson has been used (with slight variations to account for different reading abilities) with students of all ability levels in grades five, eight, and eleven. The following pages present a composite of the way this lesson has generally developed with all these groups.

These pages do not present a script, however. Instead, they offer a descriptive narrative that invites you to become involved as if you were actually participating in the lesson as a student. As you proceed through this lesson, you may also wish to take special note of (1) the kinds of material used, (2) the role of the teacher, and (3) the role of content in this approach to inquiry teaching. By so doing, you can better analyze inquiry teaching—and inquiry itself—in action.

Suppose we have been studying in an American history course the European exploration and colonization of the Atlantic seaboard of the present-day United States. Suppose further that we have now come to the point where it seems appropriate to examine life styles and the nature of society in the thirteen British American colonies on the eve of revolution. Was colonial life simply a mirror image of eighteenth century English society, or was it uniquely American? Was this colonial society a democratic society (whatever that means) or not? What was it like to live in the thirteen British-American colonies between 1750-1775? One way to use inquiry teaching to conduct this study might be as follows.

Defining a Problem or Question . . . None of us know first hand what it was really like to live in the thirteen colonies in the years just before the American Revolution. Yet, knowing something about life at that time and about the people who lived here then might give us some insight into the causes and nature of the American Revolution. Such a study might help us determine, for example, whether this revolution was really a revolt of one part of a society (the European inhabitants of English America) against another part of that society (the English in Britain), or whether this revolution was actually an international war pitting two different "nationalities," each with its own culture, self-interests, and unique past, against one another. So, what was life like in the thirteen British colonies in North America between 1750–1775? This is our immediate question! If we can answer this question, we can perhaps begin to answer the broader historical questions posed above.

Let's assume that we have defined "life" as human life and the way it was organized by individuals and groups. Let's assume further that we have defined the thirteen colonies as those occupying that stretch of land lying along the Atlantic coast of North America between the present-day states of Florida and Maine. What specific questions could we ask to help answer the question, *"What was life like in the thirteen British colonies in North America between 1750–1775?"* Here are some questions usually suggested by students:

—What did these people do for a living? for leisure?
—What kinds of houses did they live in? Why?
—What did these people consider important?
—How did these people get along with each other?

—

—

—

What other questions might be added to this list to help answer the question: *"What was life like in the thirteen British colonies in North America between 1750–1775?"* Add your questions to the preceding list in the space provided.

The specific questions listed above help define the investigation that we are about to launch. The answer to each question will serve as a partial answer to our initial question. Taken in toto the answers to all these questions will, in fact, become the answer to the question that launched our study of this topic.

. . . . *Stating Hypotheses* . . . Although some of us may know some general information related to the questions asked here, it usually proves useful to provide a common base from which to launch an investigation such as this. The list of words on page 144 includes a sample of the words commonly spoken by the inhabitants of the thirteen colonies in the years around 1750. Individually, or with others, examine this list of words. What ideas do these words suggest about life in mid-eighteenth century colonial America? Use the specific questions listed above to guide your search for answers to this question, and list here your tentative answers and the words that suggest them:

Characteristics of life in 1750 colonial America:	*Words that suggest each characteristic:*
1.	—
2.	—
3.	—
4.	—

These words suggest a number of hypotheses about colonial life around 1750. For example, if these words truly are representative of the period, it seems that farming may have been an important occupation of the time. Some agricultural-type words appear on this list, such as squash and eggplant. Weather-related words seem to be prominent—*cold snap*, for example; farmers might have been particularly concerned with the weather. The words *bluffs, back country,* and *underbrush* suggest the countryside—as opposed to urban settlements—where farms probably were located. Animals like raccoons, skunks, and gophers do not necessarily endear themselves to farmers unless as food; their appearance on this list may reflect a general concern about them that might typify a farming society. Perhaps farming was a major occupation of the colonists around 1750.

Life in the thirteen colonies had other characteristics, too. Towns appear to have existed as suggested by the words *counting house, tavern,* and *town crier.* Different social classes seem to have existed—witness the words *boss* and *indenture.* Life may have been outdoor oriented as indicated by words that suggest weather (cold snap), outdoor activities (trails, fox hunt, toboggan), and features of the land-

WORDS COMMONLY SPOKEN IN COLONIAL AMERICA—1750[1]

Word	Origin	Word	Origin
African pews	colonial	moccasin	Indian
backcountry	colonial	+portage	French
backlog	colonial	pow wow	Indian
barrens	colonial	peace pipe	Indian
bluffs	colonial	prairie	French
bogus	French	raccoon	Indian
boss	Dutch	salt lick	colonial
bureau	French	++scow	Dutch
burying the tomahawk	Indian	+++scutching bee	German
canoe	Indian	skunk	Indian
chowder	Dutch	snow plow	colonial
cold snap	colonial	squash	Indian
cookie	Dutch	stoop	Dutch
counting house	English	taking to the woods	colonial
*cruller	Dutch	tavern	English
eggplant	colonial	toboggan	Indian
foxhunt	English	tomahawk	Indian
gopher	French	town crier	English
hickory	Indian	trail	colonial
**house raising	colonial	underbrush	colonial
***indenture	English	waffle	Dutch
log cabin	Swedish	watergap	colonial
		wigwam	Indian

*a donut

**a group of people working together to build a house

***a contract binding a person to serve another person for a stated period

+to carry something overland between two waterways

++ a large, flat-bottomed boat, squared at both ends

+++ an activity in which a group of people work together to separate flax fiber from the woody stalks of flax by beating the stalks scape (barrens, prairie, taking to the woods). Furthermore, some kinds of conflict may have existed as suggested by the words *peace pipe* and *tomahawk* and the phrase *bury the tomahawk.* In fact, a great variety of different people appear to have lived in these colonies—people like Africans, French, Dutch, Indians, Swedes, English, and Germans. It appears that life in the colonies at this time was quite diverse, indeed.

Based on these words, we might infer still other characteristics of life in mid-eighteenth century colonial America. However, let us stop and review what we think at this point life might have been like for the inhabitants of the thirteen colonies in the years 1750–1775. In mid-eighteenth century colonial America, perhaps

- *farming was important*
- *towns existed*
- *people were divided into social classes*
- *it was outdoor-oriented*
- *life was dangerous*
- *different kinds of people lived there*

-

-

Add whatever other characteristics you infer about colonial life between 1750 and 1775 to the above list.

. . . . *Testing Hypotheses* . . . At this point we have some hypotheses about life in 1750–1775 colonial America, some tentative answers to our questions, some educated guesses based on very limited data. How do we know whether or not we are correct in these guesses? What can we do to check the accuracy of these hypotheses?

First, we need to identify the kinds of sources that might exist to help us validate or determine the accuracy of these hypotheses. Certainly newspapers, diaries, census data, and paintings from the period would be helpful. Court records might also help. What other sources of evidence might prove useful? List these sources here:

newspapers   diaries   property deeds
census data   paintings   bills of sale
paintings   tools   buildings   court records

-                        -

-                        -

Property deeds, bills of sale, and artifacts of the period such as tools and clothing, as well as remains of buildings that existed around that time, would also be
useful sources of information about life in colonial America. Sources such as these
can be found in many places: in an American history text, in library references, in
museums, in restorations, and elsewhere. In fact, some sources are available here for
our use in checking the accuracy of the hypotheses we have just made. Examination
of the data in these sources may turn up evidence relevant to these hypotheses.

Now we can begin to skim through these sources to see what we could find out
about our hypotheses. However, in order to make our search more efficient, we
need to take one additional step before beginning this search. We should identify the
specific evidence we imagine will prove our hypotheses accurate. In other words, for
each hypothesis we have stated, we need to answer this question: "If our hypothesis
is correct, then what specific evidence should we find that will prove it correct?"
And we might also keep in mind the question, "What don't we want to find?"
because, if we find this latter evidence, our hypothesis may be proven incorrect!

Suppose, for example, that we have some clothing worn by some people who
lived in colonial America around 1750. Suppose further that artists have been able
to reconstruct from this clothing and from paintings, diaries, newspaper accounts,
and other records of the time how some of the inhabitants of the thirteen colonies
might have appeared. These sketches could prove useful sources against which to
test our hypotheses.

What would you expect people to look like if our hypotheses about life in the
thirteen colonies were accurate? Specifically, if farming were an important occupation, what would some people be wearing, be carrying, or be doing? Would you
expect them to be dressed in fancy clothes or work clothes? Would you expect them
to be using farm tools such as a hoe, a plow, or a rake? What else would you expect
to see if a good proportion of people in the thirteen colonies engaged in farming?

Or, to test another hypothesis, how would you expect a cross section of people
to look if society really was divided into social classes? What kinds of clothing might
indicate social class: elaborate, fancy clothes for the upper or leisure classes, and
simple, plain, homemade clothing for those who were of the lower working classes?
What would these people be doing, or what symbols of occupations might they be
associated with? Would a simply dressed individual have some sort of tools, farming
tools perhaps? What other things should these people be wearing, doing, carrying, if
our hypotheses about colonial American life are accurate?

What specific evidence do we wish to find if our guesses are correct? What evidence don't we want to find if these hypotheses are accurate? These basic questions
must be asked for each hypothesis formulated about life in colonial America before
examining, indeed before collecting, any evidence. Once we have listed the kinds of
evidence (in this case, how people appeared) needed to prove our guesses valid, we
can begin analyzing the information and sources available to search for and examine
that and other relevant evidence.

The sketches on the next pages show several different kinds of people who may
have lived in colonial America around two hundred years ago.[2] What do they indicate about the hypotheses made above? To what extent does the information in
these sketches support, or refute, our hypotheses? Select several of the hypotheses

A Southern Plantation Couple

A Black Colonial Couple

A Pioneer Farm Couple

A Huron Indian Couple

A Town Artisan Couple

A Frontier Couple

from our list. Determine how you would expect people of this time and place might be dressed, what they might be doing, and what they might be carrying or using (if anything), and then examine these sketches. Note in the margin next to each hypothesis you are testing what evidence you find relative to that hypothesis.

Was farming an important occupation in mid-eighteenth century colonial America? Did social classes exist? Was life outdoor-oriented? What evidence can you find that you expected or needed to find to support these or other hypotheses? What evidence do you find that might refute them? What new ideas about life in colonial America do you get from examining these sketches?

Indeed, at least some people seem to have been farmers. One couple is already labeled as a pioneer farm couple; the woman is carrying some items, maybe produce from the farm, while the man is carrying a pitchfork! The blacksmith is hammering out some type of tool, perhaps a tool useful in farming or in clearing fields. Blacksmiths were an essential part of most farming societies.

These sketches also seem to confirm our hypothesis about the existence of social classes. The southern plantation couple appears much more elaborately dressed than most of the other couples, and the town artisan seems dressed somewhat "in between" that couple and the others. Moreoever, the dress of the Huron Indians suggests they may have been outside this colonial culture altogether. Some couples seem to be associated with work tools or activities, while others seem to indicate more leisure time or other types of non-vocational pursuits.

It certainly looks as if people did divide themselves into social classes, yet in some instances the distinctions seem a bit hazy. What does this latter thought suggest? And only one sketch seems to relate directly to farming. If farming was so important, shouldn't more of the sketches relate to farming? What does this indicate about farming—and about the artist? Some evidence here does support some of the hypotheses generated from the preceding list of words. Some evidence we might like to find regarding these hypotheses seems to be missing. And some information in these sketches may raise new questions and stimulate new ideas.

What about any other hypotheses? Was life in colonial America outdoors oriented? Was there some type of conflict or danger? Did towns exist? Examine the evidence you have collected for each hypothesis. Does it relate to that hypothesis? Does it substantiate it or invalidate it? What, then, is the fate of each hypothesis? Indicate (perhaps with a check) those hypotheses that do not appear valid in terms of this evidence. Finally, indicate (with a question mark) those hypotheses about which you can make no decision because there is little or no evidence here relative to them.

Do these sketches suggest any new ideas about life in colonial America in 1750? They seem to suggest something about male-female relationships, something about the institution of family, perhaps. They seem to suggest a wide variety of life styles, some quite regional in nature. Certainly the town artisan couple suggests the existence of a commercial or at least crafts-producing segment of society, something suggested earlier by the terms counting house and scow that appeared in our list of words. So we may have some new hypotheses, as well as new questions, about life in colonial America and perhaps even about the accuracy of our evidence. What new ideas come to mind as you study these sketches? Add these ideas to the list of hypotheses started at the beginning of this chapter.

One piece of evidence is hardly sufficient to prove or disprove any hypothesis. Additional evidence is needed. And this evidence, too, is available. We could refer now to excerpts taken from two documents written by people who lived in the thirteen British colonies during the period we are studying.[3] Select three hypotheses: the hypotheses about farming and social classes and one other hypothesis. For each hypothesis list the things that you might reasonably expect the authors of one or both excerpts to mention if, in fact, the hypothesis is accurate:

Hypothesis #1—Farming was an important occupation in the thirteen British American colonies between 1750–1775.

—

—

—

Hypothesis #2—The people in mid-eighteenth-century colonial British America were divided into distinct social classes.

—

—

—

Hypothesis #3—

—

—

—

What kinds of evidence do you expect to find in these excerpts if farming really was important in the 1750s: concern about land ownership, descriptions of farms, a discussion of laws governing landed property, or a description of the marketing of agricultural produce? What other evidence would convince you farming was an important occupation at that time? What would you want to find mentioned in these excerpts if there were distinct social classes in mid-eighteenth century British colonial America: descriptions of slavery, of different types of occupations, of plantation life, of property qualifications for voting? What else?

List the evidence you expect or need to find if the hypotheses to be tested against the evidence in the excerpted documents that follow are to be proven. Then read the excerpts to see if you can find this evidence. Use the following questions to guide your analysis of this evidence.

1. What evidence can you find to support each hypothesis?
2. What evidence do you find that tends to disprove each hypothesis?
3. What evidence that you were looking for couldn't you find?

CAROLINA*

—Eliza Lucas Pinckney
the first in the American colonies
to grow indigo successfully as a
commercial crop.
1742

Now, dear brother, I will obey your command and give you a short description of the part of the world in which I now live. South Carolina is a vast region near the sea. Most of the settled part of it is flat. . . . South Carolina is filled with fine navigable rivers and great forests of fine timber. The soil in general is very fertile.

There are few European or American fruits or grains that cannot be grown here. The country is full of wild fowl, deer, and fish. Beef, veal, and mutton are much better here than in the West Indies, though not as good as meat in England. The fruit is extremely good and plentiful. The oranges are superior to any I ever tasted in the West Indies or to those from Spain or Portugal.

The people in general are hospitable and honest. The better sort of people are polite and gentle. The poorer sort are the laziest people in the world. Otherwise they would never be poor and wretched in a land as rich as this. . . .

Charleston, the main city, is a neat, handsome place. The people who live here are polite and have a gentle manner. The streets and houses are attractively built. Both ladies and gentlemen dress fashionably. On the whole you will find as many agreeable people of both sexes here as in any other city of this size. St. Phillip's Church is very elegant and much visited. There are several other places of public worship in the town, and most people are of a religious turn of mind. . . .

[W]e have had a most charming spring in this region, especially for those who travel through the countryside. The scent of new myrtle and yellow jasmine flowers, so abundant in the woods, is delightful.

AMERICA IN 1751**

—Benjamin Franklin
Colonial publisher,
inventor, and statesman

. . . Land is in good supply in America. It is so cheap that a laborer can, in a short time, save enough money to purchase a piece of new land large enough to support a family. Thus people are not afraid to marry. For . . . they see that more land probably will be available at prices equally cheap, everything considered. Therefore marriages in America are more common and generally occur earlier than in Europe. According to my arithmetic . . . the population should at least double every 20 years.

---

*Adapted from Eliza Lucas, *Journal and Letters*, Mrs. H.P. Holbrook, ed., Wormsloe, 1850.
**Jared Sparks, ed., *The Works of Benjamin Franklin* (Boston: Whittemore, Noles and Hance, 1856). Vol. II, pp. 313–315.

But in spite of this increase, the territory of North America is so vast that it will require many ages to settle it fully. And until it is fully settled, labor will never be cheap here. No newcomers continue long as laborers for others, but instead get farms of their own. No laborers continue long as journeymen to a trade, but instead move to new settlements and set up for themselves. Hence labor is no cheaper now in Pennsylvania than it was 30 years ago, though many many thousands of laboring people have been brought over here.

It is an incorrect opinion that, by using the labor of slaves, America may possibly compete with Britain in the cheapness of its manufactures. The labor of slaves can never be as cheap as the labor of workers in Britain. Slaves are expensive. Figure the purchase price of a slave, the insurance or risk on his life, the cost of his clothing and food and the expenses of his sicknesses and loss of work. There is also loss caused by the slave's neglect of his work. (Such neglect is natural when a person does not benefit by his own efforts and hard work.) Add the cost of a driver to keep him at work and the cost of his stealing from time to time. Then compare all this expense with the wages paid by a manufacturer of iron or wool in England. You will see that labor is much cheaper there than that of Negro slaves here can ever be.

Why then do Americans purchase slaves? Because slaves may be kept as long as a person pleases or has need of their labor. By contrast, hired workers may decide to leave their masters (often in the midst of a job) and work for themselves.

To what extent are the hypotheses being tested supported by evidence from these sources? Franklin discusses the importance of land and labor while Pinckney discusses the quality of the soil and nature of farm produce, perhaps all indicative of the importance of farming. Lucas mentions different classes of people, and Franklin, too, distinguishes between different classes of people. What other evidence could you find to support or refute the hypotheses you are testing?

What new ideas do you get about life in colonial America? It does seem to be grim—a feature of life that may have been hypothesized earlier. Slavery seems to have been well-established and identified closely with race, something perhaps suggested earlier by the term "African pews" in the word list. Even though there are social classes, some people apparently can move from one to another; there seems to be some social mobility, or the hopes of it anyway. Indians are not mentioned by either author, in spite of their obvious presence and the adoption by the European immigrants of words from their language and of their foodstuffs and farming practices. What does all this mean?

Still more sources can be used to test our original hypotheses and any additional ones that we might have added to our list. For example, artists have recreated their impressions, based on actual remains, of some of the buildings that existed in colonial America during the period we are studying.[4] Assuming the accuracy of their drawings, what evidence should these drawings show to indicate, for example, that class distinctions existed in the years 1750–1775? What is there about a dwelling that provides clues to the social class of its occupants? Its size? The materials used in its construction (clapboard or brick, as opposed to rough logs or sod)? The number of rooms—and windows? The amount of land associated with the dwelling? What else about dwellings suggests class distinctions?

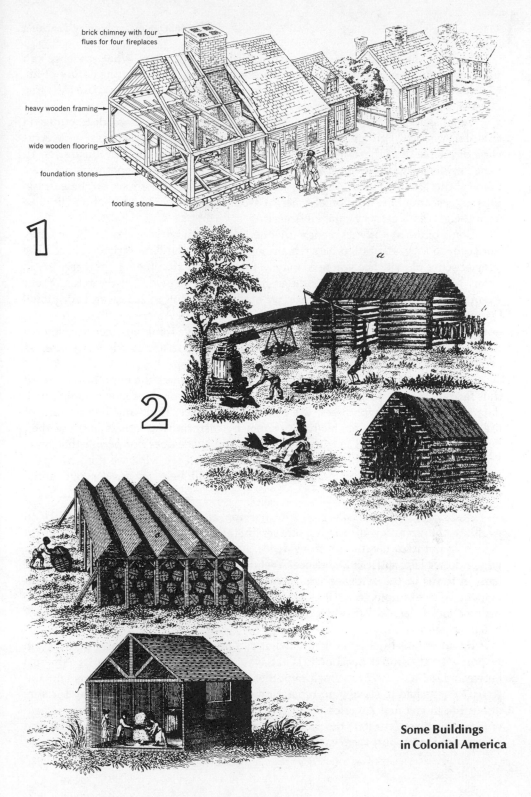

brick chimney with four
flues for four fireplaces

heavy wooden framing

wide wooden flooring

foundation stones

footing stone

1

2

a

b

d

f

**Some Buildings
in Colonial America**

153

Look at the drawings reproduced on the preceding page. What evidence can you find to substantiate or refute any hypotheses made here about the nature of life in colonial America around 1750? To help you analyze these drawings, use the same questions provided to guide your study of the documents.

What evidence do these drawings provide about social class distinctions in colonial America? Perhaps the structures depicted in illustration I suggest a different class of people than those who might have lived in the structures in illustration II. What evidence do these illustrations provide about any other hypotheses we have made about life in colonial America? What new ideas or hypotheses do these drawings suggest about life in colonial America around 1750–1775? Just what was life like in mid-eighteenth century colonial America?

Some of the hypotheses made earlier certainly seem fairly accurate. Others may not seem so accurate. Still others remain unproven by the data provided here. The very absence of evidence you need may in fact indicate that these hypotheses are in error. Moreover, our list of hypotheses has probably grown. On the basis of our examination of the available evidence, we may have hypothesized several additional features of life in mid-eighteenth century British colonial America. What can we do now to test our new hypotheses, to test further those we think are accurate, and to determine the fate of those we should discard or those about which we are, at present, still uncertain?

Obviously, more data ought to be examined to validate the hypotheses offered thus far. Textbooks, libraries, films, filmstrips, and other sources may contain much data relevant to our hypotheses. We could, for instance, find some descriptions of life in colonial America at this time written by historians or others and use their descriptions as additional sources of evidence. But space does not permit that here. So we shall have to call this investigation to a halt and see what we think we have found out about life in colonial America that will help us answer our initial question.

. . . . *Stating Conclusions.* . . . In arriving at conclusions, it is necessary to evaluate the accuracy of our hypotheses in the light of the evidence examined. Which hypotheses has the given evidence substantiated? Which are refuted? For which do we lack sufficient evidence? Weigh the accuracy of the hypotheses tested here in terms of the evidence you have collected and your inferences about this evidence. For example, to what extent were people in colonial America divided into distinct social classes? What evidence can you give to substantiate this hypothesis? What evidence refutes it?

Based on this brief investigation what can be said with reasonable accuracy in response to the initial question, "What was life like in British colonial America between 1750 and 1775?" Which hypotheses seem inaccurate? Which remain untested? If you had to stake your reputation on it, what could you now say for sure about life in colonial America about two hundred years ago? List below four generalizations that accurately describe life in colonial America during this period, and be prepared to support them with the evidence examined here.

1.

2.

3.

4.

Certainly, society in colonial America during the years 1750–1775 does seem to have been divided into distinct social classes. The range between the well-to-do, the planter or merchant, and the laborers, whites as well as blacks, appears to have been considerable. Class distinctions seem to have been closely linked with occupations and even regions of the country. Furthermore, farming does appear to have been a common form of economic activity. And finally, life seems to have been outdoors-oriented (or very much influenced by climate) as suggested by the words people used, their popular activities, their buildings, as well as by the role that land and its availability played in the development of the colonies. What other things can be said—for certain—about life in British colonial America just before the American Revolution?

But wait! How will we ever know we are correct? We could check our conclusions against still other sources mentioned earlier. Paintings might prove useful for this purpose. In other words, we could treat our conclusions as hypotheses by identifying what ought to be shown in some paintings about eighteenth century America and trying to find this evidence. We could also use the paintings to develop new ideas about colonial America. We could even use what we have found out to determine whether or not these works of art accurately represent this period.

Three paintings of life in colonial America can be found on the following pages. If our conclusions are indeed correct, what would you expect to see in these paintings: people wearing different types of clothes, outdoors or rural scenes, farming scenes? Look at these paintings to see if you can find the evidence you expect to find to validate our conclusions. What new ideas do these paintings suggest about colonial life?

Having examined these paintings, how accurate are our conclusions? Assuming the authenticity of these paintings, how accurately do they reflect life in mid-eighteenth century colonial America?

Perhaps we can feel a bit more comfortable with some of our conclusions about life in British colonial America in the years 1750–1775. Social classes? Almost certainly! Note the different indicators of class in these paintings: different clothing, housing, and occupations, for example. Farming? Of course. Outdoors-oriented? Probably. And more. Life in mid-eighteenth century colonial America was certainly cosmopolitan, socially stratified, based on agriculture and probably commerce (an emerging hypothesis at this point), closely related to the land, and, for most people, difficult. In some ways, life in this part of the world remained similar to life in Great Britain, but it differed in many important ways, too. The further one got from the coast—from the commercial cities and from the large landed estates—the less

Christ Church, Philadelphia in the mid-1700s
Courtesy of The Historical Society of Pennsylvania

typically British life appears to have been. In fact, it appears a new nation was rapidly developing—with customs, language, interests, concerns, and traits all of its own and quite different from those in England. Perhaps the American Revolution was indeed less a civil than an international war! What do you think?

THE LESSON
IN RETROSPECT

Let us stop here to review and reflect on what we have been doing. This lesson consisted of a series of learning experiences that used an inquiry teaching strategy. In general terms, we started with a problem: What was life like in British colonial America in the years 1750 – 1775? Then we broke our rather general problem into a number of more specific questions. Next, we used samples of

Flax Scutching Bee #1227
by Linton Park
National Gallery of Art, Washington
Gift of Edgar William and Bernice Chrysler Garbisch

Old Bruton Church: Virginia at the time of Lord Dunmore (detail)
by A. Wordsworth Thompson
The Metropolitan Museum of Art
Gift of Mrs. A. Wordsworth Thompson, 1899

commonly spoken words of the period to devise some tentative answers to these questions. Then we tested these hypotheses against evidence drawn from sketches of an artist's conception of people of that time, excerpts from documents, and sketches of buildings—continually adding as we did so to our hypotheses about the nature of society in this period. Next, we made some decisions about the validity of our hypotheses; we developed and stated conclusions from our investigation.

In some instances, we found our hypotheses at least partially valid; in others, the hypotheses may have been invalidated or even untested by the information we used. Some new hypotheses may have emerged as well. At any rate, we concluded something, if ever so little and tentative, about what life in colonial America probably was like. Finally, we applied our conclusions to new data contained in the paintings of life in early America. By so doing, we were able not only to further validate our conclusions, but also to generalize more accurately about life in colonial America and how this life may have related to the coming of the American Revolution and the subsequent political independence of the colonies—the very purpose we had in launching this study in the first place.

The lesson just described employs a very simple but basic strategy for inquiry teaching. As presented here, it would probably require four or five 40-minute class periods to complete. However, this lesson could be altered in any number of ways depending on the time available, the learning objectives of the teacher and students, the previous experience of teacher and students with inquiry, and the materials available for use in our classrooms.

Hypothesis Making

The question that launched this investigation appears at first glance rather vague and ill-defined. Thus, we broke it into a number of more precise, meaningful (to us), and manageable questions. Such a procedure provides not only motivation, but purpose as well. And the answers to *our* questions will serve as parts of what becomes the answer to the initial *text-given* question.

Hypothesizing answers to a question can follow many procedures. We could, for example, base this activity entirely on whatever the learner recalls about the subject at hand. Most of us think we know something about colonial America, and so do students, especially those who have already studied this period in fifth-grade history or social studies, or role played the original Thanksgiving celebration, or read *Johnny Tremain*—or watched TV!

Rather than brainstorming answers to our questions from previous knowledge, however, we provided data here in the form of a list of words to serve as a basis for hypothesizing. This approach not only gives practice and guidance in developing the skill of making inferences from data, but it also allows us to predict to some extent the kinds of hypotheses that may result so that we can have immediately available the data necessary to test our hypotheses. Otherwise, valuable time may be lost in a search that (given the limits of the school library and other available resources) may well fail to turn up the needed data and thus deflate whatever student interest has been aroused.

In a conventional social studies or history classroom, students may initially be paired off, with each pair receiving a copy of the word list. Each pair can then study the list to find answers to a different assigned question, or all may seek answers to as many of the initial questions as time allows. After five to ten minutes of discussion, the various pairs can report their hypotheses, one item per pair in turn, until all the ideas they have generated have been written on the chalkboard in the students' own words. As students report their ideas, they should give the reasons for these ideas, identifying the words on the word list and the reasoning that led them to infer the hypotheses they have made.

Thus, all students can use some given data on the topic as the basis for hypothesizing. Yet, in spite of the fact that in this sample lesson all have the same data and presumably the same amount of prior knowledge about colonial America, a wide variety of different hypotheses emerge. Why? Because, as we noted earlier, each learner has a unique background of experience, including a frame of reference and a set of concepts, that directs his or her attention to different aspects of new experience and also raises different kinds of questions to be asked of this experience. What one person sees in any body of data may legitimately be quite different from what another sees, because each individual tends to ask different questions of that data. Hence, even though the data input in this activity appears to establish a common ground for the activity, the unique backgrounds of those using the data bring forth the divergent thinking characteristic of genuine hypothesizing. What at first appears to be a highly directed activity is, in reality, very much learner-directed and individualized.

This sample lesson illustrates another essential point about the initial steps of inquiry teaching. The most productive way to initiate inquiry involves presenting students with a small sampling of data to serve as the basis for defining a problem and/or inventing hypotheses. Such data should be intriguing but brief. It should not provide answers so much as stimulate ideas or questions. A list of words, as here, or a map, a few pictures, part of a poem, letter, or document may serve these functions well. This material should not provide too much data because its primary function is to launch inquiry.

Three cautions need to be noted here, however. First, the initial data or material should be neither inaccurate nor atypical in the way it represents the subject to be studied. Neither should this data present erroneous stereotypes or do anything else to create a false impression or reinforce a stereotype that cannot be corrected in a short time or without considerable evidence. Such material might better be saved for the end of a unit, where students can use what they have learned to evaluate its accuracy. Students, as anyone, frequently focus on first impressions, and they are extremely reluctant to give them up. Their initial contact with data should open them rather than close them to further inquiry.

Second, variety is extremely important in launching an inquiry lesson. No consecutive lessons or units should begin the same way, whether in terms of media, questions, data, or student grouping. If one unit (such as that on Kiev) starts with students working in groups with photographs, the next (as this one did) might start with pairs of students analyzing a list of words or a class lecture and film, or individuals analyzing a document, or the class participating in a dilemma case study discussion. Nothing stifles learning in a sequence of inquiry teaching units any faster than starting off the same way each time.

Finally, rather than start a unit or course at the beginning point in terms of chronology, or sequence, or logic, a teacher might begin a unit or lesson by focusing first on the final point to be made, then return to the lower level data and work back to that final point in greater detail. For example, in starting an inquiry unit on causes of the American Revolution, we might first identify the results of the revolution and then backtrack to find the events and factors that led to the results. Or in discussing any event, we might raise the question of why it occurred and then return to an analysis of "the facts" before leading back to a synthesis about causes. Very often by putting first what actually emerges as the final product or material, a teacher can generate a more meaningful purpose for inquiry than anything else he or she can do.

Hypothesis Testing

Although the hypothesis testing sequence of the colonial American inquiry lesson presented here appears to be highly directed, it accommodates considerable learner self-direction as does the hypothesizing activity. All who participate in this lesson have identical information to examine. Yet a wide variety of different conclusions may be reached, again depending on the previous experience and talents of each individual. This time, however, because we have been testing the same hypotheses, a core of "answers" on which all can agree could emerge—not because one answer is absolutely correct and another incorrect, but because proper use of the process and skills of hypothesis-testing, with due awareness of the limitations therein, can only result logically in certain viewpoints regarding the hypotheses under examination. Practicing and refining the thinking skills used in this stage of inquiry are important objectives of such a learning experience.

Hypothesis-testing consists of many separate cognitive operations. Identifying the kinds of evidence needed to substantiate (or refute) a hypothesis and identifying and collecting sources that might contain such evidence launch this important part of inquiry. Either step might precede the other. In this particular lesson, you did not have to collect sources of information related to your hypotheses. Instead, we supplied this information for you. Furnishing students information is a perfectly legitimate aspect of inquiry teaching if the learners then use this information as a reservoir from which to draw only that information (evidence) relevant to their hypotheses. Such a procedure is most worthwhile if an objective of the lesson is to teach students how to read, interpret, and analyze information, rather than how to conduct a library search.

Teachers should not expect to devote equal attention to every inquiry skill in every learning experience. If they do, the series of lessons will likely become monotonous and so drawn out that the whole purpose may be forgotten before the class achieves closure. Learning is much more fun and productive in terms of knowledge and skills learned if different lessons single out only a few key skill and knowledge objectives for emphasis. Successive lessons can concentrate on different objectives instead of repeating the same ones over and over.

Once students obtain the information they need to test a hypothesis, they evaluate what they have found. Note that in this particular instance, the data used seem to have been accepted as authentic. Students rarely question the validity of data at all. Did you? The authority of the teacher or source often suffices to guarantee the acceptance of data as authentic. Again, while learning how to evaluate data may be an important objective of inquiry teaching, it is neither necessary nor desirable to emphasize this skill every single time we engage in inquiry teaching; such emphasis may serve only to detract from other, relatively more important learning objectives for a particular lesson. Experience leads us to accept as accurate and reliable many sources to which we can refer without detailed evaluation each time we use them. Students must learn when to evaluate information and sources in detail as well as how to evaluate such material.

As noted above, an investigation may result in the validation or modification of the hypotheses under study as well as the invalidation of such hypotheses. Such is the case in this particular learning experience. The hypothesis, "Society in colonial America was distinguished by a social class structure," appears fairly accurate, at least in terms of the evidence available here. That life was especially outdoors-oriented, however, may still be questionable. This hypothesis may have to be dropped, modified, or held as most tentative. Moreover, in any investigation such as this one, we may suddenly gain new insights into the subject of study as we probe deeper into the assembled evidence. These insights, posed as hypotheses, serve as occasions for further investigation as study of this topic continues.

Stating a conclusion represents an effort at closure. Determining which hypotheses are valid and which are not, and which hypotheses must be modified and how, comprise part of this operation. But students, too, must articulate a rather precise statement that ties together the significant results of the investigation. Until learners can state or demonstrate specifically what has been concluded—learned—we cannot assume that they have learned it. Hence, inquiry teaching should include activities that require the students to synthesize or pull together what they have learned and to state or demonstrate their synthesis.

Of course, if this were an actual classroom experience, more study might be necessary before drawing any firm conclusions about life in colonial America. However, what we have done here is to seek temporary closure by concluding our investigation. Then we apply our conclusions to new data—the paintings—to see if these conclusions could be affirmed and, if so, perhaps develop even deeper insights about the topic as a whole.

A textbook narrative of colonial life around 1750 could serve almost the same purpose as the paintings. It too can be read to check the accuracy of our conclusions. A text narrative also has another use. Students can read the narrative to evaluate its accuracy rather than to check the accuracy of their conclusions. They may seek to answer the question: "How accurate is the text in terms of all the evidence that we have examined?" Such an approach places the students in command and opens up additional opportunities for further study of this period and for accomplishing additional cognitive and affective objectives

commonly associated with the social studies. Inquiry teaching does not necessarily cease with a conclusion!

IMPLICATIONS
FOR TEACHING

Three additional points should be made about inquiry teaching that go beyond
the bounds of the particular lesson presented for analysis here.

Learning Materials

First, although inquiry teaching can be facilitated by using a wide variety of
audio, visual, and print media, the value of conventional textbooks for inquiry
teaching should not be underestimated. In fact, *all the instructional materials
used in the lesson presented in this chapter come from a single standard American history text!* They comprise part of Chapter 4 of Lewis Paul Todd and Merle
Curti's popular *Rise of the American Nation*.[5] This entire lesson has been organized in inquiry fashion using one standard history textbook as the *only*
instructional material!

Like Todd and Curti's text, many social studies texts today are actually
complete media kits. In addition to a narrative, most texts contain maps, charts,
and graphs; documents or supplemental written accounts such as biographical
sketches; photographs (many in color); drawings and sketches; and even word
lists (at the end of the chapter, usually, but still there nevertheless). While they
do not have all the classroom magic of sound filmstrips or sound films, these
textbooks still contain the wide range of instructional materials many teachers
usually associate with inquiry teaching. The major difference is that in a text the
materials are all bound together within a single hard cover. Even though
teachers may not have access to the multimedia they may think necessary for
effective inquiry teaching, their students usually *do* have texts. Teachers can
use most of today's conventional social studies textbooks for inquiry teaching.

The key to using textbooks for inquiry teaching lies in the word *use*. For the
most productive learning, a standard text must be *used* in a way that often
differs from that implied by its structure and probably from the way its authors
and editors intended. This suggests that a teacher must develop a fresh view of
text use in the classroom.

To use a standard text in inquiry teaching requires a teacher to do essentially
four things. First, the teacher must view the text as a resource to be used rather
than merely as a body of knowledge to be transmitted to students. Students
must treat the text as a place to go for information to generate, test, and evaluate hypotheses or as data to be analyzed for author bias, unstated assumptions,
logical argument, nature of evidence, and so on. For maximum effectiveness in
inquiry teaching, a text should be viewed as a collection of data rather than as
an authoritative answer to unasked student questions.

For example, sometimes, for a variety of reasons, the data or the media used to present the data in a textbook chapter may not appear to represent accurately the historical period or topic under study. In such cases, students can use the information presented by one media (maps, for instance) to test the accuracy of the generalizations presented in or inferred from another part of the chapter. Or, students may evaluate the data in question in terms of author assumptions or biases, for factual accuracy, and for stereotypes.

In the lesson presented here, the sketches of people show couples only; they all depict people of about the same general age. Such sketches may raise a number of questions: Did an equal number of men and women inhabit the thirteen colonies in the mid-eighteenth century? Were most or all of the colonial inhabitants married? What, if any, was the distribution by age groups and ethnicity? Moreover, the list of words cited in the text may give an impression of being ethnocentric, for it does not distinguish the specific Indian origins of the various words as it does the European origins of words. Some of these words were undoubtedly Iroquoian in origin, while others may have been borrowed from the Algonquian or Muskogean languages. If we had such precise origins, what would this tell us about life in the colonies? More importantly, because all native Americans are referred to as Indians in general, what might this suggest about European attitudes toward these people? Toward themselves? What might a listing of words in this fashion suggest about the authors of the text and about the society in which these authors lived? What might such a listing imply about the difficulties of linguistic research?

Thus, without destroying the usefulness of data that may seem on first glance inaccurate, unbalanced, or stereotypical, a competent teacher can use such data in inquiry teaching to develop important student knowledge, skills, and attitudes. Texts thus serve as springboards to further study as well as major sources of study themselves. They may serve as resources as well as sources. Using inquiry teaching with conventional texts enables teachers to escape the limitations of some texts as well as their own and their students' limitations. And using texts in inquiry teaching enables teachers to get the maximum use out of basic instructional materials, much more use than when such texts are presented solely as sources of already developed and predigested knowledge.

Secondly, to make the most productive use of conventional texts, a teacher must be willing to pick and choose from the text, to jump around, to skip some segments, and to reorder the sequence of presentation. There is absolutely no need to proceed through most texts page-by-page from the table of contents to the index without skipping anything. Nor is there any reason why a particular chapter must be studied only after all the preceding chapters have been studied. The study of any topic can be organized in many ways; teachers should feel free to organize their own study even when they have a single text as their only instructional material.

Thus, in using any one chapter, for instance, a teacher could assign first a graph or the chapter-end list of words as a basis for hypothesizing. Students may then use pictures in the chapter as one set of data against which to test their hypotheses. They could then study segments of the narrative and use other graphics in the chapter to further test their hypotheses. Finally, students could use the basic ideas of the chapter encased in the section headings as a basis for evaluating the accuracy of the chapter's thesis. This latter use might be accomplished by judging the headings in terms of the evidence contained in the chapter and in terms of the conclusions reached by the students as a result of using the information presented in the chapter. Thus, a text or chapter in a text can be broken into parts that correspond to media type (narrative, pictures, headings, etc.), and individual lessons can be built around each using a strategy for inquiry teaching as the organizing structure.

Thirdly, teachers who break away from the "same text for every student" policy and begin to use a variety of texts in each class can maximize the assets of both inquiry teaching and conventional texts. Most schools today group students heterogeneously; this means a wide spectrum of reading abilities, levels of cognitive development, and experiential backgrounds. Rather than force all students to use the same American history text, which may be far too difficult in terms of reading or conceptualization for many students in the class, a teacher ought to offer a class a variety of American history texts at different reading levels. Thus, a typical American history classroom might have five or six copies of five or six different American history texts from which students could choose.

By using multiple and multilevel texts, teachers enhance the opportunity for inquiry teaching and minimize the need for costly and difficult-to-schedule supplemental aids. In using multiple texts to study the causes of the War of 1812, for example, a teacher might have several students read one text to report what its authors claim to be the causes of the war. These causes can be classified by the entire class into different hypotheses. Then each student or group of students can use a different text to test these hypotheses against data therein and report and discuss their findings. Finally, students can return to the basic or initial text to check the evidence cited by the authors in support of the generalizations presented there. By comparing and contrasting data presented via a variety of media in a number of texts, students can develop their inquiry skills while learning about the topic at hand. Using a variety of texts in the classrooms also frees teachers from dependence on a single text and frees students from the monotony that may result from using the same text all year long.

Finally, in order to use conventional texts effectively in inquiry teaching, teachers must know and be adept at using a strategy for such teaching. The essential elements of one such strategy have been illustrated and explained here. Being restricted to "only a text" in no way inhibits inquiry teaching in a social studies or history classroom. Conventional texts (at least the best of them) have many uses indeed; inquiry teaching is one of them.

Role of the Teacher

Although inquiry is learner-centered, inquiry teaching requires considerable teacher involvement. Sometimes, especially when first used as here, this involvement may take the form of considerable and obvious (to the students) teacher guidance by means of highly structured lessons, limited and carefully preselected material, and teacher-led discussions. However, later, as students gain experience in using the skills and process that constitute inquiry, teacher involvement may become much less direct or more unobtrusive. Regardless of the extent of the teacher's apparent in-class intervention, the teacher plays a major role in any type of inquiry teaching in at least three ways.

First, this teaching strategy requires that the teacher plan or design a learning experience that will facilitate student inquiry. As suggested by the lesson presented in the preceding pages, this task includes creating and sequencing a series of activities designed to put students through the various stages of inquiry as well as collecting or preparing learning materials appropriate for these activities. Secondly, to be effective, inquiry teaching also requires that the teacher direct or guide the learning experience by asking questions, making comments or suggestions, and providing data when it is needed. Thus, in this sample lesson, the teacher or text guided the investigation through questions and directions based primarily on the operations that comprise the teaching strategy being used. These questions were specific enough to move students through the process of inquiry, but open enough to allow for a diversity of responses. Direction was also provided by the type of data introduced and the sequence of introduction. It moved from very vague isolated data to specific, detailed data all rich in potential for providing evidence relative to the variety of possible hypotheses that might be derived from an analysis of the initial data.

Finally, the teacher must evaluate. This does not mean that the teacher judges the accuracy of student hypotheses, however. On the contrary, the teacher should accept what students offer by writing their contributions on the board, in the students' own words, probing for evidence or reasoning behind their assertions ("Why?" and "So what?" are still the most productive questions any social studies teacher can ever ask!), and helping other students to build on the resulting ideas to clarify and extend them. Moreover, in order to keep the lesson moving, the teacher must continuously judge how well the students follow the inquiry process and, when necessary, explain why a particular procedure must be employed at a particular time. And, the teacher must also evaluate how well the students achieved the learning objectives for the lesson, a topic pursued in Chapter 14 of this book.

The Role of Content

Finally, any inquiry teaching lesson can proceed in a direction quite different from that planned by the teacher. Implicit in the preceding lesson are several objectives: to gain certain knowledge about life in colonial America and, more importantly, to learn how to make inferences from data and how to use a hypothesis as a search tool in problem solving. For the most part the lesson develops in line with these objectives. Nevertheless, there is the distinct possibility that this particular lesson could at any time stray in a number of directions that, while contrary to accomplishing these objectives, may imply equally or even more valuable objectives in their own right.

One such direction might involve the analysis and evaluation of the sources and the information presented in the lesson: the list of words, the sketches, and the excerpts, for example. Imagine what track this lesson might take if some students raised questions such as, "How do we know these words really were commonly used in this period?" or "On what basis were these words selected?" or "Who selected these words and why these—why not others?" Similar questions could arise about the excerpts or sketches. Students could legitimately raise many questions about the data used in this lesson. What happens to the lesson if they do?

Teachers sometimes have difficult choices to make. They can ignore student questions or put them aside until later—an ultimately devastating treatment of the questioner. This action is roughly equivalent to saying, "Your views are not important, so don't try to sidetrack me"; "Just follow me and I'll lead you to what you are supposed to discover!"; or "You don't count!" On the other hand, a teacher may decide to pursue the line of investigation suggested by student questions and then return to the lesson as planned. Or, one might scrap the original plans altogether and allow the class to pursue the lines of investigation their questions suggest.

For a creative teacher skilled at inquiry teaching, a decision to "go where the kids want to go" may be perfectly natural. And the resulting learning experience can be just as productive as the one originally planned. That is, an investigation into the authors or compilers or producers of any data being used, their qualifications, and their inferred intent, biases, assumptions, and methods can help students develop some of the same thinking skills as can a lesson that deals exclusively with subject matter. Such a study might also help students understand better some concepts of major importance (such as cultural bias or stereotyping) or even basic procedures in data gathering, analysis, and evaluation. Just because an inquiry teaching lesson goes off in a direction unanticipated by a teacher does not mean the lesson has failed or that students can't learn important skills and concepts.

In fact, the lesson presented here might easily be sidetracked into a lesson on any of a variety of topics, concepts, or skills. When students begin discussing the term *social class*, for example, we could have them brainstorm the meaning of the term, prepare a composite description that includes all their ideas, and then use their description to organize the data being studied. The lesson could conclude by revising the description of social class and by listing examples of various classes existing in colonial America at this time. Thus students can learn a transferable concept and specific subject matter information at one and the same time.

Sometimes students focus on a chapter title, picture caption, or question in a text and proceed to argue about it. When this occurs, the teacher may have them treat the data or answers to their initial question as a hypothesis by subjecting the title or question to the test of data supplied by the text itself or gathered elsewhere. For example, the following statement appears in the chapter from which the materials used in the American history lesson were drawn:

> These pioneer farm families who were of British descent still thought of them-
> selves as British, but their ties with the mother country were weakening. More and
> more they began to think of themselves as "Americans."[6]

Students could treat this assertion as a hypothesis and, perhaps in groups, investigate information about each region of the colonies in order to test the
accuracy of the statement. Their study could begin with the data supplied by
their text and expand to include data from other sources. Or, a study of this
topic could remain confined to the text and (presumably) the time already allotted for study of this content by the teacher. In using either approach we
would, in effect, be using a text statement or caption not as information to be
memorized but as a hypothesis to be tested against data.

Any inquiry lesson can easily proceed into different but equally or perhaps
even more valuable channels than that initially planned by the teacher. So can
any lesson designed to achieve any specific objectives. The decision as to
whether or not to permit this to occur depends largely on the teacher. Teachers
who are fact-oriented or unsure of how to use inquiry teaching will probably
resist such a move, proceeding as they intended. Teachers who view the
outcome of learning not in terms of facts but in terms of concepts, generalizations, and skills, or who believe that the best learning grows out of student interest, may well permit the lesson to go where the students take it. The skills or
conceptual knowledge these latter teachers wish to convey can be taught just as
easily using content suggested by the students; if this is not possible, other skills
and concepts can be taught and the originally planned objectives sought in a
later lesson. Concept and information objectives might also be woven into the
new lesson or taught at a later date. A flexible teacher, one whose security lies
in knowing how to use an inquiry teaching strategy rather than in knowing all
the answers, will find this latter course of action rewarding as well as productive.

Thus, in inquiry teaching, content serves as a vehicle as well as a goal. That
is, learning specific content or subject matter may be one objective of a sequence of lessons, but as students seek to learn this content they can at the
same time use it to develop the related skills, attitudes, values, and concepts
that constitute for many the most significant goals of social studies teaching.

SUMMARY

The lesson presented in this chapter attempts to accomplish three major goals.
First, it demonstrates inquiry and inquiry teaching in action. Secondly, it illustrates ways conventional social studies texts may be used in inquiry teaching.
And finally, this lesson illustrates the roles of content and of teachers in inquiry
teaching and learning.

This lesson also deals with many of the affective and cognitive aspects of
inquiry—those attitude and knowledge dimensions of inquiry outlined earlier.
The attitudes and values associated with inquiry are integral to this and to all in-

quiry teaching lessons not just as learning tools but also as learning objectives. This particular investigation builds on and encourages many of the attitudes essential for effective inquiry, including the curiosity of the learner, a respect for evidence as the test for accuracy, a certain tolerance for ambiguity, a willingness to suspend final judgment, objectivity as reflected in a deliberate search for both positive and negative evidence, and a respect for the use of the processes of rational thinking. Successful inquiry teaching requires students to strive toward internalizing these attitudes and carrying them beyond the classroom.

The same may be said for the knowledge related to inquiring. Students must not only learn the kinds of things they need to know about knowledge, about the tools of inquiry, and about the process of inquiring, but they must also use this knowledge as they engage in inquiry learning experiences. Involvement in a lesson such as this one on colonial America can help the students understand the tentative, interpretive, changing nature of knowledge, for their understanding of life in this period may be challenged by others and may change as their study progresses. Students should also learn to avoid making sweeping generalizations based on limited data such as a picture or two, a short list of words, or a few selected excerpts, for the conclusions based on sketchy information can pertain only to some people rather than to all. Concepts (such as social class) may be used and/or developed in this lesson. So, too, can knowledge of sources of information and of the skills necessary for successful independent inquiry.

Inquiry relies upon command of several different types of learning tools. Inquiry teaching requires helping students not only to use these tools but also to develop and refine them and to know how to use them. Its use enables us to go far beyond simply teaching the content of a lesson as an end in itself. Inquiry teaching can help students learn concepts, refine basic thinking skills, and explore a wide variety of feelings and values—all important goals of social studies teaching. And so it is to the role of inquiry in achieving these three major types of learning objectives that we can now address ourselves.

notes

1. Lewis Paul Todd and Merle Curti, *Rise of the American Nation* (New York: Harcourt Brace Jovanovich, 1977), Volume I, pp. 56, 59, 60, 53, 55, 62.
2. Reprinted by permission of Harcourt Brace Jovanovich, Inc. from *Rise of the American Nation,* Volume 1 by Lewis Paul Todd and Merle Curti, copyright © 1977 by Harcourt Brace Jovanovich, Inc., pp. 52, 54, 58, 60, 61, 66.
3. Adapted from Lewis Paul Todd and Merle Curti, Ibid., pp. 391–392 and 396.
4. Reprinted by permission of Harcourt Brace Jovanovich, Inc. from *Rise of the American Nation,* Volume 1 by Lewis Paul Todd and Merle Curti, copyright © 1977 by Harcourt Brace Jovanovich, Inc., pp. 56, 63.
5. All materials are from Chapter 4, "The Start of an American Way of Life," in Lewis Paul Todd and Merle Curti, *Rise of the American Nation* (New York: Harcourt Brace

Jovanovich, Inc., 1977), Volume I, pp. 51–69. With the exception of the words (which have been pulled from this text into a single list for more efficient use here), all materials used in this sample lesson come from this chapter. Although additional reproductions of paintings of the period (like those reproduced in this chapter) are included in this chapter, only three are reprinted here. The written text, of course, constitutes the bulk of the chapter and, while not reprinted here, can be well used in inquiry teaching as described here.

6. Todd and Curti, op. cit., p. 59.

part three

using inquiry teaching
in the classroom

8

concepts
And
Inquiry

Certainly one of the major goals of social studies teaching consists of acquiring or developing knowledge. In fact, for many educators, knowledge serves as *the* major goal of most classroom instruction. Several different types of knowledge exist, including knowledge of specifics—names, dates, inventions, and so on; of patterns or ways of dealing with data; and of more general knowledge as concepts, generalizations, principles, theories, and laws.[1] All of these types of knowledge serve as goals of social studies instruction and can be achieved as well, if not better, through inquiry teaching as they can through the use of any other teaching strategy.

Conceptual knowledge comprises one of the most important types of knowledge taught in many social studies courses. This is to say that one of the major goals of much social studies teaching is the learning of concepts. More importantly, concepts also serve as a basic tool of learning in social studies; what we inquire into and the meaning we make of experience are shaped as much by the concepts we employ as by the skills and procedures we use. Thus, concepts serve not only as goals of learning but as tools for learning in social studies.

This dual role which concepts play in learning is especially important in inquiry learning. The processes of concept-making—conceptualizing—and learning through inquiry are closely related if not virtually identical. In order to take maximum advantage of this relationship in the social studies classroom we must understand the essential nature of concepts, the process by which concepts evolve, and the relationship between conceptualizing and inquiry teaching. This chapter and the next focus on these three topics.

THE NATURE
OF CONCEPTS

A concept is a mental image of a collection of phenomena that share certain common features. It is the picture that forms in one's mind in response to a

172

particular imagined or sensed cue. One can conceptualize—invent a concept— of virtually anything, whether an object such as a desk; an institution such as family or the Presidency of the United States; a type of behavior such as aggression; an occupation such as welding; or abstract ideas such as justice, honesty, balance of power, or interdependence. Generally, a concept is triggered by or encapsulated in a word or phrase that conjures up the appropriate image. *War* is a cue-word that suggests a particular mental image of a type of violence or conflict. The word *dog* suggests an image of an entirely different concept. *Indian* and *culture* and *role* and *spatial interaction* trigger still other concepts. The list of concept cues is virtually unending.

Words are not concepts, however.[2] Words or phrases serve only as labels for concepts. Because they are so imprecise and usually mean different things to different people, words or phrases cannot thoroughly describe a specific concept. Neither can simple definitions. Concepts are much too complex for that.

A Sample Concept: Role

Concepts are complex abstractions of reality generated by individuals over time for the purpose of ordering, of giving meaning, to that experience. Of course, the degree of complexity of any particular concept depends directly on the amount of experience that has generated that concept. But regardless of its complexity, any concept has two major dimensions: a form or set of substantive components, and a structure, or pattern of relationships of these components to each other and to the whole.

Concepts may be described with some degree of thoroughness by extended outlines, essays, or similar detailed descriptions. John Stuart Mill's essay, *On Liberty,* in effect presents his image or conceptualization of this important concept. However, visual representations often prove more useful for describing concepts because they illustrate explicitly not only the attributes of a concept but also the structural interrelationships of the attributes.

A concept of *role,* for instance, can be conceived as a complicated interrelationship of many elements. *Role,* as generally defined, is a particular function or part played by an individual, institution, or process in the context of a larger setting. Such a definition, however, hardly reveals the basic attributes or structure of this concept. But a diagram can bring these dimensions of the concept into much sharper focus. A simple conceptualization of *role,* for example, might be described as in Figure 8.1.

The generalized image of *role* outlined in Figure 8.1 suggests that any role has four distinguishing components: (1) a set of special qualifications, (2) a way by which the role is acquired, (3) various types of distinguishing behaviors, and (4) certain standards of conduct expected of anyone or anything fulfilling that role. The combination and interaction of these four components, or attributes, constitute a concept of role. This concept can be used to analyze or make sense of any role in any society at any time or place, whether the role be that of citizen, parent, teacher, Senator, or whatever.

But there is more to a concept of role than the four major attributes presented in Figure 8.1. Each of the four attributes consists of a number of subordi-

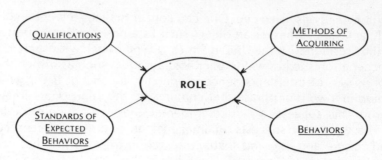

Figure 8.1. An Introductory Conceptualization of Role

nate attributes. As conceptualized here, at least two types of qualifications may be required in order to fulfill any particular role: natural qualifications or acquired qualifications. Natural qualifications are those we come by naturally as, for example, inherited traits such as ethnic origin, height, personal capabilities, or similar traits. To be a police officer, for instance, a person may have to be a certain height or age; these qualifications we possess by nature. On the other hand, one may have to achieve a certain score on a test and perhaps even live in a certain place to qualify as a police officer; these qualifications we can take action to meet by acquiring them through efforts of our own or at times with the aid of others.

A set of expected behaviors also distinguishes every role. These behaviors can be generally classified as prerogatives and prohibitions. Although the prerogatives of any specific role may be unique to that role, all roles have certain obligations and privileges no matter how formalized or apparently insignificant they are. In addition, all roles have certain standards set for these behaviors—standards that are learned in various ways, such as by trial and error, imitation or formal training; that are generated from various sources such as folkways and laws; that are reinforced by different rewards and sanctions; and that are shaped by a host of forces including custom, one's peers, and one's own view or interpretation of that role.

Figure 8.2 presents a conceptual image of *role* that articulates the attributes described here. Although this figure presents a specific image of this concept, it is not the only way a concept of *role* may be imagined. Different individuals may conceptualize *role* differently because of the way they go about it, the questions they ask, the nature of the data used, and the degree of intellectual inquiry employed. Some images of role may not include all the attributes shown here, while others may include additional or different attributes. A concept is indeed an individual impression. Yet, while various concepts are distinguished by their specific attributes and forms, and while the same concept may be imagined in different ways, all concepts are alike in possessing (1) attributes or substantive components and (2) form, or a structure of internal relationships.

Consider decision-making as another example of a concept. *Decision-making* is commonly defined as the act or process of reaching a conclusion, making a judgment, or making up one's mind. But just exactly what is this process? Decisions may be made in many ways: by the toss of a coin, by consulting

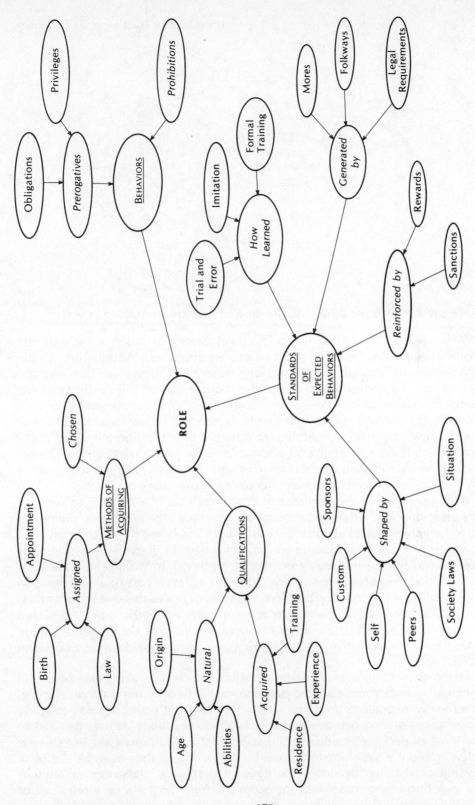

Figure 8.2. A Developed Conceptualization of Role

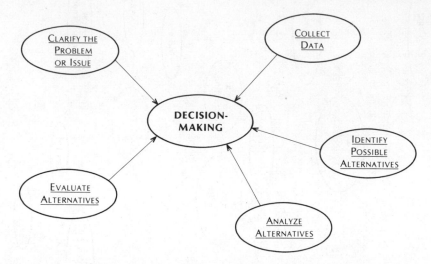

Figure 8.3. A Basic Conceptualization of a Decision-Making Process

an oracle, or by reference to a similar decision-making situation in the past. Or, decision-making may be the product of a rational process. Although many different models of rational decision-making have been suggested, one way this process might be conceptualized is presented in Figure 8.3. This figure shows rational decision-making can be conceived of as incorporating five distinct operations that feed on each other: clarifying the problem or issue about which a decision must be made; collecting information about the problem and about potential solutions; identifying all alternative solutions; analyzing the alternatives; and evaluating the alternatives to make a choice. The combination of these five operations constitutes a concept of decision-making.

Each operation in this conceptual image consists of a number of subordinate operations. In clarifying a problem, for example, one must state the objectives to be achieved and identify the obstacles to realizing them. Unfamiliar or ambiguous terms or conditions need to be clarified, as does the essential issue at hand. And finally, the problem must be broken into manageable parts for easier solution because, as in inquiry, attention to each part of a problem can help generate a solution to the problem as a whole. Just as this one aspect of decision-making consists of many subordinate parts, the other operations that constitute this concept also consist of many subordinate components. Figure 8.4 describes one way we might conceptualize a process of decision-making in some detail.

Like a concept of role, a concept of rational decision-making may be useful in making or understanding most decisions regardless of the time or place in which they were made or are to be made. This concept could be used to study the operations of Congress or of any decision-making body. It may be used to make sense of decisions made in ancient Athens, the empire of ancient Ghana, or any community anywhere in the world. This concept may even be useful in analyzing or shaping the decisions made in a specific classroom or student club, in a business or other kind of economic enterprise, or in a religious or social organization. Individuals may even use such a concept to guide their own decision-making.

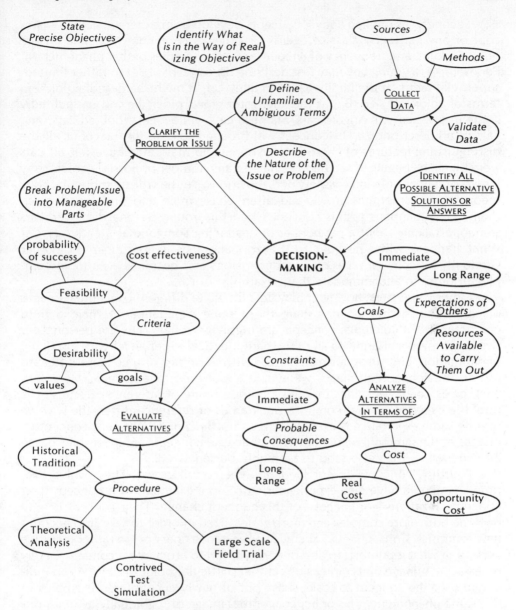

Figure 8.4. A Developed Conceptualization of Decision-Making

The Nature of Concepts

As types of knowledge, concepts possess five distinguishing features.[3] First concepts are inventions. They do not exist, ready-made, in some pure, absolute form just waiting to be discovered or learned. Quite the contrary. Individuals reduce a variety of personal experiences they have with specific phenomena that they perceive to be related to a single, generalized form by abstracting from these experiences what they believe to be the common features. The resulting generalized abstraction thus becomes their concept of this particular type of experience or phenomenon.

Secondly, as implied above, concepts develop from experience. One's concept of any particular class of events or other phenomenon depends on the number, kind, and frequency of encounters with examples of that phenomenon. For example, a young boy may first describe his concept of *cat* in rather limited, superficial terms. If the family pet is an alley cat, it might be described only in terms of color and size. But as the youngster grows older, he will undoubtedly come in contact with Angora cats, Siamese cats, yellow cats, bobtail cats, and cats of all descriptions. His concept will broaden to take into account all the distinguishing features of these cats. Whereas he may once have felt all cats were black, he begins to see them as having any number of possible colors, any length of hair or tail, and a variety of dispositions. Yet he will still note that they meow, purr, sometimes growl, and often chase mice and birds—and catch them! What happens to this concept when this youngster one day overhears someone talking about a cat burglar or describing someone as a catty person? What happens when he goes to the zoo and sees a lion, tiger, or puma? Gradually his concept takes on new dimensions and becomes even more complex in order to accommodate these examples of *cat*.

Other youngsters, however, may develop quite different conceptual images of *cat*, because they do not share these same experiences. Hence, a third characteristic of concepts: concepts are highly personal. They are personal for two basic reasons. Rarely do all of us share identical experiences with a specific phenomenon, and since our experiences with examples of a concept differ, so too do the conceptual images we evolve about these phenomena. Moreover, each of us perceives things through a unique frame of reference. Because the total life experiences that comprise our frames of reference differ, the way we see the same experience is likely to differ, thus leading to different conceptual images of the same phenomenon. Thus, because concepts are inventions based on experience, they also tend to be highly personalized.

Fourthly, concepts do not suddenly emerge full grown. They evolve over time. As people have new experiences with more examples of a concept their conceptualizations—or images—of this concept change. Their concept images become both more complex and more generalized in order to take into account new examples. Consequently, at any given instant a concept is a rather tentative version of what it purports to describe. Any effort to articulate a concept merely reveals one's image of its dimensions at that particular point in time. As an individual uses the concept to make sense out of newly encountered examples of this same phenomenon, his or her conceptual image of it gradually assumes different dimensions and becomes increasingly complex and representative of a broader class of experiences. Concepts grow and change with experience.

Finally, concepts "are never right."[4] There may be no right way to imagine or conceptualize a particular concept. Any given concept image will vary according to the experiences from which it was generated and the frame of reference of the individual doing the conceptualizing. Even, and especially, among specialists, it is often impossible to get unanimous agreement about the precise nature of a given concept. While different conceptualizations of the same concept may be remarkably similar in the basic attributes and relationship patterns, basic though often subtle differences may exist. The validity of a concept is not so much a matter of rightness or accuracy as it is the concept's power to explain or organize the countless examples of the phenomenon it seeks to represent.

A Concept of Concept

While any concept consists essentially of two parts, substance and form, concepts in general possess a number of additional distinguishing features. Psychologists[5] suggest that any concept has (1) a label in the form of a word or phrase like *role, dog, history,* or *frame of reference;* (2) a rule or definition; and (3) a set of attributes or properties that give it a unique substance just as the attributes of *role*—qualifications, methods of acquisition, standards of expected behaviors, and behaviors give that concept a substance all its own. These attributes may also include affective as well as cognitive dimensions.

Furthermore, the attributes of all concepts have (4) exemplars or specific examples. Thus, place of birth exemplifies a natural qualification for a particular role. Concept attributes also exist in (5) patterns of interrelationships with other attributes. Finally, every concept has (6) a number of generators that take the form of generalizations which trigger the concept and exists (7) in relationship to other concepts as, for example, the concept of *parent* (a role) exists as part of a larger concept of *family* (a social institution). Figure 8.5 illustrates this image of *concept* and in effect represents a concept of *concept*. To fully describe any particular concept, one must include specific reference to each of these seven basic features of that concept.

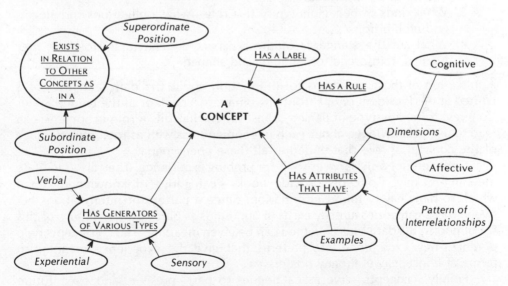

Figure 8.5. A Conceptualization of "A Concept"

Thus, concepts, as mental images, consist of both substantive features (attributes) and structure (relationships). They are, in effect, cognitive pegboards on which one can hang information in order to make sense out of it. Since concepts do play such a vital role in learning, it is not surprising that they frequently do and certainly should serve as major goals of teaching, expecially in an inquiry classroom.

CONCEPTS
AND LEARNING

Concepts in Learning

Concepts serve at least three important functions in learning. First, they generate questions which can be asked of new experience and new data. Knowing a specific concept enables one to use its attributes as questions for probing newly encountered data. Information thus uncovered may then be categorized into compartments of the concept so that meaningful relationships may be identified. For example, the concept of role described above consists, for at least one individual, of four interrelated categories or sets of attributes, each with its own subordinate attributes and exemplars. Each of these categories implies certain questions that may be asked of data.

1. What are the qualifications for this role—both natural and those that can be acquired?
2. By what procedure is the role acquired—by birth or other type of designation, or by individual choice or action?
3. What kinds of behaviors typify this role—what obligations, privileges, and prohibitions?
4. What are the standards of these expected behaviors? How are they learned, reinforced, originated, and shaped?

Application of these questions to information about the daily activities of a United States President or of a frontier woman, of a bank or of the United States Congress, or of any type of person or institution that fills a role in society, can lead to useful knowledge about each phenomenon as well as to a refined image of the concept of *role* that underlies all these phenomena.

Concepts not only serve as tools for probing experience. They also facilitate meaning-making. Concepts provide hooks—categories of knowledge—upon which to hang newly found information. Since a pattern of interrelations between these categories already exists in our minds as part of the structure of this set of hooks, the data thus collected can be given meaning. Thus, concepts help organize new experience into patterns that give the experience meaning in terms of concepts we already possess.

Finally, concepts serve as catalogues to past, present, and even future experience. Our memory consists in large part of a collection of learned or evolving concepts; it may be thought of as a personal library whose shelves hold a variety of concepts as well as generalizations, skills, attitudes, and even a multitude of specific facts. When we encounter new experience, we select from our personal library, or memory, a concept that may help us make this experience meaningful. If one concept proves useless, then we select another. If none prove useful or one very inadequate, we often proceed to revise an existing concept or invent a completely new concept in order to make this new experience meaningful. Concepts thus help us retain what we learn longer by providing structure. And as Professors Joseph Schwab and Jerome Bruner point out, structured learning not only lasts longer but is more likely to be transferable. [6]

The concepts of *role* and *decision-making* can be used to illustrate these three functions of concepts in general. For example, the concept of *role* as imagined here can be applied to information about any number or type of things perceived as probable examples of roles in order to make that information meaningful. It may, for instance, be applied to the role of *citizen* to clarify what this particular type of role means and how it functions. We can use questions suggested by this concept to analyze the United States Constitution to identify the attributes and nature of a good citizen. According to the Constitution, an individual must have certain qualifications to be a citizen of the United States. Some of these originate at birth; some may be acquired through a period of residency or by meeting certain literacy and knowledge requirements and taking an oath of allegiance. Other qualifications can be met through schooling or some type of study, or perhaps even by an act of Congress. Furthermore, citizens may engage in certain types of behaviors, including exercising such prerogatives as voting and fulfilling such obligations as military service or obeying duly enacted laws. The standards of these behaviors are shaped by many forces including custom, tradition, legal codes, and one's peers.

"Citizen" is only one type of role people play. The concept of *role* can also be applied to the part played by any member in any organization, institution, or group and could be helpful in analyzing roles such as leader, inventor, teacher, students, and so on. Furthermore, this concept can be used to analyze institutions themselves in their larger settings, institutions such as The Presidency, big business, and the frontier to name but a few. A concept of *role*, like all concepts, has a variety of uses and thus serves as an effective learning tool. This particular concept proves particularly useful in helping one analyze the multitude of roles a single individual invariably fulfills.

Concepts and Generalized Knowledge

Concepts not only generate knowledge and help to organize it, but they also serve as the building blocks of more generalized knowledge itself. Because generalizations and understandings serve as the ultimate goals of concept learning as well as triggers of concepts, a word about these forms of knowledge seems appropriate here.

A *generalization* is a statement of relationship between several concepts. As defined by Bertha Davis, it is an accurate statement that has no specific referent in time or place. [7] That is, a generalization is a statement that can generally be held true for the entire classes of things to which it refers, regardless of where or when they exist. For example, if the following statements can be considered true, they may be considered generalizations:

1. Wars are caused primarily by economic reasons.
2. A people's way of life is shaped by both its habitat and its level of technology.
3. Power and status are derived from control of the sources of production of goods and services.

Each of these statements describes a relationship between two or more distinct categories or concepts. The first describes a relationship between *wars* and *economic reasons,* regardless of time or place. The second statement describes a relationship between a people's *way of life* on the one hand and both *habitat* and *technology* on the other. And the third statement describes a relationship between *power, status, control, sources of production, goods,* and *services.*

Generalizations constitute end products of learning. They serve many purposes. For example, generalizations help to predict or explain possible relationships between similar categories of things whenever they may be encountered in the future. Generalizations also serve as a handy way of summarizing what is thought to be true about similar cases, even though these may never have been directly observed or tested. Thus, knowing the generalization that "A people's way of life is shaped by both its habitat and its level of technology" may enable a student to predict from data about a groups' life style its level of technology or its habitat. The value of generalizations lies in their usefulness in predicting, as well as in organizing, data about a variety of similar situations.

Generalizations are by no means absolute truths. The degree to which they approximate reality depends considerably upon the amount of data from which they are derived. Generalizations are at best statements that may be considered relatively true for operational purposes only, but they should still be held as tentative. Most generalizations beg for modification, as the "exception that proves the rule." Part of the value system of inquiry consists of rejecting absolutes, and generalizations are not exempt from this.

Generalizations should not be confused with understandings. Understandings are less sweeping than generalizations in that they refer specifically to some time, place, or item. Yet understandings, like generalizations, describe a relationship between two or more concepts. The following may be considered examples of understandings:

1. The Spanish-American War was caused primarily by economic factors.
2. The way of life of the !Kung is shaped by both their harsh habitat and their simple technology.
3. Power and status in old Kiev were based on the control of land.

Understandings, like generalizations, represent a product of learning, but they do not result from the final step of inquiring. Instead, understandings may be equated with the statements developed as conclusions in the preceding (fourth) step of inquiry teaching. A statement that evolves from testing a specific hypothesis may be called an *understanding* because it customarily describes a rather precise relationship between two very specific variables, and because it has specific referents in time and/or place. While understandings seem to have little predictive value, they often serve as the building blocks for higher levels of cognitive knowledge.

Generalizations evolve from understandings. If we investigate a specific war and conclude that it was caused primarily for economic reasons, and if we then investigate another war and yet another and another, reaching the same conclusion (understanding) each time, we can soon generalize about the causes of wars: "Wars are caused primarily for economic reasons." If we investigate power and status in a wide range of societies like old Kiev and reach similar conclusions, we may be able to make the generalization that "Power and status are derived from control of the sources of production of goods and services." Specific understandings on related topics may evolve into generalizations that apply to a broader range of similar cases.

Concepts and Learning

Concepts thus can be most useful in learning because they not only generate questions to ask of experience in order to give it meaning, but they also order, relate, and store for easy retrieval the information unearthed, thus saving time in learning. Furthermore, they also help summarize what we know. Concepts thus liberate individuals from the smothering effect of the masses of unorganized information that bombard us daily.

Because concepts are useful in learning, they should be and often are major objectives of learning and thus of teaching. Much of human learning consists of conceptualizing—that is, organizing what we experience into meaningful sets of categories or concepts. We do this continuously whether in or out of school. It is done on the basis of the kinds of experiences we encounter. An average individual in the course of his or her experience may conceptualize about dogs, work, school, parents, vacations, supermarkets, and other things he or she most often encounters in everyday living. Concepts like these and others formed randomly may differ considerably from person to person, but whatever form they ultimately take, they are stored in our minds for future use.

However, there is no guarantee that youngsters, if left to their own devices, will have experiences or accumulate data that will help them build concepts useful for making viable sense of their future experiences, especially in today's world of rapid change. Concepts such as dog, work, school, and vacation will at best be of only limited use in helping students deal with the wide range of social, political, economic, and cultural experiences they are bound to encounter in future years. It is precisely for this reason that schooling should deliberately assist students to develop certain useful concepts as part of their mental libraries. And that is precisely where inquiry teaching and conceptualizing come into play.

THE PROCESS
OF CONCEPTUALIZING

How we learn concepts differs considerably from how we go about learning specific facts. Concept learning involves a process whereby an individual actually invents and/or extends a mental image of something. Concepts cannot be handed to anyone to be learned beyond the level of simple recognition. In order to comprehend or understand a concept in the sense of the term *understand* as used by Bruner, an individual must invent and build his or her own concept. The individual must conceptualize.

Major Steps in Conceptualizing

Conceptualizing takes time. Psychologists have described a variety of ways in which they believe conceptualization occurs.[8] Analysis of their theories suggests that this process consists essentially of two major steps. First, one must create an initial, tentative image of the phenomenon in question. This step involves three basic operations, commencing with (1) identifying and (2) defining the concept label. Then, (3) one must invent in some fashion a preliminary image or description of the concept. This skeletal outline or hypothesis is generally incomplete, however, because the examples or experiences on which it is based are often fragmentary and limited in number. Creating this image is usually accomplished by examining one or more descriptions or purported examples of the concept in order to identify those attributes that seem to typify the concept and to develop a pattern of relationships among these common attributes.

The second major step in conceptualizing consists of applying the tentative image to examples of the concept in order to refine and broaden the concept as well as to make sense, in terms of the concept, out of these data. When an individual then examines nonexamples of the concept and identifies the attributes of the concept missing from the nonexamples, the degree of internalization or understanding of the concept becomes apparent. And as the individual applies the elaborated image of the concept to later examples and revises or reshapes his or her conceptual image, the concept continues to grow broader and expand. Conceptualizing is a never-ending, although often interrupted, process.

Conceptualizing About Situation

Suppose, for example, we wished to invent (conceptualize) a concept of *situation*. This term is used frequently in social studies and history teaching, as, for instance, "What was the situation confronting the colonies on the eve of the Revolutionary War?" or "What was the situation confronting John F. Kennedy when the existence of a Soviet missile build-up in Cuba became known?" The term *situation* is also widely used in common, everyday discussion. But what does *situation* really mean? What is a concept of *situation*?

We could go about inventing a concept of situation in at least three differ-ent ways. Looking for data in our past experience with *situations* might be one place to start conceptualizing about this concept. What do you think of when you think of the word *situation*? List, as quickly as possible, the things that come to mind when you see or hear the word *situation*:

—

—

—

Difficult? It certainly is! Trying to brainstorm an abstract idea without reference to any specific concrete, personal, or experiential data base often proves extremely difficult, if not almost impossible.

A second approach involves examining in detail two or three specific examples of the abstract concept to be developed, in this instance the concept of *situation*. We could, for example, study the situation resulting from the decision to drop the world's first atomic bomb on Japan in 1945, or the energy crisis of 1976–77, or the situation involving the ratification of the Equal Rights Amendment, to extract the common attributes of each and then to develop a generalized concept from all of these examples of *situation*. Unfortunately, such a study would require more data and time than we often have available.

Instead, let's try generating a conceptual image by analyzing what other people who have thought about the concept of situation imagine *situation* to be. First, let us start by referring to the concept rule, or definition, of *situation*. A composite of various dictionary definitions suggests that a situation means the way things are—the state of things that are occurring—a condition. This definition may provide a start, but not an especially helpful one. Often defini-tions simply don't provide useful clues to either the attributes or the structure of a concept. Having noted the definitions, however, perhaps we can dig further and find more detailed examples or descriptions of the concept. We can begin to conceptualize *situation* by studying explanations or descriptions of what other people who have thought about this concept more than we have think it is. Here, for example, is Alvin Toffler's conceptualization of *situation*:

> Every situation also has certain identifiable components. These include "things"
> —a physical setting of natural or man-made objects. Every situation occurs in a
> "place"—a location or arena within which the action occurs. (It is not accidental
> that the Latin root "situ" means place.) Every social situation also has, by definition,
> a cast of characters—people. Situations also involve a location in the organizational
> network of society and a context of ideas or information. Any situation can be
> analyzed in terms of these five components.
>
> But situations also involve a separate dimension which, because it cuts across
> all the others, is frequently overlooked. This is duration—the span of time over
> which the situation occurs. Two situations alike in all other respects are not the same
> at all if one lasts longer than another. For time enters into the mix in a crucial way,

changing the meaning or content of situations. Just as the funeral march played at too high a speed becomes a merry tinkle of sounds, so a situation that is dragged out has a distinctly different flavor or meaning than one that strikes us in staccato fashion, erupting suddenly and subsiding as quickly.[9]

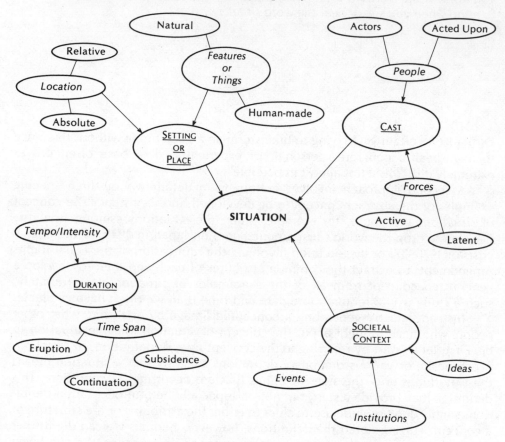

Figure 8.6. A Conceptual Image of Situation

What does Toffler identify as the essential attributes of a situation? Circle these attributes in the above selection. Did you circle the following?

physical setting	arena	context of ideas
natural objects	things	duration/span of time
man-made objects	people	erupting
place	location in society	subsiding
location		

What pattern of relationships exists among these attributes? If we were to process these elements in terms of the dictionary definitions noted above and our own ill-defined ideas about *situation*, perhaps we could generate a conceptual image such as that presented in Figure 8.6. Whereas Toffler suggests that his concept of situation consists of six basic attributes, we might mix his description with our own ideas to create a conceptual image that has only four major attributes—setting, cast, societal context, and duration—each with a number of subordinate attributes and exemplars. And we might invent a pattern to indicate the relationships among these attributes.

We (or others) might also conceptualize *situation* in a different way to suggest a different relationship of these attributes to each other. Figure 8.7 illustrates an alternative image of *situation*. This figure conceptualizes this concept in terms of three basic attributes, all existing *within* a time dimension as emphasized by Toffler, a dimension that gives different character to these attributes depending upon the nature of its inception, tempo, length or duration, and subsidence. Thus, any situation might be conceived of as a wheel, with the three main spokes—setting, cast, and societal context—supporting a rim of time consisting of the ingredients noted above.

Perhaps this image better resembles a kaleidoscope, with duration serving as the tube and the attributes representing the pieces of colored glass therein, where every turn of the tube gives new significance to the attributes and to the whole tube by rearranging them in relation to each other. Other conceptualizations undoubtedly could also be formulated to indicate additional attributes and alternative patterns of interrelationships. But this image, as outlined here, can well serve as a tentative image to grow and be fleshed out later by its application to additional examples of the concept.

And grow this image will. As individuals use their existing image of *situation* to make sense of new situations, they can also reflect on the concept itself to learn its attributes and structure as well as to broaden their image of the concept by modifying it, extending it, or otherwise altering it to make it account for a more inclusive class of phenomena all subsumed under the label of *situation*. Any concept, whether of situation or of any other phenomena, grows and changes with experience and thus becomes even more valuable as a tool of learning as one's experiential base broadens.

Of what value is a concept like *situation*? First of all, knowing this concept can help us make sense of data regarding any situation. And secondly, knowledge of this concept can help us communicate more clearly with others about the nature of any situation and thus lead to more rational social action. Thus, knowing a concept of situation (and this is true of all concepts) facilitates learning, communication, and action.

Our concept of *situation* facilitates learning in three ways. First, as noted earlier, concepts help us find important information. A concept like *situation*, for example, provides us with ready-made questions to ask of any situation we encounter, whether the situation be one in which someone is missing lunch money from a desk or a book from a locker, or what faced President McKinley as he agonized over whether or not "to take" the Philippines! We derive these questions from the basic attributes of our image of the concept. In the case of the conceptualization of situation developed here, these questions might well include the following:

1. What is the setting of this situation: its location and its features?
2. What is involved? Which people? Which forces?

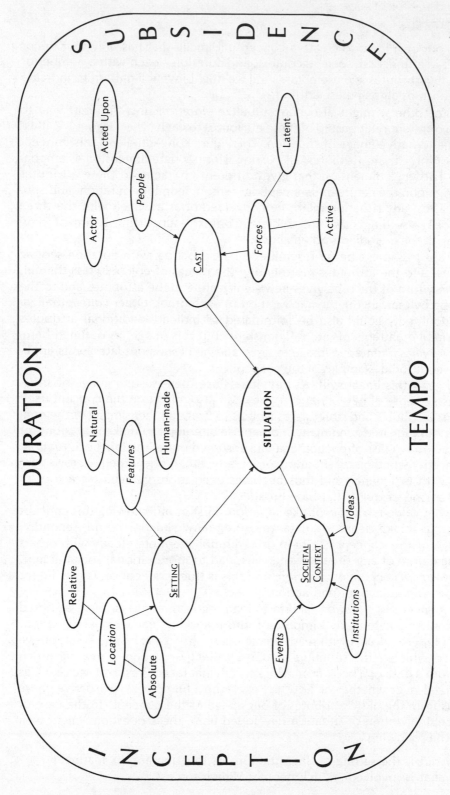

Figure 8.7. An Alternative Conceptual Image of Situation

3. What is the societal context in which this situation exists: what events, ideas, and institutions are involved?
4. How long has this situation existed? How did it originate? What has been the tempo of events? Did it slowly subside or abruptly disappear?

By using these questions, we can probe anything that seems to be a situation and produce meaningful information about it.

Secondly, a concept such as situation offers ready-made hooks for hanging the information thus collected about a specific situation. Since these hooks exist as part of a self-created pattern, by processing the information in this pattern we can give it meaning in terms of our concept. Thus, concepts not only help us find information, they also help give that information meaning.

Finally, this concept serves as an important component in a number of important historical and social science generalizations. For instance, the generalizations that relate to *situation,* according to Toffler, include the following:

- **Situations are transient—they change over time at increasing rates of speed.**
- **When things change outside a situation, the situation itself changes.**
- **Accelerated change radically alters the balance between novel and familiar situations.**[10]

These generalizations summarize and explain a great deal of information about change and about situations in the world today. Knowledge of a concept of *situation* makes them much more meaningful than they would be without some conception of *situation.*

Concepts also facilitate communication and action. Knowing a concept of *situation* helps us organize an explanation, description, or analysis of any specific situation in a way that can clearly communicate the essence of the particular example to someone else. Rational action requires complex, meaningful, well-ordered communication of data, and the knowledge of concepts is a key to both.

Concepts like *situation* thus help us make sense out of experience and also help us communicate clearly our experiences to others. Concepts provide not only a basis for action now, but also a tool for predicting or anticipating the future. All concepts are *our* creations or inventions, derived from personal experience; they constantly evolve as our base of experience broadens. Making concepts requires considerable mental effort. Conceptualizing is, indeed, thinking.

Conceptualizing and Inquiring

The processes of conceptualizing and inquiring thus seem closely related. In conceptualizing we start with a simple, tentative image of the concept in question. The tentative image, in effect, represents nothing more than an hypothesis. As we use that concept to study purported examples of the concept, we broaden or revise our conceptual image—altering the concept attributes and reaarranging them in relationship to each other as we perceive them. This is exactly what we do in hypothesis testing. Periodically, we pause to reflect on the evolving concept, to pull its components together and to articulate the image we have created—an activity comparable to the concluding stage of inquiring. And, like inquiring, conceptualizing continues by applying the concept to new examples and pseudo-examples as they are encountered, testing the accuracy of our image and altering it to account for these examples, as well as making meaningful the new examples thus encountered. Conceptualizing is, in fact, inquiring in action.

notes

1. Benjamin Bloom et al., *Taxonomy of Educational Objectives: Handbook I—The Cognitive Domain* (New York: David McKay Co., 1956), pp. 62–78.
2. See Verna Fancett et al., *Social Science Concepts in the Classroom* (Syracuse: Social Studies Curriculum Center, Syracuse University, 1968), pp. 4–5.
3. Fancett, pp. 4–8.
4. Lawrence E. Metcalf, "Teaching Economic Concepts in the Social Studies," in *The Councilor,* March 1960, pp. 30–31.
5. For example, see David P. Ausubel, *Educational Psychology: A Cognitive View* (New York: Holt, Rinehart & Winston, 1968), pp. 50, 505–524; John P. DeCecco, *The Psychology of Learning and Instruction* (Englewood Cliffs: Prentice-Hall, 1968), pp. 388–412; Peter H. Lindsay and Donald A. Norman, *Human Information Processing: An Introduction to Psychology* (New York: Academic Press, 1972), pp. 380–400, 430, 494–495.
6. Joseph Schwab, "The Concept of the Structure of a Discipline," in *The Educational Record,* 43:3, July 1962, pp. 197–205; and Jerome Bruner, *The Process of Education* (Cambridge; Harvard University Press, 1960), pp. 17–32.
7. Bertha Davis, "Conceptual Teaching in the Social Studies," in *New Approaches to the Teaching of Social Studies: A Report of the Eleventh Yale Conference on the Teaching of Social Studies, April 15 and 16* (New Haven: Yale University Office of Teacher Training, 1966), pp. 48–51.
8. Ausubel, pp. 505–524; Robert M. Gagné, *The Conditions of Learning* (New York: Holt, Rinehart & Winston, 1970), 2nd ed., pp. 121–188; Peter Martorella, *Concept Learning: Designs for Instruction* (Scranton, Pa.: Intext Educational Publishers, 1972), pp. 22–51.
9. Alvin Toffler, *Future Shock* (New York: Random House, Inc., Copyright © 1971), p. 33. Reprinted by permission of Random House, Inc.
10. Ibid., pp. 32–33.

9

---

concepts
and
inquiry teaching

Because of the close relationship between conceptualizing and inquiry, it should come as no surprise that an inquiry teaching strategy proves extremely useful for concept teaching. Inquiry teaching, more so than any other teaching strategy, enables a teacher to aid student invention and development of concepts while simultaneously helping students to use concepts to accomplish other cognitive and affective learning goals. An analysis of examples of such teaching illustrates how these goals may be achieved and suggests important implications for the use of inquiry teaching to teach concepts in elementary and secondary school social studies classrooms.[1]

CONCEPT LEARNING
AND
INQUIRY TEACHING

Concepts may be learned at several levels of cognition. At one level, ready-made concepts can be learned for the purposes of recall or recognition. Such learning usually involves the use of expository teaching and learning strategies that consist primarily of drill and memorization. At this level, students "know" a concept like they know any other specific data such as a date or name or event: they may be able to repeat it, but they probably don't comprehend it in all its detail or nuances.

At another level of learning, however, students can come to *understand* a concept, to analyze it and make it part of their own cognitive structures. This type of learning requires students to go through the process of conceptualizing their own images of the concept. Since the processes of conceptualizing and inquiring seem to resemble each other so closely, inquiry teaching can be used to aid in conceptualizing. In fact, any teacher who seeks to help students develop and understand concepts in their deepest meaning will find inquiry teaching to be the most useful of all instructional strategies for this purpose.

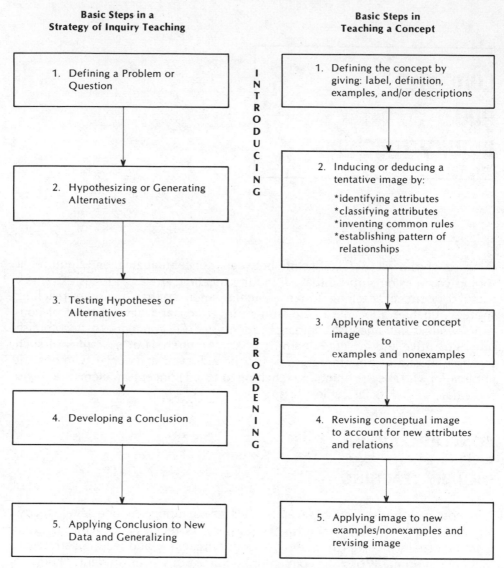

**Basic Steps in a
Strategy of Inquiry Teaching**

**Basic Steps in
Teaching a Concept**

1. Defining a Problem or Question

1. Defining the concept by giving: label, definition, examples, and/or descriptions

**I
N
T
R
O
D
U
C
I
N
G**

2. Hypothesizing or Generating Alternatives

2. Inducing or deducing a tentative image by:

   *identifying attributes
   *classifying attributes
   *inventing common rules
   *establishing pattern of relationships

3. Testing Hypotheses or Alternatives

3. Applying tentative concept image   to
   examples and nonexamples

**B
R
O
A
D
E
N
I
N
G**

4. Developing a Conclusion

4. Revising conceptual image to account for new attributes and relations

5. Applying Conclusion to New Data and Generalizing

5. Applying image to new examples/nonexamples and revising image

Figure 9.1. Inquiry Teaching and Concept Teaching

Inquiry Teaching and Concept Teaching

The strategy of inquiry teaching presented in Part Two of this book can easily be used to guide students in concept learning. As Figure 9.1 indicates, the basic steps in concept teaching and learning consist of *introducing* the concept to be learned and then *broadening* it. The former step usually involves a concentrated analysis of a concept description or of several examples of the concept itself. The latter step may involve repeated analysis of both positive and negative examples of the concept and of essays about the concept, often over an extended period of time. Regardless of the length of time devoted to this process, these steps correspond closely to the basic steps of inquiry teaching.

Introducing a concept. Concepts may be introduced in either of two ways. First, students can be provided the concept label and one or more definitions of the concept, and/or explanations of the concept, and/or written descriptions of the concept as imagined by some authority (teacher, text, or expert), in much the same way the concept of *situation* was introduced in the preceding chapter. Or students can be presented with the concept label, asked to define as best they can the label, and asked to describe the attributes of the concept as revealed in several examples drawn from their personal experiences or from textbooks or other sources. In the first approach, students *infer* the form and structure of the concept from statements about the concept. The second approach requires students to infer the essential features of the concept from uninterpreted examples of the concept itself. Either approach proves useful in forming initial, tentative images of a concept.

Introducing a concept corresponds to the step of hypothesis formation in inquiry teaching. Whether the approach is deductive or inductive in essence, students must

1. Brainstorm or otherwise identify the substantive elements (attributes) common to all given examples or noted in the definition(s) and descriptions provided.
2. Classify these elements into groups, each group having some distinguishing common feature. As this is done, it may be necessary for students to clarify or explain items they have contributed to the discussion.
3. Label each group of attributes with a word or phrase that states the feature common to the grouping.
4. Determine the relationship between each group and the other groups and among all groups and the whole. As students do this, some attributes will be perceived as basic elements of the concept, while others will be seen as examples of these attributes. Some attributes will also be seen as subordinate to, or as aspects of, other attributes. As these elements are arranged in sequential, hierarchical, causal, or some other relationship to one another, a pattern will emerge, and students will then have a structure for their concept image.
5. Describe diagrammatically, as an outline, or in some other detailed form, the resulting conceptual image in terms of its attributes, exemplars, and pattern of relationships.

Brainstorming is probably the most crucial part of this stage of conceptualizing. It is exactly what the term implies: rapid, unchallenged listing of all the various implications of a word or phrase, its synonyms, or its associated terms. The purpose of brainstorming is to bring into view or consciousness as many aspects as possible of a particular idea or object, to become aware of the various terms or behaviors associated with a particular concept label. Students may brainstorm from memory, from an analysis of specific examples, or from a given "expert" description of the concept. However, to be most effective, brainstorming should follow four simple rules: (1) whatever an individual says should be recorded (on the board or in student notes) in his or her own words as given (clarification can follow later); and (2) no one, including the teacher, should make evaluative judgments of student contributions, for critical evaluation inhibits the freewheeling aspects of effective brainstorming. Moreover, (3) ideas should be suggested at a rapid-fire, fast pace. A slowdown in the tempo usually indicates useful connections are no longer being made because, having exhausted their initial ideas, students may quite likely be straining for relationships. At this point students may begin to make wild, irrelevant comments just for the sake of saying something, and these comments will confuse rather than enlighten. Finally, (4) the time allotted for brainstorming should be relatively short (two to three or four minutes perhaps) to reduce the chances of students' stretching to find what usually turn out to be irrelevant, distracting, or completely irrational attributes or relationships. Brainstorming is a very useful tool in conceptualizing, but it serves only to initiate the process, not to conclude it.

Broadening a concept. The second major stage of concept teaching, as in inquiry teaching, involves testing the hypothesis against data. In this case the image is tested first against known examples of the concept in order to check for the existence of hypothesized attributes, to refine these attributes and modify patterns of relationships, and to identify other attributes and perhaps find new relationships among them. At the same time, of course, students will continue to learn information relative to the specific examples being used. Nonexamples of the concept must also be examined so students can note the absence of essential attributes or patterns and thus reinforce the conceptual image they are evolving. In using both examples and nonexamples, students can be guided essentially by the same questions that prove useful in testing hypotheses:

1. What attributes/exemplars/patterns do you find that you expected to find?
2. What attributes/exemplars/patterns can't you find that you expected to find?
3. What new attributes/exemplars/patterns for this concept do you find?

As students test or analyze examples in terms of the concept under consideration, they must periodically stop to review their original concept image to revise or modify it to account for new cases of the concept. Then they need to pull together their emerging or changing ideas of the concept and perhaps rearrange its attributes in relation to one another, thus modifying both the form and the structure of the concept at that point.

Finally, students should continue to apply their image to new or suspected examples of the concept as the occasion arises in subsequent study, making appropriate revisions in their image as they proceed. Thus, concept formation— conceptualizing—using an inquiry teaching strategy offers a dynamic, learner-centered, ongoing process of continuously hypothesizing conceptual images, articulating them, testing them against data in the form of examples and non-examples, revising these images in the light of the analyses, and continuing this process as appropriate thereafter.

Teaching a Concept: Two Approaches

An inquiry teaching strategy used to facilitate concept-learning may be initiated in either of two different ways. One approach permits students to articulate in a relatively open, unrestricted fashion their own initial image of the concept to be learned. The second requires students to identify or use prespecified attributes of a given concept image as a starting point for further development of the concept. In the first approach, students induce a conceptual image from bits and pieces of data they select from a variety of sources; in the second, students infer or record predetermined concept attributes from given concept definitions or descriptions and assume these to be the basic features of the concept. Both introductory techniques incorporate the initial steps of concept formation: defining the concept and creating an initial concept image. Both thus assist students in devising springboards for continued concept development that can be fostered by using the remaining steps of a strategy for inquiry teaching. And both approaches, with careful use, can lead to the same result: student development of their own conceptualizations based on repeated analysis of concept examples and nonexamples.

An open, inductive approach. The open, almost inductive, approach to concept teaching can be best illustrated by describing in narrative fashion a series of lessons that have been taught to social studies students at the intermediate and secondary grade levels. In this instance, the unit is one of a number in a world cultures course; the students are freshmen and sophomores; the topic is Africa; and the concept is *landscape*. In this series of lessons, our intent is to help students develop a concept of *landscape* while at the same time helping them to learn specific information and generalizations about the people, history, cultures, and geography of a particular part of the world.

Early in this unit, as we approach content suitable for learning about the concept of *landscape*, we can state our goal of inventing this concept. To introduce the concept we can write the concept label, *landscape*, on the board and have the class say it aloud: "landscape." Students can then suggest or find definitions: "Landscape is the ground and everything on it . . . the scenery on some plot of land . . . a scene of a place" and so on. Examples can also be given: "Landscape is what you see when you look out the window or drive through the countryside or down the road."

Then we can brainstorm about *landscape*. What does one customarily think of when thinking of the noun *landscape*? The following terms come to mind most readily:

homes	hills	roads	schools	billboards	parks
trees	erosion	swings	flatlands	valleys	factories
flowers	tall grass	shrubs	telephone poles	rivers	gravel pits

There could, of course, be many more items. But let us work with these. Which are similar to the first item, homes? Which are similar to the second item? Perhaps these could be grouped as follows:

1	2
homes	hills
schools	valleys
roads	erosion
telephone poles	flatlands
parks	trees
swings	flowers
billboards	shrubs
gravel pits	tall grass
factories	rivers

People make the items in group 1. The other items are natural. Yet, closer inspection suggests that these groups might be further subdivided as follows:

	A	B	C
from Group 1:	homes schools factories	roads billboards gravel pits telephone poles	swings parks

	D	E	F
from Group 2:	trees flowers shrubs tall grass	hills valleys flatlands rivers	erosion

Categories A, B, and C contain different classes of objects made by people: group A consists of structures that house people or property, B of structures that service people, and C of recreational structures. The remaining three groups characterize natural features of landscape: D consists of things that grow on the ground, E of surface features, and F of one way surface features change.

What relationships exist between the groups? Perhaps the image that emerges looks something like Figure 9.2. This diagram represents a tentative mental image of landscape. Obviously, it is incomplete in terms of how other people might conceptualize it. One geographer might, for instance, add a dimension of origins to the element of surface features (E) and perhaps a dimension of causes (meaning the kind of soil, temperature, and rainfall) to that of vegetation (D). Another geographer might add other attributes or rearrange the pattern described here. Certainly an image of this or any concept will be altered in time or by others as it is used to analyze a wide variety of landscapes and as one gains knowledge about other properties of the concept, *landscape*.

It is neither possible nor even desirable, however, to base the introduction of a concept solely on the past experience or knowledge of the students. In many instances students lack the experiences or information that enable them to brainstorm advantageously about certain kinds of concepts, especially the more abstract concepts such as decision-making, imperialism, or spatial interaction. Instead, students may use examples of the concept to provide them with

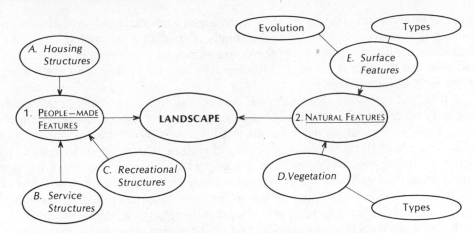

Figure 9.2. A Simple Concept Image of Landscape

some elements of the concept being introduced. For example, a teacher might present the class first with a large painting, photograph, or drawing of a landscape—or several paintings or pictures of different types of landscapes. The students can examine these examples and brainstorm a number of things they see. A list of what they observe can then be made, and the introduction of the concept of *landscape* will be well under way.

Also, other media and resources may be used to initiate brainstorming. In introducing the concept of *landscape,* a teacher might provide each member of the class with a poem about a landscape, a short essay on the subject, or even appropriate excerpts from an explorer's diary, and then have the students list the kinds of items referred to as part of the landscape in each source. Or the class might look out the classroom windows to record the different features they see as part of the landscape. Furthermore, a wide variety of sources are available to use to stimulate brainstorming about any particular concept. Whether a concept is introduced by students brainstorming out of their own experience or by class analysis of some examples of the concept, it is important to remember that this is only the first general stage in conceptualizing. The next step—the crucial one—involves broadening the concept and, in the process of so doing, internalizing it.

Broadening or testing a hypothesized concept involves using it in whatever form it has emerged from the introductory stage to analyze examples and non-examples of it. In terms of guiding students toward developing their own concepts, this means providing opportunities for students to work with data that not only reinforce the basic elements of the concept under discussion but also broaden the total concept by adding new dimensions. In so doing, the basic form and structure of the concept may be altered considerably as experience with new examples leads to modification, amalgamation, or even outright elimination of the original attributes and relational patterns. The process of refining a concept is never-ending, for the more a concept is used, the more useful it becomes; the more it is then used, the more it changes.

Broadening and refining concepts require the use of different kinds of data. Initially students should work with data that reflect the essential elements of the concept as thus far developed. Then data having other elements commonly

associated with the concept may be introduced and analyzed so that new dimensions of the concept will emerge. Finally, data that is somewhat similar but
that lacks the basic ingredients of the concept may be examined, not so much to
broaden the concept itself as to reinforce its essential elements by contrasting
them with different data.

It is quite possible, for example, that initial efforts to conceptualize will
neglect one or more dimensions of a concept that the teacher believes important. Therefore, students must be put in touch with new data, the analysis of
which may lead them to consider adding this dimension to their image of the
concept. If students fail to include a category of housing structures in their
initial image of landscape (most experts believe this to be an important part of
landscape), then we must provide the students with opportunities to use examples in which housing structures are very prominent, such as in photographs of a
farm scene or urban residential area. As a result of this experience, the students
should add a new dimension to their concept in order to provide a category to
account for this type of data.

Having thus guided the students to invent their own—admittedly spartan—
concept of landscape, we can help them broaden and refine it by having them
use this concept to explain a variety of new data. In our imagined study of
Africa, for instance, we might follow the introductory brainstorming activity described above with the following poem. This poem can also serve to motivate
student interest in the subject matter of our study, Africa, by conveying a
feeling for Africa as well as information about the continent. This poem can also
be used by students as data (1) against which to test the accuracy of their
hypothesized concept of landscape as well as (2) to generate a structure around
which to organize their information about the African landscape.

As the students read and reread this poem (preferably aloud) they should
look for answers to questions that reflect the basic attributes of the concept
image already brainstormed:

1. What is the African landscape like?
2. What people-made things can be found there?
3. What natural features can be found there?

> . . . So I came back
> Sailing down the Guinea Coast,
> Loving the sophistication
> Of your brave new cities:
> Dakar, Accra, Cotonou,
> Lagos, Bathurst and Bissau;
> Liberia, Freetown, Libreville,
> Freedom is really in the mind.
>
> Go up-country, so they said,
> To see the real Africa.
> For whomsoever you may be,
> That is where you came from.
> Go for bush, inside the bush,
> You will find your hidden heart.

Your mute ancestral spirit.
And so I went, dancing on my way.

Now you lie before me passive
With your answering green challenge.
Is this all you are?
This long uneven red road, this occasional succession
Of huddled heaps of four mud walls
And thatched, falling grass roofs
Sometimes ennobled by a thin layer
Of white plaster, and covered with thin
Slanting corrugated zinc.
These patient faces on weather-beaten bodies
Bowing under heavy market loads.
The pedalling cyclist wavers by
On the wrong side of the road,
As if uncertain of this new emancipation.
The squawking chickens, the pregnant she-goats
Lumber awkwardly with fear across the road.
Across the windscreen view of my four-cylinder kit car
An overladen lorry speeds madly towards me
Full of produce, passengers, with driver leaning
Out into the swirling dust to pilot his
Swinging obsessed vehicle along.
Beside him on the raised seat his first-class
Passenger, clutching and timid; but he drives on
At so, so many miles per hour, peering out with
Bloodshot eyes, unshaved face and dedicated look;
His motto painted on each side: *Sunshine Transport,*
We get you there quick, quick. The Lord is my Shepherd. *

Upon concluding their reading students can answer the following:

4. What attributes of our hypothesized image of landscape did you find in this poem?

— houses — mud walls   green leaves

— thatched roof dwellings   bush

— roads — service structures coastline

—

—

*Abioseh Nicol, "The Meaning of Africa," in Langston Hughes, ed., *Poems from Black Africa* (Bloomington: Indiana University Press, 1963), pp. 41–42. Reprinted by permission of Indiana University Press.

5. What new things did you find that might be part of landscape?

— *bicycles*   *cities*   *villages*

—

—

—

6. How can we revise our image to account for new attributes or examples or patterns of attributes suggested by this poem?

— *add a catagory of transportation*
— *add a catagory of collections of houses*

—

—

—

As we answer these questions, we can begin to develop a meaningful perception of part of the African landscape while we simultaneously broaden and refine our concept of *landscape*.

In continuing our study of Africa, we can refer to this concept as appropriate or continue our introduction to Africa, building it around this concept. For example, students can look at the pictures on the following pages when studying African climate regions and then, by asking the same questions used with the preceding poem, use these pictures to add attributes to their developing concept of landscape.

7. In what ways do the scenes shown in these pictures exemplify or require modifications in our concept of landscape?

—

—

—

If we wish to enlarge or refine this concept while continuing our study of Africa, we can have students analyze the following autobiographical account using the same questions listed above to analyze the poem and the photographs, being sure to conclude with the question,

Coast of Ghana   Barry K. Beyer

Northern Nigeria   Anthony Kirk-Greene

Eastern Republic of South Africa   Robert R. Griswold

Northern Tanzania   David Hamilton

8. In what ways do the contents of this excerpt illustrate or require modifications in our concept of *landscape*?

—

—

—

On the approach to Abeokuta on the narrow footpath by which we came, we got to a hilltop. From this vantage ground, one is able to see a good view of a section of Abeokuta town. The sight staggered my imagination. . . . There, in the distance, lay a sea of zinc roofs—stretching as far as the eyes could see. On entering the town, I was astonished at the size and beauty of some of the houses. . . . Most of the things that I saw were so different from what I was used to at home. There were good and wide roads; there were many more than one car; there were lorries too; there were steam-rollers used for making roads; there were street electric lights, and there was pipe-borne water supply. Every day, save Saturdays and Sundays, many students of the Abeokuta Grammar School passed along the road in front of granny's residence to and from their school: how neat, how smart, and how self-confident in their bearing . . . ! Along the same road passed, every day save Sundays, to and from their offices and shops . . . immaculately dressed people, in cars and on motor-cycles and push-bikes, who were employed in various categories such as clerks, traders, salesmen, bookkeepers, cashiers, etc., etc. I greatly admired them. . . . I visited the Olumo Rock—which is a landmark as well as a most popular object of sight-seeing for any visitor or tourist to Abeokuta to this day. I saw the River Ogun —wide, muddy, and fast flowing. I visited the railway stations . . . and saw the trains coming and leaving. I saw mercantile houses, shops and government offices, and in every one of them there were white men to be seen. I saw some of these white men on push-bikes and motor-cycles, and some as train drivers in jet-black and soot-covered suits. None of them was carried in a hammock; and they behaved more naturally, like ordinary human beings.[3]

Our study of Africa may now continue in whatever direction we or the students may elect to take it. However, we periodically need to review and revise whatever concepts we are developing—in this case, the concept of *landscape*. As we do so, we can add attributes and exemplars, rearrange them in their relationships to each other, and devise new patterns of relations among all these elements. At this point in our study of landscape, we perhaps have a conceptual image somewhat like that shown in Figure 9.3. This conceptualization certainly is much more sophisticated than the previous one (Figure 9.2), and can continue to evolve as we refer to it again and again in subsequent study of Africa or any other continent, region, or site.

Our new concept image may be used effectively to analyze the landscape of Brazil when studying that country, the landscape of Boston in studying a unit on the American Revolution, or the landscape of your own community. This same concept may even be used to make sense out of a Remington painting, a film on Asia, a selection from *The Red Badge of Courage*, one's own front yard,

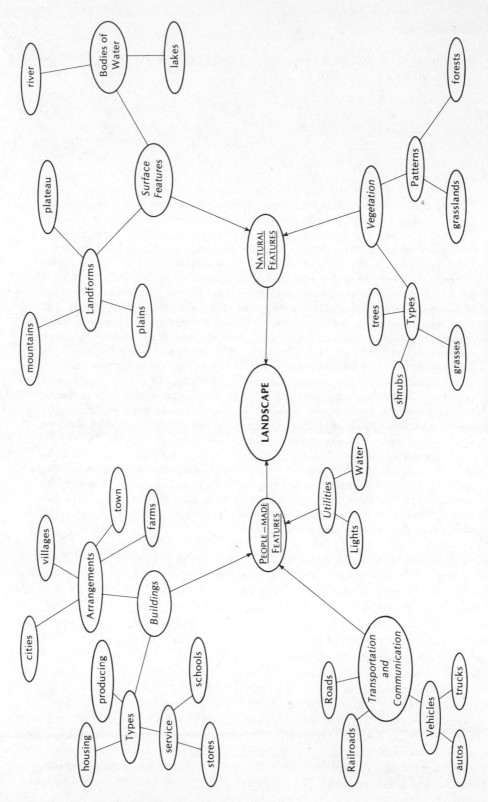

Figure 9.3. A Developed Concept of Landscape

or the battlefield at Gettysburg. It could be used to make meaningful the particular site of any event at any time or place in history.

As long as we follow certain guidelines that have proven useful in any classroom teaching, we can rearrange the materials in this sequence of activities and accomplish the same goal. First, we should start with something concrete—whether visually or experientially or personally. Second, the initial data should be brief, yet full of potential attributes of the concept being introduced. Third, in sequencing material it proves most useful to vary the media and techniques by alternating visuals with verbal material, oral presentation with silent study, and individual activity with paired or group activity. Each activity should be short in length, perhaps 20 minutes at most, and consist of a single chunk of content. Practice—analysis of a concept exemplar—should be frequent, and feedback via review and revision of the evolving conceptual image should be immediate. Finally, it proves useful to move from the simple to the complex, from the concrete to the abstract, and from the present (in time and place) to the remote. In fact, these principles underlie all effective instruction, whether concepts, skills, or simple information are being taught. The same principles apply to all content areas in addition to social studies and to all instructional strategies including inquiry teaching.

A closed, more structured approach. Sometimes in developing a concept we may wish much more structure than that suggested by the open approach to teaching a concept of landscape just described. In this instance, we might still employ a basic inquiry teaching strategy; however, while introducing the concept, we could provide the students with at least a specific skeletal outline of some attributes and a structure for the concept to be developed. Such an approach might help most when first introducing students to the process of concept formation and development; when teaching concepts to students in the intermediate grades who are beginning to move from the stage of concrete operational thought to that of more formal, abstract thinking; or when the concept to be studied is rather abstract, potentially quite complex, or more remote from the students in terms of their own personal experience.

Care must be taken in using this approach. Because it helps students identify and focus on specific attributes, this approach makes the initial stage of concept formation much easier. Yet focusing on already given concept attributes can prevent students from forming their own conceptual images. Such teaching could lead merely to memorizing the attributes as given. Teachers must be alert to this limitation and provide deliberate and repeated opportunities to use the initial concept image as a springboard for student conceptualization about the concept being studied.

If we were to use this approach in developing a concept of *landscape,* we would begin not by having students brainstorm from their own experiences or from an example of landscape, but instead by having them read an expert's description of landscape and generate the basic attributes from this description.[4] They could then add to or build on this description using the materials from the preceding pages. We used this procedure to introduce the concept of *situation* in Chapter 8.

This structured approach can be more fully illustrated by describing the introduction of another concept, that of *role*. In this instance, a class of fifth-graders once began to conceptualize about *role* in the following fashion. First, students defined from their own experience the term *role* as "a part one plays in life just like in a movie." Next they gave examples such as brother, teacher, principal, President, astronaut. Then, for homework, the students interviewed someone in their families or neighborhoods (including a sibling who was a member of the swim team, a parent, a truck driver, a lawyer, and a local political party leader) by asking each person the following four teacher-given questions:

1. How did you get this job?
2. What skills, knowledge, or other things did you have to have to get this job?
3. What do you do in this job?
4. Who decides what you should do in this job?

As can be recognized, these questions grow out of a preconceived concept of *role* similar to that presented in Chapter 8. These questions sharply delimit the initial dimensions of the concept and serve as specific guides to the concept image they are to formulate. Yet the goal here was not to replicate the teacher's conception of *role*, but merely to provide clear guidance in the initial stage of concept formation and to provide a common basis for its later expansion.

Student responses to these four interview questions were listed the next day on the chalkboard under each question:

1 *How did you get it?*		2 *What were the qualifications?*	
tried out	promoted	experience	being nice
applied	marriage	diploma	training
hired	offered	a license	wanted to do it
appointed	inherited	patience	ability
		neatness	apprentice

3 *What do you do?*		4 *Who decides what you do?*	
argue in court	run office	myself	supervisor
care for babies	cook	everyone else	the union
write	drive	bosses	family
sell things	build	company policy	laws
repair things	clean	husband	people I serve
type things	run machines	government	custom
protect	supervise others	the coach	
research			

Then the class classified the items under each question as follows:

1 **How Acquired?**	2 **Qualifications?**	3 **What Do?**	4 **Who Decides?**
Elected	*Ability*	*Keeping things going*	*Self*
marriage	*Training*	cleans	myself
desire	diploma	repairs	*Bosses*
applied for it	apprentice	protects	supervisor
tried out for it	license	cares for baby	the coach

Assigned	*Character*	*Doing things*	*Outsider*
promoted	neatness	cooks	everyone else
hired	being nice	drives	*Policy/Laws*
appointed	patience	sells things	company
inherited	wanted to	researches	government
offered to me	initiative	builds	the union
	Experience	argues in court	*Relatives*
		writes	husband
		runs machine	family
		types	
		Managing	
		runs office	
		supervises others	

Finally, the class developed a tentative image of *role* as represented in Figure 9.4. Here the students specified the attributes they had identified and some exemplars of each. They also made explicit a pattern of relationships they saw among these elements. Thus emerged a tentative, introductory concept of role that virtually replicated the dimensions considered initially by the teacher to be the essential form and substance of this concept.

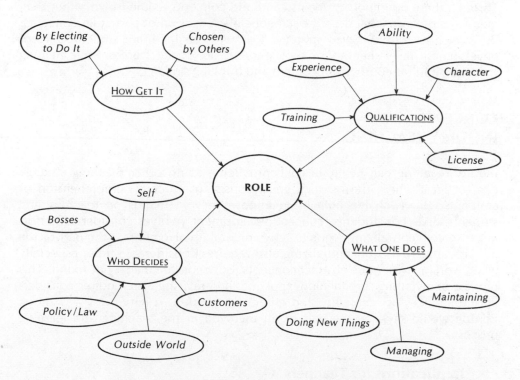

Figure 9.4. An Initial Concept of Role

But there the teacher structuring ended. Follow-up lessons enabled the students to reshape this image more freely. They role-played roles derived from their own personal experiences (brother, sister, farmer's helper, baby sitter, student, newspaper carrier, and so on) and then interviewed each other using the same questions asked in their initial homework interviews. The school principal, a custodian, a street-crossing guard, a bus driver, and a local store-keeper came to class to be interviewed. Students also analyzed material in their texts and reading books about social reformers, Presidents, and explorers. Periodically the students paused to reflect on their ideas about *role,* to revise them and to modify or add new attributes and relationships. Although the resulting concept was by no means as detailed or sophisticated as that presented in the preceding chapter, it was a step in that direction and proved extremely useful for generating questions and providing categories to make sense of any roles encountered in later material studied during the course.[5]

Thus, inquiry teaching may be used in a variety of ways to help students come to know and systematically learn how to use a specific process of concept development. The initial step of conceptualizing, or inventing a tentative image of the concept, involves the problem identification and hypothesizing steps of inquiry and inquiry teaching. The second major step of concept learning or con-ceptualizing resembles the hypothesis testing, conclusion, and application steps of inquiry and inquiry teaching. Figure 9.1 diagrams this relationship. Through these operations students can build concepts as their own rather than merely learn words that describe someone else's version of particular concepts. By using this inquiry-based strategy, teachers can facilitate student concept development in elementary or secondary school social studies while helping students simultaneously learn content and thinking skills.

CONCEPTS AND INQUIRY TEACHING

Inquiry teaching can facilitate conceptualizing as no other teaching strategy can, at least where the learning goals consist of student comprehension of concepts. But such teaching often imposes new demands on teachers and students alike. For students, concept development involves considerable effort because conceptualizing requires active mental involvement on the part of the individual learner. Conceptualizing also requires considerable time, especially when working with more abstract concepts. Concepts are made, not found. This process of inventing, broadening, applying, and revising also requires consider-able tolerance for ambiguity and especially "stick-to-it-ivity-ness"—as Brook Benton would say—on the part of all involved in the teaching and learning process.

Implications for Teachers

Using inquiry teaching to "teach" concepts has many implications for teachers as well as for students.[6] First, truly effective concept teaching using this strategy means that teachers cannot tell or give predetermined concepts to students to memorize. Rather, this approach to concept teaching requires teachers to create learning experiences that have students hypothesize conceptual images from vicarious, remembered, or actual personal, concrete experiences. Generally, this process requires close teacher guidance, at least until students have mastered the process of conceptualizing. Teachers must bring students into contact with data or experiences that contain obvious examples of some basic, commonly accepted essentials of a particular concept and then provide them with learning experiences wherein they can broaden or refine the concept as they proceed through a course.

Second, allowing students to conceptualize about anything they wish requires little if any advance planning. But facilitating student conceptualization about a specific concept requires considerable planning. In particular, the teacher must articulate an image of the concept to be taught *before* launching a concept teaching unit—not because this conceptual image is the one to be learned, but because it will serve as a guide for questions to be asked, data and examples to be selected, and learning experiences to be designed. This conceptual image may be rather sketchy and quite tentative, and so it should be considered. The concept image should be treated as a guide rather than as the definitive answer. As the lesson progresses, the teacher can join the students in examining the data used to broaden his or her initial image of the concept, just as the students refine their image. The concept lessons on role and landscape described here were based on a previously developed teacher conceptualization of these concepts. Interestingly, when these lessons ended, the teacher's, as well as the students', images of these concepts had changed.

Third, conceptual learning should not be taught by teaching one concept one day and dropping it for a new one the next. Conceptualizing takes time. It requires considerable time to introduce or "invent" a concept and repeated opportunities to examine examples of that concept before it becomes internalized. Teaching concepts really means planning inquiry experiences that use the same few concepts over and over again, with new examples and with increasing degrees of refinement. Sometimes such teaching may focus on one particular element of the concept, following it to its most precise and refined dimensions, such as examining only the alternative evaluation attribute of decision-making, for example. Other times we might study all the major attributes of a concept, first in general terms and then in increasing detail. At all times, however, concept teaching requires repeated use of concrete, personal, experiential referents or examples and periodic opportunities for student reflective analysis of the conceptual image as it is at that moment. Concept teaching, as does conceptualization, also requires a willingness to alter or modify the concept image in accord with repeated examination of new examples and non-examples.

Furthermore, developing concepts through inquiry teaching means using content as a vehicle as well as an object of learning. In concept teaching we use specific data as information from which students can generate new concepts or broaden existing concepts. As students manipulate, dissect, and rearrange this information, they learn it while they also build and learn a conceptual image that helps order this data. Thus, in concept teaching we can do several things simultaneously, including building concepts, refining thinking skills, and learning specific content.

Fifth, teachers must realize that the student versions of a concept may not be identical to their own versions of the same concept. Concepts are personal inventions; they grow out of specific experiences processed through highly individual frames of reference. Consequently, although students may use the same concept examples and participate in the same learning activities, the conceptual images they articulate may only approximate our image of the same concept. Student concepts may not include all the dimensions we feel are important, but if the examples used are appropriate, their conceptual images will approximate these dimensions. Students may not use the teacher's words to describe a concept's essential elements, but they will use words meaningful to them. If given repeated opportunities to analyze concept examples, students will gradually broaden their images of the concept and eventually evolve a rather complex structure of interrelationships and insights. They will thus develop their own images of the concept. Concepts not only evolve but they evolve differently for different individuals.

In addition we need to realize that, while concept teaching can provide a set of categories to bring order out of chaos, concepts can also constrain or restrict future learning and thus future action. Concepts can serve as blinds to new ways of looking at experience and hence can stifle creative, divergent thinking. Thus, we need to help students develop alternative concept images of the same phenomenon, just as we need to help them develop multiple hypotheses for testing.

Finally, concepts can be broadened—developed or expanded—in several ways. We can introduce a concept by a label or an example, identify its major attributes, and move immediately to examine examples and nonexamples one after the other. We can review and reflect on the evolving concept as we proceed, modifying it and enlarging it in the process. Such an approach might be exemplified by a study of the concept of *revolution:* we (1) could introduce this concept via a detailed study of the American Revolution; and then (2) help the students broaden the concept that emerges from this initial study by using the concept image to analyze the Glorious Revolution, the Russian Revolution of 1917, Castro's Cuban revolution, the Reformation, the Agricultural Revolution, the Industrial Revolution, and other purported examples of the concept. We can conclude this study by (3) using our evolved concept to evaluate the model of revolution presented by Crane Brinton in his *Anatomy of a Revolution,*[7] if we so choose, or by examining the extent to which a current event may or may not be a revolution. After each study we can reflect on what we learned about the specific event or example and also about the concept we are developing. Upon completion of this study, we can then turn to other content, to study other concepts, if we so choose. This approach has the advantages of focusing for a specific time on a single concept and eliminating distractions in the form of intervening, nonrevolution-related content and concepts. However, this approach may require us to give up a strict chronological or national study of our subject in favor of topically arranged, cross-cultural studies.

A second approach mixes the development of a number of concepts throughout a course as the data seems appropriate. Thus, we can introduce the concept of *revolution* in our American history study of the American Revolution and then drop it until we come to the election of 1800, where we can use our tentative concept image to make sense of the Jeffersonian Revolution. We may then drop this concept in favor, for example, of a concept of decision-making when we study the Louisiana Purchase and the War of 1812. However, we can revive our study of *revolution* by examining other revolutions in American history as they pop up in our course—events such as the Jacksonian Revolution, the Populist Revolt, the Industrial Revolution, the Civil Rights Revolution of the 1960's and other examples or nonexamples of this concept. And we can continue to introduce and study other concepts in this same fashion as we move chronologically through a study of America's past. This approach permits us to maintain a chronological continuity if this seems desirable, and it also provides variety in terms of learning goals. However, this approach also disrupts sustained focus on a given concept by attending to other content and concepts between the study of data illustrative of any given concept.

Of course, both approaches may be combined and used as appropriate. Some concepts can be introduced and broadened immediately and then returned to much later in order to reinforce them and provide opportunities for students to continue to broaden them. Others may be introduced, dropped, and examined sporadically thereafter as students encounter appropriate content. Such variety has many benefits, especially when a course focuses on only four or five concepts. Regardless of which approach we select, we should not confront students with large numbers of concepts to "learn" in catalog fashion; instead we should focus in depth on a small number of significant concepts in order to facilitate full student conceptualization of them.

Selecting Concepts to Teach

Although it appears possible to teach any concept in some form to students at virtually any grade level, the desirability of so doing remains an open question. If students are to conceptualize about ideas such as imperialism, democracy, and the like, they must be able to engage in the operations that typify at least the initial stage of Piaget's formal abstract thinking[8]. Yet students at almost any grade level can conceptualize, albeit in somewhat simplified form, about more concrete concepts, using personalized or experiential data as vehicles for concept formation. What we ask students to conceptualize about depends on many factors. Therefore, in designing concept-centered curricula or courses, the most pressing task involves deciding which concepts *should* be taught and in what sequence these concepts *can* be taught.

Just as social studies teachers lack the time to teach all the concepts they might like to teach, so, too, do we lack agreement about which concepts should be taught in social studies and what sequence is most effective for introducing them. Which concepts should we teach? Certainly, if we wish students to learn on their own, we ought to stress certain procedural or methodological concepts such as hypothesis testing, deducing, generalizing, and the like. But we also ought to stress certain substantive concepts. Yet there are literally hundreds of substantive concepts that might be considered legitimate learning objectives for any social studies or history program. Which should we select?

A number of significant efforts have attempted to answer this question. One of these identifies and classifies certain concepts according to their parent social science disciplines.[9] According to this approach, concepts of *role, group,* and *acculturation* may be classified as primarily sociological, while concepts such as *region, link,* and *spatial interaction* are essentially geographic in nature. Another effort to identify useful concepts divides them into categories of substantive ideas, methods of dealing with ideas, and values.[10] This scheme classifies concepts such as *power, scarcity, change, conflict,* and *group* as substantive or content concepts, regardless of their parent disciplines. *Causation, analysis,* and *interpretation* are considered methodological concepts. Value concepts include *empathy,* the *dignity* of individuals, *loyalty,* and similar values and attitudes. These concepts are often offered as instructional goals because, as core concepts of different disciplines, they prove useful—or have proven useful—in making sense out of life in a rapidly changing world.

Still another way of looking at concepts identifies certain concepts—called action concepts—as being a most useful basis for rational citizenship. According to Professors Shirley Engle and Wilma Longstreet, *conflict, power, valuing, interaction, change,* and *justice* constitute the most basic of these action concepts.[11] This type of concept involves processes, rather than things, and human interaction—or at least action. Although as ill-defined as most other concepts, these concepts might well serve as useful learning goals and structural frameworks for history or social studies instruction.

Professor Edwin Fenton suggests yet another way of classifying concepts for the purpose of determining those most worthy of classroom instruction: the role they play in learning.[12] As he points out, some concepts seem more useful than others in processing data. Certain concepts, for example, seem so all-encompassing that they are almost useless as a guide to learning. Such concepts Fenton describes as *universal* and *macro*-concepts. Because they are so broad or all-inclusive, they must be broken down into more basic concepts before becoming useful learning tools. *Culture, society,* and *political system* exemplify such very broad concepts. These and others like them may serve best only as storage bins—purely descriptive, catch-all categories for storing certain kinds of general information—or as structures for organizing courses of study, teaching units, or research. But they do not enable one to zero in on specific data with any precision at all. Thus, they are not in themselves desirable as learning goals.

A more useful type of concept generates questions that provide immediate help in analyzing data in specific detail. This type of concept Fenton describes as an *analytical* concept. *Decision-making,* he asserts, is such a concept, and so, too, are concepts like *comparative advantage, role, market, areal distribution, change, resolution of conflict,* and *leadership.* Each may be part of a larger concept (landscape may be part of the concept of *region,* for instance), but each is useful in and of itself because the questions to which it gives rise are questions that are more likely to organize data and to produce meaningful insights than are questions based on broader concepts. Indeed, these analytical concepts serve as basic tools of learning.

However, another type of concept also proves useful in learning, and this type should also be considered as a goal of concept teaching. These concepts might best be described as *micro*-concepts, for in effect they serve as the foundations upon which rest the analytical concepts described by Fenton. Micro-concepts include such concepts as *site, situation, cost,* and *role.* Micro-concepts are restricted in what they encompass, but one cannot deal with concepts such as *areal distribution* or *spatial interaction* unless concepts such as *site* and *situation* are clearly understood. Knowledge of certain micro-concepts seems prerequisite to the development and use of higher level analytical or action concepts.

Figure 9.5 outlines one sequence of basic concepts that could be used as the basic structure for a K–12 social studies curriculum. The first set (*I*) includes micro-concepts that serve as the foundations on which are built the second, or more analytical, set of concepts (*II*). The final set (*III*) of multidisciplinary con-

I

MICRO-CONCEPTS

GEOGRAPHY	ECONOMICS	POLITICAL SCIENCE	SOCIOLOGY AND ANTHROPOLOGY
Site	Price	State	Role
Situation	Cost	Law	Status
Scale	Money	Sanctions	Norm
Boundary	Producer	Legislative	Family
Resource	Consumer	Executive	Group
Landscape	Goods	Judicial	Class
Link	Services		
Node	Exchange		
Flow			

II

ANALYTICAL CONCEPTS

Areal distribution	Scarcity	Decision-making	Cultural change
Areal association	Market	Leadership	Acculturation
Spatial interaction	Allocation	Citizenship	Assimilation
	Production	Power	Accommodation
			Social mobility

III

MULTIDISCIPLINARY CONCEPTS

Change	Comparative advantage
Institution	Interdependence
System	Conflict resolution
Justice	Multiple causation

Figure 9.5.   A Sequence of Concepts

cepts involve some knowledge of all preceding concepts. A clearly articulated K–12 history or social studies curriculum might well consider introducing and reinforcing those concepts listed as Set *I* in the elementary grades. Then, while continuing to use and broaden these same concepts in the middle school grades, concepts from Set *II* could be introduced. Finally, action-oriented, multidisciplinary concepts (Set *III*) could be introduced and used in the senior high school curriculum. Continued reinforcement and expansion of previously introduced concepts and systematic use of these multidisciplinary concepts at the appropriate grade levels could provide a very useful conceptual structure for a total K–12 curriculum, as well as valuable learning for students.

Regardless of how one views concepts, different types of concepts do serve different functions. Some are so narrow and restricted that they serve as hardly more than definitions. Others seem so broad and all-embracing that they may best be used to store information and/or structure courses of study. Some are static, descriptive mainly of the state or condition of an object. Others are process or action concepts, and as such are extremely complex and sophisticated. Some are strictly discipline-based, while others are multidisciplinary. Some are descriptive. Still others may serve more analytical purposes.

The concepts cited in Figure 9.5 are obviously not the only concepts of import. But unquestionably they are substantive concepts useful in analyzing data. Such concepts are extremely useful in making sense out of experience. Consequently, these concepts should be considered both as tools and as objectives of learning.

In spite of the apparent value of building curricula around one or more of the preceding sets of concepts, it is ultimately the individual teacher, department, or school system that selects the concepts on which to focus. All too often concepts selected for instruction tend to be either simple, descriptive concepts (such as *island, desert,* or *school*) or extremely broad concepts (such as *society, region,* or *political system*). Most of these in themselves seem of questionable value, for they are either so narrow as to be barely definitions or so broad as to be virtually incomprehensible. Concepts selected for instruction must be chosen on the basis of specific criteria. The following questions articulate one set of criteria for this purpose:

1. Is this concept meaningful to students at this grade level?
2. To what extent is this concept useful in making sense out of present or future experience?
3. Can this concept be well-illustrated through the content we wish to or must teach?[13]
4. How far removed is the concept from easily observed examples?
5. How applicable is the concept to a wide variety of instances, generalizations, or other concepts?
6. How precisely delimited is the concept at present? Are its attributes fairly well agreed-upon by most observers?[14]

Criteria implied by these questions help eliminate from consideration concepts that are either too broad or too narrow and enable us to select those that will be most valuable to students in explaining a wide range of data and experience.

Concepts, in sum, are the keys to inquiry. They not only shape what we learn, but they are shaped by what we learn and how we learn. Hence, concepts must serve as objectives as well as tools of learning and teaching. Conceptualizing, making concepts, is a learner-centered process; it requires students to be active investigators instead of passive receivers. Because the processes of conceptualizing and inquiry are so closely related, a strategy of inquiry teaching can well serve as a strategy for concept teaching in the social studies classroom.

notes

1. For a summary of various models of concept teaching see Peter Martorella, *Concept Learning: Designs for Instruction* (Scranton, Pa.: Intext Educational Publishers, 1972), pp. 52–82; Peter Martorella, *Concept Learning in the Social Studies* (Scranton, Pa.: Intext Educational Publishers, 1971), pp. 90–107.
2. From John Fraser Hart's, "Selected Concepts in the Geographic Analysis of Rural Areas," *Social Education,* 30:8 (December 1966), pp. 607–609.
3. Adapted from Obafemi Awolowo, *The Autobiography of Chief Obafemi Awolowo* (Cambridge: Cambridge University Press, 1960), pp. 36–37. Reprinted by permission of Cambridge University Press.
4. By using excerpts from Hart's, "Selected Concepts in the Geographic Analysis of Rural Areas," op. cit.
5. For plans and materials for teaching concepts such as landscape, role, resources, citizen, and the like, see Barry K. Beyer, *Virginia: A TV Social Studies Experience* (Richmond, Va.: State Department of Education, 1973).
6. See Barry K. Beyer and Anthony N. Penna, "Some Implications of Concept Teaching," in Barry K. Beyer and Anthony N. Penna, eds., *Concepts in the Social Studies* (Washington: National Council for the Social Studies, 1971), pp. 88–91.
7. Crane Brinton, *Anatomy of a Revolution* (New York: Random House, 1965), rev. ed.
8. A useful explanation of Piaget's theories may be found in Barry J. Wadsworth, *Piaget's Theory of Cognitive Development* (New York: David McKay Company, 1971), and in Herbert Ginsburg and Sylvia Opper, *Piaget's Theory of Intellectual Development: An Introduction* (Englewood Cliffs: Prentice-Hall, 1969).
9. For an example of a discipline-based classification scheme, see *A Conceptual Framework for the Social Studies in Wisconsin Schools* (Madison: Wisconsin State Department of Public Instruction, 1964).
10. The research of the Syracuse Social Studies Curriculum Center suggested this type of classification as outlined by Roy A. Price et al., *Major Concepts for Social Studies* (Syracuse: Syracuse University Social Studies Curriculum Center, 1965).
11. Shirley H. Engle and Wilma S. Longstreet, *A Design for Social Education in the Open Curriculum* (New York: Harper and Row Publishers, 1972), pp. 46–95 passim.
12. Edwin Fenton, John M. Good, and Mitchell P. Lichtenberg, *A High School Social Studies Curriculum for Able Students: Final Report of USOE Projects H-041 and H-292* (Pittsburgh: Carnegie-Mellon University Social Studies Curriculum Center, 1969), pp. 25–26.
13. Beyer and Penna, p. 92.
14. Adapted from Edith West, "Concepts, Generalizations and Theories: Background Paper #3," as published in Peter H. Martorella, *Concept Learning: Designs for Instruction,* pp. 46–47.

10

Thinking Skills and Inquiry Teaching

Of all the skills that social studies courses customarily claim as instructional objectives, none are as important as those classified as thinking skills. Virtually all social studies courses purport to teach students, to some degree or other, the basic cognitive skills of information processing so that they will be able to make, apply, or evaluate knowledge at various levels of abstraction for a wide variety of personal, academic, and civic purposes. Mastery of these skills not only affects one's degree of success in schooling, but also lies at the heart of a self-fulfilling and contributing life in our twentieth and twenty-first century world.[1]

Of all the teaching strategies available for use in the social studies classroom, inquiry teaching seems by far the one best suited to teaching basic thinking skills. Conventional recitation or expository teaching strategies—by their rigid classroom environments, teacher-dominated patterns of discourse, and emphasis on student memorization and recall—generally inhibit student mastery of the wide range of thinking skills they might be learning in social studies courses. Moreover, such strategies, when they do focus on thinking skills, tend to emphasize low level skills or to treat instruction in these skills as extraneous exercises and problems unrelated to the content or learning sequence being used in the classroom. Inquiry teaching, however, provides not only a framework for instruction in thinking skills of all types, but also facilitates learning of these skills as an integrated part of the content flow of classroom learning. This chapter suggests ways for teachers to use inquiry teaching to teach directly a wide range of thinking skills as an integral part of content-focused lessons in the social studies classroom.

THINKING SKILLS AND INQUIRY TEACHING

As noted in Chapter 3, thinking consists essentially of two distinct levels of cognitive operations: (1) macro-thinking procedures or processes such as those that comprise the major steps of inquiring (or its variants like decision-making or problem solving); and (2) the very specific micro-skills of interpretation, extrapolation, analysis, and so on that constitute the macro-thinking processes. Inquiring necessitates the use of both types of thinking, and inquiry teaching offers innumerable opportunities for instruction in and practice of these skills.

Inquiry Teaching and Thinking

Inquiry teaching facilitates the learning of thinking skills in at least four ways. First, inquiry itself provides a framework within which the various specific thinking skills of interpretation, analysis, and so on are brought to bear on data or experience. Hypothesis formation, for example, requires learners to use the skills of translation, interpretation, analysis, extrapolation, and synthesis in various patterns or sequences to posit a potential solution to a problem or possible answer to a question. By moving through a process of inquiring, from problem identification to application of a conclusion, students have a ready-made structure for purposefully employing and practicing—and learning—specific thinking skills.

Secondly, because inquiry teaching puts students in situations where they must engage in inquiry, use of this teaching strategy requires students to draw upon the whole range of thinking skills and processes in order to succeed in their inquiry. For example, in order to determine the probable causes of the American Revolution, students in inquiry teaching must infer connections between disparate events and conditions, collect data about these variables, analyze these data for a variety of potential relationships, and so on. The only way they can arrive at their own judgment about possible causes or even evaluate the accuracy of the judgments of others is to think! So inquiry teaching creates a need to think as well as a framework in which purposeful thinking can occur.

Thirdly, inquiry teaching provides an opportunity to teach and to learn thinking skills within the content flow of the teaching-learning process rather than as an appendage to it. When students confront data that needs interpretation, the opportunity then exists to provide instruction, as well as practice, in how to interpret; when students find it necessary to analyze data, perhaps for bias or unstated assumptions, the opportunity is there to provide explicit instruction in ways of identifying bias and assumptions. Thus, inquiry teaching enables us to teach and learn skills simultaneously with teaching and learning substantive knowledge without interrrupting the flow of the content.

Finally, inquiry teaching gives purpose, or motivation, to skill learning. Faced with an assignment to analyze or evaluate an event or situation, students quickly recognize their need to know or learn how to complete their tasks satisfactorily. Their motivation to learn skills appropriate to the task assigned is thus enhanced by inquiry teaching; when the teacher then comes to their aid by providing instruction in how to do it, he or she is meeting a specific need of which the students are acutely aware. Students perceive such instruction as helping them accomplish the larger, content-related goal, rather than as a meaningless exercise in itself.

Thus, inquiry teaching actually can facilitate the teaching of thinking skills simultaneously with content learning or concept development without interrupting the flow of content in a series of lessons. As students move through the steps of inquiring by using a sequenced body of information, they can be provided instruction and practice in specific skills as part of their use of this content without diverting their attention either from the content being studied or from the overall inquiry process being used. As they practice a thinking skill using the content they are supposed to be studying, they can learn more about the content—and more content itself—as well as move further toward mastery of the particular skill or process being taught.

Systematic Teaching of Thinking Skills

Students do not learn how to think merely by being told to think. By merely requiring students to accomplish some content-related goal by using whatever skills they already possess, we must not assume that we are teaching or that they are learning those skills. Such practice really amounts to testing skills, rather than to teaching skills.[2] Teaching thinking skills, as indeed the teaching of any skill, requires systematic, deliberate, sustained instruction, as well as repeated practice. And it also requires careful student reflection about the skill being taught and practiced. Mastery of thinking skills doesn't just happen; it comes about as a result of purposeful teaching and learning.

Teachers can use several strategies within the context of inquiry teaching to provide students direct instruction and guided practice in thinking skills. A simple strategy of *rule—example—demonstration—application* serves this purpose well. Such a strategy requires:

. . . a teacher (text, film or other media) to
1. define the skill,
2. explain the specific operations that constitute the skill, and
3. demonstrate the skill;

. . . and the students, with decreasing teacher guidance, to
4. practice the skill repeatedly using a variety of appropriate data in different settings, and
5. reflect on and analyze what they have been doing—in essence, examining the skill as and after they use it.

Although all steps in this strategy are important, the final step is perhaps most crucial. At this point students can reflect on the various operations that comprise the particular skill they have been practicing and, by verbalizing what they have been doing, can (1) not only raise the elements of the skill to a level of conscious analysis but (2) also internalize these elements.

Thus, to some extent this five-step skill-teaching strategy may be used at any point within an inquiry lesson to teach a skill students need in order to complete one of the steps in the study in which they are engaged. Although this strategy may not appear to be inquiry-oriented, it actually represents a rough modification of inquiry teaching. The initial three steps set up a hypothetical model or explanation of a specific skill in the form of someone else's interpretation of the skill. The final two steps of the strategy provide students the opportunity to test this "hypothesis" in practice, to adapt it to their own needs, and to internalize it.

Furthermore, this strategy may be modified to make it even more inquiry-oriented in structure and thus even more valuable for teaching thinking skills. Such a modification simply requires us to use the final two steps of the above strategy to launch a sequence of skill-teaching activities, and then to come back to the same two steps to conclude the activities. Thus, as shown in Figure 10.1, students may engage in a learning activity that requires use of a particular skill without any prior introduction to that skill. Upon completion of this activity, they can then infer the operations or steps they followed in order to derive rules that can be consciously followed in using this same skill again in the future. These inferred operations or rules may be treated as hypotheses that students can then use to complete another activity that requires the same skill for answering a new set of questions or resolving a new problem.

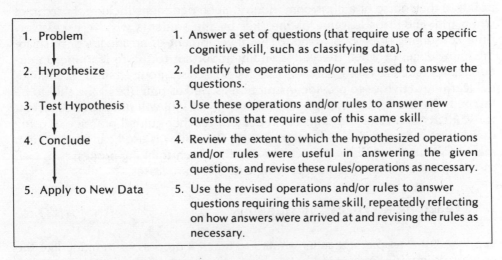

1. Problem | 1. Answer a set of questions (that require use of a specific cognitive skill, such as classifying data).

2. Hypothesize | 2. Identify the operations and/or rules used to answer the questions.

3. Test Hypothesis | 3. Use these operations and/or rules to answer new questions that require use of this same skill.

4. Conclude | 4. Review the extent to which the hypothesized operations and/or rules were useful in answering the given questions, and revise these rules/operations as necessary.

5. Apply to New Data | 5. Use the revised operations and/or rules to answer questions requiring this same skill, repeatedly reflecting on how answers were arrived at and revising the rules as necessary.

Figure 10.1. An Inquiry Strategy for Teaching Skills

Such an activity may even include instruction consisting perhaps of defining the skill and providing some examples of basic operations or rules that constitute the skill. Upon completion of this activity, students may reflect again on the rules hypothesized originally and modify or add to them as their experience dictates. Additional opportunities to use the student-generated rules, to discuss how well they work, and to modify or refine them will enable students to move toward mastery of the skill. Thus, students can hypothesize the elements of a skill, test the hypothesized elements by using them with different data, reflect on the skill, revising their knowledge of its elements, and then apply these elements as they understand them to new data. Throughout a course of study, students can periodically reflect on the nature of a skill over and over again.

Either the more didactic strategy of *rule—explanation—demonstration—application—reflection* or an inquiry strategy as outlined above may be used to facilitate student mastery of cognitive skills. Regardless of the strategy used, students must receive (1) instruction about the nature of the skill and the rules and operations of which it is comprised; (2) repeated guided opportunities to practice the skill; and (3) opportunities to reflect on what they did as they used the skill, dissecting it to identify the steps they used and the rules that guided their progress through these steps. Instruction, application, and reflection are absolutely essential steps in teaching thinking skills, whether organized in didactic or inquiry fashion.

TEACHING THINKING SKILLS THROUGH INQUIRY TEACHING

The systematic teaching of thinking may be extremely beneficial at certain points in the course of a classroom inquiry. Such occasions include those times when trial-and-error learning of the skill by the students will be excessively time-consuming or probably lead to the development of erroneous or misleading knowledge, or when the skill is vitally important to future learning. In circumstances such as these, teachers can develop class, group, paired, or individual learning activities to provide instruction as well as practice in the skill to be learned. Obviously, one experience with any given skill will not prove sufficient for students to master the skill, but repeated, teacher-guided practice in using the skill as well as student reflection on how the skill was used can lead to such mastery. Such direct instruction can be used to teach thinking processes as well as the specific thinking skills that comprise these processes.

Teaching a Process of Thinking

Suppose, for example, a teacher wanted to teach a process of thinking like the process of inquiring presented in this book. One way to introduce this process might be to (1) list, with student help, the basic steps of the scientific method as students have learned it in their science courses; (2) have students read the story "It Was Obvious" to identify examples of these steps; (3) discuss the nature and purpose of each step in the process and what had to be done by the central character in the story to execute each step; and (4) give students an opportunity to apply and reflect on this process themselves. This, in fact, is the structure of the initial chapters of this book that are designed to introduce to you the nature of inquiry!

This approach might be especially useful to undertake early in a course that frequently uses a strategy of inquiry teaching. For instance, suppose we teach a course in American history and wish to begin the course by focusing on the geography of the United States. We can easily introduce students to a strategy for inquiring as described above and then have students apply this process to a spatial problem. This application can serve several purposes: (1) to practice, with teacher guidance, the process of inquiring; (2) to learn information about specific features of America's topography, climates, and mineral resource and population distribution; and (3) to provide motivation and direction for the study of American history that will follow.

To accomplish such goals, the teacher might have pairs of students use a question guide like the accompanying Inquiry Guide to analyze a number of maps depicting the spatial distribution of various features of the United States. [3] Students individually or in pairs can overlay these maps one on another—the actual materials from which this example is drawn consists of student sets of translucent maps—and compare the data shown on each to answer the questions. As they do so they will not only learn specific information about the geography of the United States—but they will also practice and learn a process of inquiring. You, too, might use the maps on the following pages to answer the questions on this Inquiry Guide just to see if they do accomplish these goals!

Students might answer these questions completely before discussing any of their answers, or they might periodically report and discuss their answers as they proceed through the questions. Regardless of when such discussion occurs, reflection on *how* the students arrived at their answers is crucial for them to become conscious of and learn the skills and process in which they are engaged. Thus, in the follow-up discussion of this particular activity, students should discuss how they arrived at their answers as well as the substantive answers themselves.

In effect, the questions in this activity take students through the essential steps of inquiring. In reflecting on these steps, students should note that question 1 basically involves the skills of comprehension—of translating symbols into verbal form and of interpreting information shown by these symbols. Question 2 provides the problem for the inquiry that follows by asking, "What is one reason why people congregate in certain places in the United States today and not in other places?" Student answers, regardless of whether they are "closeness to water" or "nearness to resources" or "in a favorable climate," constitute hypotheses. Note that this question asks for only one response; it capitalizes on a typical student willingness to be satisfied with a single answer to questions of this type (recognizing, of course, that in an entire class we will get a number of different responses to this question and therefore a number of hypotheses to be tested). At the same time, this question produces a student-generated focus for the questions that follow, thus allowing considerable student freedom in dealing with the content presented.

Subsequent questions or directions carry the students through the remaining steps of inquiring from hypothesis testing (questions 3–6), to hypothesis evaluation (questions 7–8), and then to stating a conclusion (question 9). Finally, item 10 suggests a need for additional data not only to corroborate student findings but also to test geographical or historical hypotheses untestable by the data on these maps. This last item thus launches students into their study

INQUIRY GUIDE

1. Examine Map 12, *Population Distribution* 1970. How could you best describe the way in which people seem to be distributed throughout the United States today?

   a. Compare Map 12 with Map 1, *The United States Today*. Note that in some places large numbers of people live close together. In which of the following states does it appear that the people live closest together?

      (1) Alaska   (3) Colorado
      (2) New Jersey   (4) North Carolina

   b. Very few people live in some places. In which one of the following states do people appear to be most scattered?

      (1) Kentucky   (3) New Mexico
      (2) Pennsylvania   (4) Wisconsin

2. Examine Map 12. The population of the United States in 1970 seemed to be distributed unevenly over the land. What is one reason why people congregate in certain places in the United States today and not in other places?

3. If your answer to Question 2 is correct, then you should be able to find people congregated in large numbers in certain places in the United States. For example, if you gave as your reason "closeness to water," then you should expect to find large clusters of people living (1) along large rivers, (2) around large lakes, and (3) along the seacoasts. If the reason you gave in answer to question 2 is correct, list the kinds of places in the United States where you should be able to find large concentrations of people:

Use the maps to answer the following:

4. List the places where there are large clusters or groups of people that are located where you expected to find them, according to the list you made in answer to question 3:

POPULATION DISTRIBUTION 1970

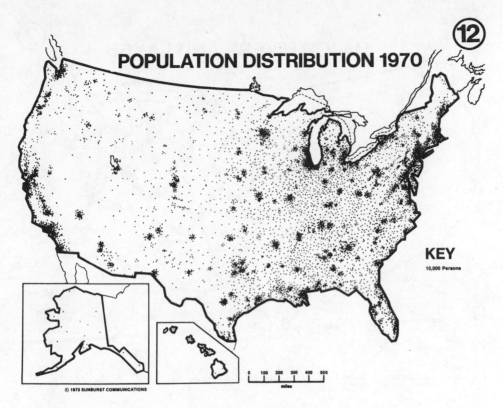

KEY

10,000 Persons

0 100 200 300 400 500

miles

© 1973 SUNBURST COMMUNICATIONS

(12)

THE UNITED STATES TODAY

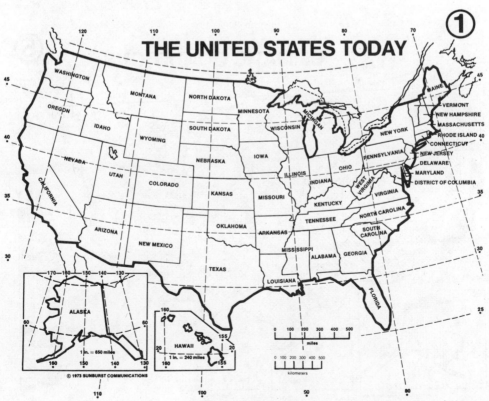

(1)

0 100 200 300 400 500

miles

0 100 200 300 400 500

kilometers

© 1973 SUNBURST COMMUNICATIONS

MAJOR RIVERS AND LAKES

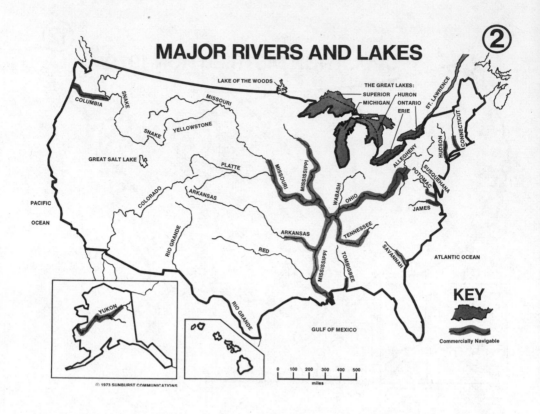

②

COLUMBIA

SNAKE

MISSOURI

YELLOWSTONE

SNAKE

GREAT SALT LAKE

PLATTE

COLORADO

ARKANSAS

MISSOURI

MISSISSIPPI

WABASH

OHIO

LAKE OF THE WOODS

THE GREAT LAKES:
SUPERIOR   HURON
MICHIGAN   ONTARIO
            ERIE

ST. LAWRENCE

CONNECTICUT

HUDSON

ALLEGHENY

SUSQUEHANNA

POTOMAC

JAMES

PACIFIC

OCEAN

RIO GRANDE

ARKANSAS

RED

TENNESSEE

SAVANNAH

ATLANTIC OCEAN

MISSISSIPPI

TOMBIGBEE

RIO GRANDE

GULF OF MEXICO

YUKON

KEY

Commercially Navigable

0 100 200 300 400 500
miles

© 1973 SUNBURST COMMUNICATIONS

CLIMATIC CONDITIONS

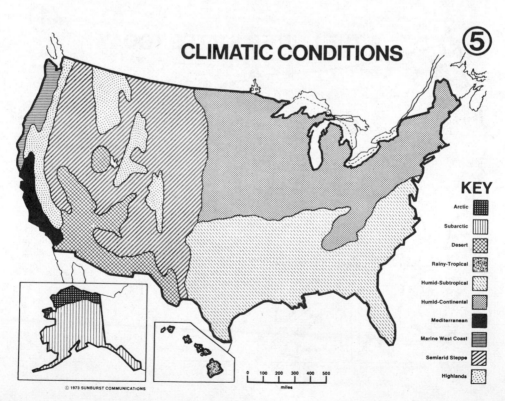

⑤

KEY

Arctic

Subarctic

Desert

Rainy-Tropical

Humid-Subtropical

Humid-Continental

Mediterranean

Marine West Coast

Semiarid Steppe

Highlands

0 100 200 300 400 500
miles

© 1973 SUNBURST COMMUNICATIONS

224

5. a. List any places where large groups of people ought to be, according to your answer to question 3, but in fact are not:

   b. What reasons may explain this?

6. List any places where there are large clusters of people that are *not* where your answer to question 3 says they should be:

   b. What reasons may explain this?

7. Does your answer to question 2 explain why all clusters of people are where they are today?

8. If your answer to question 2 completely explains all the clusters of people, go directly to question 9.

   If your answer to question 2 does not explain the way all people are distributed throughout the United States, list here some other reasons that might help explain why Americans seem to congregate where they do (check your answers to 5b and 6b).

9. Write a sentence that best explains why the population of the United States is distributed the way it is. Be prepared to explain your reasons for this statement.

10. List sources other than these maps that you could use to find out if your statement in question 9 is accurate:

of American geography and history by giving them the opportunity and reason to apply their conclusions to new data.

Before this next study gets underway, however, a student review of the steps that they have followed in this activity will reinforce their knowledge of the basic process of inquiring—exactly what the activity seeks to develop. By comparing these steps with those of the scholar in the tale analyzed earlier, and by analyzing what the students did to complete each specific step in this activity, students will come to understand more clearly the nature of inquiring and move a step closer toward mastery of this process of ordered thinking.

By engaging in the type of activities described here, whether they involve the use of maps, documents, poems, statistics, or other type of media, students in any social studies or history course can take an initial step toward learning the cognitive operations that constitute inquiry while they also develop important insights into the specific content they are studying. These activities can further assist students by raising questions that serve to organize continued study of content. Follow-up activities can then be designed to reinforce their learning of the general steps of inquiry by having them go through the steps to resolve content-related problems.

Learning activities designed to guide student inquiry may vary considerably in the complexity and degree of direction provided. Some may resemble the preceding map activity. Others may be like the Inquiry Guide presented on pages 227–228. Some may be teacher-prepared, while others may be student-designed. Some may constitute merely oral classroom activities, while others may involve elaborate take-home or in-class written activities. Whatever their form, the directions given for inquiry learning activities should require students to systematically move through the basic steps in the process of inquiring.

An Inquiry Guide like that presented on the following pages can serve as an all-purpose guide. It proves useful in dealing with all problems or questions students may choose for inquiry in virtually any social studies or history content. This guide can thus be used repeatedly throughout a course (although certainly not on a weekly basis) to help students practice and learn how to employ the basic steps in the process of inquiring.

The Inquiry Guide obviously may not contain the types of inquiry questions that suit every teacher. But it certainly can be modified to do so. As it is, this guide serves well as the basis for a three student, self-directed inquiry into a given or self-developed question. The questions in it may be reordered or new questions added to duplicate those described earlier in this book, depending on teacher or student goals. The Guide may culminate in a written or even audiovisual report if teachers or students would prefer. It may be extended to require some type of student action based on the completed inquiry. However it or some variant is used, having students *sign* the completed Guide generates significant student motivation for and commitment to the study; when completed by triads, such inquiry guides also prove extremely useful in helping teachers and students achieve similtaneously a wide variety of the knowledge, skill, interpersonal, and affective goals for which inquiry teaching is so well suited.

Similar guides or activities, becoming less and less structured as students develop their inquiry skills, can provide additional opportunities to practice and analyze the entire process introduced here or selected steps within this process. The result? Skill learning simultaneously with the use and learning of specific content, the development of generalized knowledge, and perhaps even the de-

INQUIRY GUIDE

DIRECTIONS: Complete the following as directed.

1. QUESTION:

2. HYPOTHESES:	A. NEW IDEAS (HYPOTHESES):
a)	d)
b)	e)
c)	f)
3. EVIDENCE NEEDED (if hypotheses are accurate):	B. EVIDENCE NEEDED (if new hypotheses are accurate):
a)	d)
b)	e)
c)	f)
4. EVIDENCE THAT COULD PROVE HYPOTHESES INACCURATE:	C. EVIDENCE THAT COULD PROVE NEW HYPOTHESES INACCURATE:
a)	d)
b)	e)
c)	f)
5. POSSIBLE SOURCES OF EVIDENCE:	D. ADDITIONAL SOURCES OF EVIDENCE:
1)	6)
2)	7)
3)	8)
4)	9)
5)	10)

6. Review the list of sources in item 5 for additional ideas about the evidence you might expect to find in these sources relative to your hypotheses (listed in #2). Add any ideas about evidence to the list you started in #3 and #4.

7. Look at the sources and other materials available to see if you can find the evidence you listed in #3 and #4. Mark a (✓) by any hypothesis for which you have found evidence that proves it correct, and list this evidence under the hypothesis. List new ideas in block A and test those by completing items B–D.

8. CONCLUSION: List below three hypotheses that seem to prove accurate from the data you have examined. List under each conclusion the key evidence that supports it:

1)

2)

3)

Be prepared to justify these choices for the class.

Signatures:

_____

_____

_____

velopment of useful personal interaction skills and more positive attitudes toward learning and the subject being studied.

Teaching Micro-Thinking Skills

Specific micro-thinking skills may also be taught directly using the approaches outlined above and as part of an overall inquiry lesson or sequence of lessons. These learning experiences may be guided by teacher questions and explanations communicated orally, by written skill guides, or by tape recordings, captioned filmstrips, or other audiovisual media. Students may engage in these activities individually or in pairs, triads, or groups depending on the additional instructional goals set for the activity. Follow-up discussion of the skills being taught and used can provide the necessary instructional clincher!

Inference-making and classifying are two skills of central importance to thinking and thus to inquiry teaching and learning. Inference-making is involved in almost every act of thinking, including interpretation, extrapolation, analysis, and synthesis. Our inferences serve many functions. Most inferences actually serve as hypotheses, for they are based only on limited data or experience. Sometimes inferences serve as conclusions when they have been generated from and tested against a considerable amount of evidence. All inferences, however, serve as a basis for some type of follow-up behavior or further thinking. Eventually, what often starts as an inference becomes a piece of knowledge when it is proven (or accepted as) true by experience or by some other validating procedure.

Classifying involves the systematic categorizing of data according to perceived or given similarities, patterns, or characteristics. By classifying data we can make—infer—general statements about the data being classified and thus develop testable hypotheses or test generalizations. The skills of inference-making and classifying in a very real sense underlie almost all productive thinking and learning. Inquiry teaching provides numerous opportunities to teach and use these skills while students engage in the content selected for study.

Teaching inference-making. To *infer* means to deduce—to extrapolate or interpolate—from evidence. We make inferences by making connections between given data and what we already know or believe about something that seems in our minds to be related to that data. We make inferences constantly and naturally. Students of all ages make inferences, depending of course on the degree of abstraction of the data and of the inference sought and on the nature of their previous learning. Students do not need instruction in how to make inferences *per se* so much as they need systematic instruction in how to make *logical* inferences and in how to judge the rationality of inferences already made.

Instruction for making logical inferences may take many forms. One procedure essentially involves helping students become conscious of the three steps involved in inference-making: (1) examining the available data or evidence, (2) using the basic features of the data to search one's memory for any ideas or data related to the evidence, and then (3) stating a connection between what one knows or believes about this data and the problem or task at hand.

Another procedure for helping students learn to make logical inferences consists of aiding them to reflect systematically on the extent to which the connections they posit are reasonable or not. Once students have articulated an inference, we can guide them in evaluating the accuracy of their inferences in terms of the logic of their reasoning, the appropriateness of their recalled knowledge, and the quality of the assumptions on which their reasoning is based. Such instruction thus requires helping students to make and state inferences; state the data, knowledge, or assumptions behind these inferences; and reflect critically upon the data and reasoning used in generating their inferences.

For example, suppose we want to help students improve their skill of inference-making while they study the photographs and drawings of the artifacts used to launch the inquiry study of Kiev in the Prologue. We might do this by creating a series of written questions that pairs of students could complete as they study two of the artifacts used in this activity. The objects are pictured on the next page for easy reference here. Our questions might be arranged as in the Inference-Making Guide (pp. 232–233). Once students have completed this skill guide, we can discuss how they got their answers, how they made the inferences they did, and then continue with the lesson at the substantive level by discussing their inferences as hypotheses about life in the society represented by the artifacts. Thus we can engage in skill teaching, content learning, and knowledge building almost simultaneously and in uninterrupted sequence.

We might launch this inference-making activity, especially if this were the students' first encounter with an activity of this type, with remarks such as the following.

An inference is an idea that comes to you or that you invent about a topic or in answer to a problem or question when you see or hear certain information about that topic, problem, or question. To "infer" something means to make a connection between something before you and something you already know or believe. To make an inference you must (1) examine the information you have, (2) search your memory for anything you might know about that same information and for any ideas related to what you know about it, and then (3) state a connection between what you know about information like that and the problem or question you are working on. The connection you make must be reasonable. That means it must follow logically from the knowledge or assumptions you have.

For example, suppose you have a picture of a sandy desert-like region. You might infer that few people would live permanently in the area because you already know or believe that deserts lack the plentiful supply of water needed to support large permanent settlements. Your inference is based on something you already know about what you see in front of you. It has followed logically from what you know.

The idea, "few people would live in this region," constitutes an inference. It may or may not be accurate because you have little information to go on so far. But

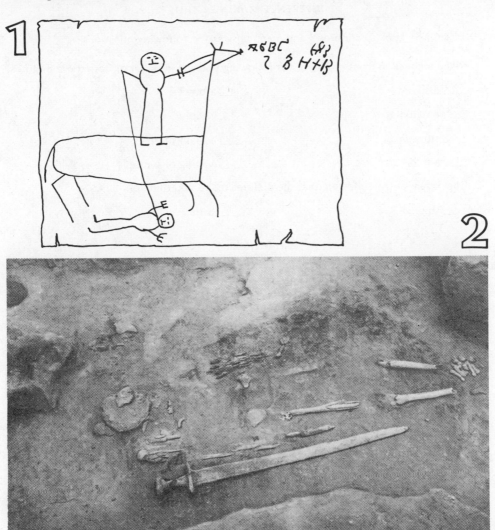

it does seem logical given what you believe to be true of reasons such as, "deserts lack water." You can check the accuracy of your inference by testing it against more data later. At the moment, it is important to figure out how to make inferences that are logical—that follow reasonably from the data available. How well can you make logical inferences? Use the Inference-Making Guide in examining the artifacts shown here.

Thereupon students can proceed to complete the guide as directed. This procedure carries through the general strategy of skill teaching outlined earlier in this chapter. The above introductory remarks note the skill label, define the skill, and give an example. The questions on the guide help students systematically make and examine inferences as they apply the steps explained by the teacher to the given data. Item 1, however, does not require inference-making; rather, it involves simple translation, requiring students merely to tell what they

INFERENCE-MAKING GUIDE

DIRECTIONS: Look at pictures 7 and 8 and answer the following questions:

1. Place a check in front of any of the following you *see* in either or both these pictures:

_____ a sword   _____ a bowl

_____ an animal   _____ people

_____ stones   _____ a blacksmith

_____ a river   _____ writing or symbols

2. Check any of the following that the pictures make you think of:

_____ shields   _____ armor

_____ graves   _____ spears

_____ cows   _____ potatoes

3. Select one of the items you checked in #2 above and write it here:

_____

a) What do you see in the pictures that makes you think of this item?

b) What do you already know or believe about these things that makes you think of the item you checked?

c) How do your answers to a and b make you think of the item you wrote above?

4. Check any of the following that the pictures bring to your mind:

_____ farming   _____ cooperation

_____ warfare   _____ friendship

_____ craftsmanship   _____ peace

5. Check any of the following that the pictures make you think of:

_____ danger   _____ backward

_____ primitive   _____ friendly

_____ resourcefulness   _____ pagan

6. Select one of the items you checked in #5 and write it here:

    _____

   a) What in the picture makes you infer this?

   b) What do you already believe or know about what's in the picture that makes you
      infer this item?

   c) Why do you think your inference makes sense?

7. List one rule you could tell someone to follow if he/she wanted to be able to answer
   questions 2, 4, or 5:

8. Check any of the following that you infer from the pictures:

   _____ teachers or schools   _____ belief in life after death

   _____ people specializing in   _____ a lack of leisure time
         certain jobs
                                           _____ peacefulness
   _____ the tropics

9. Circle one of the inferences you made in #8. Explain in a sentence or two why you made
   this inference.

10. List here two or three other things these pictures make you think of:

actually see in the pictures—to translate, as it were, pictorial data into words without changing the meaning of the original data. Thus, the activity guide starts where the students are, with what they actually see, not with what they interpret it to mean.

Most of the remaining items call for inferencing or justifying the inferences made. These items move in a sequence from making inferences about physical objects (item 2), to making and justifying inferences about conditions (items 4 and 5), to making and justifying inferences that may involve certain value-laden judgments. Item 8 asks the student to infer larger ideas related to these pictures. Items 3, 6, and 9 provide decreasingly detailed guidance in a process for making inferences, while items 7 and 9 require students to indicate the rule being taught by stating the rule (item 7) and explaining how they apply the rule (item 9). Thus the items on this thinking guide move back and forth between making inferences and reflecting on how they were made. Students get practice in making inferences and receive instruction in how to make logical inferences. As this activity progresses students not only develop new insights into the subject or content being studied, but they also have an opportunity to pull together their perceptions of *how* they have been doing what they have been doing.

After students complete all the items on the Inference-Making Guide, the entire class should discuss their responses, especially those to items asking for reasons why they made the inferences they did. In answering these questions, students must articulate what they see in the pictures, what they know or believe to be true about what they see, and the reasons for the connection they posit between what they see and what they "know." Students must, in other words, think in terms of their perceptions and their premises. In answering item 5 by checking the word *danger*, for instance, students must articulate their reasoning that led to this choice. They may note that they see what they believe to be implements of war (spears and swords) in the photographs; that people make or use such instruments in self-defense, or in attacking other people, or perhaps even in hunting; and that all of these occasions involve a certain amount of danger. Hence, they infer that life in a society that had implements like these probably had a certain amount of danger in it! Is this a logical line of reasoning?

Student analysis of answers to a set of questions such as those in the Inference-Making Guide can help answer this question as well as help students articulate the rules for judging the logic of inferences they might make or encounter in the future. Consideration of these items helps students become conscious of the operations that constitute inference-making, the subject of item 7. Articulating these operations provides a valuable step in learning this skill just as practice in using the skill for both procedures reinforces each. In subsequent lessons the teacher can quiz the students on these rules, give them positive and negative examples of inferences drawn from verbal or visual data and ask them to state why such examples are either logical or illogical inferences, and provide them further opportunities to practice this particular skill with additional instruction, reflection, and discussion.

Providing instruction in thinking skills as described here neither interrupts nor detracts from the content or other objectives of an inquiry lesson. In fact, use of such a skill activity can enhance the learning of information and the achievement of other kinds of cognitive or affective goals toward which this lesson might be directed. For, not only must the students manipulate and examine the content of the lesson in order to answer the activity questions, but in so doing they build a bridge from the skill focus to the content focus of the lesson by completing items 8 and 10. These final choices could serve, in effect, as hypotheses, or they could suggest additional hypotheses. Discussion of student responses on these items can thus move the focus of the activity forward to its content function in the overall strategy of inquiry teaching for which it was originally designed—that of making hypotheses about life in the place where these objects were uncovered. This skill activity on inference-making proves most useful, in fact, *before* the students offer hypotheses about the nature of life in this place about 1,000 years ago because it gives them guidance in the first steps in hypothesizing—making logical inferences from given data and making connections between given and observed data and what one knows or believes to be true because of previous learning or experience.

The skill of classifying. A similar approach may be used to teach students the skill of classifying or categorizing information. For students just learning to employ this skill, we can ask them to decide whether or not specified data should be included in a given class; for example, which of the following may be classified as animals: dog, tree, cat, sparrow, corn stalk, turtle? As students master this class exclusion skill, they can then be asked to engage in class *in*clusion categorizing—to classify data into classes that are also included in other classes. The answer to the following question illustrates this skill: If Paris is in France and France is in Europe, is Paris in Europe? Finally, an even more complex task of classification may be undertaken by categorizing data with overlapping attributes. For example, given that some wives are scientists and that wives are women, we can classify some women as scientists. Students can learn to classify data by moving gradually from excluding data from a given class, to including data in multiple classes and, finally, to classifying data with overlapping attributes.

A variety of techniques may be used to provide instruction and practice in classifying, including (1) giving students a set of data and then asking them to classify these data under appropriate given labels; (2) giving students data already grouped and having them provide the category label that tells the feature common to all the data in a given group; or (3) providing data and asking students to classify them by several different criteria and to provide labels for whatever groups they devise. This last type of classification, the multiple classification of the same data, proves especially useful, and also difficult, for it forces students out of prevailing mind sets and thus enables them to gain new insights into the data being used.

Classifying data is not an end in itself. One classifies data for a purpose: to test a hypothesis, to make an inference, or to complete some other task. Thus, students should conclude a classifying activity by making some statement about what is revealed or suggested by the results of the categorizing in which they have engaged. They can do this by making a generalization suggested by the set of categories they have made or choose from a list of generalizations. The generalization should be supported by their classification of the given data.

Instruction and practice in classifying data may be as integral a part of any inquiry teaching strategy as the teaching of any skill. The activity on page 237, for example, suggests one way a teacher can provide instruction and practice in classifying data while simultaneously helping students to test hypotheses and to generate inferences that can serve as additional hypotheses for testing.[4] As students employ these skills, they also learn about a specific historical topic, in this case about the Civil War in the Classifying Information activity on pp. 237–238.

Classifying information according to a single criterion, such as by seasons in the Classifying Information activity, gives useful but limited insight into that information. Repeated classification of the same information according to different criteria can provide additional insights, however. Questions 3, 4, and 5 on the activity did just that. The Civil War battles listed on the activity can be successively classified in terms of duration of fighting, location, victor, and other categories. Each time these battles are classifed according to a new criterion students can infer a significant statement about the military course of the Civil War or about the parties to that war; these inferences may then serve as useful hypotheses for testing against textbook or other information.

LENGTH OF FIGHTING	WINNER	
	South	North
1 day		
2–5 days		
more than 5 days		

Figure 10.2. Multiple Classification Matrix

We can and should go beyond single criterion classification, however. Students should be asked, especially in the secondary grades, to classify the same information in several categories simultaneously in order to infer relationships among several variables at once. They can, for example, classify the major battles shown in this activity in terms of victors and length of fighting and then state any relationships they infer among these variables. Use of a matrix such as that shown in Figure 10.2 will facilitate such analysis. Students can even classify these same battles in terms of winners *and* length of fighting *and* section of the country (north, border states, south) where the battles occurred in order to identify even more sophisticated relationships. Classifying data in a variety of ways using a number of variables can help students infer or test previously inferred relationships among data—and making relationships is a basic analytical skill.

The Classifying Information activity on pp. 237–238 could also serve a number of other functions in inquiry teaching, as well as provide instruction in the skill of classifying data. We might use this activity, for instance, to launch a study of the military aspects of the war by using the generalizations developed

CLASSIFYING INFORMATION

Starting in 1861, Northern states fought Southern states in a Civil War. The North won the Civil War. Southern states that fought to set up a separate government lost the war. Look at Chart #1 below of major battles in this war. The chart has three columns: *Time, Place,* and *Winner.* Notice that the battles appear on the chart in order of time from 1861 through 1865.

CHART #1. MAJOR BATTLES OF THE CIVIL WAR

Time	Place	Winner
1. July 21, 1861	Manassas, Virginia	South
2. April 6–7, 1862	Shiloh, Tennessee	North
3. May 1, 1862	New Orleans, Louisiana	North
4. August 29–30, 1862	Manassas, Virginia	South
5. September 16–17, 1862	Antietam, Maryland	North
6. December 13, 1862	Fredericksburg, Virginia	South
7. May 1–4, 1863	Chancellorsville, Virginia	South
8. May 23–July 4, 1863	Vicksburg, Mississippi	North
9. July 1–3, 1863	Gettysburg, Pennsylvania	North
10. September 19–20, 1863	Chicamauga, Tennessee	South
11. November 23–25, 1863	Chattanooga, Tennessee	North
12. May 5–12, 1864	The Wilderness, Virginia	North
13. July 22–September 2, 1864	Atlanta, Georgia	North
14. December 15–16, 1864	Nashville, Tennessee	North
15. December 22, 1864	Savannah, Georgia	North
16. March 29–April 5, 1865	Appomattox, Virginia	North

You can classify information in a variety of ways. To classify means to put all information that is alike in a group or category of its own. Chart #1 classifies the major battles in the order of time. Suppose you wanted to test the hypothesis "Most Civil War battles occurred during the warm weather months." You could list these battles according to the different seasons of the year (fall, winter, spring, and summer) to see how many occurred during each season. Let's test this hypothesis by classifying the above battles according to the seasons in which they occurred. On Chart #2, list the battles in the space under the seasons in which they occurred.

CHART #2. CLASSIFICATION OF THE BATTLES.

FALL September–November	WINTER December–February	SPRING March–May	SUMMER June–August

Now answer the following questions:

1. Assume that the spring and summer months are the warm weather months of a year. Is the hypothesis, "Most Civil War battles occurred during the warm weather months," correct? _____

2. What is one reason for your answer to question 1?

    _____

    _____

3. List three ways other than by seasons that you could classify the information on Chart #1.

    a._____

    b._____

    c._____

4. Classify this information in one of these ways on another sheet of paper or in your head. What is one thing this tells you about the Civil War?

    _____

    _____

    _____

5. Repeat what you did in item 4 for two of the other ways of classifying this information you listed in item 3. When you have done this, list what seems to be true about the military events of the Civil War.

    a._____

    b._____

by the students as hypotheses to test by a follow-up study of a text and other materials. When used in this fashion, this activity thus serves triple goals: learning of information about this War, skill development, and hypothesis formation. If we engage the students in small group follow-up testing of their generalizations/hypotheses, then a host of other knowledge, inquiry, and interaction objectives can also be accomplished.

SUMMARY

Inquiry teaching certainly provides numerous opportunities for the direct teaching of thinking skills and processes in the context of the course content without interrupting either the content sequence or the sequence of steps employed in an inquiry teaching strategy. Ways to teach only three of these processes and skills have been described here.[5] But the techniques presented here may be useful in providing direct instruction in all skills and processes of thinking. Such instruction can become an integral part of inquiry teaching, not as an exercise in itself but as a means to other goals. Such teaching can also result in improved student motivation and learning of content and concepts, as well as the mastery of thinking skills and processes.

notes

1. See for example, James P. Shaver, "A Critical View of the Social Studies Profession," *Social Education,* 41:4 (April 1977), pp. 300–308. See also Dana Kurfman, ed., *Developing Decision Making Skills* (Washington: National Council for the Social Studies, 1977), esp. pp. vi, viii, 1–4.
2. Harold Herber, *Teaching Reading in Content Areas* (Englewood Cliffs: Prentice-Hall, 1970), pp. Vi–viii.
3. Adapted from E. Perry Hicks and Barry K. Beyer, *United States Inquiry Maps* (Pleasantville, New York: Sunburst Communications, 1973). Reprinted with permission. Four of the 14 maps that comprise these materials are reprinted here. In their original format these maps are each 8½ x 11" in size and are printed on translucent paper so they can be overlaid one on another. Skill activities like the activity reproduced here are available for students in intermediate and secondary grades.
4. Adapted with permission from Anthony N. Penna, "The Civil War and Reconstruction: The Response of Government—Two Curriculum Units for Slow Learners" (D.A. Dissertation, Carnegie-Mellon University, 1969), pp. 211, 290.
5. Additional techniques for teaching basic skills in social studies may be found in Barry K. Beyer, *Back-to-Basics in the Social Studies: Implications for the Classroom* (Boulder: Social Science Education Consortium, 1977).

11

Reading, Writing, and Inquiry Teaching

Reading and writing are without doubt among the most important of all the learning skills that students can, and indeed must, master. The nature of these important skills and the crucial role they play in learning, in social studies as in most other subjects, makes systematic instruction in these skills highly desirable. Furthermore, inquiry teaching offers an excellent vehicle for accomplishing this important goal.

Inquiry teaching and reading and writing are mutually reinforcing. Reading and writing can be used with ease to move the process of student inquiry along from problem identification through its various steps to conclusion and final application. A strategy of inquiry teaching may also be well used to provide and guide classroom instruction in reading and writing. In fact, inquiry teaching provides a means by which and a framework in which instruction in these skills can be wedded with content learning and thinking skill development, as well as with the achievement of other common classroom learning goals.

READING COMPREHENSION
AND WRITING

Reading and writing are among the most widely used learning techniques which we require students to use in our classrooms. Instruction in these skills thus proves useful in social studies courses as in most other courses. Reading serves as the principal means through which students collect information. Reading and writing together constitute the major means through which students communicate to others in the formal educational setting what they have learned, are learning, or need to learn. Without considerable competency in reading comprehension and in writing, students can barely survive, let alone succeed, in most social studies and other classrooms today.

Moreover, reading comprehension and writing should be important teaching goals because they are, in essence, thinking. Indeed, these processes

240

constitute thinking in action. Both require the mental processing and manipulation of information, including the evaluation and selection of alternatives, inferring relationships, and testing hypotheses. Reading comprehension and writing thus prove to be handy vehicles for teaching thinking, for they are in themselves acts of thought.

Reading comprehension is a complex cognitive process. It is, in effect, not a single skill, but a collection of skills. As Nila Banton Smith has written, reading comprehension involves thought-making as well as thought-getting.[1] This process consists of determining what a source says literally (translation), what its author means by what he or she says (interpretation), and what the source means to the reader (extrapolation, application, synthesis, or evaluation)?[2] In reading we seek to identify and make relationships by using the skills of analysis and synthesis in two ways: on the one hand in relating one sentence to another, one paragraph to another, and one idea to another; and on the other hand relating what we read to what we already know and expect or wish to find.[3] We infer meanings, posit relationships, and uncover bias and unstated assumptions; we evaluate what we read and seek meaning in terms of our own perceptions and past knowledge. In short, reading comprehension involves a complex processing of information and ideas; this, in effect, is thinking.

Apart from the psychomotor act of putting pen to paper or the editing acts of punctuating, spelling, or arranging words in grammatically acceptable form, writing, too, is thinking. In fact, writing is also a process rather than a single skill. Generating, organizing, and expressing ideas with clarity and precision involve synthesizing ideas, choosing evidence relating to the ideas, sequencing the evidence in a reasoned order, and explicitly stating perceived relationships among the evidence and/or between the evidence and a thesis or point we wish to make.[4] Writing, done well, involves making and communicating meaning by choosing and relating ideas and information and presenting the evolving synthesis in clear, logical form. Thus, writing, like reading comprehension, is an act of thinking.[5]

Just as the use of inquiry teaching provides an opportunity to directly practice and learn thinking skills and processes, so too does this teaching strategy offer opportunities for improving student skills of reading comprehension and writing and thus, indirectly, the skills of thinking. But unless teachers give explicit in-class attention to instruction in reading and writing, the specific skills that constitute these processes stand little chance of being developed and learned. Social studies teachers must therefore provide direct, systematic instruction in reading comprehension and writing if they want to help students master these essential communication processes in the social studies classroom.

READING COMPREHENSION AND INQUIRY TEACHING

Although reading is often the most frequently used information gathering tool used in social studies, instruction in the process receives relatively little attention in these classes or in any subject matter classes beyond the fourth grade. Yet a considerable proportion of social studies students report that they experience more difficulty with reading vocabulary and comprehension than they do with learning the facts contained in what they read.[6] In other words, while students feel they have little difficulty in "getting the facts," they do admit difficulty in making sense—or meaning—of what they read. Teachers ought to provide instruction in vocabulary and reading comprehension while they teach for knowledge and other learning objectives. They can do so with relative ease and convenience. This instruction can be provided in three different places in a lesson: (1) when giving a reading assignment, (2) as students are doing their reading, and (3) in a follow-up discussion of a reading assignment. Attention to reading at each of these three points can provide instruction in reading while keeping the focus on the content of the course. It can also be done without interrupting the development of the inquiry or the substantive flow of the lesson. At the same time, this instruction facilitates learning of thinking skills as well.

Introducing Reading Assignments

Teachers can help students improve their reading comprehension in the following ways: by alerting them to the vocabulary and organization cues commonly used by texts, filmstrips, or oral presentations to call their attention to what the authors consider important; by helping students deal with unfamiliar or new technical terms that appear in the reading; and by helping students develop a specific purpose for reading.

Texts use a variety of typefaces or colors to call a reader's attention to major ideas. Similarly, authors or lecturers use words such as *first, second, third,* and so on to alert readers and listeners to the major points they intend to make. Filmstrips and films often insert title frames or subtitles to distinguish one important topic from another. Students should be alerted to these cues and should be taught to skim assignments for cues like these to help them improve their reading (as well as listening and viewing) comprehension. A prereading search to skim a reading assignment for headings and other cues can help students identify the main points and the general structure of the ideas to be presented in what they are about to read.

Social studies and history, like other disciplines, have their own technical languages; many words have highly specialized meaning—words like *mercantilism, civil rights, allocation, squatters, culture,* and *technology.* All too frequently we assume students know the meanings of technical and subject-specific words when, in fact, they do not. Even though texts attempt to deal constructively with such words, most lists of new or unfamiliar words are still found at the end of a chapter rather than preceding the chapter content. Yet students need to know, or at least have some idea, of the meanings of new or technical words and phrases before they come across them in their reading, or at least when they encounter them in their reading.

Teachers can help students in at least three ways to master the vocabulary of the social studies. We can, for example, have students use dictionaries, glossaries, or other sources to identify the meaning of the words in a chapter-end list of key words to know *before* they do the assignment in which these words will appear. We can also alert students to techniques of defining words in the context in which they appear in a text. Many social studies texts now provide a number of aids to this end. Some present the definitions of new words in marginal notes or in footnotes; sometimes definitions may be presented in appositional or parenthetical statements immediately following the word in question. Occasionally the sentence immediately following a new word may provide its definition, explain it, or illustrate it by giving an example or two. Context clues, found by noting how the word is used in relation to other words, can also help students generate at least a tentative meaning for an unfamiliar word.

We can also assist students in developing tentative definitions by having them analyze new words in terms of prefixes and suffixes, as well as by looking for root words. Mercantilism, for instance, can be broken into *mercant* or *merchant* and *ism*. Students can derive a working definition by combining the meanings they understand from these two groups of letters. Students can also give examples of new words and, as a class, generate tentative definitions of the words from the examples. These definitions can then be refined as the students use the words in subsequent reading and engage in follow-up class discussion of what they have read. Assisting students to find or develop definitions of key words before or as they read, rather than after they read, not only makes their reading easier but improves reading comprehension. If teachers would provide prereading instruction and repeated supervised practice in vocabulary learning, students could overcome one of the most common difficulties they face in social studies learning.

Finally, purposeful reading (just as purposeful listening or viewing) assignments are by far more productive of learning than assignments lacking any clearly defined goal. An assignment to "read pages 140 to the top of 149" does not provide nearly as useful a guide to comprehension as does an assignment to read these same pages "to find three features of life in the United States between 1820 and 1850 that may have contributed to the westward migration of Americans in that period and be able to give two examples of each"! Such an assignment, of course, is strictly teacher-given and directed, but not all purposes for reading need be teacher-generated.

Students can also establish their own purposes for reading by using the assigned materials as a basis for raising their own questions or generating hypotheses about the material to be used. Prior to beginning an assignment, students can skim a text (or filmstrip) to identify the main ideas that apparently will be "covered" in the material by noting subheadings, italicized words or phrases, photographs, maps and charts and their captions, introductory and concluding paragraphs, and any questions included in the material. Topics suggested by these items can then be recast as questions or hypothetical statements. Or, without looking at more than the title, the introductory paragraph, or the first few frames of a filmstrip, students can brainstorm questions that they imagine might be answered or that they would like to have answered in the material that follows. Students can then complete the assignment to answer the questions or test the hypotheses they have raised. Such purposeful reading generates more motivation and offers greater guidance than does reading to cover a specific number of pages without anything in particular to look for. Regardless of whether the purpose for reading is teacher-given or student-developed, purposeful reading sharply enhances student comprehension.

Guiding A Reading Assignment

Instruction in how to read—or view or listen—can proceed simultaneously with the act of reading, viewing, or listening itself. Such instruction actually provides assistance in thinking and in moving through a body of content as well as it aids students to learn about the content being studied. The type of guidance most productive of these goals seems to be that which helps students to distinguish carefully between (1) what a source says literally, (2) what the author of the source appears to mean, and (3) what the source means to the reader given what the reader already knows or wants to know about the content or subject of the source. These distinctions actually represent the different major thinking skills that constitute reading comprehension: the skills of translating, interpreting, and higher levels of thinking. Teachers can aid in the development of these skills by having students answer questions that require the use of these three skills in sequence while they read or view appropriate learning materials.[7]

Standard reading guides offer one method to provide instruction in reading while students read. Such guides, for example, can be used in conjunction with any of the materials (the list of laws, or pictures of artifacts, or excerpts from sources) used in the lesson on old Kiev presented in the Prologue. Suppose, for example, we prepared such a guide for use with the list of laws from old Kiev. Such a guide might consist of questions like those on page 247.

The first several questions in the Reading Guide merely require students to employ the skill of translation—of putting a communication into another form without changing its meaning. Questions 1 through 3 in the guide can be answered by direct reference to the laws themselves; the answers exist in the laws. Students need only find a word appearing in the law list that is also given as a possible answer in the Reading Guide; they do not have to know the meaning of any of the possible answers to the questions on the guide. An effective reading guide might start with two or three questions such as 1–3 that relate to items at the beginning, in the middle, and toward the end of the material being used by the students. Such questions will start the students at the lowest level of reading comprehension by reading what the source actually says as opposed to what it may mean. They also require the students to read through the entire selection at this level of comprehension simply to answer the questions.

Question 4 asks students to reflect on *how* they are answering the questions up to this point; it requires them to reflect on the skill they have been using. Their answer to this question represents a rule for using the skill of translation. How do you know your answer to question 3 (or 2 or 1) is correct? Because it (the list of laws) *says so!* This answer is the rule to translating information: the source literally says the answer. Questions such as number 4 interspersed throughout a reading guide help students reflect on the skills they are using to answer the substantive questions, and by so doing they focus students' attention on skill learning while students at the same time engage in content learning.

While question 5 involves only a literal translation of the data contained in the laws, it also requires students to compare data. Students must also translate the value of the different coins into numbers so they can arrive at a correct answer. Questions requiring students to examine several pieces of information, even at just the literal level, can enhance their familiarity with this information before they move on to establish meaning.

The remaining questions require students to deal with the meaning of the laws. Question 6 requires students essentially to classify the laws according to four given categories. Classifying data, as noted earlier, is a skill essential to interpreting information. Questions 7 and 9 require students to determine what certain laws mean, to interpret them. Items 8 and 10 then ask for the reasoning behind their responses to questions 7 and 9 because we cannot really determine the validity of an interpretation until the reasons or evidence for it have been made clear. These items offer students an opportunity to tell how they arrived at their answers to items 7 and 9. Because they are open-ended items, 8 and 10 also serve as effective springboards for follow-up discussion of this Reading Guide.

Questions 11 and 12 require students to use their skills of analysis and synthesis. Question 11 asks students to identify evidence that relates to a specific generalization—to determine the relationships of segments of data to a given idea. Question 12 asks students to develop a generalization that explains (or relates) the laws as a whole. Thus, a guide incorporating questions like these helps students to move from simple translation skills, through the skills of interpretation, to higher level skills of application, analysis, and synthesis, and to learn about the content being studied in the process.

The types of questions suggested here differ in one significant way from typical end-of-chapter or workbook questions. Each question (with the exception of items 4, 8, and 10) provides guidance for students by giving options from which to choose a correct answer. According to some reading specialists, providing such options actually provides instruction in how to answer the question, and thus provides guidance in reading comprehension. These options, in effect, imply rules for reading. Answers to items such as 4, 8, and 10 then give students the opportunity to indicate whether or not they have understood the rule in use. Reading specialists also suggest that further guidance in reading can be provided by indicating next to each question on a guide like this one the page and column number where students can find the answers to literal level questions—such as (12, 1) for page 12 column 1, for example—or page numbers within which information can be found from which given interpretations can be derived (i.e., 12–14).[8] Answer keys may also be provided so that students can check the accuracy of their own answers upon completing their reading guides.

Of course, alternative types of reading guides may also be devised to provide instruction in reading comprehension. Instead of providing a series of multiple choice questions, for example, we can offer students a list of statements and ask them to check those for which they can find support in a specific reading assignment, Thus, with reference to the list of laws on old Kiev, we might present the following statements:

_____1. A grivna was a coin.

_____2. In time of war, all slaves had to join the army.

_____3. Judging from these laws, the people of this place were more interested in freedom than in protecting property.

_____4. The people who made these laws probably considered religion more important than property rights.

_____5. The steward was considered more important than a free worker on the prince's estate.

SOME LAWS

These laws refer to amounts of money. The grivna was a coin like a silver dollar. A rezana was 1/50th of a grivna. Think of a rezana as a two-penny piece.

Laws

1. If anyone kills the prince's steward, he must pay 80 grivna.
2. If anyone kills a free worker on the prince's estate, he must pay 5 grivna.
3. If anyone kills a peasant or a herdsman, he must pay 5 grivna.
4. If anyone kills a slave who is a teacher or a nurse, he must pay 12 grivna.
5. If anyone kills the prince's horse, he must pay 3 grivna; for killing a peasant's horse, 2 grivna.
6. If anyone kidnaps another man's male or female slave, he must pay 12 grivna to the owner.
7. If anyone beats a peasant without the permission of the prince, he must pay him 3 grivna; if anyone beats a sheriff or another assistant to the prince, the fine is 12 grivna.
8. If anyone plows beyond the boundary of his property, the fine is 12 grivna.
9. If anyone steals a boat, he must pay 30 rezana for the boat and a fine of 60 rezana.
10. If a slave runs away from his owner and someone hides him but the owner finds him, the owner receives back his slave and 3 grivna for the offense.
11. If anyone cuts a man's leg and the leg is cut off or the injured man becomes lame, the injured man's son must avenge his father.
12. In time of war all males in the city shall become a part of the army. The peasants of the countryside shall surrender all of their horses and join with the army. The prince shall supply the weapons.
13. If a member of the local guild commits a crime and is not caught, the other members of the guild must pay for the offense.
14. If an indentured laborer runs away from his lord, he becomes the lord's slave. But if he departs openly to complain of an injustice on the part of his lord and goes to the prince or to the judges, they do not make him a slave but give him justice.
15. If a peasant dies without male descendants, his estate goes to the prince. If there are daughters left in the house, each receives a portion of the estate; if they are married, they receive no portion.
16. If a mustache or a beard is forcefully cut off, the offender must pay 12 grivna.

READING GUIDE

DIRECTIONS: Circle or write the correct response to each of the following items with reference to the laws listed opposite.

1. What was a *grivna?*

    a) a coin   b) a Russian peasant   c) a prince   d) a farm

2. What was the penalty for killing a peasant's horse?

    a) 5 grivna   b) 2 grivna   c) 5 rezana

3. Who was to pay if a member of a local guild committed a crime and was not caught?

    a) his wife   b) the government   c) other members of the guild

4. How do you know your answer to question 3 is correct?

5. Which crime has the highest penalty?

    a) stealing a boat   c) hiding a runaway slave
    b) killing the prince's horse   d) killing the prince's steward

6. Most of the laws listed here deal with:

    a) freedom   c) property
    b) religion   d) women

7. What did the people who made these laws probably consider most important?

    a) freedom   c) property
    b) religion   d) women

8. Explain one reason for your answer to question 5:

9. Who did the people who made these laws probably consider most important?

    a) a peasant   c) a slave who is a teacher
    b) the prince's steward   d) a free worker on the prince's estate

10. Explain one reason for your answer to question 7:

11. Which of the laws listed here support the idea that ownership of private property was important in this society?

    a) Laws 6, 8, 9   c) Laws 1, 5, 16
    b) Laws 7, 12, 14

12. Which of the following statements do these laws suggest is correct?

    a) These people had a system of formal education.
    b) These people lived along the sea coast.
    c) These people followed the Moslem religion.
    d) These people believed in freedom and equality for everyone.

_____6. Most of the people who lived in this place engaged in long distance trade.

_____7. The people who lived in this place were divided into social classes.

_____8. These people did not believe in the saying, "An eye for an eye, a tooth for a tooth."

Students could use these statements to guide their reading of the laws, checking those for which they found evidence in the laws and, if required, writing the reasons for their selections. They could also be asked to rewrite those statements for which they found no support in the laws into statements that the laws did support.

Again, it is important to note that the statements in the preceding list are not random. Like the questions in the Reading Guide, these statements reflect specific reading skills. The first two statements can be verified by a simple literal reading of the laws; to decide on their accuracy requires only reading at the translational level. Statements 3–5, however, require interpretation on the part of the students. To verify the remaining statements students must employ the skills of application, analysis, synthesis, and/or evaluation—skills that comprise the highest level of reading comprehension.

Reading comprehension guides may also be constructed following the major steps in an inquiry teaching strategy. An initial question might ask students to select a statement that represents the general or main idea of a passage, and subsequent questions could ask students to identify evidence from the passage that supports the main idea they have selected. Further questions would ask students to select examples of this idea or of related ideas presented in the passage. Such questions may be in the form of multiple choice items and/or completion items. Regardless of the type of questions asked, to be most effective in guiding reading comprehension, the items chosen must require students to translate and interpret what they are reading as well as to apply, synthesize, or evaluate it.

By devising multiskill reading comprehension guides built on these principles, teachers can, in effect, instruct students in reading skills without having to work individually with each student. We can also diagnose specific reading comprehension problems by noting the types of questions that students find difficult to answer correctly. Furthermore, such guides can provide reading instruction before students are asked to use the data being studied in the appropriate step of inquiry. This procedure helps ground students firmly in the content presented, thus facilitating learning of this content and of knowledge derived from its use.

Follow-up Instruction

Teachers can also provide instruction in reading comprehension and thus help students further develop their thinking skills by conducting a follow-up discussion or activity. For example, students can compare their answers to reading guide questions with those of a partner. In this case, each pair of students would come up with a single set of answers upon which they agree. (Of course, as in completing the guide, students should have constant access to the source material being used [in this case the list of laws] so that they can use the content they are presumably learning rather than try to recall it from memory. For, if students were to fill out a reading guide without access to the material and erred, we would wonder whether they have faulty memories or poor reading skills.) Groups of pairs then can repeat this activity. Finally, the entire class can engage in a discussion of those questions that caused disagreement. The teacher can also use open-ended questions like items 4, 8, and 10 as entries for probing student knowledge of the data studied and as springboards to return the learning activity to the next step in the inquiry strategy being used.

At this point it is crucial for the teacher and students to discuss *how* they arrived at their answers as well as the nature of the answers themselves. By so doing the teacher can make the students conscious of the skills being taught. And the students can discuss the rules they have devised or discovered for answering each type of question, thus engaging in a form of self-teaching of these skills.

By using some or all of the procedures suggested here, teachers can provide systematic instruction in reading throughout a course without detracting from the flow of the content or the sequence of steps in the inquiry teaching strategy. In fact, by so doing, reading instruction becomes purposeful and meaningful because it enables students to handle the data they need to proceed to the next step in inquiring—and thus students view this instruction as a most helpful activity rather than as a meaningless task. Such instruction furthermore facilitates student development of thinking skills such as translation, interpretation, and application—an important goal of inquiry teaching, as well as of social studies instruction in general.

WRITING AND INQUIRY TEACHING

Instruction in writing, while not a common goal of many social studies classrooms, offers considerable potential for facilitating student learning of content, development of knowledge, and refinement of thinking skills. Furthermore, instruction in writing can both use and reinforce student inquiry. As noted earlier in this chapter, writing elicits, and indeed is, thinking. Moreover, one learns as one writes. In the process of writing, writers gain insights into a subject that they did not have when they started writing.[9] Teachers can thus use student writing as a tool of student learning and thinking, as well as a device for facilitating inquiry teaching and learning.

Yet writing poses several significant challenges for students and teachers alike. In addition to the problem of producing grammatically acceptable, correctly spelled, and accurately punctuated prose, students seem to encounter two major problems: (1) generating ideas and information to write about and (2) organizing their ideas in a meaningful fashion. Teachers, on the other hand, encounter problems in managing the evaluation and feedback responsibilities occasioned by giving frequent writing assignments to the large numbers of students they teach daily. Fortunately, however, the use of inquiry teaching strategies provides solutions to both sets of problems.

Introducing Writing

As in teaching reading comprehension, instruction in writing may precede the actual writing, may occur simultaneously with that writing, and may also occur as a follow-up to student writing. Prior to extensive student writing, teachers may provide direct instruction in ways to generate and organize ideas in writing by using either of the skill teaching strategies outlined in Chapter 10. As teachers and students focus on improving what they write and how they write it, weaknesses in sentence structure, punctuation, and spelling will gradually disappear. Attention to the following three tasks proves most useful in helping students launch writing assignments.

Generating ideas to write about. One type of assistance that teachers can provide to improve student writing (and thinking) consists of teaching students how to generate ideas about which to write and how to find data useful in supporting these ideas. Writing specialist Linda Flower and psychologist John R. Hayes have identified a number of such techniques.[10] For example, students can brainstorm and list as rapidly as possible everything they associate with a topic or assertion about which they are to write; they can brainstorm from memory or by skimming their notes, texts, or other sources such as dictionaries or a thesaurus. Then students can pull additional ideas or data out of each item. They can, in effect, brainstorm implications and the synonyms or opposites of key words generated in the first brainstorming round. They can also brainstorm possible causes and consequences of selected items on their lists. After classifying the resulting collection of data, students can invent generalizations to provide direction and substance for their writing. When brainstorming does not prove as productive as desired, students can anticipate questions their readers might ask or objections that may be thrown up by those who oppose the position they wish to take; they can use the results as data for their writing.

To illustrate this brainstorming procedure, suppose you assign students to write to this assertion: "Slavery was the most important cause of the Civil War." Focusing on the words *slavery, cause,* and *Civil War* students might brainstorm the following list of words:

roots	factories	*Uncle Tom's Cabin*
economics	cotton cloth	sectional differences
plantation	cotton gin	petitions
slave codes	abolitionists	speeches
economic system	underground railroad	

Next, students can refer to the above words and phrases and think about the things they associate with each word, as for example:

economics: employment
cheap labor
cotton picking
tariffs
cotton for factories

abolitionists: underground railroad
back to Africa
emancipation
moralistic
William Lloyd Garrison
The Liberator

Students can also think of causes and or consequences of each key word in terms of *slavery* and the *Civil War:*

economics: would have to pay more for
labor if no slaves
what to do with slaves if
freed?
slave revolts—Nat Turner
John Brown's raid
fighting in new territories

abolitionists: idealists
desire for political power
violence
breaking laws
Dred Scott decision

Similar ideas and data can be generated from any of the words or phrases initially brainstormed by thinking of motives, implications, synonyms, and so on.

At an appropriate point students may then classify the items generated into categories they devise. For example, some of the items listed here might be classified as follows:

Opposition to Slavery

Peaceful	*Subversive*	*Violent*
petitions	underground railroad	John Brown's Raid
elections	back-to-Africa movement	fighting in new
books—*U.T.C.*		territories
The Liberator		slave revolts
abolition speeches		

Students can also invent additional categories to accommodate the other data listed above, as well as new ideas or data generated as the classifying proceeds. In doing this, they will begin to articulate ideas inferred from their manipulation of the data about slavery as a cause of the Civil War. These ideas may then be stated as assertions:

- Because Northern abolitionists threatened to take away the South's much needed source of cheap labor, sectional division resulted.
- Opposition to slavery began in the form of peaceful protest and education and grew to more active, eventually violent, efforts to end slavery.

Such statements may also serve as the basis for making even more general inferences to use in turn as organizing ideas for an assigned essay or paragraph. This technique is far more than an exercise in memory, for it involves using a number of higher level thinking skills as the process of writing gets under way.

Structuring writing. Secondly, we can teach students various ways to organize their ideas and information in writing. Attention to structuring writing should begin with the paragraph, the smallest unit of writing that expresses and supports an idea complete in itself. Paragraphs are the building blocks of larger pieces of writing.

Probably the most useful device for teaching intermediate grade students to organize paragraphs, or for helping older students improve on this skill, is what has been called the *hamburger paragraph*. As indicated in Figure 11.1, a well organized paragraph resembles a hamburger. Whereas the hamburger has a top and bottom roll enclosing a piece of meat, a paragraph has a topic sentence and a concluding sentence enclosing something substantial, generally facts and evidence supporting these facts. Just as the top roll introduces a hamburger, the topic sentence introduces or states the main idea of the paragraph; and as the bottom roll helps to hold the hamburger together, the concluding sentence ties up the paragraph by explaining the significance of the main idea in terms of the information provided in the "meat" of the paragraph. And whereas we often embellish the meat of a hamburger with onions, ketchup, pickles, mustard, or other condiments to make it more palatable, so too do we add to the basic facts that constitute the "meat" of a paragraph—explanatory statements, examples, and statements explicitly relating these assertions to the main idea of the paragraph itself.

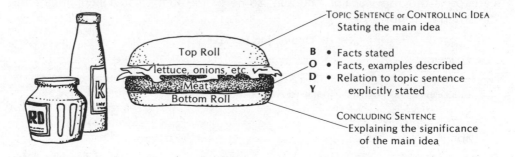

Figure 11.1. A Hamburger Paragraph

By explaining this concrete analogy to students and illustrating it on the chalkboard before they write, and by using it repeatedly as a guide in writing and evaluating paragraphs, and even using the term when making assignments—"Write a hamburger paragraph to explain or criticize this statement . . . "—we can help students learn how to better organize their writing.

Of course, an essay can be viewed as nothing more than an extended paragraph just as a hamburger enlarged may become a *Big Mac®* or some similar item. In effect, an essay may become a giant hamburger enclosing a "tower" of related hamburgers in which the bottom roll of each serves as a transition to the next. The entire creation can be extended into a maxiburger—or paper—of heroic proportions!

Obviously, this format for organizing a paragraph or essay is rather unsophisticated. Many types of paragraphs or essays exist that would not adapt to this model without modification. However, because of the power and simplicity of the hamburger image, it serves as a most useful beginning, especially for upper elementary school students or even older students experiencing difficulty with writing paragraphs. Once students have mastered this form, they can learn more sophisticated and more powerful ways to structure paragraphs and essays.

Inquiry itself also offers a useful format for structuring a paragraph or essay. As illustrated in Figure 11.2, the topic sentence of the hamburger essay may be considered a tentative assertion about a subject or, in effect, a hypothesis. The body of the paragraph then presents evidence to support or refute this hypothesis; it presents information, illustrative examples, and explanations or arguments carefully sequenced to speak about the hypothesis. Finally, the conclusion presents a new synthesis and states the significance of this synthesis as either a modification of the original hypothesized assertion or as a completely new idea generated by the evidence and line of reasoning presented in the body of the writing.[11] Such a format can be used to organize a single paragraph or an extended essay or research paper.

A Hamburger Paragraph	An Inquiry Paragraph
TOPIC SENTENCE	HYPOTHESIS
Stating the main idea	A sentence making a tentative claim about a subject
BODY	EVIDENCE
Facts stated Examples described Explicitly related to the topic sentence	Data, explained and illustrated elaborating, supporting and/or refuting the hypothesis — and Data anticipating criticisms of the hypothesis, Arranged in sequence leading to a conclusion — Explicitly relating arguments to the hypothesis
CONCLUDING SENTENCE	CONCLUSION
Explaining the significance of the main idea in terms of the evidence and arguments presented.	A new systhesis incorporating the evidence and argument with a revised hypothesis (if needed) and A statement of the significance of the conclusion.

Figure 11.2. Alternative Paragraph Stuctures

Using inquiry as a model for writing offers several advantages over the hamburger model. The hamburger analogy describes writing essentially in terms of the structure of the finished product. If anything, it provides a sort of target towards which students can move as they write. The inquiry model of writing, however, describes both a product and a process of writing. Use of this analogy with students thus allows the teacher to provide guidance in writing while the student writes rather than waiting until a product has emerged for evaluation.

Writing to an audience. Students need to be as much aware of the audience to whom they write as of what they wish to write about. In fact, attention to the interests, concerns, and knowledge of an intended audience can help immeasurably in communicating clearly what the student wishes to say. Attention to this third point will be most useful in improving student writing.

Writing specialists claim that students should write to specific readers with unique concerns or to generalized audiences with certain common traits.[12] In writing to the former type of audience, the student must provide new information that the audience does not know and use examples relevant to what that audience can be expected to know. In writing to the latter type of audience, students may assume that its members generally know the same information that the students know and that they have the same experiential background as the students do.

In both instances, however, students must realize that what their audiences don't know is how the information chosen relates to the main idea or point intended. As a result, students must continuously explain this relationship and anticipate their readers' desire to know the significance of what they write. Moreover, student writers should also know that their audience is probably impatient; it wants to know quickly what the gist of the writer's main idea is and whether it is worth reading about at all. Therefore, student writers must state clearly at least the essential point they propose to make and tell why it is significant. If students learn to take an imagined audience into account, their paragraphs or essays will more likely reflect the characteristics of well-structured writing outlined in Figure 11.2 because they will not only provide information but also clearly state a main idea, tell why it is significant, provide relevant information, and show explicitly how this information relates to their main idea.

Teachers can instruct students in the techniques and models presented here in a variety of ways prior to making writing assignments. For instance, a teacher can lead a class through these techniques as the students verbally prepare a paragraph for the teacher or volunteers to write on the chalkboard. Students working in groups or pairs can then practice these techniques as they write paragraphs on their own as part of specific, teacher-given assignments. Helping students to generate ideas to write about, to plan structured writing, and to write to a specific audience leads to vastly improved student writing—all while dealing with content and data.

Guiding the Process of Writing

We can also provide instruction in writing as students actually write, both implicitly through the nature of the writing assignment itself and explicitly through the procedure and context used to carry out the assignment.

Organizing writing assignments. The directions a teacher gives for a written assignment shape the product that results from that assignment more than most of us realize. Well-organized student writing can be developed by clear, well organized writing assignments. In giving writing assignments, teachers should follow at least five guidelines:

1. Specify exactly what is meant by the key action words used in the assignment so that students know what is required by the verb that directs the assignment. *Tell* or *mention* may mean a mere listing of items. *Explain* or *describe*, on the other hand, may require detailed descriptions, definitions, examples, and explicit statements relating these examples to a major organizing idea or topic. If students know in advance what such words require, their writing will more likely reflect these requirements.

2. Specify the number of points, major facts, or ideas to be presented in an assignment. "Explain two causes of the Civil War" leads to better writing than does, "Tell about what caused the Civil War." Specific directions set the parameters for student writing, help students budget their time, and indicate the extent to which the teacher requires "coverage" or in-depth analysis.

3. Give students a purpose for writing. Rather than always describing (in effect repeating or reporting), have students write to persuade or convince someone of the truth or falsity or importance of something or to stimulate some specific action on the part of their readers. Students can also write to solve specific problems rather than merely describe the problems themselves. Purposeful writing, just as purposeful reading, produces the best learning.

4. Have students write to assertions rather than to topics or subjects. An *assertion* is a sentence that says something significant about a topic. In writing to a topic, a student must invent a direction or point to make of his or her own. However, an assertion implies a sense of direction or purpose of its own; in writing to an assertion, a student must only prove or disprove, illustrate or explain the extent to which the claim made in the assertion is accurate or inaccurate. The assertion, "Slavery was the excuse—but not the cause—for the Civil War" is much easier to write to than the topics, "Slavery and the Civil War" or, "Causes of the Civil War." Writing to convince someone of the accuracy (or inaccuracy) or an assertion provides one way to give students a purpose for writing and thus to enhance the quality of their thinking and writing.

5. Use—and make known to students—precise systems for evaluating student writing. For example, one could declare that, for every five points in an essay, a student must state and explain a major idea, present at least one appropriately explained example, and provide a clear, step-by-step explanation of how this idea is directly related to the organizing idea of the entire paragraph or essay. Students can then use this scoring system to guide their writing as well as to evaluate it after they have completed it.

Writing assignments made in line with these guidelines not only help students organize their writing in well-structured fashion but also produce writing that is substantively richer than the "buckshot essays" ("If you write enough you're bound to say something significant") that result from vague, imprecise assignments. Clear directions actually provide guidelines and instruction in writing and produce better quality writing than do vague directions.

Writing while learning. Professor A.D. Van Nostrand and his colleagues at Brown University have devised an approach to teaching writing that provides instruction in generating and structuring writing while students actually engage in the writing process.[13] In adapting this approach to social studies teaching, students can (1) start with a topic or subject; (2) collect information about it from texts, notes, photographs, or any other media; (3) infer a general relationship among the pieces of information thus collected; and (4) use this inference as an organizing idea for a paragraph or essay. Here they can present a carefully reasoned sequence of information relevant to this organizing idea, always explaining how the information used is related to this idea (perhaps in causal, sequential, chronological, spatial, or some other way). Students can then conclude their paragraphs by stating the hypothesis or organizing idea in a form more fully developed or modified as a result of what they have presented or learned in the process of writing the paragraph. An activity built on this approach for use with the photographs of old Kiev used in the Prologue might proceed as in the following Writing Guide. This guide refers to the photographs of artifacts on page 3–4 in the Prologue.

The Writing Guide on pages 257–258 includes both directions to the students telling what they should do (right-hand column) and explanations of the reasons for completing each step as directed (left-hand column). Although this particular guide is designed to use with the study of old Kiev presented in the Prologue, the format of the guide may be adapted to use with any content and, in simplified form, to use with students at any secondary school level. This approach to writing has two assets: it helps students generate their own ideas to write about using the content of the course, and it helps them organize their writing. This activity also calls for considerable thinking. By using the technique, subject matter learning and skill development can proceed simultaneously in the social studies classroom.

Integrating writing with inquiry. Writing guides such as the one presented on pages 257–258 can be used in a number of places in inquiry teaching not only to provide instruction in writing but also to carry forward various steps in inquiry teaching. Such an activity may help students generate hypotheses, find new data about a topic, or evaluate specific hypotheses representing a variety of points of view. For example, students can use a writing guide such as this one to write about a topic before they study it in detail; they then can use their paragraph as a hypothesis to submit to the test of data presented on the subject through their text, a lecture, or a film. Students can also use this approach to write a paragraph in the middle of a unit in order to generate new insights into a specific topic that comprises a portion of the unit being studied. Students can even write about a given topic from different points of view and thus generate multiple generalizations about that topic. Finally, students can use an initial assertion (Step 3 in the Writing Guide) as a search tool to uncover additional data as they study. This approach to writing can be used to launch a series of inquiry

WRITING GUIDE

PURPOSES:

DIRECTIONS:

GIVEN A
TOPIC

STEP 1: *Subject:* Life In This Place Around 1,000 Years Ago

COLLECT
RELEVANT
DATA

STEP 2: List below 5–6 ideas or pieces of information about what life was probably like in this place 1,000 years ago. Use the items in the photographs to get your ideas or information. You do not have to write these as sentences. Just jot down the ideas or bits of information that you select as you look at the pictures. Two sample items are already listed to help you start your list:

— *had military activity and weapons*

— *coins had faces of people*

—

—

—

—

—

—

FIND OR MAKE
A TENTATIVE
RELATIONSHIP AMONG
THE ABOVE DATA

STEP 3: Now, write a sentence that explains one way in which all (or almost all) of the above ideas and information seem to be connected or related to each other. Your sentence should not list the above items. Instead, it should be a new sentence that summarizes how you think the above data relate to each other:

USE YOUR
SENTENCE AS AN
IDEA AROUND
WHICH TO ORGANIZE
A PARAGRAPH

STEP 4: The sentence you have just written may serve as an idea about which to write a paragraph. This paragraph should state and explain or prove this idea. Write a paragraph that uses this sentence as an organizing idea. Use at least four pieces of information or ideas from the above list to explain, illustrate, or prove your organizing idea. Be sure to connect each piece of information to your organizing idea:

PRESENT, AND
EXPLAIN DATA
RELATING TO YOUR
IDEA AND TELL
HOW IT IS RELATED

WRITE YOUR
CONCLUSION—
A REVISED FORM
OF THE MAIN
IDEA OF THIS
PARAGRAPH AS
YOU SEE IT NOW

STEP 5: Finally, write a sentence that summarizes the main idea of this paragraph as you see it now. This sentence should *not* repeat the sentence you wrote in Step 3. It should instead extend that sentence to reflect why you have learned as you wrote the paragraph.

lessons, to generate new insights in the middle of a series of lessons, or to conclude an inquiry study. Thus, instruction in writing and inquiry teaching can go hand-in-hand to provide instruction in thinking as well as in content learning.

Follow-up Instruction and Feedback

Instruction in writing should not cease with student completion of a paragraph or essay. Rather, instruction can continue in follow-up discussion and revision of student writing using techniques similar to those described in the preceding pages for teaching thinking and reading comprehension. Much of this follow-up can be peer-centered and student-generated. Students can be given opportunities to review, evaluate, discuss, reflect on, and revise their own and their peers' paragraphs, essays, and papers. Such follow-up relieves the teacher of the necessity for reading and annotating every piece of writing assigned, although it does not relieve the teacher of the responsibility for providing appropriate instructional guidelines for such student-generated feedback. Some of these guidelines can, in fact, be built into the very writing procedure used by the students.

Student-centered feedback. The research of Professor Daniel Fader at the University of Michigan and of other writing specialists suggests that frequent practice with attention and immediate feedback by peers may eliminate the need for constant teacher feedback and still provide the instruction requisite for improved writing. Students can be paired or grouped in triads to jointly write a single paragraph or essay. Members of a group can then exchange or read aloud to each other their contributions; they then review the writings, suggest changes, and rewrite them in view of peer comments. [14] Taking another approach, students can work independently or in partnerships using self-instructional activities monitored by peers who are further along in the course or who have already successfully completed the course. [15] In either of these approaches, students can check not only for accuracy and completeness of substance but also for structure and style. By following such procedures, demands on teacher time will not appreciably increase and students can still secure the feedback necessary to improve writing.

To facilitate student-centered follow-up, a teacher can provide students with feedback guides tailored to each specific assignment or general enough to be relevant to most writing assignments for a given course. Such guides might consist of questions that focus student attention on the essential features that have been the object of instruction. For example, the Paragraph Evaluation Guide on page 261 may be useful in guiding student evaluation of a "hamburger" paragraph. With slight alterations, this guide can also be used to evaluate a short essay as well.

In using a paragraph evaluation guide, a student first summarizes his or her own paragraph (retaining this summary for use later) and then trades paragraphs with an assigned or self-selected partner. Next, each student reads the other's paragraph completing the items required on the guide. Then students discuss their evaluations with their partners, reviewing one paragraph at a time. Here they first compare their summaries—the evaluator's perception of the paragraph's main idea with the author's summary of what he or she intended the paragraph to say. Where there are significant differences, the evaluator can propose changes that might communicate more clearly the point intended by the author. These changes can be identified by reviewing the evaluator's comments to item 2, b–f on the paragraph guide and by a careful explanation of the reasons he or she has for any suggested improvements or changes. After reviewing one paragraph, the students can reverse roles and evaluate the second paragraph in similar fashion. To conclude this learning activity, students can (1) discuss as a class ways to resolve any common writing problems: (2) list two or three suggestions made by their evaluators that they think would lead to better writing; and (3) rewrite their paragraphs to incorporate suggested changes and/or review as a class the substance of the paragraphs, noting especially corrections for any substantive errors. This type of review of a writing assignment can thus move substantive learning forward as well as provide additional instruction in writing.

Evaluation guides such as the one illustrated on page 261 may be used with papers and essays as well as with paragraphs. And they may consist of a wide variety of questions or tasks. For more advanced students, the following list of questions may form the nucleus of a writing feedback guide:

1. What is the topic sentence of this paragraph?

2. What evidence, facts, or arguments does the author give to support the topic sentence? List these here:

3. Does the order in which this evidence or argument is presented lead to the conclusion or not? If the sentences should be rearranged, do so by numbering the sentences in the order you suggest. Be prepared to explain the reasons for this new sequence to the author.

4. Does the author tell the significance of her or his main point? Is the conclusion a more fully developed statement of the main idea?

5. In your opinion, what is the best way to state the main idea the author is trying to make? Write a sentence stating this idea here:

Teachers who wish to stress the relationship between inquiry and the structure of a paragraph or of an essay can provide students with a writing evaluation guide, similar to the preceding, that underscores this relationship by asking,

1. What is the hypothesis (organizing idea) of this paragraph?

2. To what extent does the author prove or support his/her hypothesis?

    a. What evidence does the author give to prove or support the hypothesis?

    b. Does the author explain how each piece of evidence given connects to the hypothesis? Check where this could be done better.

3. What is the author's conclusion? In what way does this conclusion differ from the author's original hypothesis (organizing idea)?

PARAGRAPH EVALUATION GUIDE

Author_____   Date_____

Reader_____

1. On a separate sheet of paper write a one-sentence summary of your paragraph. What is the main idea you are trying to get across? (Keep this summary for use later.)

2. Now, exchange paragraphs with another student and complete or answer the following:

   a. Write a one-sentence summary of his/her paragraph here (What seems to be the author's main point?):

   b. Does his/her paragraph have a topic sentence? Write it here:

   c. List below the evidence or reasons he/she gives to support the topic sentence:

   d. Put a check by any piece of evidence that is not clearly linked to the main idea.

   e. In what ways does the content of the concluding sentence differ from that of the topic sentence?

   f. List any errors you find in the information included in this paragraph:

   g. Circle any words that are spelled incorrectly or any incorrect punctuation. Help the author correct these errors.

   h. List one suggestion for improving this paragraph:

Other useful writing checklists may be easily devised. To use any such checklist, students may exchange papers, read each other's papers carefully answering the questions on the guide, and then meet together to make comments, offer suggestions, and point out problems or errors. Common problems can then be discussed by the entire class, and students can rewrite their assignments to correct their errors or build on these assignments with particular attention to remedying in revised papers the type of errors noted earlier. Thus writing, as reading, can be integrated with oral communication—for both are expressions of "inner speech"—and discussion can complement the skills of reading and writing.

Additional feedback guides. Finally, students can use other techniques to generate instructional feedback. They can, for instance, use a point system to identify weaknesses or strengths in student paragraphs or essays. To develop such a system, a teacher might assign a paragraph a specific number of points. For example, if we decide to use a 10 point scale for each paragraph, we might distribute the points in this fashion:

1 point for the topic sentence or major assertion

3 points for a supporting fact or argument, as follows:

  1 point for stating the fact or argument

  1 point for a relevant example

  1 point for explicitly relating the fact or argument to the topic sentence or assertion

3 points for a second fact or argument (as above)

1 point for a concluding statement that explains the significance of the main idea or assertion

2 points distributed (as desired) for accuracy of content or specific grammatical errors (such as spelling or punctuation or noun/verb agreement or similar aspects of writing), or for appropriateness of content examples, etc.

A point system of this sort reinforces the "hamburger paragraph" structure described earlier in this chapter. Thus, in using it students reinforce their conceptualization of an appropriate structure for paragraphs. Of course, this distribution of points is entirely arbitrary and based on certain assumptions that all teachers might not share. Other point systems may work just as well. The major advantage of this system is not to be underestimated, however: use of a point system that reinforces the writing structure being taught not only enables students to evaluate peer writing as objectively as possible but it also provides a useful guide for them as they engage in their own writing.

Students can also outline a partner's writing to provide instructive feedback. This involves (1) listing the main idea, (2) listing the steps in the argument given to support this idea, or (3) listing the evidence given in support of the idea, and (4) indicating how the evidence relates to the main idea. Such a procedure helps students identify important omissions in a piece of writing as well as to identify substantive errors. By using these or other techniques, a teacher can engage students in providing useful instructional feedback to one another while they discuss content at the same time. Teachers may also wish to collect student papers and their revisions for purposes of spot-checking or other diagnosis (but not for grading). Instruction can then be provided appropriate to the problems or weaknesses exhibited in the student writing. But it is not necessary for a teacher to examine closely or grade every paper or writing sample if some of these other procedures are used.

MANAGING INSTRUCTION
IN BASIC SKILLS
THROUGH INQUIRY TEACHING

Instruction in reading comprehension, writing, and thinking simultaneously with the study of a given body of content can be conducted effectively without added burden through the use of a strategy of inquiry teaching. Systematic instruction in each of these skills can be provided as the skills are needed to accomplish other substantive or procedural goals; such instruction gives purpose to skill learning, enhances motivation[16], and improves subject matter learning.[17] This instruction can thus facilitate student inquiry and at the same time serve as an integral part of an inquiry teaching strategy.

However, emphasis on skill teaching often appears to require considerable time, a commodity in short supply for the teacher who teaches approximately 150 students daily. While attention to skills does take time, finding this time is not as impossible as it may appear at first sight. In fact, the amount of time required is not nearly as much as one might suspect.

Because of already overcrowded social studies curricula, most teachers have problems in finding additional time to teach reading and writing while also seeking to accomplish more conventional social studies goals. But reallocating time already devoted to social studies teaching for teaching these basic skills *is* possible, and therein lies at least a partial solution to the time problem. We can make time for systematic student instruction in reading comprehension and writing during social studies classes in at least three ways.

First, we can make writing and reading do double duty in our courses by using them in place of some of the verbal activities we already use. Students can read instead of listening to lectures or oral reports by other students. Instead of reporting orally or discussing, students can write anytime they must process information or communicate ideas or information to others. And whatever they read or write can serve as a springboard for further study rather than merely as an end in itself.

For example, we might use the brainstorming or inferencing procedures presented in this chapter to introduce a social studies unit. Students can thus write about a topic *before* they read or study it in detail. To do this they can skim the unit in our text(s)—an important skill in developing reading comprehension—and list (in effect, brainstorm) some bits of information about the unit topic. Then they can write a paragraph explaining an assertion they have invented from the data they collected. Their concluding or summarizing statements can thus serve as hypotheses to test against detailed reading of the text assignment; collecting information that supports and/or refutes their hypotheses will provide a student-defined purpose for reading. (Reading specialists repeatedly tell us that purposeful reading is the most efficient reading.)

To continue such an integrated effort, students can next revise their hypotheses in light of the data they find in their texts and then use their modified hypotheses as organizing ideas for revised paragraphs. Through group or peer discussion of their findings before revising their writing, they can develop and test new insights about their topic under study. Subsequent group evaluation of the revised paragraphs can clarify these insights even more, as well as provide students additional instruction in writing. In a final class discussion, students can analyze, evaluate, or extend the concepts and generalizations they have invented. Thus, when reading and writing instruction are integrated with content study in an inquiry framework as described here, all components become mutually reinforcing, and little additional time will be needed for each.

A second way to find time in class for instruction in reading and writing involves eliminating some of what we now do in our courses. Rather than continually covering topics, we should perhaps concentrate more on *un*covering; we can take more time on fewer topics and substitute depth for breadth, thus allowing us to engage in skill teaching while we investigate selected content.

Finally, taking a longer view of the time available to us may also "give" us the time that instruction in reading and writing requires. We need to be aware that time spent in teaching these skills in one course may enable other teachers in later courses to concentrate more on substantive learning goals because by then students will have better developed the thinking and communicating skills requisite for more sophisticated learning. Thus, attention to the articulation of skill and content teaching across social studies courses can help us reallocate time in some courses for additional attention to reading and writing.

Cooperative action among teachers can also enable us to make maximum use of our time to prepare materials for skill teaching. Obviously no single teacher can prepare all the reading, writing, and thinking guides (at least in the formats suggested here) needed for all their courses over the period of a year. But teachers of the same course working in groups can prepare such guides over the course of several years or, if fortunate, in summer workshops. One teacher in the group—or a pair of teachers—can design a sequence of several reading guides (perhaps for every fourth chapter); another teacher or pair of teachers can design a sequence of writing guides for every third chapter; another team may design a sequence of guides for specific thinking skills for intervening chapters. By trading their guides, trying them out, and revising and adding to them—using the principles presented here and in other sources on these topics—teachers can build a reading, writing, and thinking skill program that is sequential within a course or perhaps throughout a curriculum. These guides should be included in every social studies and history curriculum.

We need to note five other points regarding skill teaching. First, skill activities need not be long. We too often confuse quantity with quality. In the case of writing, for example, short but frequent supervised practice proves most effective. Therefore, frequent (bi-weekly) writing and rewriting of paragraphs and one or two page essays will provide sufficient opportunities for practice and instruction as students use their writing to move through their study of content. Long research papers seem most dysfunctional as traditionally assigned. But such papers can be very useful learning devices if introduced at the beginning of a course as a short 3-5 page paper, revised and rewritten to different specifications and lengths as the course progresses. By developing a short research paper as a series of drafts on a continuing basis, students will receive systematic instruction in writing as well as training in research. Such instruction can be a continuing effort rather than the more typical culminating "test" it so frequently is.

Second, instruction in basic skills means precisely that—teaching, not testing. Thus, students must have ready access to the data or content they need to use as they engage in the skill being taught. Reading guides should be filled out as the students read, not after they have completed their reading. As students write, they should have free access to all the data germane to their topic and be encouraged to refer to it freely. Specific skill teaching activities require this same procedure. Skill teaching should not turn into measuring the memory.

Third, frequent instruction and practice means frequent feedback. This takes time. But it does not have to be teacher time, and it most certainly does not have to involve grading. We must be alert to the difference between testing skills and teaching them, as pointed out by Herber. Grades simply do not provide the type of instructive feedback that leads to improvement in reading or writing. But guided feedback via peer group discussion serves this purpose well.

Fourth, follow-up analysis of the skill or process being introduced or practiced is an absolutely crucial step in skill learning. Such analysis may be easily combined with discussion of the content under study so that the development of knowledge and the learning of skills can reinforce each other. What is important in this follow-up is that at some point students give attention to how they arrived at the answer or decisions they have generated, for by so doing they can thus identify the rules that guide the operation of this skill or process. Such follow-up may take a number of forms. Combinations of students or student pairs or triads, for example, might compare answers to teacher questions, resolve any discrepancies by reference to the data they have been using, and then report their findings to the entire class. The class, in turn, can check the findings of each group who, in turn, can report how they arrived at their answers. This provides a focus on the skill being studied. Articulating a set of rules for answering questions offered by the teacher or skill guide can then reinforce the student understanding of the nature of the skill and also provide another round of instruction in this skill. Repetition of activities that use these guidelines provides continued instruction, practice, and reinforcement in the skill, and thus helps move the students toward mastery of the skill.

Finally skill teaching, as described in this and the preceding chapter, offers rich opportunities to develop a multitude of cognitive, affective, and interpersonal objectives, as well as to improve the skills of communication and thinking. Such teaching also offers opportunities for teachers to engage in learning with their students as they provide this instruction. It may prove most enlightening and useful, for example, for a teacher to complete a writing assignment or engage in reading while students do the same, if for no other reason than to demonstrate the value of these processes. Such activity on the part of a teacher also provides one way of indicating that these activities are *not* busy work but important ways to learn and that they form part of the learning process. A teacher who writes the same assignments as the students and puts his or her paper into the class hopper for student evaluation may not only improve his or her writing skills but also get enough of a feel for such an assignment and what it takes to complete it to become more alert to the types of instruction the students need—or perhaps spot flaws in the assignment that call for its revision.

Reading and writing and thinking skill lessons should not be viewed as exercises or as ends in themselves. Instead, instruction and practice in these processes should be a means to an end and openly presented as such. Student reading and writing should be integrated where appropriate in a sequence of learning activities designed to develop knowledge and achieve other affective and cognitive goals as well.

SUMMARY

In order to become proficient in the basic skills and processes of reading comprehension, writing, and thinking, students must have careful instruction, engage in frequent supervised practice, and receive immediate instructive feedback—all in the context of the content in which these skills and processes are to be used. Inquiry teaching provides not only an overall framework wherein such instruction can occur naturally, without interrupting the content flow of a study, but also a highly motivating framework for the teaching and learning of these basic skills.

The basic steps of inquiry can serve as a structure for writing paragraphs and essays just as they serve as one structure for developing reading comprehension. And inquiry teaching itself can be used as a strategy for teaching specific basic skills as students (1) use a skill to answer content questions; (2) hypothesize rules for what they did to find their answers; (3) test these rules by using this skill again to answer other content questions; (4) reflect on, add to, and revise their rules in a follow-up discussion; and (5) continue to apply and revise the skill rules as they have opportunities to employ the skill throughout their course.

Inquiry teaching proves to be an extremely useful strategy for helping students master cognitive skills as well as learn content. By its very nature, this teaching strategy offers an opportunity and framework for teaching thinking skills and the associated processes of reading and writing while students simultaneously learn information and develop higher level conceptual and generalized knowledge. More so than any other teaching strategy, inquiry teaching intertwines skills and content so that each reinforces the other without interrupting the flow of learning.

notes

1. Nila Banton Smith, *Reading Instruction for Today's Children* (Englewood Cliffs: Prentice-Hall, 1963), p. 264.
2. Harold Herber, *Teaching Reading in Content Areas* (Englewood Cliffs: Prentice-Hall, 1970), pp. 62–63.
3. William S. Gray, "The Major Aspects of Reading," in Helen M. Robinson, ed., *Sequential Development of Reading Abilities* (Chicago: University of Chicago Press, 1960), p. 17.
4. James Gray, "The Problem" (unpublished paper, Berkeley: University of California, n.d.), p. 6.
5. Gray, pp. 1–6; Josephine Miles, "The Use of Reason" (unpublished paper, Berkeley: University of California, 1964); Russell G. Stauffer, *Teaching Reading as a Thinking Process* (New York: Harper and Row, 1969); and A.D. Van Nostrand, "English I and the Measurement of Writing," in Ben A. Green, Jr., ed., *Personalized Instruction in Higher Education: Proceedings of the Second National Conference Held by the Center for Personalized Instruction* (Washington: The Center for Personalized Instruction, 1976), pp. 23–27.
6. Melvin Michaels, "Subject Reading Improvement—A Neglected Teaching Responsibility," *Journal of Reading,* IX:2 (October 1965), pp. 16–20.
7. Herber, op. cit.
8. Ibid.
9. James Gray, "The Problem" (unpublished paper, Berkeley: University of California, n.d.), p. 6; A.D. Van Nostrand, *A Functional Writing Model* (Providence: Brown University, 1976); "Functional Writing Course Catching on at College Level," *New York Times,* November 24, 1976.
10. Linda S. Flower and John R. Hayes, "Problem-Solving Strategies and the Writing Process", in *College English,* 39:4 (December 1977), pp. 449–461.
11. Josephine Miles, "The Use of Reason" (unpublished paper, Berkeley: University of California, 1964).
12. Richard E. Young, Alton L. Becker, and Kenneth L. Pike, *Rhetoric: Discovery and Change* (New York: Harcourt, Brace and World, 1970), pp. 171–180, 203–211, 218–225. See also Flower and Hayes, op. cit., pp. 18–20.
13. Van Nostrand, *A Functional Writing Model;* A.D. Van Nostrand et al., *Functional Writing* (Boston: Houghton Mifflin Co., 1978).
14. Daniel Fader, *The New Hooked on Books* (New York: Berkley Publishing Co., 1976), pp. 7–38.
15. Van Nostrand, "English I," op. cit., pp. 23–27.
16. See William Purkey, *Self Concept and School Achievement* (Englewood Cliffs: Prentice-Hall, 1970); James Block, ed., *Mastery Learning: Theory and Practice,* New York: Holt, Rinehart and Winston, 1971), pp. 13–28.
17. See the studies by Fay (1950), Krantz (1957), Sepp (1965), Hilsom (1961), and Schuler (1963) cited in Thomas H. Estes, "Reading in the Social Studies," in James Laffey, ed., *Reading in the Content Areas* (Newark: International Reading Association, 1972); see also Dorothy Leggitt, "Measuring Progress in Reading Skills in 9th Grade Civics," *School Review* 42 (November 1934), pp. 676–687.

12

Values
And
Inquiry Teaching

Inquiry teaching serves affective as well as cognitive learning goals. It can be used to develop personal and societal values, feelings of self-worth, and attitudes and feelings of empathy and tolerance. In fact, the strategy of inquiry teaching described in the preceding pages corresponds closely to the basic instructional strategies of the most significant affective teaching approaches used in social studies classrooms today.

Affective education focuses essentially on values and feelings. Values are those things people prize. Values serve as standards of behavior, as well as criteria for judging and choosing. They are, in effect, abstract ideas—concepts—revealed and expressed through human action and speech. Values underlie and give purpose to human behavior; human behavior, in turn, shapes values.

Educators classify values in a number of ways. Some identify values in terms of their relationship to cultural phenomena—as aesthetic (relating to beauty), ethical (relating to what is right or wrong), logical (relating to truth), and economic (relating to utility). Values may also be viewed as personal, group, or societal; individuals possess personal values, while at the same time they share other values with reference groups and society as a whole. And many times these values differ and come into conflict with each other.

Values can be described in other ways, too. Some values may be described as procedural (critical thinking might be such a value), others may be more behavioral (such as "not speaking until spoken to"), and still others may be substantive (such as thrift and respect for authority, for example).[1] Professor Jack Fraenkel classifies values as either instrumental, as a means to an end (honesty, for instance), or as terminal (the ultimate values held by individuals,[2] such as respect for human dignity). Substantive values have also been viewed as either sacred or secular. Traditional societal ideals (in the United States, ideals of freedom of the press, speech, assembly, and so on) are sacred values. In the United States, values like the Judeo-Christian work ethic and a belief in the future are secular values.[3] Regardless of how one classifies or analyzes values, there can be no doubt that values of many different types play crucial roles in our lives and therefore serve as important educational concerns.

Affective education seeks to facilitate the development of human and societal values through a variety of approaches. Value development or acquisition has two major dimensions: cognitive and feeling. That is, value development first involves the articulation and conceptualization of specific value ideas or concepts. To value something, an individual must have some knowledge of its meaning, its attributes, and its relation to other potential values. Developing a concept of a value is a part of the judgment-making process whereby worth is attached to that concept. In this sense, the process of valuing is essentially a cognitive act.

But valuing also possesses a feeling dimension. Concepts or things take on value to the degree one feels an attachment for them, to the extent one prizes them. This attachment to a value possesses some degree of cognitive commitment and a high degree of feeling.

The affective domain thus embraces dimensions of both cognition and feeling. To effectively facilitate affective learning goals, a teaching strategy must address itself to both aspects of valuing. Inquiry teaching does just this.

INQUIRY TEACHING AND VALUES: THE COGNITIVE DIMENSION

Many different values-education strategies compete for classroom use today. Of all these strategies, however, three seem to receive widespread attention at all grade levels, especially in the social studies classroom. These three strategies are *values clarification, values analysis,* and *moral reasoning.*

Although these strategies often seem to differ considerably from one another they are really more alike than different in the techniques and materials they employ. They share many commonalities in rationale, teaching approach, and learning objectives. All are student centered. They view values as developing from within the individual and they treat values education as essentially helping individuals to articulate and clarify these values and to arrange them in some type of hierarchy as guides to behavior. All attempt to elicit from students value-related statements or behaviors and then to subject these behaviors or responses to student examination by reflection or analysis. All are essentially cognitive, although feeling plays a role in each. The focus of each strategy is on analyzing and understanding what is valued in terms of reasoning, consequences, and individual well-being. All can and do deal, directly or indirectly, explicitly or implicitly, with a variety of values—individual as well as societal, instrumental as well as terminal. Most importantly, each of these strategies is built essentially on the strategy of inquiry teaching presented here. Perhaps the fact that these approaches to affective education share a common inquiry strategy not only reflects but shapes their essential commonality.

Values Clarification and Inquiry Teaching

Today the term *values clarification* seems to encompass at least two different approaches to values education. On the one hand, values clarification refers to a highly cognitive process of articulating, examining, and choosing values, a process proposed some years ago by Professors Louis Raths, Merrill Harmin, and Sidney Simon.[4] At other times, values clarification refers to a highly humanistic, almost intuitive process designed to generate and sustain feelings of self-worth, pride, and serenity, a process popularized in more recent years by Sidney Simon and his colleagues.[5] Raths' approach rather than Simon's more clearly approximates the essential steps of inquiry teaching described here.

Theory and rationale. As originally defined by Raths, Harmin, and Simon, *values clarification* involves becoming aware of what one values, examining the implications of these values, and often ranking selected values in some hierarchy of significance or importance. This approach to values education is based on the assumed rationality of human beings.[6] Proponents of this approach claim that, through repeated examination of one's preferences, beliefs, and attitudes analyzed in terms of alternatives and their consequences and implications, individuals will adopt and affirm a set of values that will enable their future choices to be more reasonable, humane, positive, and just than they otherwise would be.

Raths' cognitive approach to values clarification employs a seven step process.[7] According to this approach, in order for anything to be considered a value, it must be:

1. freely chosen,
2. from alternatives,
3. examined in the light of their consequences; and
4. prized,
5. affirmed,
6. acted upon,
7. over and over again.

These seven criteria not only constitute the process of *valuing,* but serve also as a teaching strategy for clarifying and developing values. By helping students to engage in these operations teachers can help them articulate, examine, and redefine their values—in effect clarify their values—and adopt and internalize selected values in an integrated pattern.

Raths' seven steps of values clarification closely resemble the basic steps in a strategy of inquiry teaching. Using his approach, an individual identifies a *problem* involving the need for some type of value decision or choice and then hypothesizes *alternatives*. The alternatives are then *tested* against information about their possible consequences and other implications and a choice is made and affirmed—a *conclusion* is reached. Finally, the choice can be *applied* (though in classroom practice it seldom is) through some type of affirming action to future situations involving a variety of competing values. As this action occurs again and again, the value in question moves around in relationship to other values until it is fitted into a position that an individual finds in acceptable relationship to other values he or she holds. Thus, by confronting repeated choice situations involving particular values, an individual can enlarge or revise his or her understanding of a value, modify its position relative to other values held, and, indeed, endow it with worth. Or at least, this is what the values clarification rationale affirms.

In using this process, students articulate, share, and discuss in an informal, nonthreatening classroom atmosphere their attitudes, beliefs, preferences, and other indicators of their values. Sometimes they do this individually, in small groups, or as an entire class, but generally any values clarification activity involves some combination of these techniques. In so doing, students participate only when they choose to and, while they may be questioned, they are never (supposed to be) put into a confrontation situation where they are required to defend a position or attack another's position. The teacher plays an unobtrusive role, guiding students generally through a series of verbal activities, encouraging volunteers to share ideas, responding occasionally with clarifying questions designed to make students evaluate or reflect on their remarks, and providing opportunities for students to express and reflect on various value positions they might have.

As in inquiry teaching, the key to successful use of this values clarification strategy consists of helping students become aware of and confront any gaps between what they claim or would like to believe and the way they actually behave. Once such an awareness has been created, the students' natural desire to close the gap provides intrinsic motivation to pursue the thinking process through to a conclusion or choice and to apply the choice in later situations. According to Raths, as students repeatedly engage in this process, they become more positive, purposeful, consistent, and enthusiastic in their behavior.[8] As a result, we should expect them to develop an integrated value system that enables them to make a wider variety of value choices and resolve a wider variety of value issues or dilemmas with more positive results than they otherwise might. This is the ultimate goal of this approach to values clarification.

Teaching techniques. Many techniques and activities have been devised to help teachers implement the process of valuing described by Raths.[9] For example, students may create a Pie of Life by listing the activities they engage in during a typical day, determining the amount of time spent in each, and dividing a circle to indicate these events in proportion to the time devoted to each. They thus produce a pie graph to visually describe the way they distribute their time in a given day or other period of time. Then students can write out or state orally something they learned in examining the "pie," decide on something they might like to change (to get more leisure time, perhaps, or to budget their time "better"), and make a contract with themselves to carry out this intention.

Other values clarification techniques include making and reflecting on a personal Coat of Arms, Rank-Ordering given data and explaining the ranking, and listing and sharing statements that describe what students are able to do, believe in, or hope for. Newspaper articles also prove to be most useful launching pads for values clarification, as illustrated by the Value Sheet on page 273.[10]

This guide presents students with a story about one type of value-laden behavior. A series of questions then guides them toward taking a position, reflecting on their position, and noticing possible inconsistencies between their beliefs and actions. Similar value discussion sheets may be built around poems, short stories, quotations, cartoons, and items of similar nature that present value-laden issues or incidents. Proponents of the values clarification approach to affective education have devised scores of other imaginative techniques useful in helping students clarify what they consider important to them.[11]

These techniques and materials are not ends in themselves, however, in spite of the fact they are often treated as such by many teachers. Overemphasis on these techniques, especially in isolation from one another, often obscures the basic valuing process they are designed to facilitate. Use of any one of these techniques in isolation of the others rarely carries an individual through all seven steps of values clarification. Different techniques need to be used to focus on the choosing steps, the affirming and prizing steps, and application. For instance, the Values Voting technique (raising hands to indicate a position in a series of questions) gives students an opportunity to choose freely from alternatives and to affirm their choices publicly, but it must be coupled with other techniques to carry the valuing strategy to its final step.

The strategy of Twenty Things I Like to Do by itself carries a person through only part of the valuing process, but in combination with the Contract technique, the entire process can be completed. An outline of this process illustrates the relationship between values clarification techniques, the process of values clarification, and the process of inquiry teaching: [12]

TECHNIQUE	VALUING PROCESS	AN INQUIRY STRATEGY
1. Listing 20 Things I Like To Do	• *Choosing Freely*	
2. Coding these items in terms of consequences, costs, time required, and so on.	• *from alternatives* • *examined in the light of their consequences*	*Problem* *Hypothesis* *Test*
3. Ranking the items in terms of preference		
4. Reporting or discussing one of the top ranked items	• *Affirming and* • *Prizing*	*Conclude*
5. Making a contract to, in a specified period, engage in one or more top ranked but seldom engaged-in actions	• *Acting* • *Repeatedly*	*Apply*

Values clarification and inquiry. Values clarification relates to inquiry teaching in three additional ways. First, values clarification techniques can be used to introduce and motivate inquiry investigations into social studies content. Many of the techniques like the Pie of Life, or Twenty Things I Like to Do, or the Values Voting technique can be used to launch the study of a history or social

---

VALUE SHEET

Illegal Behavior

DIRECTIONS: Write out answers to the questions below. Later, you will have a chance to discuss your answers with a small group of students. You need not reveal your answers to anyone if you choose not to do so.

New Rochelle, N.Y., Oct. 27—When the red light turns to green and reads "Thank you" at any one of the automatic toll booths of the New England Thruway here, it does not always mean what it says. At least not if the motorist has short-changed the machine or dropped lead washers or foreign coins into it.

The state police reported today after a two-week campaign against toll cheaters that they had arrested 151 persons. They have been fined in City Court from $25 each for first offenders to $250 for multiple offenders.

Lieut. Thomas F. Darby reported that the offenders included a clergyman, a doctor, a dentist, an atomic scientist, lawyers and quite a number of engineers, advertising men and salesmen.

What the offenders did not know, the lieutenant said, was that new toll-booth glass with one-way vision prevented them from seeing watchful troopers inside.

Neither did they know, the lieutenant continued, that the license plate of each offender was recorded, along with the objects he dropped into the machine.*

* * * * * * *

1. Under what circumstances would you try to pass a toll machine without properly paying the fee? Check the most applicable reply below.

_____Only if I was certain that I would not be caught.
_____If I felt I had a good chance of not getting caught.
_____Never, under any circumstances.
_____Only if I needed the money desperately, like for family food supplies.
_____(Write any other choice that better suits you.)

2. Among the 151 persons arrested, there was only one clergyman, doctor, dentist, and atomic scientist. On the other hand, there were several lawyers, engineers, advertising men, and salesmen. Do you think this means that persons in the first group of occupations are more honest than those in the second group? Discuss.

3. Do you think this behavior is serious? Do you think these persons are likely to be dishonest in other ways that would be more serious? Discuss.

4. Return to Question 1 and put an X by the reply that you would make to this: Under what circumstances would you keep a dime that was returned in error in a phone booth?

5. How do you account for any differences in your answers to Questions 1 and 4, if any?

6. Are you clear about how you feel about illegal behavior? Discuss.

---

* © 1961 by The New York Times Company. Reprinted by permission.

studies topic. In a study of life in the middle ages or of life in a particular culture or country, for instance, students can complete a Twenty Things I Like to Do activity and then use their lists as hypotheses to see to what extent some of their preferences might resemble those of people in the area or culture being studied. Or, students could list items they could not live without, rank order them, and then study the lives of people from other areas or cultures to prepare similar lists for them, and to compare the two lists in order to infer the values, resources, and other attributes of that culture. Using the technique of completing unfinished questions about a topic to be studied ("In this society, I wonder why . . . " or, "In this society, I would expect . . . ") can also help students generate their own questions to guide their study of a topic.

Values clarification techniques can also be used in the context of a substantive unit to generate data or at the end of a unit to summarize or pull together the substance of what the students have been studying. At the conclusion of a unit, for example, students could complete a Twenty Things I Like to Do activity from the point of view of an individual living in a time or place the class has just finished studying. Comparison of this list with a similar list they generate for themselves could help them not only clarify their own values, but also clarify the substance of the unit they have studied. Making a Coat of Arms to illustrate what people in a specific culture, region, or time, or people of a specific social class, ethnic background, or occupation might put on their coats of arms (in terms of what they were good at, liked best, were proudest of, hoped for most, and so on) could also tie up the substance of a unit of study as well as set the stage for a similar activity related to the students themselves. The potential these techniques have for introducing and concluding the study of substantive units seems unlimited.

Values clarification relates to inquiry teaching in yet a third way. Inquiry teaching requires an informal, trusting, nonthreatening classroom atmosphere, just as does values clarification. And use of values clarification techniques in the classroom can help create and reinforce an atmosphere that facilitates the risk-taking associated with hypothesizing and other operations of inquiring. Moreover, the technique called Focus Grouping can prove useful in substantive as well as values clarification activities, especially in inquiry teaching. By putting students in triads, giving each limited but uninterrupted time to report his or her opinions of some aspect of the content being studied, having the listeners repeat what one speaker says before proceeding to the next, and so on not only facilitates a sense of self-worth but also helps develop listening skills and enhance content learning. Thus, values clarification built on the seven step process of valuing outlined above can help students develop their skills of thinking as well as clarify their values.

The strategy of values clarification thus parallels inquiry teaching both in its sequence of steps and in its essential features and rationale. Both strategies emphasize (1) informed choice; (2) deliberate, reflective examination of alternatives; and (3) the application of a choice to new data. All of these operations require students to use a variety of thinking skills ranging from extrapolation and inference-making to analysis, application, and evaluation. Moreover, both strategies count on cognitive disequilibrium to move the learner through the steps of the learning process. Use of the values clarification strategy (not just isolated techniques but the entire strategy) can reinforce the cognitive goals of inquiry teaching while inquiry teaching may be used to facilitate clarification of student values.

Values Analysis and Inquiry Teaching

Values analysis is generally less personal, moving frequently toward societal problems and choices concerning values. This approach to affective education also seems more closely related to inquiry teaching than does the strategy of values clarification proposed by Raths, Harmin, and Simon.

Theory and rationale. Values analysis seeks to help students think systematically, and often in rather abstract terms, about values issues so they will be able to make intelligent personal and social decisions in the future.[13] This approach to values education aims to provide students with a set of skills, knowledge of values, and commitment to a process of decision-making that will enable them to direct their future in a way that should be "best" for everyone. It is based on the assertion that intelligent social action—the ultimate goal—requires thinking and analysis of facts and values before such action occurs.[14]

Teaching process and techniques. The values analysis teaching strategy proposed by Professor Jack R. Fraenkel seems to encompass the essential ingredients of the several different teaching approaches to values analysis that exist today.[15] In essence, this strategy engages students in a step-by-step examination of (1) the facts of a value-laden situation or dilemma; (2) the alternative choices available; (3) the consequences, both short and long range, of each alternative; and (4) the evidence, in terms of both data and reasoning, that suggests the probability of these consequences.[16] In this strategy, students can use a variety of data retrieval charts or questions to examine values issues in order to make a choice that reflects their informed judgment about the "best" or preferred action to take. The issues investigated may be personal in nature and directly relevant to the lives of the students, or they may be more societal in orientation.

Figure 12.1 presents a values analysis teaching strategy devised by Fraenkel. This strategy clearly resembles the inquiry teaching strategy presented in this book. It commences with a dilemma or issue, just as a problem launches inquiry. The articulation of alternative solutions or actions corresponds with the hypothesizing step of inquiry teaching. The extrapolation of consequences corresponds to the testing stage of inquiry teaching as does the next step that involves gathering reasons and evidence to support the probability of the occurrence of the inferred consequences.

Assessing the various alternatives in terms of their imagined consequences approximates the evaluation step of inquiry teaching where students judge the validity of hypotheses in the light of the evidence examined; the difference here is that students judge the *preferability* of a course of action in terms of probable consequences, rather than judging the accuracy of a hypothesis in terms of evidence collected. Next, in inquiry teaching students conclude their inquiry by revising, accepting, or rejecting a hypothesis they have been testing; in the values analysis model presented here they decide which alternative should be chosen. Although this approach to values analysis does not include a final, action component as does inquiry teaching, students could easily *apply* their decision to a real life or experimental situation to determine the extent to which the anticipated

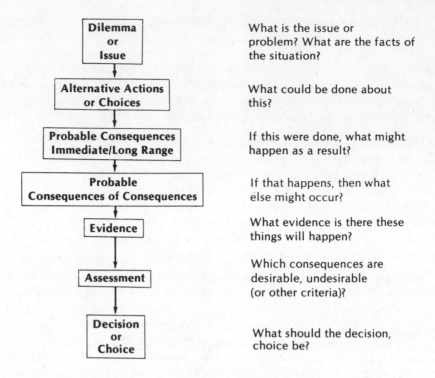

Figure 12.1. A Values Analysis Strategy [17]

consequences and results occur, to validate further the efficacy of their choice, or to broaden their conception of the values involved in the issue or dilemma being studied. Indeed, students can easily move from the final step of deciding on an alternative to planning a course of action that would aid them in realizing their action or policy choice. This is the ultimate goal of employing values analysis in the classroom. This values analysis strategy replicates the essential steps of inquiry teaching. The two strategies mutually reinforce each other.

The essence of values analysis, as presented by Fraenkel, consists of carefully distinguishing among statements of fact, inferences, and values, and of deliberately examining alternative choices of action in terms of their multiple consequences, whether long or short range—both single consequences and the consequences of these consequences. To achieve these ends, values analysis requires a teacher to have students examine and test the inferential claims involved in an issue, as well as the factual claims made about the issues, and to infer and compare the values that underlie the actions or statements related to an issue. Students must also evaluate the suggested alternatives by examining their posited consequences in terms of the individuals or groups that might be touched by each alternative if it were chosen and by the various points of view through which one might view the issue, whether legal, moral, aesthetic, political, or whatever. Thus, this strategy involves a very deliberate process of intellectual analysis that not only refines student understanding of certain values but also facilitates the development of their skills of thinking and of inquiry.

A values analysis activity. Values analysis can focus on student-centered issues, on issues of societal import, or on issues that emerge from any social studies content being studied. Such analysis can be conducted into issues having ethical, legal, aesthetic, logical, economic, or other dimensions. For example, suppose in our study of Kiev, we wished to have the students engage in a values analysis activity. We could present them with an issue or dilemma like that which follows as the basis for such an activity.

THE STEWARD'S DILEMMA

On orders of the prince the royal steward was inspecting the prince's fields to north of the city. It was a bright, sunny day. As he rode along the rutted road, the steward marvelled at all the land which he supervised for the prince. But he also remembered the prince's reminder to "Be sure you supervise it wisely—or your head will roll."

"Oh, what a way to go," he thought!

Suddenly the steward stopped short!

"What's this?" he wondered. There, not a hundred feet away, was a poorly dressed peasant farmer pulling down the wooden rails that marked the boundary of one of the prince's unused fields.

Quickly the steward hid behind a tree to watch. By now the peasant had finished pulling down the rails and had dragged them into a pile behind some nearby trees. Then he returned to his plowhorse and began to plow his field. But as he plowed, he came right across the boundary onto the prince's field! In no time at all, the peasant had plowed a good portion of the prince's field so that the steward could not tell where the peasant's field ended and the prince's began. In fact, the entire plowed area soon looked like it all belonged to the peasant.

This clearly was against the law! A peasant was taking the prince's land. The steward knew the prince had not given permission to do this. In fact, the law stated a large fine for just such an act. This should be reported at once!

But wait! Who was the peasant?

The steward gasped in amazement! It was his brother, Sergi! Sergi, the poor one—the brother whose work at home had made it possible for him to get an education and be chosen to work for the prince.

Sergi, the poor one—whose family lives from hand to mouth each day—the man with how many children? At least ten, the steward thought. How could he, the prince's steward, report Sergi to the prince? How could he report his own brother?

What should the steward do?

Once students read and discuss this story, they can brainstorm alternative actions that the steward could take. Such alternatives might include the following:

1. tell the brother to stop
2. wait until Sergi leaves and replace the rails
3. help Sergi move the fence to the end of the newly plowed land
4. ignore the whole thing
5. report what has happened to the prince but don't tell him you saw Sergi do it
6. tell the prince the entire story

Other alternatives can also be imagined.

But what is likely to happen as a result of each alternative action? The students could use a data retrieval chart to identify the various things that might happen to the steward, Sergi, Sergi's family, the prince, and to other landowners and peasants for each alternative open to the steward. They could then analyze each consequence in terms of the evidence and reasons that suggest it might occur. Next, they could evaluate each alternative and its consequences in terms of legal, ethical, economic, demographic, and any other criterion. At times students may go even further to infer long range consequences, or what is likely to happen to each individual involved in the long run if the immediate consequences they predict occur. And they may also attempt to infer the extent to which any of the consequences they predict are likely to happen. After ranking the alternatives in the order preferred, students could indicate and justify their choice of actions.

In completing this or any values analysis using the strategy described here, students might work as a class under the direction of the teacher using a chalkboard to record their findings, or they could work individually, in pairs, or in small groups using charts for recording their information. Regardless of which approach they use, the teacher plays a major role in designing and conducting the learning experience and in probing student ideas for evidence, reasoning, and inferring.

Values analysis and inquiry. Values analysis lessons or activities not only are guided by an inquiry teaching strategy but can fit well into a course or unit of study that is built on the inquiry strategy presented here. Such lessons may launch a unit of study, be used in the midst of a unit of study, or conclude a unit. When used to initiate a unit, they can also serve to motivate further inquiry and even to establish a purpose for studying the subsequent unit—for by treating as a hypothesis the student choice of action that concludes a values analysis lesson, students can proceed to study the unit to test the validity of their hypothesis. Wherever values analysis activities are used they can help students develop their skills of thinking, refine their concepts of selected values, and learn new content-related information or generalized knowledge. Values analysis and inquiry can be, and indeed are, mutually reinforcing.

Moral Reasoning and Inquiry Teaching

The theory of cognitive moral development proposed by Harvard Professor Lawrence Kohlberg suggests yet another approach to values education. Current public concern about ethics and morality in public and private life make his research and ideas concerning how people reason about moral issues particularly attractive to social studies teachers and administrators alike.

Theory and rationale. For the past twenty years or so, Kohlberg and an increasing number of researchers have been investigating the ways that individuals make decisions involving moral issues. As a result of his research and study of philosophy, Kohlberg claims that, as individuals mature, the way they reason about moral issues evolves through at least six distinct stages—from an initial, very self-centered, reward/punishment stage of reasoning, through stages where concern for one's image and for law and order predominate, to higher stages of concern for the societal welfare and for principles such as justice and human dignity.[18] Described briefly, these stages are as follows:

Stage 1 **Punishment and reward.** An individual's decision about a moral issue is based on a desire to avoid punishment or win a reward.

Stage 2 **Reciprocity.** An individual's decision is based primarily on a "you scratch my back and I'll scratch yours" type of reasoning.

Stage 3 **Desire for approval by others.** At this stage an individual wants to "look good" to his or her significant others, to be well-thought of.

Stage 4 **Law and order.** An individual here seeks to obey constituted laws, rules, and authority, and thus to maintain law and order.

Stage 5 **Social contract.** An individual's decisions at this stage are based on an asserted contract among all members of a society, a contract that implies the right to change these relationships in the interests of the society.

Stage 6 **Universal principles.** At this stage individual decisions reflect a sophisticated conception of justice, equality, and human dignity—principles that apply equally to all.

Kohlberg and his colleagues claim further that the conventional level of moral reasoning, at least in middle-class America, consists of Stage 3 and Stage 4 thinking. Most children until age 10 or so reason at Stages 1 and 2; individuals tend to move into Stage 3 reasoning by the age of 13, and to Stage 4 by the middle teens. Movement to Stage 5 reasoning occurs as individuals enter their early twenties. Stage 6 reasoning evolves sometime after that if it evolves at all, for only a fraction of the individuals tested to date seems to exhibit this type of reasoning as a predominant stage of moral reasoning. However, it should be noted that many adults never move beyond Stage 2 reasoning and that movement from one stage to another may vary in rate according to socio-economic and other factors.

In sum, Kohlberg argues that as individuals mature they change in the way they go about reasoning out moral dilemmas. People gradually—and naturally—move from an "I" centered type of reasoning to a "we" centered (me, my friends, and others around me) reasoning to a "they" level (others, many of whom I do not know or who are not immediately connected to me in time or space) of reasoning. One might decide to take or not take a specific action at any of the stages of reasoning that Kohlberg has identified.

According to Kohlberg's theory, moral reasoning does not simply involve a question of one moral precept at a time; it is never whether or not to be honest in taking an exam, for example. Questions that call moral reasoning into play involve several moral principles in conflict with each other, such as whether to be honest in taking a test when by so doing failure seems assured, thus preventing one from fulfilling an implied contract with one's teammates to be eligible for the big tournament game Saturday. Moral dilemmas involve competing value claims: honesty, friendship, the sanctity of promises and contracts, respect for law, and so on. The ways a person reasons out decisions regarding these competing claims changes qualitatively over time.

Movement from one stage to another seems to be governed by certain principles, according to Kohlberg. Each individual, he asserts, reasons primarily at one stage of thought. However, an individual can understand all stages below his/her current stage of reasoning as well as his/her own stage of reasoning and the *next highest* stage of reasoning. Moreover, individuals are attracted to the next highest stage of reasoning because that stage helps them resolve dilemmas they cannot adquately—justly—resolve at their current stage of reasoning.

To illustrate this last—and crucial—point, assume that two individuals both reason at Stage 3 on moral issues; both evidence special concern about how their actions make them look in the eyes of those whose respect they value. Assume further that they disagree on what action to take in a situation involving whether or not to cheat on an exam. One feels it is justified in order "not to let the team down." The other feels it is not justified because it "would let my parents down." Appeal to Stage 3 reasoning will not help these individuals resolve this dilemma. But Stage 4 reasoning, involving respect for rules and law, does help resolve the dilemma because cheating on a test is clearly against school rules. In arguing or discussing the moral issues involved in why one should engage in a certain type of behavior to resolve a moral dilemma, individuals gradually come to appreciate the fact that the higher stage of reasoning proves a more adequate basis for making action decisions. And they gradually move toward this higher stage of reasoning.

Movement through the stages of moral reasoning thus seems to occur as an individual has opportunities to confront problems that contain distinctly moral issues—questions of right and wrong, good and bad; has opportunities to articulate his or her own stage of moral reasoning, hear reasoning at the next highest stage; challenge this next higher stage of reasoning, and defend and examine his or her own stage of reasoning. In other words, individuals move through the stages of moral reasoning as they engage in stage-related discussions of moral issues. As they do, they develop—and need to develop—a broader societal perspective, develop their abilities of abstract thinking and empathizing (to consider others beyond those in one's immediate circle one must be able to abstract), and become increasingly adept at focusing on larger issues or principles implicit in value-laden situations. Such development, Kohlbergians claim, results in the integration of one's values into a hierarchy of related values based on an increasingly sophisticated concept of justice that, according to Kohlberg, underlies all moral behavior in all societies.*

Teaching techniques and strategies. At least nine different approaches have been suggested to facilitate the cognitive moral development of students in a classroom or group setting. Of these, the moral discussion strategy developed at Carnegie-Mellon University provides one useful way to wed cognitive development with values education. [19] Like the values analysis and values clarification approaches described above, this process also elicits an essentially cognitive response. Unlike the values analysis strategy, however, this moral

---

*There is obviously more to Kohlberg's theory—and to criticism of this theory—than is presented here. For a more detailed explanation see citations 18 and 22 in the Chapter-end Notes.

reasoning strategy may not always require systematic analysis of issues in a deliberate, step-by-step fashion. Yet this strategy can be, and often is, even more systematic than that of values analysis. Unlike the seven step values clarification strategy, moral reasoning emphasizes direct confrontation between different stages of reasoning as the principal method of fostering growth. Moreover, unlike both of these strategies, moral reasoning focuses on just one specific type of value, the ethical. But like both of the previously described strategies, this moral reasoning discussion strategy corresponds closely to a strategy for inquiry teaching.

Figure 12.2 presents a teaching strategy designed to facilitate the development of an individual's stages and skills of reasoning about moral issues or dilemmas. This strategy requires students to identify a moral issue in a dilemma story and then to justify in a discussion the choice of action recommended to resolve the dilemma. The parallels between this strategy and inquiry teaching seem most obvious. Presenting the dilemma here corresponds to identifying a problem in inquiry teaching. Choosing a position corresponds to hypothesizing, while the small and large group processes of articulating, ranking, and critically evaluating reasons for the recommended choices constitute, in effect, the testing of hypotheses against evidence and logic. The final step that brings closure to the process corresponds to the concluding step of inquiry teaching. Although this strategy provides no obvious action-related step as does Raths' values clarification strategy, it can be used repeatedly throughout the year to engage students in a sequence of discussions involving the same basic issues (those involving friendship and authority, for example). When it is so used, students in effect receive practice in applying their thinking to new situations and in revising or otherwise altering their reasoning and the facts they take into account.

This strategy employs a very specific type of instructional material, a moral dilemma, that may be presented in oral or visual form or as a written story. A well-constructed dilemma features a central character (who may be an individual or group of individuals) in a problematic situation. The situation must involve two or more issues that generate moral conflicts (as friendships or other roles of affection, property, contract or promise, punishment, and authority). It must also require the central character to make a moral choice, a choice involving a decision about the right thing to do. The *Steward's Dilemma* presented on page 277 reflects these attributes.

If we were to employ the moral reasoning strategy described here with a dilemma like the *Steward's Dilemma*, we might initiate our lesson by asking some questions that would set the stage for the discussion to follow. We would attempt to get the students to think about situations and issues such as those to be presented in the dilemma story. Thus we might ask such questions as, "How many of you have ever seen a friend or relative do something that might not be considered right?" or, "How many have ever seen someone break a law?" And so on. Once the students had talked a bit about these situations we would have them read (or listen to a reading of) the dilemma story and clarify the basic facts of the story. Then we would ask a volunteer to state the dilemma confronting the steward, and, if the rest of the class agreed with this view, we would ask

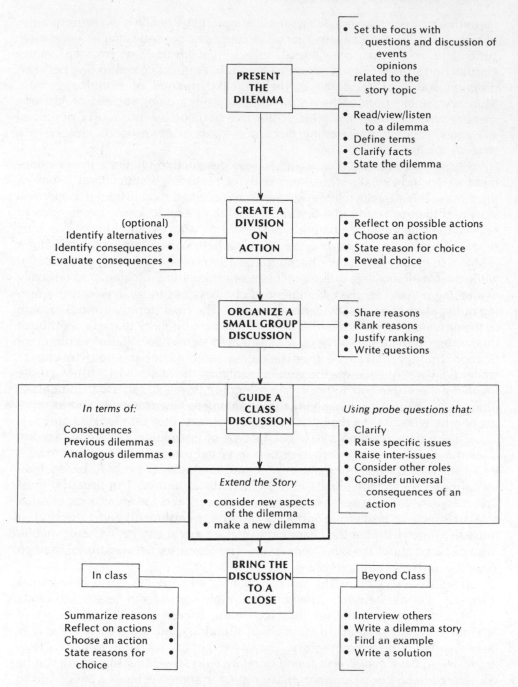

PRESENT THE DILEMMA

- Set the focus with
    questions and discussion of
        events
        opinions
    related to the
        story topic

- Read/view/listen
    to a dilemma
- Define terms
- Clarify facts
- State the dilemma

CREATE A DIVISION ON ACTION

(optional)
- Identify alternatives
- Identify consequences
- Evaluate consequences

- Reflect on possible actions
- Choose an action
- State reason for choice
- Reveal choice

ORGANIZE A SMALL GROUP DISCUSSION

- Share reasons
- Rank reasons
- Justify ranking
- Write questions

GUIDE A CLASS DISCUSSION

In terms of:

Consequences
Previous dilemmas
Analogous dilemmas

Using probe questions that:

- Clarify
- Raise specific issues
- Raise inter-issues
- Consider other roles
- Consider universal
    consequences of an
    action

Extend the Story

- consider new aspects
    of the dilemma
- make a new dilemma

BRING THE DISCUSSION TO A CLOSE

In class

- Summarize reasons
- Reflect on actions
- Choose an action
- State reasons for
    choice

Beyond Class

- Interview others
- Write a dilemma story
- Find an example
- Write a solution

Figure 12.2. A Strategy for Guiding a Moral Discussion

each student to write down at least tentatively the action they think the steward
should take and one reason for taking that action.

After having several volunteers state their reasons for the actions they recommend, we could then divide the class into groups. Most likely we would make the groups homogeneous, each group consisting of 4–5 students all of who recommended the same action for the steward to take. In a short meeting each group could listen to the various reasons given by each member for his or her position, rank the reasons in the order the group prefers, and then tell why their first-ranked reason is preferred. After the class reconvenes, each group could report, and students could engage in a critique and discussion of the reasons given for the various positions. To conclude, students representing one position could summarize reasons given by those representing another position until all reasons articulated had been reviewed. Then all could reflect on what they had heard and write the choice of action they now prefer and the best reason they had or had heard for that action.

No attempt would be made to collect papers, vote, or identify individual student choices. The class would probably close with students still arguing about what the steward should do and why. However, they could also be assigned to interview three other students or their parents to see what course of action they would recommend for the steward and the reasons for their recommendations. A discussion of their findings might launch class on the following day.

Like the values clarification strategy described earlier, this moral reasoning strategy is designed to emphasize the gap that may exist between one individual's stage of reasoning about a value issue and another individual's higher stage of reasoning. But it goes a step further than this. By acknowledging Hilda Taba's observation that effective moral education requires teaching "in situations that stir feelings and loyalties,"[20] this strategy deliberately attempts to create learning situations that will bother individuals cognitively—that force them to confront the inconsistency or inadequacy of their own reasoning about a moral issue. Thus, in small groups students hear reasoning they might not expect but in a context that supports the same position they took. However in the follow-up large class discussion, students might find their own reasoning challenged by others. They would then have the opportunity to reply to or to challenge still other reasons reported by other groups. An atmosphere of confrontation thus replaces the atmosphere of mutual support that characterizes the small groups. By creating such disequilibrium and confrontation, the strategy seeks to facilitate movement from one stage of reasoning to another and thus to make individuals more socially aware and more capable of socially beneficial actions.[21]

This strategy, like the values analysis strategy, also emphasizes the analysis and evaluation of action alternatives in terms of the different people involved as well as in terms of consequences. Indeed, most student reasoning is couched in terms of consequences. "The steward should tell the prince because if he doesn't he'll lose his job—not to mention his head!" or "The steward should not tell because he wouldn't want to see his brother jailed or his family starve!" are common student remarks made in discussing the steward's dilemma. However, unlike the values clarification and values analysis strategies, this moral reasoning strategy employs specific types of questions during the large group discussion to probe student thinking about consequences. These questions also serve other important purposes: (1) to focus student attention on moral issues they might otherwise ignore, (2) to require students to deal with these issues in increasingly more sophisticated ways, and (3) to help students get outside of themselves and develop broader societal perspectives. These questions probe student reasoning from a variety of angles and push them to stretch their thinking in ways they might not otherwise do.

Probe questions such as those just described play an important role in guiding moral dilemma discussions. Four types of probe questions prove extremely useful to this end. These types of questions and samples of each related to the *Steward's Dilemma* are:

1. BEST REASON probe (this type of question serves best to launch a large group discussion of reasons for a specified action).

   Example: What is the best reason for the steward to report Sergi?
   What is the best reason for the steward *not* to report Sergi?

2. ISSUE RELATED probe (this type of question forces students to think about specific issues they might otherwise not think about in discussion of a dilemma).

   Example: What obligation does the steward have to his brother Sergi? to Sergi's family? to the prince?
   Which obligation is most important? Why?

3. A ROLE SWITCH probe (this type of question requires students to look at the dilemma issues from the point of view of a variety of other people involved in the dilemma and thus helps to extend their societal perspectives).

   Example: From the point of view of Sergi, what should the steward do? From the point of view of Sergi's wife and family what should the steward do?

4. UNIVERSAL CONSEQUENCES probe (this type of question helps students to generalize about the principles and issues implicit in the dilemma).

   Example: When is it ever right to tell on someone?
   When is it ever right to break a contract?
   When is it ever right to break a law?

Questions like these, used in this sequence, may be adapted for use with any dilemma to guide a moral discussion to increasingly more sophisticated levels of analysis. They also stimulate student thinking about moral issues, thus gradually facilitating stage change.

Values analysis techniques and strategies can also easily be incorporated as an important part of a moral dilemma discussion. Having students make a commitment to action prior to examining alternatives sometimes closes students to change and thus inhibits interaction and exchange in follow-up discussion.

Therefore, after students discuss the facts of a dilemma but before they make even a tentative choice of action, they could brainstorm some alternative courses of action and analyze them in terms of their consequences for the people and/or groups involved in the situation—just as occurs in values analysis. Then the students can choose the action they believe the central character or group should take. Group discussions of the reasoning behind these choices could then follow.

Use of a Dilemma Analysis Sheet as on page 287 proves useful in conducting such an analysis. This chart may easily be adapted for use with any values or moral dilemma. As used here with the *Steward's Dilemma,* it may serve as a lead in to a moral reasoning discussion. Students can enlarge the chart to add the names of more people involved in the situation as they perceive it, or the teacher can suggest additional names for their consideration (such as Sergi's family, the prince, other peasants, or other nobles who own large estates). Students in each group can examine the consequences for a single alternative for the two given characters (in this instance, the steward himself and Sergi) and one or two other characters of their own choosing, thus giving each group something unique to contribute to the follow-up class discussion as well as a common point of departure. Or a group can examine consequences of all alternatives for only one character.

Additional space on this chart can also be provided by using the reverse side of the chart to accommodate more than the four alternatives for which this chart provides space. Use of a chart such as this one provides excellent opportunities for small group analysis of alternatives and consequences prior to a large class discussion of action recommendations and the reasons students have for making such recommendations—the essence of a moral reasoning discussion as described in the preceding pages.

Values clarification techniques may also be incorporated in the strategy presented above for directing moral reasoning discussions. Many values clarification techniques, such as Values Voting for instance, may be used as warm-up activities prior to presenting students with a dilemma story. Examples of such techniques have been given above. The technique of Focus Grouping may also be used in the small group discussion stage of this strategy. This technique not only guarantees that each member of the group receives an opportunity to air his or her views, but it also guarantees more careful consideration of a wider variety of reasons for various recommended actions. Furthermore, requiring members of a group or class to repeat the essence of a speaker's comments before they in turn speak can help teach listening skills as well as diffuse emotionally charged arguments.

Thus, the moral reasoning strategy presented here emphasizes a high degree of self-reflection, student interaction, and analytical thinking. Although not nearly as teacher directed as is values analysis, this strategy requires that the teacher play a major role in guiding the class through its basic steps. Furthermore, this strategy clearly requires students to examine alternatives in the light of their consequences from various points of view as they seek the "best" or "right" thing to do.

Moral reasoning and social studies. Kohlberg's theory has important implications for the substance of social studies and history education, as well as for strategies used in facilitating affective education in social studies courses. It has been argued that the Declaration of Independence articulates Stage 5 reasoning, setting forth as it does a social contract theory of society and government.[22] This theory is then codified in a Stage 4 law and order type of reasoning in our federal and state constitutions. We might suggest, however, that the political system that operates in the context created by these two types of documents functions basically in terms of Stage 2 and 3 reasoning. If these assertions and Kohlberg's claims are accurate about the stages of reasoning through which children progress and the fact that the highest stage of reasoning that an individual can comprehend is only one stage higher than his or her own stage, then the implications for what students are taught in social studies courses and the introduction to specific content are far-reaching (and generally unacknowledged), indeed. Inquiry strategies thus seem most relevant to developing moral reasoning. Indeed, moral reasoning and inquiry appear to be very closely related both as substance and as a strategy of teaching in social studies.

Values Education Strategies and Inquiry Teaching

Values clarification, values analysis, and moral reasoning strategies resemble each other in many ways. All three emphasize reasoned reflection as an approach to valuing. All seek to clarify values by analyzing the consequences of recommended or preferred actions. All aim to sensitize individuals to value issues and to improve the adequacy of cognition regarding values. And all seem to aim toward the development of more integrated value systems in the belief that such systems lead to more desirable social and individual behavior, behavior that is more acceptable in a democratic society.

Moreover, all of these strategies seem to be based on the same principle of learning—that of creating cognitive disequilibrium. The heart of each strategy consists of making students aware of a gap between "the creed and the deed" as Simon calls it or between "is and ought" as Kohlberg refers to it. Helping students become alert to the existence of this gap makes them more inclined to move to close this gap, to bring their actions *closer* to what they profess to value. Although each strategy attempts to accomplish the goal with different techniques, all strive to have students articulate and examine their own values in order to clarify, refine, and order them.

These strategies are alike in other, more subtle ways, also. All reflect the values associated with rational decision-making and with an idealized democratic and humanistic society. For, while each of these strategies seeks to help students develop an awareness of their own values, whatever they may be at that particular point in time, each also seeks to have students adopt some of these values as the very basis of their own lives and behavior. The goal is to help students first to understand a particular value at the highest level of cognition within their capabilities and then to accept those that are better—more socially

DILEMMA ANALYSIS SHEET

1. What is the problem facing the steward?

2. List below some possible things the steward could do to resolve this problem:

List below some of the people who might be affected by what the steward might decide to do. Tell what would happen to each, if the steward chooses each possible action.

	The Steward	Sergi	Sergi's Family	Other Peasants	
a)					Now
					In the future
b)					Now
					In the future
c)					Now
					In the future
d)					Now
					In the future

ALTERNATE ACTIONS

3. Which of the actions above do you think the steward *should* take?

4. Why?

acceptable, more just and functional, more likely to be in the interests of the larger democratic society. Whether an individual's ultimate values result from natural development or individual choice, these strategies all seek to move—or help move—students toward some set of socially acceptable values. Finally, all of these strategies reinforce and complement a strategy of inquiry teaching. Indeed, each of them requires students to move through some version of the basic steps of inquiry.

Values clarification, values analysis, and moral reasoning teaching strategies share a number of limitations, also. Each lacks sufficient research to support its claims of classroom effectiveness in accomplishing its stated goals.[23] None are directly related to specific types of social action behaviors, nor is their use sufficient in and of itself to bring about the types of behavior sought by a public that seems generally to favor the teaching of values in the schools. While all approaches claim to be educationally worthwhile, little evidence exists at this time to indicate their claims can be fully realized.

While these strategies share many common features, so too do they differ in significant ways. Values clarification, for example, stresses the acceptance of personal values at their existing stage of expression, while values analysis places more emphasis on problem exploration and exploration of consequences, both immediate and long range. Moral reasoning, on the other hand, directly challenges values at their existing stage of expression by raising points of view often quite opposed to an individual's point of view while maintaining the unresolved nature of the conflict as an acceptable aspect of the process.

Furthermore, while the values clarification and values analysis strategies often emphasize teacher-to-student interaction, the moral reasoning strategy described here emphasizes student-to-student interaction. While values clarification and values analysis deal with a variety of values, the moral reasoning strategy deals primarily with issues of right and wrong. In values clarification and moral reasoning, individuals articulate values positions and defend or critique such positions; in values analysis, students dissect and analyze value implicit behavior.

Finally, values analysis and moral reasoning probe thinking and reasoning, while values clarification tends to avoid any deep, challenging cognitive probing. While values clarification stresses the need for a supportive classroom atmosphere, moral reasoning discussions use such an atmosphere to create a confrontation between individuals espousing different points of view. Values clarification stresses action, while values analysis emphasizes rather detached analysis of consequences of suggested actions, and moral reasoning focuses primarily on reason giving, challenging, and evaluating. Both of these latter approaches, however, imply action.

In sum, while these strategies represent somewhat different approaches to values education, and while they do have serious limitations and shortcomings, they also share much in common. Used to their fullest potential they can complement and reinforce each other. Indeed, as closely related as they are to inquiry teaching, these values education strategies may be easily used to reinforce the major goals of inquiry teaching as well.

FEELINGS, VALUING, AND EMPATHY

Values clarification, values analysis, and moral reasoning appear at first to be primarily cognitive in nature. However, these approaches to values education also have another dimension, for values and valuing involve feeling and feelings as well as understanding. These and other approaches to values education acknowledge this relationship between feeling and valuing and between feelings and values in several ways. In one approach, feelings serve as the subjects of study. In other approaches, feelings and the act of feeling are treated as integral parts of the values and attitudes that may serve as goals of classroom instruction and learning. Inquiry teaching provides a useful instructional strategy for dealing with both of these ways of treating feeling in the classroom.

Values and Feelings

Although values clarification, values analysis, and moral reasoning all have feeling dimensions, feeling plays a quite different role in each. One end of the spectrum of values education strategies that exist under the values clarification umbrella seeks primarily to elicit feelings rather than to analyze them. This approach, popularized by Sidney Simon and some of his colleagues, involves primarily the use of techniques designed to evoke in individuals feelings of pride, personal worth, wonder, and caring—to produce, in effect, an emotional high. It does not seem to devote much attention, however, to systematic cognitive analysis of these feelings once they have been elicited.

Simon claims that the goal of this type of values clarification is to nourish the ego, to promote humaneness, and to sensitize people to each other as individuals. Some techniques, such as discussion and sharing of things people excel at or their contributions to the classroom or community, often result in the development of very positive individual feelings on the part of those involved. However, other techniques, as for example discussion of such topics as, "What the world would lose if I were to die today," or the use of the Partner-Risk, Life-Line, or Epitaph exercises, can produce just the opposite.[24] The major goal of such techniques seems to be to enhance individual self-confidence and ego strength. Thus, Simon's approach to values clarification deals with feelings not so much for purposes of analysis as to make people simply feel better by reviving their own sense of dignity and worth.

Feelings also play a role in values analysis in a way quite different from that of values clarification. In values analysis, students are asked (once the facts at issue have been clarified) to infer for purposes of analysis the feelings implicit in a situation or exhibited by a character or individual under study.[25] In using this strategy, students are also often asked to relate personal experiences and feelings to the topic under discussion. Sometimes students compare these feelings to those of the character under study. Sometimes they analyze these feelings to find out why they exist. And sometimes, once these feelings are articulated, students leave them alone.

In moral dilemma discussions, student feelings often surface in the form of heated discussions, having been neither deliberately evoked nor analyzed. Of course, the more intensely one feels about a course of action and its supporting reasons, the more one may become involved in a values or moral discussion—at least to a point. A moderate amount of such feeling stimulates thinking and involvement in an exchange about the reasoning behind a recommended action, but a high degree of feeling often inhibits a rational exchange or sidetracks the discussion altogether. Feelings aid moral dilemma discussions but rarely serve as their subjects.

Thus, all three values education strategies described in the preceding pages deal with feelings in some way. Yet they use these feelings for a variety of purposes. Like values clarification, the moral reasoning strategy often evokes feeling as a vehicle for carrying a discussion rather than as an end in itself. Like values analysis, moral reasoning discussions use feelings to stimulate discussions as a means of getting at stages of reasoning rather than as subjects of analysis or introspection. All three treatments of feeling and the resulting feelings play a useful role in values education in social studies depending on the goals and objectives of the curriculum.

Exploring Feelings

Social studies teachers can help students explore feelings in a variety of ways. Teachers can contrive situations (or capitalize on existing situations) that produce a feeling—perhaps of curiosity, affection, anger, or something similar—and then have students step back and reflect on what they felt. Or, students can examine a situation that involves some emotion on the part of several persons other than themselves and then analyze in a relatively detached way the feelings the people expressed. In both instances, analysis of the feelings evoked can lead to an awareness of the values that underlie the situation. Both of these approaches involve two general steps: (1) becoming aware of a feeling and what it means; and then (2) analyzing that feeling to identify the values and attitudes behind it.

Calling up a feeling. Teachers can call up feelings to study in several ways. They may first use instructional materials that present the feelings of various characters or groups. Autobiographical accounts, film biographies, role play of historic individuals, poems, and narratives prove useful for this purpose. By using these materials, students can identify specific feelings, speculate about what they were or are like, and, to some degree, delimit the nature of that feeling and its underlying value base. This approach has the advantage of avoiding sensitive issues of personal privacy. Yet at the same time it often fails to help students develop a clear understanding of the feelings—or values—under study.

Teachers can also attempt to elicit certain types of feelings in their students and then use the resulting feelings as subjects of study through classroom simulations or role play. For example, to develop an understanding of what it *felt like* to be a farmer in the American midwest between 1880 and 1935, one might well use the game of *Farming,* originally developed by the High School Geography Project.[26] In playing this paper and pencil game, students come to experience the frustrations, successes, doubts, and worries that typified the lives of commercial farmers who lived at the mercies of the weather, shifting national and international markets, changing consumer tastes, a fluctuating industrial economy, and other uncontrollable and often unpredictable forces. In fact, many students who take part in this game of planting and harvesting finally just quit in frustration when they sense they can't win—exactly as did many thousands of farmers in the real-life situation. This approach to calling up feelings results in much greater awareness of the essence of a particular feeling and condition than does the more indirect study of evidence about how a certain group or individual felt.

An even deeper apprehension of a feeling can occur when students develop in themselves a specific feeling from normal classroom activity rather than from a simulated activity. Such was the type of feeling engendered by the now classic "brown eyes/blue eyes" experiment over a decade ago. In this instance, some students experienced discrimination for reasons over which they had no control; a teacher treated children with brown eyes in one way and those with blue eyes in the opposite fashion. Then she reversed the way she treated each group. Such treatment produced intense feelings on the part of the students as they became acutely aware of how it felt to be a victim of discrimination.[27]

Analyzing feelings. Once a feeling has been apprehended students can then explore the feeling and its implications. Although a number of strategies have been devised for guiding such analysis, most have been derived from the work of curriculum specialist Hilda Taba.

Taba's basic strategy involves exploring how an individual feels or felt and the reasons for that feeling. It also attempts to link feelings of others read about to the life experience of the students when they do not base their analysis directly on their own feelings. This strategy generally proceeds as shown in the table on page 292.[28]

In using this strategy, teachers customarily use these eight basic questions only if students do not voluntarily deal with the points on which they focus. Certain sequences of questions (questions 2 and 3 and questions 6–8) usually need to be repeated several times in order to evoke a variety of responses. However, rather than probe student feelings directly, as called for in items 6–7, teachers may, of course, ask students whether anything like the incident or feelings under discussion ever happened to someone they know. Questions 3 and 8 cap this line of questioning, for each asks students to get beyond the feelings under discussion to probe the values or attitudes that underlie such feelings—one goal of such analysis.

This feelings-analysis strategy represents a modification of an inquiry teaching strategy, for here students identify an incident and a feeling, hypothesize what the feeling was like, and then test their perception against other cases that involved similar feelings. In responding to this strategy, students

Teacher	Student	Teacher Follow-through
1. What happened?	Restates facts.	Sees that all facts are given and agreed upon. If students make inferences, asks that they be postponed.
2. How do you think . . . felt?	Makes inferences as to feelings.	Accepts inferences.
3. Why do you think . . . would feel that way?	Explains.	Seeks clarification, if necessary.
4. Who has a *different* idea about how . . . felt?	Makes alternative inferences and explanations.	Seeks variety, if necessary. Asks for reasons, if necessary.
5. How did . . . (other persons in the situation) feel?	States inferences about the feelings of additional persons.	Seeks clarification, if necessary. Encourages students to consider how other people in the situation felt.
6. Have you ever had something like this happen to you?	Describes similar event in his/her own life.	Insures description of event.
7. How did you feel?	Describes his/her feelings. May reexperience emotions.	Seeks clarification, if necessary. Provides support, if necessary.
8. Why do you think you felt that way?	Offers explanation. Attempts to relate his/her feelings to events s/he has recalled.	Asks additional questions, if necessary, to get beyond stereotyped or superficial explanation.

move from simple analysis of the feeling in terms of their own experience (as well as in terms of the experience of another character) to a deeper examination of what underlies such feelings in themselves or others. Although intermediate grade social studies teachers find this approach especially useful in their classrooms, it proves well-suited for use in any activity involving the analysis of feelings.

Feelings and Values

Feelings and feeling are more than types of affect, simply to be studied in and of themselves or as a means of probing for deeper, value-laden meanings. Values themselves incorporate a dimension of feeling, an emotional dimension with which primarily cognitive approaches to values education sometimes fail to deal. Feeling and the resulting feelings seem to be related to values in at least two major ways.

Valuing, for example, consists of attaching some degree of preference or commitment to some object, condition, or ideal standard of behavior. This attachment is in part cognitive, a result of the rational process of *understanding* the nature and implications of whatever is valued for both the individual and the larger society. Such attachment is also emotional; it may be intuitive or culturally ingrained or the result of conscious, deliberate choice. This attachment consists of a sense of commitment to or preference for whatever is valued. This feeling may vary in intensity depending on the position of the particular value in relation to other values held by an individual. Attaching worth to something is external to the behavior, object, or condition valued, i.e., attachment or commitment is generated by an individual and is not part of whatever is valued.

Yet many things we often value (especially such abstractions as patriotism, loyalty, honesty, and empathy) also themselves consist of certain feelings. Or at least they give rise to certain feelings that only they can generate. These feelings may not initially be part of one's conceptualization of the value per se but merely an individual's feeling transferred to what is valued. In time, however, they become so closely identified with the value concept as to be an integral part of its meaning for the individual.

Comprehending values thus involves both feeling and understanding the feelings associated with such values as well as knowing the cognitive attributes of the value concept itself. Inquiry teaching can be used to help students experience and analyze these feelings and thus come to understand as fully as possible the meaning of such value concepts. In fact, if it is true as Raths, Harmin, Simon, and others[29] insist, that values cannot be given to anyone, then inquiry teaching may be the most useful of all forms of instruction in values education.

Teaching Students to Feel

One of the most, if not the most, important elements of affective education is the ability of students to feel what someone else feels—to see things as another does, with the same intensity, degree of commitment, and perception as does that other individual or group. Students' inabilities to engage in values analysis or to move to higher stages of moral reasoning frequently result from their inability to "see things as others see them," to get inside another point of view. The younger the students, the more restricted their experiences have been; consequently when they express value preferences or articulate values, they as often as not cling with unusual tenacity to the value articulated. They confirm their belief rather than submit it to examination and analysis or hold it open to change. Helping students become aware of the broad range of human experiences available offers one way to prevent this "freezing." And helping students learn how to empathize and to develop a willingness to empathize plays an important role in achieving this goal.

Empathy consists of comprehending something by feeling and understanding it from the point of view of someone else. If one has empathy for another culture, for instance, one knows and feels issues and things from the point of view of a member of that other culture. In order to exercise or express this understanding, to empathize, one must get inside the phenomenon to be understood (whether another culture, an individual in an unusual situation, or whatever). To exhibit empathy for another culture, for example, students must get into that culture (without their own personal or cultural preferences getting in the way) to the point where they understand and feel things as individuals in that culture do. Empathy involves knowing and feeling; these two dimensions are virtually inseparable. As a value, empathy additionally involves a commitment, a willingness and a predisposition to put one's self in another's shoes when the occasion requires. It is, therefore, important in teaching (about) this value to deal with the feelings as well as the more cognitive attributes associated with empathy.

Helping students learn empathy and give it worth cannot be accomplished solely by analysis or by moving in and out of a subject. Rather, development of this value requires repeated practice at (and reflective analysis of) empathizing with a wide variety of situations. Reproducing the "brown eyes/blue eyes" experiment described above or using the game of *Farming* or any appropriate simulation provides an excellent vehicle for initiating such an experience. Once the empathy-producing experience has been developed as a point of reference, students can then explore both the topic in which they are involved and the nature of empathy as a concept.

Another way to develop empathy involves engaging students in learning experiences that stimulate what some literary scholars and teachers call the *sympathetic imagination.*[30] This can be accomplished through the use of literature, biographies, diaries, vivid newspaper accounts, or similar sources with a specific discussion strategy based on inquiry teaching. Thus the goal becomes one of *feeling* what it is like to be a victim of discrimination—or what it was like to be a farmer in the 1930's—or what it was like to be at Breed's Hill in 1775. This means students must get inside a character, situation, or culture without bringing their own preferences or interests into play; they must get involved in the subject rather than stand back and pull it apart from a distance. Students must get to the point where they can answer the question, "Why did X do what he/she/they did?" or, "What made X feel this way?" from the perspective of that person rather than judge whether a particular action was or is desirable or determine what they themselves might have done in a similar situation.

Dealing with motives and feelings of others is the goal of any strategy aimed at teaching empathy, but confronting these topics is not the first step in such a strategy. Instead, students need to move gradually toward this goal. An inquiry strategy proves most useful in this regard. For example, students can read, view, listen to, or otherwise study information about any event as seen through the eyes of an actor in the event and answer questions like those on the following page, beginning with factual questions.

This strategy (p. 295) works as well with documents, newspaper accounts, autobiographical accounts, and other historical and social studies data as it does with literary sources. By using this sequence of questions, teachers can help students get inside a character or event and thus develop empathy for those involved. Starting with a search for specific data about the individual— "the facts of the case," so to speak—(in question 1), we can focus on the odd or unusual or unexpected (question 2) in order to pique the students' curiosity and

Questions	Inquiry Steps
1. What did X do? or	*(Gathering information—*
What happened in Y?	from a source—translating
or What does X propose?	and interpreting data)
2. What seems unusual,	(Stimulating the student's
extraordinary, different,	imagination and curiosity—
etc., about this?	motivating)
3. How did X feel?	*(Hypothesizing)*
3.1 What *statements*	
or *actions* suggest	
this?	
3.2 What *words, sounds,*	(Hypothesis testing and
rhythms suggest this?	concluding)
4. What does the author think	*(Hypothesizing)*
or feel about this?	
4.1 What *data* used	
suggests this?	
4.2 What *words, sounds,*	(Hypothesis testing and
rhythms suggest this?	concluding)
5. Why did X (or the author)	*(Hypothesis testing,*
do/propose what he/she did?	*evaluating, and concluding)*
5.1 What connections do you	
see between his/her feelings	
and actions?	
5.2 How might these feelings	
have shaped X's motives?	

to motivate inquiry. Responding to such a question stimulates the students' imaginations and leads them to move psychologically closer to the central character being discussed. We can then move to an exploration of the character's feelings (question 3) by exploring the substance of the character's actions or words and the way the character (or author) uses words and/or actions to express him or herself. From here, if we wish, we can (question 4) go on to explore the feelings of the author of the source if the author is someone other than the character we are studying. Here students can look on the source as an expression of someone else's feelings and beliefs, assumptions and concerns, as well as a statement about a specific incident or subject or character. The final question brings us to the target of our inquiry: empathizing with the character under study by inferring the motives for his or her actions, proposals, or statements. This is the most crucial part of any learning activity that aims to develop empathy.

Follow-up discussion of feelings and motives attributed by students to the character(s) under study may be useful, too. By focusing on the relationship between the character's inferred feelings and his/her actions (question 1) and motives (question 5), students can get even further into the character and his/her culture and move toward a deeper empathy for the character, situation, or culture being studied. Asking students to discuss how *they* feel about this same situation enhances empathy while initiating analysis. However, further comparative or evaluative discussion of the character's actions, feelings, or motives (What could/should X have done? What might you have done in this situation?) puts further distance between the students and the character or situation, thus exposing the character or situation to more analytical dissection while involving the students in articulating their own feelings or values. Neither enhances empathy or the ability to empathize, although both techniques may be useful in gaining insight into the character or situation under study.

Empathy, like similar feelings, is easier to experience or express than it is to analyze. Yet analysis may actually help students develop such a feeling if approached in the manner described here. The essence of this strategy involves moving in sequence from the students' natural responses (responses they might not articulate until asked but that are usually there, nonetheless) to their more distant analytical responses. Inquiry teaching provides a useful way for doing precisely this, just as it serves as a basic strategy for values clarification, values analysis, or reasoning about moral issues. The relationship between feelings and knowing, and thus action, seems basic to all learning.

AN INTEGRATED APPROACH TO VALUES EDUCATION

Values education has many dimensions. The three approaches discussed in this chapter represent the most significant of these approaches in social studies today. Often they are viewed as antithetical to each other. In reality they are not. Instead, they compliment each other in many ways. Indeed, these three approaches to values education seem to be different facets of the same coin.

Although values clarification, values analysis, and moral reasoning strategies generally stress cognitive processes and goals of understanding and knowing, each possesses an element of feeling. Values clarification and moral reasoning seem to focus more on valuing than does values analysis, whereas values analysis appears much more detached than do the former. Indeed, values analysis seems to be primarily *about* values rather than valuing in nature. All three approaches, however, employ what is essentially an inquiry teaching strategy to accomplish their diverse goals, and in this sense they are much more closely related than they appear at first sight.

Methodologically, values clarification, values analysis, and moral reasoning strategies are so closely interrelated that they may well be considered as mutually reinforcing rather than as opposed to each other. Values clarification strategies can create the classroom atmosphere essential for the free and open discussion upon which moral reasoning is based; the cognitive abilities developed by the moral reasoning strategy described here seem most useful in values analysis; in turn, the deliberate analysis of value issues in terms of the wide variety of criteria employed in examining and judging consequences seems essential to effective moral reasoning and to values clarification. Any of these strategies can be used to introduce or motivate a unit of study, to help students unearth new information, and to facilitate student synthesis or evaluation. The

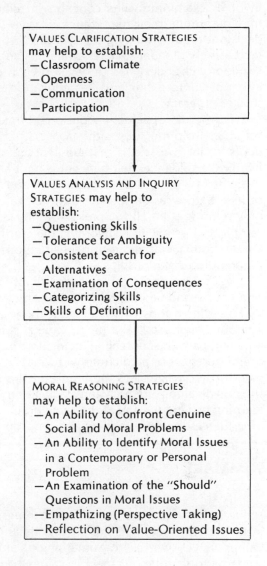

EXAMPLES OF ACTIVITIES

Focus Groups
Computer Game
Nonlistening Game
Voting Questions

VALUES CLARIFICATION STRATEGIES
may help to establish:
—Classroom Climate
—Openness
—Communication
—Participation

Value Incidents
Value Assumptions

VALUES ANALYSIS AND INQUIRY
STRATEGIES may help to
establish:
—Questioning Skills
—Tolerance for Ambiguity
—Consistent Search for
  Alternatives
—Examination of Consequences
—Categorizing Skills
—Skills of Definition

Moral Dilemma Stories
Role-Taking Exercises
Reviewing Alternatives
  and Consequences of
  Moral Problems

MORAL REASONING STRATEGIES
may help to establish:
—An Ability to Confront Genuine
  Social and Moral Problems
—An Ability to Identify Moral Issues
  in a Contemporary or Personal
  Problem
—An Examination of the "Should"
  Questions in Moral Issues
—Empathizing (Perspective Taking)
—Reflection on Value-Oriented Issues

Figure 12.3. A Model for Using Three Values Education Strategies [31]

model described in Figure 12.3, developed by Professor Ronald Galbraith, suggests one way of integrating these three approaches in the classroom.

Moreover, each of these approaches by itself tends to speak to only one aspect of values and values education. But values education involves more than analyzing value concepts to understand the consequences of acting upon them and more than clarifying the nature of these value concepts. It also involves how much worth we will give these value concepts as standards of behavior and thought, how committed we will be to them as guidelines for action. And this involves examining value concepts in relationship to one another so that we may determine their importance relative to other values we may hold. Such decisions require thinking at increasingly sophisticated levels of abstraction and increasingly broader societal awareness and empathetic understanding. Teaching approaches designed to develop each of these skills or conditions can be integrated into a single values education component for any coherent social studies program.

Furthermore, values lessons ought not to be viewed as ends in themselves, set apart from the substantive aspects of teaching and learning. Stroking students for its own sake is as fraudulent and may be as damaging as any negative learning experience. Self-concept is built as much, if not more, by success at a difficult task as it is by compliments and positive treatment from significant others. Setting aside specific days for values clarification or moral reasoning only reinforces an all too prevalent impression that students should "do as we say but not as we do." Divorcing the clarification and analysis of feelings and values from social and historical situations unduly fractures any sense of their inherent interrelationships.

Values lessons ought instead to fit into the context or flow of the substance of a course and be integral to it. They may thus do triple duty by getting (1) at various dimensions of values education, as well as (2) at knowledge of the content being used, and (3) at various skills and processes of thinking. After analyzing a values or feeling incident or moral dilemma, students can compare their inferences or predictions with what actually occurred; in this way they can gain further insight into the nature of the subject under study as well as into their own value systems. Values education can thus carry forward a substantive learning experience and at the same time achieve important goals in the realm of student self-understanding and development.

SUMMARY

Values and valuing are two different things. A value is something to which we attach worth. Valuing is the process by and the degree to which an individual values—gives worth—to something. Values education consists of helping students to learn about specific values concepts as well as of helping them to attach worth to these concepts.

Values clarification, values analysis, and moral reasoning are the most important, but not the only, of many values education strategies available for use in the social studies classroom.[32] They should not be viewed or treated as competitive in nature. For best results, these strategies may be used together as an integrated approach to values education. By combining appropriate emphasis on feelings as well as on values and valuing with an inquiry strategy basic to all, teachers can facilitate development of student skills of thinking, conceptualizing, and expressing, as well as student awareness, understanding, and refinement of basic values and feelings—all essential goals of social studies teaching and learning.

notes

1. Edwin Fenton, ed., *Teaching the New Social Studies in Secondary Schools: An Inductive Approach* (New York: Holt, Rinehart and Winston, 1966), p. 42.
2. Jack R. Fraenkel, "Teaching About Values," in Carl Ubbelohde and Jack R. Fraenkel, eds., *Values of the American Heritage: Challenges, Case Studies and Teaching Strategies* (Washington: National Council for the Social Studies, 1976), p. 155.
3. J.W. Getzels, "The Aquisition of Values in School and Society," in F.S. Chase and H.A. Anderson, eds., *The High School in the New Era* (Chicago: University of Chicago Press, 1958), p. 149.
4. Louis E. Raths, Merrill Harmin, and Sidney B. Simon, *Values and Teaching*, 2nd ed. (Columbus: Charles E. Merrill Publishing Co., 1978).
5. Sidney B. Simon, Leland Howe, and Harold Kirschenbaum, *Values Clarification: A Handbook of Practical Strategies for Teachers and Students* (New York: Hart Publishing Co., 1972).
6. Raths et al., pp. 26–29, 200–226.
7. Ibid., pp. 26–29, 47–49.
8. Ibid., pp. 6–8, 248–249.
9. Ibid., pp. 38–196; Simon et al.
10. Raths et al., pp. 88–90.
11. Simon et al., op. cit.
12. Simon et al., p. 30.
13. Fraenkel, p. 150.
14. Ibid., p. 165.
15. Maurice P. Hunt and Lawrence E. Metcalf, *Teaching High School Social Studies* (New York: Harper and Row, 1968); Byron G. Massialas and C. Benjamin Cox, *Inquiry in the Social Studies* (New York: McGraw-Hill, 1966); Donald Oliver and James P. Shaver, *Teaching Public Issues in the High School* (Boston: Houghton Mifflin, 1966).
16. Fraenkel, pp. 171–208.
17. Ibid, p. 204 (adapted) with permission of the National Council for the Social Studies.
18. Lawrence Kohlberg, "The Cognitive Developmental Approach to Moral Education," *Phi Delta Kappan*, LVI:10 (June 1975), pp. 670–677.
19. Barry K. Beyer, "Conducting Moral Discussions in the Classroom," *Social Education*, 40:4 (April 1976), pp. 194–202. This strategy has evolved from research conducted at Carnegie-Mellon University by Frank Alessi, Edwin Fenton, Ronald Galbraith, Thomas Jones, George Westergard, and the author.
20. Hilda Taba, *Curriculum Development: Theory and Practice* (New York: Harcourt Brace and World, 1962), p. 45.
21. See also Ronald E. Galbraith and Thomas M. Jones, *Moral Reasoning: Teaching Strategies for Adapting Kohlberg to the Classroom* (Anoka, Minn.: Greenhaven Press, 1976).
22. Edwin Fenton, "The Implications of Lawrence Kohlberg's Research for Civic Education," in B. Frank Brown, ed., *Responsible Citizenship* (New York: McGraw-Hill Book Co., 1977), pp. 103, 110–112.
23. Elizabeth L. Simpson, "Moral Development Research: A Case Study of Scientific Culture Bias," *Human Development*, 1974, Vol. 1, pp. 81–106; Jack R. Fraenkel, "The Kohlberg Bandwagon: Some Reservations," *Social Education*, 40:4 (April 1976), pp. 216–222.

24. Simon et al., pp. 177–188, 304–305, 308–313.
25. Fraenkel, *Teaching,* p. 165.
26. Available as part of the High School Geography Project materials from The Macmillan Company, Inc., New York City.
27. "Brown Eyes/Blue Eyes," *Christian Science Monitor,* September 15, 1971.
28. Reprinted and adapted with permission, from Alice Duvall, Mary C. Durkin, and Katherine C. Leffler, *The Taba Social Studies Curriculum: Grade 5—United States and Canada—Societies in Transition* (Copyright © 1969 by Addison Wesley Publishing Company, Inc.), pp. xxviii–xxx.
29. Raths et al., pp. 26–29, 41–46.
30. I am indebted to Professor Jan Cohn of Carnegie-Mellon University for assistance in clarifying this strategy.
31. Ronald E. Galbraith, George Peabody College for Teachers. Reprinted by permission of the author.
32. Douglas P. Superka, Patricia L. Johnson with Christine Ahrens, *Values Education: Approaches and Materials* (Boulder: Social Science Education Consortium, 1975).

Part FOUR

Inquiry Teaching and the Curriculum

13

Planning
For Inquiry
Teaching

The way we organize teaching shapes to a considerable degree not only how, what, and how well students learn but often whether they even care to learn at all. This is as true of inquiry teaching as it is of any other type of teaching. The most productive inquiry teaching is not a hit-or-miss affair. It is well-organized teaching built directly on how one learns by rational problem-solving. If we wish our students to learn how to think or inquire as well as to be disposed to think and to inquire, then our teaching must encourage and facilitate student use of the process, skills, attitudes, and knowledge associated with inquiry. This means, in essence, that we must organize individual lessons, units, and entire courses around a strategy of inquiry teaching.

DAILY LESSON PLANS
FOR INQUIRY TEACHING

The strategy described in the preceding pages offers a very practical framework for guiding a sequence of daily classroom lessons in any social studies subject. Moreover, this type of teaching provides a framework within which teachers can combine a wide variety of instructional materials and techniques to help students accomplish a number of diverse cognitive and affective goals. As students move from identifying a problem to testing and evaluating hypotheses and to applying their conclusions to new data, we can use lectures, oral reports, library research, and textbook discussions to provide data for student analysis. In the same way, we can use simulations, primary sources, and case studies. An inquiry teaching strategy can unify a variety of media and methods into a coherent pattern to help students develop higher levels of thinking as they engage in learning how to learn on their own.

Effective daily inquiry teaching doesn't just happen. It requires organization and advanced planning because teachers as well as students require guidance in the use of this strategy. Specific detailed daily lesson plans that articulate the major objectives of the lesson and the steps in a strategy of inquiry teaching can provide this guidance and help make true student inquiry a classroom reality.

Daily lesson plans represent the most detailed level of planning for teaching. These plans make it possible for a teacher to carry out and achieve the intended goals of a unit or course. Preparing such plans requires a sort of dry run through a sequence of lessons before actually teaching these lessons. This effort consists of imagining how a lesson or number of lessons would ideally proceed in order to accomplish the prescribed objectives. In inquiry teaching, such plans cannot be simple content outlines or mere notes to "discuss," "show," or "cover." Nor can they consist only of a list of activities in which students may engage. To be most useful, inquiry lesson plans must state (1) the primary objectives of the lesson, (2) the key operations (questions, directions, and so on) to be performed by the teacher and students in order to move from one step in the inquiry process to the next, and (3) the key statements or actions by the students that will indicate when such moves can be made.

The specific format for these daily lesson plans may vary according to what seems to work best for a particular teacher. Inquiry teaching plans may be as specific or detailed as is necessary to facilitate the desired learning experiences. For teachers unaccustomed to inquiry teaching, plans may be quite detailed— written as if to direct another teacher how to conduct the lesson. But for a teacher who has a feel for inquiry teaching and knows how to use the process to its fullest potential, plans need not be too elaborate.

Planning A Sequence of Lessons

Realistic daily lesson plans (that is, plans that are likely to work in a classroom) can be prepared in four steps. First, we must select and state the major overall learning goals of the unit to be studied. Next, we must briefly outline in sequence the steps through which the students should proceed in order to accomplish these goals. Then we can estimate the time each activity or step will require in order to determine what we might reasonably expect to accomplish in a class period of a given length of time. Only after having completed these three steps can we finally translate our sketchy sequence of activities into specific and detailed objectives and plans for each daily class.

Learning and teaching goals most appropriate for inquiry teaching have been outlined in Chapter 4. These goals do not consist merely of learning information supplied by a teacher, film, or text. Expository teaching will serve this type of goal much better and far more efficiently. Inquiry teaching, on the other hand, seems best suited for accomplishing higher level cognitive goals and a variety of other goals as well—goals such as concept development and the growth of thinking skills and affective development—in a context that reinforces and facilitates their realization rather than inhibits them. Selecting the exact goals for a unit or course must be based on consideration of a number of factors including the nature of the students for whom the instruction is designed; the nature of society today and in the future; the characteristics of the subject matter involved; what we know about how people learn; administrative considerations including the availability of materials; teacher competencies; and, of course, one's philosophy of education.[1] Such decisions may be individual, departmental, or even administrative. Planning daily lessons cannot proceed until appropriate goals and unit outlines have been developed.

Once appropriate teaching goals have been articulated, we can turn to outlining a sequence of learning activities that will provide the overall structure of our lessons and help us generate the specific lesson plans we need to conduct such daily lessons effectively. One useful type of outline specifies the purpose, content, media, student grouping, and the activity for each discrete step in the sequence. The result is, in effect, an outline of the learning steps, or modules, that will constitute the unit. Such an outline may be constructed by following these basic guidelines:

1. Build each module around the place it fits in a strategy of inquiry teaching. Although any series of lessons is obviously grounded in content, the key to planning modules is the role each plays in carrying student learning through a process of inquiring. Therefore, the major concern in planning at this point should be constructing a sequence of modules to move students through the steps of problem identification, clarification, hypothesizing, testing hypotheses, stating conclusions, and applying conclusions to new data.

2. Build each module to require no more than 15–20 minutes to complete (about the limits of the attention span of even the best students). Thus, any 40–50-minute class period may consist of at least two distinct modules. This practice stimulates and maintains student motivation. Obviously, such time limits cannot always be adhered to in practice, nor are we always able to complete certain types of activities in a short time span. However, using these figures as an average helps us produce crisp, varied lessons that generate student interest and involvement.

3. Focus each module on a single media—and vary the media. If one module requires students to write, the next might involve discussion, and the one that follows might be built around pictures. Thus, in any single 40–50-minute class period, students will engage in at least two mini-lessons using at least two media. Again, this procedure stimulates motivation and keeps learning alive. Such a practice should not be structured beyond reason, however. There are times when the same media may be useful as a basis for successive modules.

Let us assume we are to prepare lesson plans for the short inquiry sequence on Kiev that opened this book—a study to which we can add some other materials on reading and values clarification presented in subsequent chapters of this book. A module outline for this sequence of lessons might resemble the Module

Outline on pages 306–307. The column headed *Purpose* lists the basic and subordinate steps of inquiry teaching in a sequence that moves from a problem statement to the application of our conclusion to new data. Note that the media used to communicate information generally varies from module to module, as do the ways we propose to group the students as the sequence of lessons unfolds. This module outline provides a quick overview of how we want our sequence of lessons to unfold. It serves as a useful guide in writing the daily plans that must next be prepared.

Before preparing such daily plans, however, we must determine how many modules will constitute each daily lesson. We must guess at the time each module will require to complete. Thus, module one (the teacher showing students objects on an overhead and asking them to infer what people were like who made or used these objects) might take only five minutes or so, since its purpose is primarily motivational. The second module would require even less time. But the next two modules might involve considerable time, perhaps ten minutes for module 3 and 10–20 minutes for module 4, including reporting time. Thus, perhaps our first 40–50 minute class (for average tenth-graders, at least) can include the first four modules.

The remaining modules seem to fall nicely into a sequence of daily lessons characterized by a variety of media and moving step-by-step through the inquiry process. The second class can include modules 5–8, the first two of which require only a short time. Module 9 by itself may form a third daily lesson, while modules 10, 11, and 12 may become a fourth 40-minute lesson. Each of the remaining pairs of modules may also constitute separate daily lessons. Thus, it seems reasonable to believe that these sixteen modules may constitute about six class days of lessons. The first class can be devoted to clarifying the problem and hypothesizing, the next three to testing our hypotheses, the fifth class to evaluating our hypotheses and drawing conclusions about their validity, and the final lesson to applying our conclusions to new data.

Writing Daily Lesson Plans

Daily lesson plans differ from a module outline in two important ways. Whereas a module outline is cast in general, rather sketchy terms, a daily lesson plan is much more specific and detailed. And while a module outline serves a planning function, daily lesson plans serve as actual guidelines for carrying out a learning activity in a classroom on a given day with a specific group of students. Module outlines are statements of general intent. Daily lesson plans constitute guidelines for action.

Effective inquiry lesson plans translate the general ideas sketched in the module outline into specific classroom learning activities. These daily plans consist of learning objectives stated in terms of observable student behaviors or the products of student behaviors, of specific teacher actions or moves, and of specific student actions or moves. The sample plans that follow illustrate one format for such plans. They constitute the daily plans for the six-day inquiry sequence contained in the preceding module outline for the study of Kiev

A Module Outline

General Goals:
To state accurately at least five major features of life in old Kiev
To interpret information contained in visual and written sources
To synthesize generalizations from specific data
To be willing to work cooperatively with others

	Purpose	Content	Media	Student Grouping	Activity
1	Motivation	Artifacts (paper clip, pencil, penny, etc.)	Overhead projector	Class	If you found these shapes in an ancient place . . .
2	Problem	What was life like in this place about A.D. 1000?	Teacher	Class	Listen
3	Problem Clarification	Statement	Board	Class	Define terms and subquestions; which are testable?
4	Hypotheses	Objects made by people	Artifact Photos	Groups	What was life like for these people?
5	Identify Sources	Memory sources/evidence	Board	Class	What types of sources will help check our ideas?
6	Identify Needed Evidence	If . . . then	Board	Class	If (what you say is true), then what should you find in the laws?
7	Test 1 (Skills)	Laws	Handouts	Pairs	Reading comprehension
8	Test 1	Laws	Handout	Class	What evidence can you find? What can't you find? What new ideas do you get?
9	Values Lesson	Steward's Dilemma	Handout	Class, Groups	Complete the values sheet.

		Steward's Dilemma	Discussion	Group, Class	What should the steward do? Why?
10	Moral Dilemma Discussion				
11	Identify Needed Evidence	If . . . then . . .	Board	Class	If what we said was true then what should we find in the documents?
12	Test 2	Primary sources	Reading	Individual	What evidence can you find? What can't you find? What new ideas?
13	Evaluate Hypotheses	All data and evidence	Board	Groups	Which hypotheses are supported or not supported?
14	Conclude	Hypotheses	Paper	Class	Accept / Modify / Reject } Pick 4–5
15	Identify Needed Evidence	If . . . then . . .	Board	Class	If what we said was true, then what should we see in the pictures?
16	Apply to new Data	Buildings and paintings	Slides	Class	List 5 features of life in old Kiev

presented in the Prologue. In these plans, the first column in each plan describes what the teacher should do. The second column indicates what the students may say or do in response. Only key teacher and student actions are indicated here. It should not be assumed that the responses indicated here are the only acceptable ones; they represent merely what we expect, hope, or need to happen for each lesson to progress as we would like it to.

FIRST DAY

Defining a Problem and Hypothesizing

Objectives:

1. Given a question, to state at least five questions, the answers to which will help answer the initial question.
2. Given pictures of artifacts, to infer and state—giving appropriate reasons and evidence—at least three possible characteristics of the society that produced or used these artifacts.
3. When in a group, to be willing to engage in cooperative investigation of given data.

Materials:

- pencil, paperclip, penny, pair of pliers, other small objects
- overhead projector
- photographs of artifacts from Kiev around A.D. 1000

TEACHER	STUDENTS

INTRODUCTION AND MOTIVATION

1. Project objects (pencil, paperclip, penny, pliers, etc.) on overhead. Ask the students to assume they found these in a dig (explain if necessary) and to guess what the people or society was like that made or used these things.	These people were . . . These people had . . .
2. Have the students explain why or how they make the inferences they do.	Ex.: "Anyone who can make and shape an object like that (paper clip) must have fine tools . . . because . . ."

CLARIFYING THE PROBLEM

3. Introduce the Kiev artifacts by noting some years ago archeologists	

uncovered these items dating back about 1,000 years. Ask: *What was life like in this society?* Have the students define *life* and *society* and suggest questions the answers to which will help answer the main question. List all questions on the chalkboard.

life—the way people lived
society—a group of people

What did they do for a living?
What kind of houses did they live in?
What did they eat?
What did they consider important?
. . .

4. Have the class select those questions that might be testable using artifacts.

HYPOTHESIZING

5. Divide the class into groups of 4–5. Give each group a set of pictures. Have volunteers describe literally what they *see* in several pictures. Then have each group list on scrap paper answers to the questions on the board. (Allow about 8–10 minutes for this activity.)

STATING HYPOTHESES

6. Have each group in turn report one hypothesized feature of this society. List them on the board. Continue until all groups have exhausted their lists. Encourage students to tell *why* they think their guesses are accurate.

These people were . . . because . . .
- farmers—farm type tools
- lived near trees—used wood in tools
- warlike—had weapons, soldiers
- educated—had writing

CLASSIFYING

7. If time permits, have students classify the items on the board into self-defined categories.

8. Record on a ditto master the items and questions on the board. Make copies to be distributed in the next class.

SECOND DAY

Testing Hypotheses

Objectives:

1. Given a list of self-generated hypotheses, to state at least five types of sources that might provide information to use to check the accuracy of these hypotheses.
2. Given a reading guide and list of laws from the society being studied, to answer correctly questions calling for translation, interpretation, and higher level thinking skills.
3. Given a list of hypotheses, to infer the kinds of evidence that ought to exist if these hypotheses are accurate.
4. When paired with another student, to be willing to engage in cooperative investigation of given data.

Materials:

- Reading Guide for list of laws*
- list: Some Laws**

TEACHER	STUDENTS

Review

1. Hand out the ditto of the hypotheses made in the previous class. Review them briefly.

TESTING HYPOTHESES

Identifying Needed Evidence

2. Have the students identify the kinds of evidence they need to find if their guesses about life in this place are accurate.
   Ask: If these people really were . . . (for example, farmers), what evidence should exist that will convince you they (were farmers)?
   Ask: If these people really were (for example, warlike), what evidence should exist?
   Treat only 3–4 hypotheses like this

Possible responses:
   . . . perhaps remains of farms
   remains of fenced plots
   old tools used for farming
   . . . perhaps castles or forts
   having as heroes great warriors
   many weapons

---

* See Chapter 11
** See Epilogue

so students get the idea of using the "if . . . then" statement to infer evidence.

3. Ask: Where can we find these types of evidence?
(Allow only 5 minutes for this.)
Have the students list some sources they might use to find this evidence.

museum   a book on the world
a text   around A.D. 1000
a book on coins a book on
documents   archeology

4. Tell the students you have a partial list of laws which governed the people who lived in this place. Ask: *If the features you have listed really are correct, what kinds of laws would these people have had? What kinds of laws would you expect to find on this list?* List answers on the board.

If warlike . . . a draft law
                    a law about rights of
                    soldiers
If farmers . . . a law about property
                    laws about the sale of
                    crops
                    laws regulating plant-
                    ing . . .

Collecting Evidence

5. Pair the students. Give each pair a list of laws and a reading guide. Direct each pair to complete the reading guide and sign their names.

6. Have pairs of students exchange their completed reading guides, compare answers, and arrive at answers all four can agree on. Allow them to refer to the laws.

7. Reconvene the class to discuss only those questions on which there was disagreement. Have the students tell how they found or arrived at their answers (in order to articulate rules for reading).

8. Ask the class to look for the laws they wanted to find to prove their hypotheses accurate. Have volunteers report their findings and tell how the laws they select support their hypotheses. Have the students list any kinds of laws that are missing or any that seem to refute their guesses.

they . . . engaged in trade and
                 commerce, because . . .
          . . . lived in cities, because . . .
          . . . valued property

Analyzing and Evaluating Evidence

9. Have the students go over their hypotheses to determine, on the basis of the evidence just seen, which seem accurate, which do not, and which remain yet untested. Require evidence from the laws to support student opinions.

STATING A TENTATIVE CONCLUSION

10. Have the students identify what they feel are probably the major characteristics of this society. Circle these on the dittos.

Based on the evidence we have seen so far, these people
were . . .
believed . . .
considered . . .

DEVELOPING NEW HYPOTHESES

11. Have students state new ideas about this society and add these to their lists. New questions may also be added.

they . . . had social classes
. . . had slaves
. . . and so on

THIRD DAY

Values Analysis and Clarification

Objectives:

1. Given a list of laws, to state the social hierarchy of a given society and describe some functions of one member of this social structure.
2. Given a values dilemma story:
    • to state a dilemma facing a character
    • to list alternative actions that might resolve the dilemma
    • to list likely consequences of each alternative
    • to choose, giving reasons, a preferred alternative
3. When in a group, to willingly accept others points of view.

Materials:

• *The Steward's Dilemma**
• Values Analysis Guide**
• lists of laws and hypotheses from previous classes

---

* See Chapter 12
** See Epilogue

Review

1. With reference to the laws distributed in the previous class, have
   the students list each type of person
   named and rank them in the order
   of their presumed importance.
   Have the students tell what they
   think was the main job (function)
   of the *steward*.

Prince   Guild member
Steward   Peasant (herdsman)
Sheriff   Indentured servant
              Slave

The steward was the manager of the
prince's household, property, finan-
ces, and so on. He was responsible for
maintaining the prince's income.

INTRODUCING A DILEMMA

2. Introduce the dilemma story by
   asking the class (1) if anyone ever
   heard of someone who saw a friend
   or relative do something illegal and
   did not know what to do about it,
   (2) how that person might have felt,
   and (3) if it is ever right to do anything illegal.

3. Distribute *The Steward's Dilemma*.
   Have the students read it silently.
   Clarify any difficult words (perhaps: *peasant* or *plowhorse*); have
   the students recap the story and
   describe the Steward as they
   imagine him. Have a volunteer
   state the steward's dilemma.

What should he do about Sergi—tell
the prince, keep quiet, or what?

Identifying Alternatives and Consequences

4. Have the class brainstorm all the
   things they can think of that the
   steward could do. List these on the
   board.

List of
alternatives:
a) tell the steward
b) don't tell, but get Sergi to stop
c) pretend he never saw it
d) go back at night and put up the
   fence
e) talk to Sergi about it
f) change the map of the prince's
   land
. . . etc.

Identifying Alternative and Consequences, continued

5. Have the students identify all the people directly and indirectly involved in this situation; list these across the top of the board.

6. Distribute the values analysis guide. Divide the class into as many groups as there are alternatives. Assign each group an alternative and direct them to think of all the consequences that might occur to all those involved if that alternative were followed. Ask how each character might feel if that alternative were chosen.

7. Have the groups report. Briefly list the consequences in the matrix on the board as reports are given. Encourage others to add anything omitted.

the steward/Sergi/Sergi's family/the prince/other peasants/other land owners/etc.

Making a Tentative Choice

8. Have the students reflect on the alternatives listed (and any other new ones suggested). Then have them write the alternative action they think the steward *should* follow and write one reason for their answer. Have several volunteers state their choices and reasons for their choices.

9. Assign the students to check with three fellow students or members of their families before the next class to see what they think the steward *should* do. Students will discuss all action recommendations in the next class.

FOURTH DAY

Moral Reasoning/Hypothesis Testing

Objectives:

1. When in a group, to willingly accept the points of view of others and contribute to completion of a group goal.
2. In a class discussion, to state and respond—giving reasons—to reasoning for and against a variety of recommended solutions to a value dilemma.
3. Given a discussion of alternatives, to choose a preferred alternative and give one or more reasons for that choice.
4. Given documents of the period, to state and explain evidence relative to the hypothesized features of this society.

Materials:

- excerpts from documents*
- values analysis guide from previous lesson**
- ditto list of hypotheses from first and second class

TEACHER	STUDENTS

Moral Reasoning

Review

1. Have students review the dilemma and list some of the choices open to the steward.	. . . he could "see nothing . . ." . . . he could speak to Sergi . . . . . . he could report to the prince . . . etc.
2. Have two or three volunteers report some alternatives recommended by those they interviewed and the reasons they give for their choices. (Allow only 5 minutes for 1 and 2.)	

Reasoning About Choices

3. Have the students reread their own choices and reasons as stated on the values guides. Permit them to make any changes they wish. Then, by a show of hands, identify the students who selected each alternative. Divide them into groups of 3–5 according to the alternative chosen. Have each group do the following (write these directions on the board):
   a) listen to and list the reasons given by all members for choosing that alternative
   b) select what you think are the two or three best reasons
   c) write the reason why they think these are the best reasons
   d) select someone to report to the class
      (allow 10 minutes or so for this step)

4. Reconvene the class (with students facing each other in a circle or hollow square). Have various spokespersons report to the class. Encourage all students to offer ideas, to challenge reasons given, to offer their own reasons for the alternative they chose. Use the following questions to guide the discussion, where appropriate:
   a) What obligation does the steward have to the prince? to Sergi? to the law? to Sergi's family?

---

*See Prologue.
** See Epilogue

REASONING ABOUT CHOICES, CONTINUED

b) Which obligation is most important?

c) From the point of view of Sergi (of the prince? of Sergi's wife and family?) what should the steward do?

d) When, if ever, is it right to break a law—or to "tell on" anyone, even a relative?

(allow 10–15 minutes for this step)

Making a New Choice

5. Close the discussion by having the class state all of the alternatives being presented and the reasons they heard given for some of them. Then have the students write on the back of their values analysis guide the alternative they now think the steward should follow and one reason why he should take this action.

HYPOTHESIS TESTING

Identifying Needed Evidence

6. Tell the students you have some excerpts from some documents written at this time by some people like the steward from this place. They can read these to find out what the prince—or life here—was like.

(Students will have expressed concern in the values discussion about knowing more about the prince and how he might react to various actions the steward could have taken.)

7. Students can also read these excerpts to test the accuracy of their previous hypotheses.

Ask: *If the features you have checked earlier really are correct, what will these documents be about?* List these on the board.
Or ask: *If the prince is like what you think he might be like, what will these sources say about him?*

. . . about war, perhaps
. . . attacks on other peoples
. . . about trade with other peoples
. . . the prince and how he ran the country

Collecting and Analyzing Evidence

8. Direct the students to read the excerpts and state any of this evidence they find as they come across it.

9. Have students report their findings.

The prince helped the poor—they did have social classes.

This was a time of war and violence;
there probably were warriors around.
Schools existed.
Some people were Christians.

10. Conclude by asking students to review the ditto handout of hypotheses to report at the next class on
those that were most accurate in
view of the data examined so far.

FIFTH DAY

Developing a Conclusion

Objectives:

1. Given hypotheses about life in this place around 1,000 years ago, to evaluate
   their accuracy in terms of the available evidence.
2. Given evidence relating to hypotheses about life in this place, to state at least
   3 hypotheses justified by the evidence.
3. Given tested hypotheses, to synthesize them into a unique communication
   accurately describing life in this society about 1,000 years ago.
4. Given an opportunity to discuss life in this society, to voluntarily give reasons and evidence in support of one's conclusions and to challenge reasoning and evidence given in support of conclusions of questionable validity.

Materials:

- ditto list of original hypotheses and revisions
- student notes
- data used in class (as needed)

TEACHER	STUDENTS

Review

1. Have the students refer to the
   original question being investigated
   and to the subordinate questions.
   Ask volunteers for answers to several questions upon which the class
   might all agree. Allow just enough
   time to stimulate thinking about
   this topic, but stop the discussion
   before more than several answers
   have been offered.

What was life like in this society?

DEVELOPING CONCLUSIONS

Evaluating Hypotheses

2. Divide the class into groups of 4–5 students. Direct each group to focus on a different set of hypotheses and to decide which were supported, refuted, or untested by the evidence. They should be prepared to justify their decisions. (Allow 10–15 minutes for this.)

3. Reconvene the class. Have the groups report their results. Encourage contributions by all students —challenges as well as support. List the various hypothesized features or modifications thereof in columns on the board.

Definite Features	*Questionable Features*	*Untested Ideas*
had a system of formal education	lived by the sea	?
farming was important		
definite social classes		

Stating a Conclusion

4. Have the class agree on the three or four most accurate hypothesized features of this society. Require evidence to support their decisions.

The major characteristics of this society were . . . because . . .

5. Have each student write a sentence that answers the initial question: *What was life like in this society?* Have volunteers read their sentences and discuss any which the students wish to discuss. Indicate that in the next lesson, the class can visit this site (via slides) to find out even more about this place, including where it is. They should think about what they would expect to see there given today's conclusions.

(The question of the location of this site will have risen by this time)

SIXTH DAY

Applying Conclusions to New Data

Objectives:

1. Given conclusions about major features of life in this society 1,000 years ago, to state (infer) evidence that should exist in buildings and art if these conclusions are accurate.

2. Given slides of structures and art work from this site dating to A.D. 1000, to identify evidence that supports, refutes, or requires modification of stated conclusions.
3. Given conclusions and new data, to be willing to modify, reject, or otherwise alter such conclusions in the light of new evidence.
4. Given information about a specific society, to state at least three relationships inferred among selected features of this society.

Materials:

- slides of buildings, art work from old Kiev
- sentences from previous lesson

TEACHER	STUDENTS

Review

1. Have the students restate the conclusions they reached as a class in the preceding lesson. List these on the board.

APPLYING CONCLUSIONS

Identifying Expected Evidence

2. Introduce the slides. Ask the students: *If our conclusions about this society of 1,000 years ago are accurate, what will we see in the structures there or art works to convince us of our accuracy?* Probe for explicit statements about how what they may see will confirm (or refute) their conclusions (i.e., How do you know a Christian church when you see one?).

Perhaps the students will say:
. . . Christian churches
. . . portraits of warriors
. . .

Collecting and Analyzing Evidence

3. Project the slides slowly talking about each as it is shown, focusing on its relation to any of the conclusions under consideration. What new ideas arise?

STATING CONCLUSIONS

4. Have the students restate the 3–4 conclusions that they, as a class, believe to be most accurate in terms of the data so far examined.

Based on the evidence we have seen, this society . . .

EXTENDING THE STUDY TO NEW AREAS

5. Have the students suggest how and why the various features they identified related to each other— Christianity and commerce and warriors, for example.

6. Then, have them indicate how they could test the accuracy of these hypothesized relationships.

Perhaps by examining more data about this society or by looking at similar societies around A.D. 1000 (in China, in the West African Sudan, in Western Europe, or in North or South America); or by starting to build a concept of feudalism or of social stratification or of division of labor; or by raising questions about cultural exchange, the independent invention of institutions, and so on. The course text might be a good place to start or continue this investigation.

The study suggested in these lesson plans is very simple, indeed. Such a study could easily move in a number of directions quite different from those suggested here. Additional content and materials could be used. Any number of different objectives could be sought. However, the important thing to note here is the way this particular set of lessons is organized. These six lessons use an inquiry teaching strategy and the format of the plans reflects this structure.

These lesson plans involve students in a series of learning experiences that require them to define a problem for investigation, to make and test hypotheses, and to draw some valid conclusions about the accuracy of their hypotheses—conclusions that they then apply to new data relevant to the initial problem. Moreover, each lesson fits into a larger context of learning. Each carries forward in terms of skills, knowledge, and affect the lessons that precede it and leads into the lessons that follow. In no single lesson will the students engage in all the steps that constitute the inquiry. But used in sequence, these plans will involve a class in the basic steps of inquiring.

Daily lesson plans may be more or less elaborate than those outlined here. Considerable practice and success in using inquiry teaching in the classroom may obviate the necessity for more detailed plans. However, for anyone unfamiliar with a strategy for inquiry teaching, detailed plans may be necessary until the basic steps in the strategy have been internalized. These plans help us focus deliberately on selected aspects of inquiry and keep us from getting so bogged down in content that our lessons revert to lecturing or lesson-hearing. Preparing detailed daily plans also helps ensure that materials appropriate to our objectives and to the requirements of our lesson may be secured or prepared, that students may be arranged in classroom activities in ways to maximize learning, and that possible student reactions may be anticipated and provided for. Finally, detailed lesson plans for inquiry lessons provide the kind of guidance needed to ensure that the essentials of student inquiry receive the attention necessary to accomplish the goals and objectives of inquiry teaching in our classrooms.

There is one very important point to remember, however. No set of lesson plans should be considered rigidly prescriptive. No teacher need slavishly follow the items in a plan if student questions or curiosity or interests lead the unfolding lesson into areas that differ from the original plan. The teacher, above all else, must remain flexible. Lesson plans are guides, not orders. Teachers should feel free to deviate from plans when it appears appropriate to do so, because skill, concept, and affective objectives can be achieved through the use of many different bodies of content.

USING AN INQUIRY STRATEGY AS A STRUCTURE FOR COURSES

While a module outline based on that presented above provides an important element in planning for daily inquiry teaching, such an outline is not the point from which inquiry course planning properly begins. Just as the daily lesson plans are detailed expansions of the sequence of learning activities sketched in a module outline, so is a module outline a detailed expansion of a unit or course of study. The essential starting place for inquiry teaching, as with all classroom teaching, is the course or unit of study. For maximum classroom effectiveness, inquiry teaching requires the organization of instruction into courses or units that are themselves organized around an inquiry teaching strategy.

In using an inquiry teaching strategy as the organizational structure for a unit or course, the basic elements of this strategy may be subsumed under the three basic components of any organized teaching experience: an introduction, a body, and a conclusion. The introductory phase of an inquiry study involves developing a purpose for inquiring. The body of such a study consists of hypothesizing, testing hypotheses, and evaluating them. The conclusion involves tying up and perhaps applying the entire study. An introduction and a conclusion are essential to any extended study, just as they are to even a daily sequence of lessons. No useful inquiry can be undertaken without a purpose, and the function of the introduction is to develop this purpose. Likewise, no inquiry is complete without making its meaning explicit, and this is the main function of the conclusion.

An inquiry strategy, arranged in the form of an introduction, a body of study, and a conclusion, provides a convenient framework for organizing any history or social studies learning experience. Just as this strategy provides a practical guideline for structuring daily classroom lessons, so, too, can it serve as a basic structure for units of study requiring several weeks or months of study. In addition, an inquiry teaching strategy may also serve as the fundamental framework for a single semester or year-long course of study, or even a sequence of courses in an entire curriculum. Inquiry teaching has benefits far beyond the carrying out of specific daily learning experiences.

Structuring Inquiry Courses

Any course of study at any intermediate grade or secondary grade—or any sequence of courses at these grade levels—may be built around the strategy of inquiry teaching presented in the preceding pages. Take a typical world regions or world cultures course, for example. Such courses normally include content about several regions of the Third World, including the Middle East, Latin America, Africa, southern Asia, Southeast Asia, and eastern Asia. If we were to organize such a course in inquiry fashion, we might launch it by developing hypotheses about these regions or peoples in general and then use content about each of these regions to test our hypotheses. A series of concepts and/or general statements about Third World cultures could emerge as one final product of this inquiry.

A course such as this might be introduced by a short unit designed to raise questions about people as a whole and especially about the peoples of the Third World. The main question to emerge might be, "What are the peoples of the Third World like?" This leads to a whole host of other basic questions such as "What do they look like? Why? How do they behave? What do they believe?" And these in turn lead to questions like "Why do they do the things they do and believe what they do? How did they come to do or believe these things? What do they want to do or believe in the future . . . and why?" Questions like these can serve as excellent problems for classroom study. Answers to them will certainly help students gain a clearer understanding of peoples from cultures different from their own and thus gain insights about people in general and themselves in particular.

Once a problem for investigation has been articulated and refined, a course may be organized in one of several ways: either in a largely cumulative fashion, or in a way best described as additive, or in some combination of the two. Analysis of three types of inquiry course structures follows.

An Additive Inquiry Course Structure

In an *additive* inquiry framework, each major content unit directly relates to the initiatory problem, and students may study it independently of all other major content units. Integration of all these units occurs in a final concluding unit by, in effect, adding together the conclusions of each unit to develop a number of general statements relative to the initiatory questions or problems.

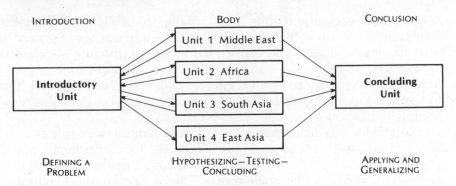

Figure 13.1. An Additive Inquiry Structure

Suppose the introductory unit is used to launch a course organized as in Figure 13.1. Having identified a major question to investigate ("What are the people of the Third World like?") the students can then hypothesize an answer and proceed to test their hypotheses by in-depth studies of each individual region included in the course. Students may perhaps first focus on the Middle East. Here, using selected concepts, they can test their original hypotheses against content in the form of pictures, items from newspapers, or excerpts from travellers' accounts about this region. They might commence the unit by stating, "If the people of the Third World are _____(original hypotheses), then the people of the Middle East should be _____." Then students can study data about the habitat, ethnic groups, political structures and processes, economic features, and other aspects of this region to test their propositions. Finally, they can bring the unit to a close by drawing conclusions about the validity of their hypotheses and by making statements such as, "The peoples of the Middle East are _____ because _____. They aspire to become _____ by _____," and so on.

Students should then hold these conclusions in abeyance as they turn their attention to content about a second region. Referring to their initial questions, they may examine selected data about the peoples of Africa and hypothesize answers to the same questions. Study of this region may proceed exactly like that of the preceding region, but it should end with a series of statements relative to hypotheses about the peoples of Africa: "The peoples of Africa are _____ because_____. They aspire to become_____by _____." Again storing these conclusions for later consideration, the students may proceed in the same manner to study content about the next region and to investigate in a similar manner each of the remaining areas or cultures to be studied.

When all the regions included in the course have been studied, the students may collect their conclusions about each region and add them up—integrate or synthesize them—into a series of statements generally applicable to or descriptive of all regions. Thus, the students progress from the introductory unit to unit 1, then return to the questions or ideas hypothesized in the introduction and apply them to unit 2, returning to the initial questions or hypotheses each time before going on to each of the other units. Finally, to conclude, they pool the conclusions developed in each unit and weave them into a series of generalizations that encompass all they have learned. This additive structure is formulated on the basic steps of inquiring—moving from problem identification to general conclusion. A course organized in this fashion has direction and purpose. It can lead to a solution of a problem or to an answer to a question that is worthy of classroom investigation.

This pattern for organizing content need not be limited to a single course. A sequence of courses, indeed even an entire K–12 curriculum, may be organized in the same way. For example, let us assume that the course on world cultures just outlined is a ninth-grade course. The concepts and generalizations developed at the conclusion of this course could easily be used to initiate a study of European history in the tenth grade and of American history in the eleventh grade. A one-semester, twelfth-grade course in the humanities or on some special topics, such as current problems, ecology, or ethnic studies, might be used to test and elaborate these conclusions still further. A final course in the sequence might synthesize the conclusions of each of the preceding courses, weaving them together and refining them to develop generalizations and concepts about human behavior in all times and places with special reference to the contemporary scene.

A course or sequence of courses organized in this additive fashion offers a very high degree of flexibility, continuity, and reinforcement. It is extremely flexible because, with the exception of the introductory and concluding units, there is no special sequence in which the individual content units must be studied. Hence, units may be added, dropped, or shuffled around for any reason whatsoever (such as relevancy of content, availability of materials, or student interest) without interfering with the overall learning goals. Students may enter the course at almost any point without any serious handicaps. This structure also offers a certain continuity by providing a common starting point for each unit in the form of reference to the initial problem or question. It builds in periodic review and summary by using previously developed ideas, skills, and knowledge again and again. Comparison and contrast are made easy by the parallel structure of its major units and by the opportunities in the concluding unit for pooling comparable information from each of the preceding units. Above all, this framework gives the entire sequence a common purpose and a unifying thread. It allows learning to go somewhere.

A Cumulative Inquiry Course Structure

A second inquiry framework for organizing a course or curriculum may be much more cumulative and integrative than that just described. In a *cumulative* structure, each unit grows directly out of and builds on the preceding unit, the entire sequence culminating in a complete synthesis, and perhaps application, of the accumulated products of all the learning experiences.

Figure 13.2 depicts a cumulative structure. Here students develop a purpose for study in the introductory unit. The second unit then consists of an

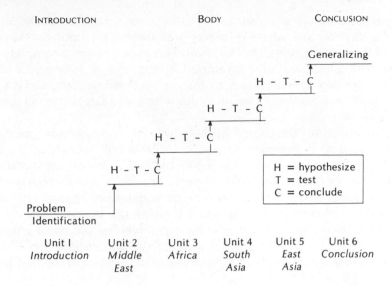

INTRODUCTION BODY CONCLUSION

Generalizing

H – T – C

H – T – C

H – T – C

H – T – C

H = hypothesize
T = test
C = conclude

Problem
Identification

| Unit I | Unit 2 | Unit 3 | Unit 4 | Unit 5 | Unit 6 |
| Introduction | Middle East | Africa | South Asia | East Asia | Conclusion |

Figure 13.2. A Cumulative Inquiry Structure

in-depth study of a body of content used to hypothesize solutions to the initiatory problem and to test these hypotheses. Study of each succeeding unit offers an opportunity to modify, reject, or add to the conclusions already formed as the students progress toward conceptualizing or generalizing about the subject under investigation. The entire structure builds on the basic operations of inquiry teaching from identifying a problem to hypothesizing (H), testing (T), and concluding (C), to final generalizing (or conceptualizing).

A course of study about various world cultures, as described earlier, might be easily reorganized in this cumulative fashion. The same introductory unit could be used to initiate this study. After identifying some questions for investigation, the students could engage in an in-depth study of information about the Middle East. A limited amount of data about this region and its peoples could be examined in order to hypothesize answers to the questions raised in the introductory unit. Then more data may be examined in greater detail to test the validity of these hypotheses and eventually to draw conclusions about them. These conclusions may take the form of statements to the effect that, "The peoples of the Middle East are _____ because _____. They aspire to become _____. They are becoming _____." And so on.

The first and second units thus resemble their counterparts in the additive structure. But in this cumulative structure the students do not put aside the conclusions developed in one unit before starting the next. Instead, they treat these conclusions as hypotheses to be submitted to the test of the evidence about the peoples and cultures of the next region to be studied (Africa, in this hypothetical course of study). As the students proceed, they may modify, expand, or even drop these conclusions altogether, developing new or additional ones as they repeat this process of using the conclusions generated in one unit as hypotheses for the next. The concluding stage of this sequence requires them to develop final conceptual or general statements that embrace all the evidence examined in the preceding units.

The usefulness of a framework such as this is not limited to single courses. Just as is the case for the additive inquiry framework, a cumulative structure may be used to organize a sequence of several courses, or even a complete K–12 curriculum. The generalizations developed at the end of a one-year course might well be treated as hypotheses to test in succeeding courses. Thus, one course may build directly on all that precedes it and lead directly to what immediately follows.

The generalizations developed in this study of world cultures might, for example, be used as hypotheses to test in subsequent courses in European history or American history. They could be tested and appropriately modified by studying the ancient Greeks and Romans or the inhabitants of various medieval European kingdoms. In a following course, the conclusions that emerge in this process could be further tested by applying them to the study of colonial New Englanders, the Jamestown settlers, Southern planters, or yeoman farmers and frontiersmen. Thus the entire sequence can lead to the articulation of useful concepts and generalizations about human behavior and human beings, regardless of time or place.

Because this inquiry structure is highly cumulative, it is somewhat more sophisticated, though no less flexible, than the additive inquiry framework. The major content units (such as the units on the Middle East, Africa, and others cited in the above example) may be arranged in whatever order the students or teacher wish, and the students may enter the sequence at virtually any point without being handicapped in terms of concept and skill learning. Yet this framework makes advanced planning quite difficult. The teacher cannot be positive of what content to have available for the next unit until the exact nature of the hypotheses to be tested in it are known; these become known only at the conclusion of the unit then under study. Thus, either a considerable range of data must be kept available, or the teacher must be able to predict with some accuracy what data will be needed.

This organizational framework offers considerable opportunity for constant comparison and reinforcement. As students test the ideas developed in one unit against new data in the next, similarities in data can be readily identified, and common underlying themes or features gradually become more apparent. The entire process leads to a gradual building or broadening of knowledge and skills culminating directly in high-level intellectualization of the topic under study. Such a framework seems particularly suited to concept development, for it provides repeated opportunities to study examples of concepts introduced in previous units and thus to broaden student images of these concepts throughout the course.

A Sequential Inquiry Course Structure

Although the additive and cumulative structures provide two basic frameworks for inquiry-oriented courses or curricula, the essential elements of these two patterns may be combined in a number of different ways. One of these variations merits particular attention. It combines the idea of cumulative modification of conclusions with the pooling of conclusions developed in the study of a number of discrete bodies of content. For our purposes here, this structure may be best identified as a *sequential* inquiry course structure.

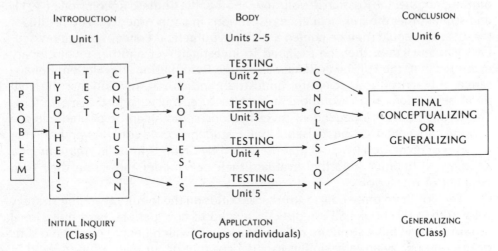

Figure 13.3. A Sequential Inquiry Structure

This sequential framework (Figure 13.3) requires first that students define a problem for inquiry and examine a body of relevant data in order to hypothesize and test solutions, developing some tentative answers (conclusions) in the process. Then small groups of students, or even individual students, may simultaneously investigate different bodies of new but related evidence in order to test further the conclusions developed in the initial unit. Finally, all students may report and examine the conclusions of each independent inquiry and generalize or conceptualize about the results.

The sequential inquiry structure may be used to organize a study of virtually any topic or theme. The study of Third World cultures described above may easily be organized along these lines. Students can develop a problem and then study as a class one cultural region in order to hypothesize and test solutions. Their conclusions may then be tested further by small groups, each studying a different region of the world. The concluding unit brings all students back together to share the results of their investigations and to develop some general statements applicable to all the regions examined.

This same structure might also be used, for example, to organize a study of revolutions. Such a study might commence with a brief look at some contemporary event that purports to be revolutionary (an invention, a discovery, or a significant achievement such as the landing of astronauts on the moon). Students could hypothesize about the nature of revolutions: "What are they like? What causes them? What kind of results do they have?" They would build a simple conceptual model of this phenomenon. Then they might examine evidence about the American Revolution in order to test, broaden, and revise the hypothetical model.

At this point, the class could be divided into several teams, each examining data about a different revolution in order to test the hypothesized concept. One group could study data about the French Revolution, another the Glorious Revolution, another the Russian Revolution, another the Chinese Revolution of 1911, and still another the independence revolutions in Latin America. The results of these studies could then be pooled and the hypothetical concept image revised. Each student could then be assigned to investigate yet another revolutionary event (such as the European Renaissance; the Reformation; the Harlem Renaissance; the agricultural, scientific, industrial, and atomic revolutions; the civil rights revolution; and revolutions in architecture, music, and transportation). The results of these independent investigations could again be pooled and the existing conceptualization revised. Finally, students could study several existing theories of revolution (such as that presented by Crane Brinton in *Anatomy of a Revolution*) in order to further evaluate their own model and refine their own concept of revolution.

Each of these three course structures builds on the inquiry teaching strategy presented in this book. All are directly related to how people learn by rational inquiry. The additive structure reflects the way in which people pool the results of discrete but essentially similar experiences that occur over a long period of time (usually interrupted by numerous totally unrelated learning experiences). The cumulative structure approximates the more deliberate, step-by-step process through which individuals tackle persistent problems that concern them directly. The sequential framework, often used by those engaged in theorizing about selected questions or problems, represents a practical combination of the essential elements of both of the other approaches.

A teacher might wish to use all three frameworks in the same course. If so, the additive framework might be used to structure the first unit or segment of a course so that students can gain experience in using the skills of inquiring without getting too deeply involved in the complex interrelationships of the content. The cumulative framework may then be used for students to experience the progressive aspects of working out solutions to problems involving closely interrelated data. Finally, the sequential framework would provide an opportunity for completely independent inquiry—the necessary culminating experience in any course or curriculum designed to teach students how to learn on their own.

It should be noted at this point that organizing a course in terms of any of these structures does not preclude using concepts and skills as organizers as well. The most effective courses (or units or lessons) are those that have multidimensional structures and goals. Content forms one part of any course; concepts and skills, as well as affect, may form other parts of the same course. The sequence in which all of these components are arranged can be based on an inquiry teaching strategy that enhances rather than limits the learning of selected conceptual, skill, and affective goals.

We can thus organize a unit or course using any of the inquiry structures outlined above and include selected concepts that can structure student study of each segment of the unit or course content. A concept of social class can be introduced in the introductory unit, for instance, to develop hypotheses about the structure of the society being studied, as well as to develop a tentative image of this particular concept; subsequent study of other cultures will provide opportunities to broaden the concept while the concept is used to test further substantive hypotheses developed in the initial unit. Additional concepts can be introduced in succeeding units and reinforced and broadened as the course proceeds. Skills, too, can be integrated into any of these inquiry structures in the same way. Skills associated with analyzing data, for example, may be taught in the first unit and then used as students find them appropriate in later units. Concepts and skills can provide the internal structure of units and courses that are built on a process structure of inquiry.

USING INQUIRY TO ORGANIZE UNITS

One basic difference between a unit of study and a course is the length of time devoted to each. A course usually requires a semester or year to complete. A unit may require anywhere from one week to several months and generally exists as one of a series of units that constitute a course. Yet in terms of structure, a unit is nothing more than a minicourse. To be effective, it should be organized just like a course—that is, it must have an introduction and a conclusion, as well as a body of content. The same inquiry frameworks for structuring courses can be used to organize units for inquiry teaching. Repeating the specific characteristics of these three frameworks is unnecessary, but a description of several different sample units built on one or more of them may be helpful.

Let us take a unit on a Third World culture, for example. Suppose we wish to organize a five-week study of Africa, one of a series of units on various world cultures. Suppose further that we will focus on people, and that the purposes of the study include learning something about people and their culture and developing the skills of thinking. General statements about Africa may be treated as hypotheses for testing in the next unit on South Asia.

The first unit might be introduced by helping students articulate their image of Africans in response, perhaps, to a series of pictures that challenges them to pick out only those people who are inhabitants of the region, or perhaps in response to the question, "What comes to mind when you think of Africa?" The stereotyped view that will certainly emerge may then be challenged by some statistics or a film that depicts the wide variety of peoples who call Africa home. The students will express curiosity about these people and perhaps even about the material. From here, they can move immediately to a study of some specific African peoples and cultures.

Our hypothesized typical African may be tested against information about several different groups of Africans, each selected for study because its culture represents a feature common to many Africans. The students could first study the Yoruba of Nigeria, hypothesizing about the nature of this culture on the basis of limited evidence, and then test these hypotheses by analyzing Yoruba music, art, folklore, tradition, history, social customs, and so on. Then they might draw some conclusions about the Yoruba relative to these hypotheses: either their hypotheses are valid, or they need to be added to, modified, or dismissed.

Thereupon, the students could turn their attention to another group, perhaps the Ganda of Uganda. Again, they would hypothesize about these people and then test their hypotheses by analyzing the behavioral and institutional expressions of Ganda culture. Conclusions could then be drawn about the validity of their hypotheses. Similar studies can be made of other Africans, too, such as the Ashanti and the Kikuyu.

Finally, our unit may draw to a close by having the students pool their conclusions regarding each group of people and compare them to their original image of typical Africans. Certainly this image will need to be modified in view of the evidence just examined. Important and more valid generalizations about Africans will emerge. Although these represent the conclusion of this unit, they may also be treated as hypotheses about peoples of the Third World in general and submitted to the test of data about the inhabitants of South Asia in a following unit, if the course is so organized. This sample unit is built on an additive framework. It proceeds from an introduction that generates a problem for investigation to hypotheses that are tested by a number of different sets of data—in this case data about different peoples of Africa. Then the conclusions of each test can be pooled and generalizations derived. In diagram form, this unit might be depicted as in Figure 13.4.

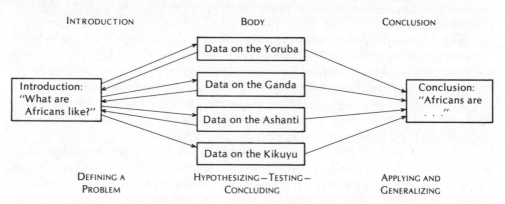

Figure 13.4. A Unit Using an Additive Structure

By way of another example, suppose we wish to organize an inquiry unit about leadership in America along the lines of a sequential framework. Such a unit might be introduced by having students articulate a problem for study: "Why do some people become leaders while others do not?" The entire class might attempt to identify why they think certain of their schoolmates have attained positions of leadership in school affairs: the head cheerleader, the president of the dramatics club or student council, the football captain, the features editor of the school paper, and so on. Evidence could be sought by checking records and perhaps by interviewing these leaders and other students. The class could conclude this phase of the inquiry by making some general statements as to how people become leaders. These statements may then be considered hypotheses for further study.

Thereupon, each student could look into the life of a different American. Representatives of all aspects of life might be studied—from the field of politics: George Washington, Martin Luther King, Barbara Jordan, Thaddeus Stevens, Dixie Lee Ray, Shirley Chisholm, Thomas E. Dewey, John F. Kennedy; from the arts: Frank Lloyd Wright, Beverly Sills, Earl (Fatha) Hines; from labor and business: John L. Lewis, Andrew Carnegie, Caesar Chavez; and from other areas of society: Harriett Tubman, Jane Addams, Jonas Salk, Daniel Hale Williams, Lucretia Mott, Betty Friedan, Orville and Wilbur Wright, and even Wyatt Earp. Each student could test the class statements about the determinants of leadership by seeing to what extent these factors are evident in the career of his or her subject.

Upon reconvening and pooling all conclusions, the class might develop a general list of leadership attributes to then check against the original hypothesis or perhaps against excerpts from Machiavelli's essay on leadership, *The Prince*. Or students might be asked to apply their conclusions by preparing a critique of James MacGregor Burns' description of Franklin D. Roosevelt as both "a lion and a fox." Or they might even use the criteria they develop to appraise the potential or career of a prominent local or national contemporary leader.

This unit could vary in length depending on the amount of time allotted to independent research and on the number of students who must report on their findings. Regardless of its length, however, the unit may be considered an example of the sequential inquiry structure. The students develop a problem, work out and test a tentative solution, and then investigate one or more new bodies of data relative to the same problem before pooling their conclusions and revisions and applying some general statements regarding the initial problem. Diagrammatically, the unit might look like that in Figure 13.5.

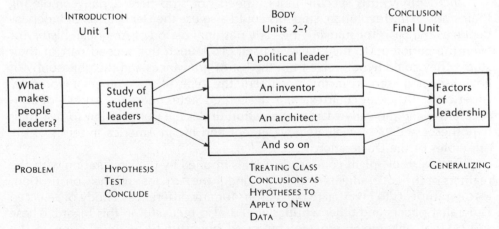

Figure 13.5. A Unit Built on a Sequential Inquiry Structure

Either of the units discussed above can be organized just as easily along the lines of any inquiry framework. The point is that any one unit of study must be as carefully organized as an entire course of study. And inquiry units may be organized just like inquiry courses. The only difference between units and courses is the scope of what is being studied and the time devoted to this study.

One additional point may be useful: in designing an inquiry unit (or course for that matter) it is not always necessary or desirable to start at the chronological or logical beginning of the topic to be studied. In fact, it often proves extremely useful for motivational as well as organizational purposes to start a unit with something from the middle or end of the topic under study.

For example, instead of introducing an American history course with the conventional study of Columbus and the explorers, we could begin with the Declaration of Independence. Using the list of grievances and philosophy of government contained in this source, students could generate hypotheses about the causes of the American revolution. Then they could study the settlement of the 13 colonies and the subsequent colonial period not just to cover this period as is so often done, but to test their own hypotheses about the causes of the event that gave birth to their country. This study would be much more purposeful, self-directed, and relevant than the usual method of study.

Students could conclude their study by evaluating the accuracy of their original hypotheses and any others later invented or discovered in terms of the evidence uncovered from their texts and other instructional materials. They could also evaluate the Declaration as a historical document and apply their conclusions to additional data in the form of relevant statements by individuals of the period (both colonial and English) and by historians as well. Thus, an inquiry study of early American history could well be organized around a single document that would provide continuity and purpose to learning. At the same time it would allow, indeed require, students to develop and practice the skills of inquiry as they gather information, develop concepts, and form generalizations pertinent to the subject.

Incidentally, this specific inquiry need not stop here. Upon completing their study of the revolution, students could also use the Declaration of Independence as the basis for studying the early national period of American history or even the period up to the Civil War itself. To launch this second part of their study, they could hypothesize from the list of grievances and the philosophy of government presented in this document the type of government favored by Americans. Then they could examine the United States under the Articles of Confederation and the early years of the nation under the Constitution to test their hypotheses and/or to evaluate government and life in America in terms of the principles of the Declaration.

Such a study might contrast the ideals implied by the Declaration with the realities of the governments established under the Articles and the Constitution, leading students to investigate the reasons for any differences. Study of selected Federalist papers and other writings would also be useful in this regard. These sources not only would provide continued opportunity for instruction in the skills of inquiry but also would enable students to develop generalizations, or hypotheses, about social and political change, human motivation, the structure and functions of government, and so on. Using a strategy of inquiry teaching to study these topics (or any others) can provide the opportunity to achieve a variety of learning goals simultaneously and can make learning more purposeful and student-centered than is typical of conventional exposition.

SUMMARY

Inquiry teaching has many facets. Among these, its organization or structure is most crucial. If a course or unit of study does not require students to define a problem, hypothesize answers, test their hypotheses against a variety of data, draw reasoned conclusions, and apply these to new data to synthesize a valid generalization or conclusion, inquiry will probably not occur in the daily classroom learning experiences. If the teacher does not carefully design the daily lessons to require students to engage in these same operations, inquiry surely will not occur. Carefully planned courses, units, and daily lessons built on a strategy of inquiry are essential to effective teaching.

Designing inquiry learning experiences involves three major activities, each involving increasing attention to the details of a strategy for inquiring. First, courses and/or units must be conceptualized that are organized in terms of the basic steps of a strategy for inquiry teaching. Next, modular outlines of more specific learning experiences must be prepared to sequence the activities that carry out the goals and objectives of the course or unit. These modular outlines, organized in terms of the inquiry operations through which students are to proceed in the classroom, provide the basis for the more precise planning of daily lessons that follows. Preparing these daily lessons constitutes the final step in planning for classroom teaching. Such plans specify the teacher and student actions that will carry out in a classroom setting the various steps of inquiry as students move to achieve the daily, unit, and course goals and objectives. The strategy of inquiry teaching described in the preceding pages may well be used as a structure for each of these three levels of teaching plans. When so used, the climate of thinking and learning to think will be sharply enhanced, as will the imaginative potential of the course for which it serves as a framework.

notes

1. Ralph Tyler, *Basic Principles of Curriculum and Instruction* (Chicago: University of Chicago Press, 1949), pp. 1–43; Bryce B. Hudgins, *Learning and Thinking* (Itasca, Ill.: F.E. Peacock Publishers, 1977), pp. 1–63; Hilda Taba, *Curriculum Development: Theory and Practice* (New York: Harcourt, Brace and World, 1962), pp. 76–99, 112–129, 145–147.

14

EvaluatinG
InquirY

Evaluation plays as important a role in inquiry teaching as it does in any other type of teaching. Measuring student achievement provides a basis for determining the degree of student mastery of learning objectives, both cognitive and affective. Measures of student achievement also provide a basis for improving instruction by supplying information useful to diagnose student learning needs, as well as to identify the strengths and weaknesses of classroom instruction and learning materials. By measuring what students have learned from their participation in a sequence of inquiry lessons, teachers can secure much needed insights not only into the quality of student learning, but also into the quality of their own classroom teaching. This chapter describes procedures and items that have proven useful in evaluating inquiry in the social studies.

EVALUATION AND
INQUIRY TEACHING

Most classroom teachers measure the learning outcomes of their instruction regularly. Those who use inquiry teaching strategies do not find themselves relieved from this important function of teaching. Instead, the very nature of their teaching often requires even more attention to classroom evaluation than that undertaken by teachers who employ more conventional teaching strategies. Concern about evaluation results not only from the frequent need to justify the value of inquiry teaching as a classroom strategy, but also from the nature of the learning outcomes that distinguish inquiry teaching from other approaches. Thus, teachers who use inquiry teaching must, from the start, be alert to the importance of evaluation.

For most inquiry teachers, evaluation is an ongoing and highly subjective, informal process. We continuously evaluate what we are doing as a lesson unfolds as we try to determine whether or not the students have reached a certain stage in the learning process so they can profitably proceed to the next stage. Sometimes we evaluate by observation, at others by questioning. In each instance we look for indications that what we have been doing or seeking has been achieved by the students. For this reason, detailed lesson plans are useful; if we think out and note the key learning operations in which we want students to engage and the things they will say or do to indicate they are ready to undertake these operations, then our on-the-spot evaluation need not be a hit-or-miss affair, and our teaching will have that much more effect. The degree of success we experience in inquiry teaching directly reflects the extent to which we consciously evaluate what we and the students in our class are doing as we move through the various steps and procedures of the teaching strategy we are employing.

However, on-going evaluation often seems subjective and highly intuitive. At best it leads only to rather impressionistic judgments about student achievement and the quality of classroom instruction. Because this type of evaluation fails to generate replicable evidence that can serve as a basis for reflection and analysis, such efforts have limited use in determining overall student achievement or in refining or revising the instructional procedures or materials used in an inquiry lesson. Fortunately, more formal methods exist for these purposes.

To be most effective, formal teacher evaluation of the products of inquiry teaching must consider two factors. First, we must distinguish carefully between the various types of objectives to be evaluated toward which our inquiry teaching supposedly was directed. And second, we must realize that we can measure what students have learned, or at least how their behavior has changed (presumably as a result of a classroom learning experience), either by asking them to tell us directly or by having them demonstrate whatever they have learned indirectly by some other type of observable or measurable behavior. Precisely identifying the objectives to be evaluated and selecting the evaluation procedures and instruments appropriate to measuring these objectives provide the keys to successful evaluation of inquiry learning and teaching.

The types of learning objectives commonly sought by most inquiry teachers can be classified into two basic categories. The cognitive objectives of inquiry teaching include knowledge of generalizations, patterns, concepts, and specifics, and mastery of cognitive skills—including thinking processes like inquiring, decision-making, or problem-solving as well as the microthinking skills defined by Bloom and his colleagues. The second category of objectives has an affective nature, consisting of values and valuing, attitudes, and preferences. In order to determine how successful a particular inquiry unit or course was in facilitating the learning of any of these objectives, teachers must be able to devise, select, use, and judge the evaluation procedures appropriate to each of these types of objectives.

MEASURING
COGNITIVE LEARNING

Educators still use paper and pencil tests most often to measure the cognitive outcomes of instruction. Usually these tests consist of a combination of objective and essay items, arranged in some sequence—usually chronological, topical, or by degree of difficulty—with the objective items generally preceding the essay items. Such tests can easily provide a measure of student learning in inquiry teaching, as well as a measure of the effectiveness of the teaching itself. However, because of the complexity and diversity of the cognitive objectives for which inquiry teaching can be used and the problems inherent in testing for such objectives, the nature, preparation, and use of classroom tests for inquiry teaching differ considerably from those employed to measure the learning outcomes of more conventional teaching.

Like most teachers, inquiry teachers generally must prepare their own chapter, unit, midcourse, and final exams to consist either of self-designed items or items copied from texts, workbooks, other tests, or any of a dozen other sources. In order for these tests to accurately measure student achievement from inquiry teaching, care must be taken to ensure the reliability and validity of these tests—to ensure that these tests consistently measure the types of learning objectives they are intended to measure. This requires attention to the structure of the tests themselves, to the types of items included on them, and to how such tests are prepared and evaluated.

The Structure of Inquiry Tests

Like any valid test, a valid inquiry test must have three characteristics. First, in the distribution of test items or points, the test should directly reflect the emphasis given to objectives sought in the unit or chapter being tested. Thus, if a third of the students' time and effort was devoted to study of a particular topic (presumably because that topic was important enough to warrant that much time and effort), then a third of the test items or points should be devoted to measuring knowledge of that topic. If a unit of study required equal attention to five major topics, then each of the five should receive equal attention on the unit test.

Second, test items should reflect the various levels of knowledge and skills taught. Many teacher-made tests tend to evaluate only the lowest level of knowledge and skills in spite of the best of intentions, often in contradiction to our stated instructional objectives. For example, a study some years ago of 50 teacher-made tests in science and social studies revealed that 81% of the test items measured knowledge of specifics, while only 11% of the items measured knowledge of understandings and 8% measured skills.[1] Since inquiry teaching seeks to develop a variety of cognitive skills and knowledge at varying levels of complexity, tests used to measure the outcomes of such teaching must measure both the level and the distribution of the cognitive objectives toward which the teaching is directed.

Finally, an effective test must be valid and reliable. That is, a test must measure what it is supposed to measure (validity) and do it consistently so that several different evaluators would arrive at the same score and interpretation of the results (reliability). Thus, a good inquiry test, as any test, ought to include questions appropriate to the objectives to be measured, questions that will elicit the types of knowledge and skills intended.

Of course, like any test, an inquiry test must also have variety; it ought to include several types of questions, not only because some types of questions measure mastery of certain skills or kinds of knowledge better than others, but also because variety in types of test items enhances student interest and motivation. Tests must also be useable—easy to administer, score, and evaluate. Tests, furthermore, should be challenging. They should not be so taxing as to discourage students, but neither should they be so easy as to "be a breeze." A test that is too easy fails to measure the upper limits of student learning and achievement. Tests should challenge students to reach as well as ask them to repeat or demonstrate where they now are.

Although tests may be organized in any number of formats, some formats seem more appropriate than others for evaluating inquiry teaching. Probably the most useful inquiry test format consists of two basic parts: one part measures knowledge and the second measures skills. Such a test reflects the following structure:

Part I. Knowledge

1.1 Specifics
1.2 Patterns
1.3 General/Conceptual

Part II. Skills

2.1 Microthinking Skills
—Comprehension
—Application
—Analysis
—Synthesis
—Evaluation
2.2 Process Thinking Skills
—Problem Definition
—Hypothesizing
—Evidencing

One might add a third part to this structure—application. Whereas questions in Part I might measure recall and recognition of knowledge, and those in Part II might measure a student's ability to use specific thinking skills, this third set of items could require students to apply previously learned knowledge to new information, thus measuring use of various types of knowledge and skills simultaneously. By organizing a test into the components suggested here, a test can permit students to do first what they usually seem most anxious to do—to pour out all the information they have learned and demonstrate their degree of mastery of the skills taught. Then they can build on their data base of remembered knowledge and skills by applying them to new data or problematic situations. A two or three part test as described here serves as an excellent organizational pattern for any unit, midcourse, or final exam in inquiry teaching.

Within each part of this test format, questions can be arranged in a variety of patterns. As suggested above, questions might progress from the lowest level of difficulty to the highest: from knowledge of specifics to knowledge of generalizations; from translation, interpretation, and other skills of comprehension to evaluating in terms of given or self-generated criteria. At the same time, the content of the questions can be organized in chronological sequence, or topically, in order of difficulty (from more concrete to more abstract, for example), or according to the sequence of class presentation of the unit goals. Objective questions may precede essay questions, and questions calling for recognition may precede those calling for recall. Thus, useful inquiry tests have many dimensions.

The structure of a test is important to teachers and students alike. A well-structured test facilitates student completion and actually reinforces learning, while a random mix of different types of questions results only in student confusion and, almost certainly, poor performance. Moreover, a well-organized test built according to these guidelines facilitates evaluation of teaching and student achievement by compartmentalizing items of similar levels of difficulty and content. Thus, analysis of these items leads more readily to the recognition of weaknesses in teaching or unit materials, as well as to a more precise analysis of deficiencies in student achievement.

Planning An Inquiry Test

To ensure that the objective part of an inquiry test measures all critical cognitive learning objectives without overemphasizing or omitting any single objective, teachers can use a matrix like the Test Planning Chart on page 339 to plan their tests. Such a matrix can divide the test items into any number of categories depending on the objectives sought. This particular matrix divides the test items into two kinds, those measuring knowledge and those measuring skills. It furthermore divides each set of items according to the topic and/or media studied in the unit being tested.

Test items in Part I are coded according to type of knowledge and content. Those in Part II are coded according to skill level and the media (map, written test, document, graph, etc.) with which each skill is used; they can also be coded according to the course content that will be included in the media to be used (if one so desires). This particular test plan could even be extended to include the components of inquiring whenever they serve as the instructional objectives. The value of such a plan lies in the fact that it calls a teacher's attention to the different types and levels of cognitive objectives that can be sought, and thus should be measured, in an inquiry teaching unit. Such a matrix thus helps a teacher develop objective tests which are more likely to reflect the levels and distribution of knowledge and skill objectives taught in the particular segment of the course to be evaluated.

In using a matrix such as this, a teacher can employ the following procedure:

1. List the major content topics or subtopics to be tested under *Content Areas* down the left hand side of Part I of the matrix.
2. List the media (maps, documents, etc.) the students used or studied in the unit under *Media* down the left hand side of Part II of the matrix.

TEST PLANNING CHART

(Cognitive Objectives)

PART I. KNOWLEDGE ITEMS

CONTENT AREAS	1.10 Specifics	1.20 Ways & Means Patterns	1.30 Conceptual & Generalized	Total %
Total %				100

PART II. SKILL ITEMS

MEDIA and/or CONTENT	2 Comprehension	3 Application	4 Analysis	5 Synthesis	6 Evaluation	Total %
Total %						100

3. Key the media to specific content from the unit, if desired.
4. Determine the weight to be assigned each content topic and media to be tested (in terms of percentage of the total test).
5. Determine the weight to be assigned to the various levels of knowledge and skills to be tested (in terms of percentage of the total test).
6. Review the unit to be tested in order to guard against omitting any skills or topics that received significant attention in teaching. Check also the unit objectives to see that all objectives, if taught, are reflected in the test plan.
7. Finally, determine the distribution of test items by content or topic, levels of knowledge, and media and skills by placing in appropriate boxes of the matrix the number of test items to be prepared for each. Be sure the number of items reflects the weights assigned to each component of the list.

Use of this procedure can lead to the creation of a test that much more validly measures teaching and learning than a test prepared in some other less structured fashion. Suppose, for example, that we wish to construct a test for a unit of study that emphasized three major topics. Suppose too, that in teaching about these topics we wanted students to learn both specific and generalized knowledge, as well as a knowledge of patterns and of ways and means of dealing with this information. Assume, finally, that we also intended to teach students the skills of comprehension using graphs and the text narrative, as well as the skills of analysis and application. We want our test to be a valid measure of these goals.

Now, suppose that our test requires about fifty minutes and that we have decided to make it 60% objective and 40% essay. Within these limits we also want the test to measure the types of skill and knowledge objectives noted here and to give approximately equal weight to these two major types of objectives. A test plan for the objective portion of a test based on these specifications might resemble the one in Figure 14.1.

According to this sample test plan, the objective portion will consist of 30 objective questions, 15 devoted to knowledge and 15 devoted to three specific skills. Each item will be worth two points. Thus, this portion will comprise 60% of the test and, we estimate, can be completed in about 25 to 30 minutes, figuring an average of one minute to complete each item. Our test items are distributed as equally as possible over the content topics (5 each) and media (3–4 each) to be tested. They reflect the emphasis given the different levels of knowledge and skills in class.

In setting up this part of the test, we can arrange the items so that we first measure student knowledge of specific information across all topics, then their knowledge of patterns across all three topics, and finally their generalized or conceptual knowledge of the three topics. Four sets of skill questions can follow, each set referring to a given graph or paragraph. The questions within each set can progress from translation through interpretation to synthesizing questions in the proportions indicated in our plan.

TEST PLAN

(30 Objective Questions)

CONTENT	Part I. KNOWLEDGE				MEDIA	Part II. SKILL			
	Specifics	Patterns	General	Total		Translation	Interpretation	Synthesis	Total
Topic 1	2	1	2	5	Graph #1	2	1	1	4
Topic 2	2	2	1	5	Graph #2	1	2	1	4
Topic 3	2	1	2	5	Paragraph #1	1	1	2	4
					Paragraph #2	1	1	1	3
Total 30%	6	4	5	15	Total 30%	5	5	5	15

Figure 14.1. A Sample Objective Test Plan

Finally, the essay portion of the test can require students to answer two questions. One question will ask them to recall knowledge learned in the unit by describing some specific event, condition, or topic studied. A second will require them to explain how some event in this unit was related to another event they have previously studied, thus giving them an opportunity to demonstrate their skills of application and analysis. Each question will be worth 20 points to maintain the planned balance between thinking skills and knowledge. Thus, our test plan will reflect the learning objectives of the unit as well as the distribution of the information studied in the unit. In its final form, then, our test may be organized like that in Figure 14.2.

Part I. Objective Items

A. *Items Measuring Knowledge*

Level of Knowledge	Topics 1	2	3	Question Numbers
Specifics	2	2	2	1–6
Patterns	1	2	1	7–10
Generalized	2	1	2	11–15

B. *Items Measuring Skills*

	Graph #1	Graph #2	Paragraph #1	Paragraph #2
Translation	2	1	1	1
Interpretation	1	2	1	1
Synthesis	1	1	2	1
Question No.	16–19	20–23	24–27	28–30

Part II. Essay Items

#1   One essay measuring recall of knowledge
#2   One essay measuring skills of analysis and application

Figure 14.2. A Sample Inquiry Test Structure

Of course, inquiry tests may be any length, and the distribution of essay and objective items may vary according to the objectives of the unit to be tested and the time available to the teacher for grading the tests. Whatever their length or objective/essay proportion, inquiry tests must reflect in the level and distribution of test items the knowledge and skill goals of the unit being tested. To facilitate preparing these tests, teachers can use a test plan like the one presented here to relate content and media with the skills and types of knowledge to be tested. A valid and reliable inquiry test requires attention to all the goals of a unit or learning experience. Careful advanced planning using the procedure described here can help assure the creation of such tests.

Selecting Appropriate Test Items

While careful test planning is essential to effective evaluation in inquiry teaching so, too, is the selection of test items that are appropriate to the learning objectives we wish to measure. Many different types of test items can and should be used to measure student achievement of knowledge, skill, and process objectives because different types of questions seem better suited to measuring certain objectives than do others. Each type of item also has its own unique advantages and weaknesses. By using a number of different types of items on a test, we maximize the balance and validity of the test while, at the same time, provide a variety to challenge and interest the students. In so doing we can construct a test that provides a much more valid measure of inquiry teaching and learning than a conventional, one-type-of-question test.

Measuring knowledge. Both objective and essay questions can be used effectively to measure knowledge of specifics, patterns or trends, and concepts, generalizations, or principles. Among the more useful types of objective items for this purpose are multiple choice, matching, completion, and true-false/ correction questions. Of course, each of these types of questions has its own strengths and weaknesses. Each must be carefully prepared in terms of clarity, accuracy, and completeness, and each must be constructed and placed in a test so as to avoid providing answers to other questions on the test. Inquiry tests can use each of these types of questions to good advantage in measuring student knowledge.

For example, multiple choice items can be easily used to measure knowledge of specifics, as illustrated by questions 1 and 2 below:

1. The majority of people who lived around 1,000 years ago at the site studied in our unit were most likely:

   a) farmers.
   b) merchants.
   c) nobles.
   d) fishermen.

2. England is to Europe as which nation is to Asia?

   a) Australia
   b) Mainland China
   c) Japan
   d) Korea

A modified type of true-false question may also measure various types of student knowledge. Such questions not only require students to indicate whether the statement is true or false, but also (to eliminate the element of guessing—the fundamental weakness of this kind of question) require students to correct any statement they decide is false, as in the following items:

1. The majority of people who lived around 1,000
   years ago on the site studied in this unit were
   merchants.   1. _____

   _____

2. England is to Europe as *Japan* is to Asia.   2. _____

   _____

If a student decides either of these statements is false, he or she must mark an *F* in the space after the number and write on the line under the statement a word that could replace the *italicized* word (or phrase) to make the statement true.

Knowledge of patterns or relationships may also be measured by objective items. One of the most useful objective items for this purpose is the outline question. In essence, this is a multiple choice question with a variety of different options to be used in answering the question. For example, the outline below omits a number of items.[2] Students can write in the spaces provided in the outline the words or phrases from the list that best fit on each line in terms of the overall idea of the outline:

benefits enjoyed   no free elections
freedom from taxation   no services provided by government
informed voting   opportunity to take part in government
little past experience with democracy   reasons for accepting the lack of
                                                               freedom

CITIZENSHIP

I.   Citizenship in a democracy
     A. _____
         1. Protection of individual rights
         2. _____

     B. Responsibilities owed
         1. _____

         2. Respect for law

II. Citizenship in a dictatorship
     A. Examples of lack of freedom
         1. _____

         2. No real guarantee of personal liberty
     B. _____
         1._____

         2. Promise of a "better life"

This type of question seems especially useful for measuring student knowledge of patterns of information and relationships. It may be more or less open depending on the objectives to be tested. Such a test item could consist of various phrases, including both specific examples and general statements, interspersed with a series of lines that correspond to the position of some of the given words in an outline, as in the preceding example. Students could then be asked to place these items on the lines to indicate a meaningful interrelationship of the ideas expressed. An even more open type of question could merely list some information and permit students to devise their own outline indicating the relationships they see in this information. This type of question must always deal with information students have already studied, however; if it did not, the question would test an analytical skill rather than existing knowledge.

Student knowledge of concepts and generalizations may also be measured by objective questions. A multiple choice question similar to that below, for example, measures student knowledge of a previously studied generalization:

Which generalization is most accurate in terms of the information about world population growth studied in this unit?

    a) The amount of available food is directly related to population growth.
    b) The more people can afford children, the more children they have.
    c) Smaller families reflect higher income and educational levels of parents.
    d) Large families are necessary in both preindustrial and industrial societies.[3]

To measure knowledge of a concept, students can also be given an example of a concept and asked to identify from a list of concepts the one that the example best illustrates, as in this question:[4]

Each item below consists of a statement. From the list which follows each statement choose the concept most closely related to it.

1. Franklin D. Roosevelt's speaking ability and his excellent radio voice won him considerable public support.

    a) decision-making   c) leadership
    b) ideology   d) citizenship

2. Medieval peasants were expected to bow to the lord of the manor.

    a) leadership   c) role
    b) norms   d) social class

Students might also be asked to identify from a list the major attributes of a concept studied in class or to recall these attributes from memory and list them in answer to a completion question.

Multiple choice and other objective questions can be used to measure knowledge of cause and effect relationships, chronological relationships, comparative relationships, and principles as well as the basic components of any methodology or even more specific name-place-date knowledge. However, in selecting or constructing such questions, caution must be exercised to avoid providing clues to the answer by the wording of the question stem, to minimize guessing, and to avoid the use of double negatives and phrases used in class or in the text. Objective questions may serve in many ways to evaluate knowledge, but such questions must be carefully prepared.

Contrary to general belief, essay questions per se do not necessarily measure only thinking skills or even only higher level thinking skills. In fact, the best that researchers can say about what essay questions measure is that they seem to measure a student's "ability to compose an adequate answer to a question in effective prose"[5]—often under considerable time pressure. Questions requiring essay answers can measure various types of knowledge as well as the various thinking skills that they are more commonly assumed to measure.

To measure knowledge of specific information, for example, essay questions can be devised that require students to define a given term or feature of a given event or topic and/or to describe a given feature of a topic they have studied. Questions like the following require only that the student recall and present previously learned specific information:

1. The Industrial Revolution was a change from the *domestic system* of production to the *factory system*.

    a) Define each italicized word.
    b) Describe three reasons why this change occurred in England.

2. Describe three features of life in Kiev around A.D. 1000 and give two bits of evidence that illustrate each of these features.

Similarly, questions can measure student knowledge of concepts and generalizations. Students can be asked to describe in essay form their image of any previously studied concept, or they can be given a generalization learned in class and be asked to explain its meaning and to give examples to illustrate their explanation. However, essay questions that require students to describe, explain, or prove anything they have just completed studying actually test only remembered knowledge rather than higher level cognitive skills other than those associated with reading comprehension and clear, concise writing.

Student mastery of concepts or generalizations may best be measured by asking students essay questions that require them to apply what facts, concepts, generalizations, and/or skills they possess to new data. To evaluate students' knowledge of a concept of landscape, for instance, the teacher could ask them to describe a landscape shown in a photograph of an outdoor scene. Students could also be asked to describe, given what they see out the classroom windows, the landscape of their school site. Or they could draw an ideal landscape.

To measure their knowledge of a concept of role, students could describe the degree to which a certain person was successful in fulfilling a particular role. Such questions are quite sophisticated and require students to use what they know for a purpose. In essence, these questions require students to engage in the final stage of inquiring—to apply a concept or generalization to new data to make it meaningful. The degree to which they delineate the various dimensions of the specified concept or generalization may serve as a measure of how well they know the concept or generalization.

Measuring thinking skills. Just as objective and essay items can be used to measure student knowledge, so too can these same types of questions serve to measure student mastery of thinking skills and processes. However, when used for these latter purposes, objective and essay questions differ in two important ways from those used to measure knowledge of information or generalizations. First, skill questions should be accompanied by some data for immediate reference to which students apply the skill being evaluated. Second, this data should be unfamiliar to the students. If these two conditions are not met (if students are required to recall previously learned data or if they must use data already studied in class), skill questions based on these data will most likely reflect existing knowledge of the content rather than the ability to use the skill.

The most effective skill question on a test consists of two parts: some type of data for students to work with and a series of questions designed to have students use specific skills to make sense of the data. The questions might present the data via graphs, maps, paragraphs, photographs, cartoons, charts, or some other media, depending on the type of media used in the unit being tested. The questions accompanying any set of data may test a variety of skills, and these questions may be either objective or essay in design.

Objective questions that evaluate mastery of thinking skills are in effect the same kinds of questions used in teaching thinking skills.* When using such ques-

---

* See Chapter 10.

tions on a test, teachers should start with those requiring use of the simplest cognitive skills and proceed to those requiring the most complex cognitive operations. Thus, a series of skill questions referring to data the student has not studied or seen might start with questions designed to measure a student's ability to translate information—to read what the given data literally says. Subsequent questions might then test the skills of interpreting the data, then of extrapolating from the data, and finally of generalizing about the data. The following questions exemplify such a sequence of skill questions:

Africa's share of the world's output of selected minerals is shown on the following graph. Each △ represents 10% of the world's total output of the specified mineral:

Diamonds	△ △ △ △ △ △ △ △ △ ◿
Cobalt Ore	△ △ △ △ △ △ △
Gold	△ △ △ △ ◿
Copper	△ △ ◿
Chromite	△ △ ◿
Tin	△ ◿

1. Based on the above graph, what percentage of the world's supply of chromite is produced in Africa?

   a. 2½%
   b. 25%
   c. 50%
   d. 75%

2. Which of the following interpretations of this graph is most correct?

   a. Africa produces more diamonds than any other mineral.
   b. The production of gold is Africa's third greatest source of wealth.
   c. More copper is produced in Africa than chromite.
   d. Africa is a major producer of the world's supply of gold.

3. In the years following the discovery of a large supply of cobalt ore in Alaska and its production for world use, the number of symbols for cobalt on the above graph will probably

   a. Increase
   b. Decrease
   c. Remain the same
   d. Disappear

Question one requires students only to translate what the graph says. Question two requires them to tell what the graph means—to interpret it. Question three requires students to go beyond the data—to extrapolate. In addition, if we want to find out if students could use the skills of synthesis, we could ask them to generalize about this data:

4. Which of the following conclusions can most accurately be supported by this graph?

   a. Africa is a major producer of several mineral resources.
   b. Africa produces most of the world's mineral resources.
   c. Mineral production is Africa's greatest source of wealth.
   d. Producing minerals in a major part of Africa's economy.

Questions designed to test the students' ability to use other skills may also be added. A number of questions such as these that require students to translate, interpret, and synthesize data may be used with any set of data on any test if the intent is to evaluate how well students know specific thinking skills.

   Sometimes, especially in testing skills or components of a thinking process such as inquiry, data can be built into the stem of an objective question itself, as in the following questions designed to measure student skills of inferring the logical consequences of a hypothesis (question 1), of separating relevant from irrelevant information (question 2), or of altering hypotheses in the face of additional data (question 3): [6]

1. If the hypothesis, "The success of the Protestant Reformation attempts to change the Catholic Church was due to the support of the rising merchant class," is valid, all of the following statements will be supported by the data EXCEPT:

   a. Many merchants joined Protestant churches.
   b. Many merchants realized increased profits after the Reformation.
   c. Many merchants donated money to support leaders of the Reformation.
   d. Many merchants had disagreed with the Catholic church's prohibition on charging interest.

2. Which of the following grievances drawn up by the common people of a French town in 1788 would you include in your notes if you had asked the question "Did the French people revolt against their government in order to obtain more freedom?"

   a. We wish to see the laws reformed.
   b. We wish to see taxes paid in proportion to income.
   c. We wish to see a law requiring officers to charge us with a crime in order to hold us after arrest.
   d. We wish the abolition of taxes that harm commerce and industry.

3. Suppose you had begun with the hypothesis, "Chinese leaders instituted the communes in 1958 in order to carry out the goals of Communism," and then found the following statement in the decree establishing the communes. What would you do with your hypothesis?

   a. "The purpose of the people's communes is mainly the all-continuous leap forward in China's agricultural production. The communes will complete the building of socialism ahead of time and carry out the gradual transition to Communism."

   a. I would not change my hypothesis.
   b. I would change my hypothesis to, "China instituted the communes to allocate more human resources to agriculture."
   c. I would change my hypothesis to, "Chinese leaders instituted communes to promote economic growth and to promote the goals of her ideology."
   d. I would change my hypothesis to, "Chinese leaders instituted communes to increase their control over the people."

Questions requiring essay answers can also be used to measure student mastery of particular thinking skills or processes. In order to measure student mastery of inference-making skills and the skill of synthesizing generalizations, we might use the following question:

Africa's share of the world's output of selected minerals is shown on the following graph. Each △ represents 10% of the world's total output of the specified mineral:

Diamonds	△ △ △ △ △ △ △ △ △ △
Cobalt Ore	△ △ △ △ △ △ △
Gold	△ △ △ △ △
Copper	△ △ △
Chromite	△ △ △
Tin	△ △

1. Using just the information on this table, what is the best general statement you can make about Africa's mineral resources? Explain at least two reasons, using evidence from the above graph, to justify the statement you have made.

2. Explain, giving at least one hypothetical example in each case, at least three ways in which a sudden change in political or economic conditions in Africa might affect any non-African nations who produce any of the minerals shown on the graph.

Other types of essay questions can be used to measure student mastery of thinking processes, including the process of inquiring:

DIRECTIONS: Read the following statements. What problem(s) is/are implied by this collection of statements?

a. European colonial administrations built, staffed and financed elementary and secondary schools throughout their colonies in Africa after 1900.
b. Europeans employed Africans on plantations and in mines for more wages than Africans had ever before earned after 1900.
c. European colonial administrations supervised the building and financing of roads, hospitals, and bridges throughout their African colonies after 1900.
d. After 1945 Africans in increasing numbers began to demand the end of European rule in Africa.
e. After 1945 Africans used political agitation, violence, and even guerrilla warfare to achieve independence from European control.
f. By 1977 approximately 50 independent nations existed in Africa.

DIRECTIONS:
1. Write one problem or question implied by the above statements.
2. List three explanations, any one of which might be a possible solution to this problem or answer to this question.
3. Select one of these possible answers or solutions. Explain at least three kinds of evidence that might relate to this possible answer or solution and tell specifically how such evidence would validate or invalidate this answer or solution.

The above question attempts to measure a student's abilities to identify a problem, generate a hypothesis (infer and synthesize data), and infer the logical consequences of the hypothesis—all skills essential to the process of inquiring.

Data can thus be included in questions requiring essay responses in order to measure student skills as well as knowledge. In effect, this type of question (as illustrated by the two preceding questions) requires students to apply their previously learned knowledge (of specific information and the processes of dealing with information or concepts and generalizations) and their higher level skills to a set of given but unfamiliar data. In such cases, the data should be similar to what the students have been using in class, but not the same data they have seen before. The skills and conceptual knowledge tested ought to be skills and concepts taught in the unit being evaluated. To answer this type of question, students must be able to give meaning to the data presented in terms of previously learned generalizations and/or concepts. And this, in turn, requires use of the specific higher level thinking skills of application, analysis, synthesis, and evaluation as well as the skills associated with clear, well-organized, concise writing.

Almost any kind of data may be used in application-type essay questions. For example, to measure student achievement in a course studying the growth of cities in America, we might create an essay question that gives students population figures and sets of maps showing the shape and size of the urban area of a single city in four different time periods; to these we could add sets of maps for the same periods showing where different types of people (professional workers, skilled workers, etc.) lived and perhaps the major transportation arteries. Our question would then ask the students to first *describe* the changes they note in this city over the period covered by the data and then *explain* what probably accounts for the changes noted. Student answers will require use of the concepts and information learned in the course as well as of the skills of analysis and snythesis. Or, to take another example, assume students have been studying the social aspects of American history and have written a family history as part of their coursework. We could measure their cognitive achievement by giving them a brief but specific family history and ask them to write an essay analyzing the family described in terms of any number of selected concepts (taught in the course) such as social mobility, ethnicity, social class, technology, values, and value conflict. Similar essay questions can be constructed using cartoons, songs, poems, and other data.

Application questions such as these have a number of disadvantages as well as advantages: they cannot generally be answered in 20 minutes or so; rather, they generally require considerable thought and planning before the writing occurs. These questions often serve best as take-home questions or questions that are major parts of extended—two to three hour—tests.

These questions also serve double duty: they measure both remembered knowledge and skills. Precisely because of this, however, another difficulty arises. Poor student performance in answering the questions may result from either or both the lack of substantive knowledge about the cases given and/or the inability to use the skills tested; consequently, a teacher may not be able to identify the precise nature of the deficiency. Thus, such questions must be used with caution in diagnosing specific student achievement.

As in measuring student knowledge, one or two items on a single test simply cannot secure a valid or reliable measure of a student's degree of mastery of a specific skill. Instead, we need to ask four, five, or even more questions measuring the same skill with different forms of data that use content other than what the class studied. Thus, as in the sample test planned in Figure 14.1, we might include four different sets of skill questions, each built around a form of data studied in class (paragraphs and graphs). Each form would contain information not yet studied, and each set of skill questions would measure similar skills across all four items and in the same sequence. Thus, question 1 for each set would measure the skill of translation (as does one other question on this sample test), providing a total of five translation questions. Student performance on these five questions will provide a much more reliable measure of their abilities to perform this skill than would their answering of only one or two translation questions. Any skills test must include a number of items measuring each skill to be evaluated if we are to obtain a reliable evaluation of student achievement or of the validity or reliability of our questions.

Sources of Test Items

Even though few skills tests exist ready-made for any particular body of content to use in history or social studies inquiry teaching, it is not necessary for teachers to invent such questions completely from scratch. Many useful sources of skill items do exist from which teachers can cull or adapt items for their own tests. The National Council for the Social Studies distributes a booklet containing many items for measuring critical thinking skills.[7] The annual New York State Board of Regents examinations in comprehensive social studies contain a wealth of validated essay and objective skill and knowledge items in American, European, and non-Western history as well as in economics, government, sociology, and other social studies subjects.[8] Careful selection of items from these tests can provide a bank of questions useful for measuring a wide variety of cognitive learning objectives.

In many instances, however, teachers do find it necessary to write their own items. This task can be made easier by adapting already existing questions to the level of knowledge or skills to be tested or by using as models existing questions already keyed to specific skills or levels of knowledge. The questions included in this chapter may serve as models, as may sample questions contained in Bloom's *Taxonomy of Educational Objectives,* Norris Sanders' *Classroom Questions: What Kinds?*, and a number of other similar sources.[9] In order to prepare questions designed to elicit specific skills by using content-related data, one can seek out sample questions from these sources, alter the wording to fit the desired subject and ability levels of the students, and rewrite the options accordingly. Thus, the task of preparing inquiry test items can be made much easier, with more valid and reliable results.

Evaluating Inquiry Tests

While careful planning and preparation of inquiry tests may contribute to the development of an effective instrument, we cannot be sure of the validity of the test items we have selected or created until we have analyzed student performance on the test itself. As teachers, we often make a number of assumptions about classroom tests—whether self-designed or commercially produced—that have considerable impact on our interpretation of these tests. We assume, for example, that our students can read with comprehension the questions they are asked; often they cannot. Inadequate answers may, in fact, reflect deficiencies in reading rather than in content mastery. In addition, we often assume that a question clearly measures a variable we have specified, when it actually may not.

Sometimes we ask questions that require knowledge of two different types of information as in the question, "Which of the following presidents supported a policy similar to that of the Monroe Doctrine?" (followed by the names of four presidents). Such a question requires student knowledge of both the Monroe Doctrine and the foreign policies of each of four presidents. Failure to answer the questions correctly could at best result from lack of knowledge of any one of these areas; which ones, however, will likely remain forever unknown to us.

We also assume students have the knowledge needed to answer an essay question that calls on them to apply this knowledge to explain some other phenomenon (the details of which students may be required to call up from memory). When they are unable to answer a question of this type satisfactorily, we cannot be sure of the cause of their failure—whether lack of the original knowledge, knowledge of the phenomenon to be explained, or mastery of the skill of explaining.

In sum, we too often assume that the questions we use will measure the skill or knowledge we intend them to measure; in fact, they may not. Tests can measure a whole variety of variables including the student's long distance eyesight, astuteness at cribbing, friendships with others who took the test in earlier classes, physical health and alertness, and luck. Tests designed to evaluate the products of inquiry teaching are especially vulnerable to the weaknesses of the assumptions noted here. Careful evaluation of student responses to our test items as well as analysis of the items themselves provides a most useful final step in creating valid inquiry tests.

Although a detailed statistical analysis of test responses provides the most reliable data about item validity, classroom teachers frequently lack the time to undertake such analyses. They can, however, undertake less time-consuming forms of analysis that may help them spot unreliable or invalid items, knowledge of which can help them revise their tests to make them more accurate when used again in the future.

Teachers may use two simple methods to gather information useful for evaluating a test. First they can ask one or two colleagues to rate their test items in terms of levels of knowledge or nature of the skills being evaluated by each. If the colleague rating corresponds with the author's intent on an item, the chances of the item being reliable are enhanced. But if the two analyses disagree, it may well be that the item does not reliably measure what its author intended it to measure.

Second, a teacher can undertake a quick analysis of student responses to each item on a test in order to identify any questions that seem to produce odd

ITEM ANALYSIS

Item	Top Third	Bottom Third	Item	Top Third	Bottom Third	Item	Top Third	Bottom Third
1 a			8 a			15 a		
b			b			b		
c			c			c		
d			d			d		
2 a			9 a			16 a		
b			b			b		
c			c			c		
d			d			d		
3 a			10 a			17 a		
b			b			b		
c			c			c		
d			d			d		
4 a			11 a			18 a		
b			b			b		
c			c			c		
d			d			d		
5 a			12 a			19 a		
b			b			b		
c			c			c		
d			d			d		
6 a			13 a			20 a		
b			b			b		
c			c			c		
d			d			d		
7 a			14 a			21 a		
b			b			b		
c			c			c		
d			d			d		

or unusual results. To this end they can use the following procedure with the Item Analysis chart reproduced on page 353. After grading all the student answers, the teacher can

1. Rank the papers from lowest score to highest.
2. Divide the answer papers into thirds (or, if exceptionally large classes are involved, into reasonable proportions so you have at least 15 papers in the top and bottom sets of scores). Put aside all papers other than those in the top and bottom sets, or top and bottom thirds.
3. Indicate on an item analysis sheet the total number of students in the top and bottom sets being analyzed.
4. For each set of papers, top and bottom, go through each answer sheet marking in the appropriate place on the item analysis sheet each response to each question chosen by that student.
5. Total the responses to each possible answer to each question asked (incorrect responses as well as correct.).
6. Examine each question in terms of the number of students giving different responses in order to identify test items in which

   a) more students in the top third chose a particular incorrect response than did those in the bottom third.
   b) none or almost all of the students in both thirds missed a question or chose a particular incorrect response.
   c) the responses of students in the upper third cluster around one incorrect response, and responses of students in the bottom third cluster around another incorrect response.

7. Analyze the items thus identified for such things as two possible correct responses, give-away cues, ill-defined terms in the question stem, confusing use of negatives, and other possible flaws.

The following chart illustrates how this procedure works. The chart displays the results of a test item analysis conducted on questions 1–4 of a test taken by 30 students.

Item	Top Third(10)	Bottom Third(10)
1 a		I
(b)	JHT IIII	JHT III
c	I	
d		I
2 a		II
b	III	III
c		II
(d)	JHT II	III

Item	Top Third(10)	Bottom Third(10)
3 (a)	JHT III	III
b		I
c	I	JHT I
d	I	
4 a		
(b)	JHT	JHT II
c		
d	JHT	III

Figure 14.3. Sample Item Analysis

The correct responses for each question are circled. The marks after each letter represent the number of students selecting that option as their answer to that particular question. Analysis of these responses indicates that

1. Question 1 was a relatively easy question that did not discriminate significantly between students who did well on the test and those who did not do well. Almost every student answered it correctly. Perhaps its major function was as a confidence-builder. Starting tests with several "easy" questions—questions that students of all abilities can answer correctly—is a useful motivating (and fear reducing) device.
2. Question 2 discriminates nicely between the top and bottom thirds of the class, since a significantly higher proportion of students in the top third than in the bottom third answered it correctly. However, we ought to look at option b—something in it attracted an unusual number of top students. Maybe there are two correct options here!
3. Question 3 discriminates between top and bottom students. However, since a great many students in the bottom group selected option c, we should examine that option. Perhaps the wording or something that happened in class gave the impression to "the less prepared" that it was correct. Again, maybe we actually have two correct options in this question.
4. Question 4 does not discriminate well at all. Fewer students in the top third answered the question correctly than did students in the bottom third. Perhaps there is something in option d that makes it correct, too. Or perhaps the intended correct option is worded in such a way that it misled the better-informed students.

And so on. Such an item analysis does not tell why students selected certain options, nor does it indicate faulty questions per se. But it does alert us to potentially troublesome questions. In this instance, further examination of questions 2, 3, and 4 seems warranted by this item analysis. Problems of content or wording may exist within these questions and their associated options about which we were unaware until we made this test analysis. Or we may have done something in class that counters our intent in these questions.

Although a test analysis like this is somewhat inadequate, it is much better than no analysis at all. Furthermore, such an analysis does not take too much time. A pair of students could, in fact, compile the results in a very short time. And the analysis itself can help spot possibly flawed test items. Once analyzed, poor items can be replaced or rewritten. The revised items can then be tried another time to determine their validity. As long as a teacher remains aware of the possible weaknesses of any teacher-made tests and tries to design, select, evaluate, and revise test items appropriate to the objectives he or she seeks in inquiry teaching, these tests will become increasingly valid and reliable measures of the cognitive outcomes of inquiry teaching.

Classroom measures of student achievement are also extremely useful in evaluating inquiry teaching. Analysis of the results of well-constructed inquiry tests can help a teacher identify weaknesses or omissions as well as strengths in the teaching strategy, materials, and activities employed in class. Such analysis can also identify some objectives that need additional attention, some that are being achieved well, and some with unanticipated outcomes that may or may not warrant additional attention. Evaluating the cognitive results of inquiry teaching serves as one of the best, albeit indirect, measures of the quality of inquiry teaching available to classroom teachers.

MEASURING AFFECTIVE LEARNING

Evaluating affective outcomes of inquiry teaching may be accomplished by using the same types of instruments and procedures generally used in measuring affective outcomes of any other type of instruction. We may use paper and pencil instruments that require students to respond to questions or items in such a way as to indicate their values, attitudes, or feelings about a specific subject or issue. We may also use observational techniques to compile evidence of specific behaviors that may reflect student attitudes and values. Regardless of the type of evaluation conducted, however, measuring student attitudes and values requires the same careful planning, design, and appraisal of evaluation instruments, procedures, and results as does the measurement of cognitive learning.

Guidelines for Measuring Affect

For the most accurate and reliable measure of attitudes, values, and feelings, evaluation should follow at least four guidelines. First, the evaluator must determine what specific evidence will indicate the existence of a given attitude, value, or feeling. Next, the evaluation must allow the subjects or respondents as much choice as possible. Third, the evaluation ought to be repeated over a period of time both to identify the basic pattern of student attitudes and values as well as to identify changes in these attitudes and values. Finally, the evaluation must be carried out in a setting that does not unduly influence its results. Failure to adhere to these conditions will make the results of any evaluation of affect highly suspect. Each of these guidelines requires some additional explanation here.

The most crucial aspect of any measure of affect involves the type of evidence selected as indicative of the attitudes, values, or feelings under study, for these aspects of affect cannot normally be observed directly. Instead, people most often evidence their values, attitudes, and feelings by how they behave and, to some extent, what they say. Thus, in order to identify an individual's attitudes and values, one must search out observable behaviors or other types of evidence from which to infer the existence of a particular value, attitude, or feeling. Making such inferences is, of course, risky. However, some educational researchers have identified certain types of evidence that do seem to be useful value indicators.

Overt behavior provides the most reliable clue to peoples' values, attitudes, and feelings. The way we behave or act, especially in circumstances involving the same basic issues, reveals what we consider important to us. If we dislike something, we do what we can to avoid it. We may even make disparaging remarks about it. Given a choice of coming into contact with it or avoiding it, we will consistently do the latter. If we like something, we may go out of our way to do it. We may buy books about it on our own. We may talk about it all the time. We may even become a kind of expert on what we enjoy, a person our friends turn to when they need information about or help with the activity. By engaging in behaviors such as these, we reveal our likes or dislikes, values, attitudes, and feelings.

Other more indirect value indicators also exist. Raths, Harmin, and Simon, among others, assert that some more reliable indicators include expressions of aspirations, opinions for or against something, interests, feelings, beliefs, and worries.[10] Statements regarding preferences also reveal an individual's attitudes, values, and feelings. These indicators serve, in effect, as proxies for the more overt value-laden behaviors described above. Efforts to measure affect within schools most often seek evidence about these less direct types of indicators as a first step to identifying the attitudes, values, and feelings of students.

In attempting to identify student attitudes, values, and feelings, teachers must do more than clearly define the types of evidence they can accept as indicative of any given value or attitude. They must also collect this evidence in various situations, using procedures that permit students considerable choice and that do not bias student responses. Forcing students to choose among limited options on a paper and pencil instrument or even in an actual situation may provide a clue to the relative importance for that student of values implicit in the choices, but a limited choice does not allow for expression of what may be even more basic values held by the student. Moreover, attempting to measure how students feel about a particular subject, teacher, or topic in the class taught by that teacher may not reveal the student's true attitudes or feelings but only those the student thinks the evaluator wants to find. For the most reliable results, a measure of affect must be administered in a setting that students do not connect directly with whatever is being evaluated.

Just as in measuring cognitive objectives, so in measuring affective outcomes of instruction must we realize that no single behavior or response can be interpreted as conclusive. A variety of behaviors that reveal a consistent pattern of responses must be observed or recorded in order to determine the extent to which an individual holds a particular value, attitude, or feeling. Student possession of a given attitude or value cannot accurately be inferred from a single overt behavior or a response to a single test item. And a change in student values or attitudes requires a series of measures administered prior to instruction, at the conclusion of instruction, and some time after the conclusion of instruction. Values and attitudes are slow to change; they involve many complexities. Therefore, measurement of these attitudes and values must encompass an extended period of time and seek to identify many value indicators and behaviors.

Techniques for Measuring Affect

A variety of procedures exists for identifying student attitudes, values, and feelings. Formal procedures involving paper and pencil instruments or interviews predominate. But informal procedures such as observation and anecdotal records also prove useful. Several examples of each procedure may suggest techniques useful in evaluating student achievement of the commonly sought affective goals of social studies instruction.

Paper and pencil measures. Paper and pencil measures of affect range from open-ended, virtually free-response measures to highly structured, restricted choice measures.[11] Among the most open types of items for free-response instruments are those that ask respondents to list, to complete an unfinished statement, or to respond to a picture, poem, or an unfinished case study or values dilemma.

Asking students to list a specific number of things they enjoy doing most or list the three school subjects they like best provides some inferred insight into their basic attitudes and values. Negative listings can also be used as a device for identifying positive attitudes and values—if one is willing to infer that what a student prefers is the opposite of what he or she reports as a dislike. Students can also be asked to complete sentences such as the following:

1. American history is _____ .

2. When I enter my social studies class, I feel _____

   _____ .

3. Reading my social studies textbook makes me _____

   _____ .

4. I think George Washington was _____ .

Such statements may not always elicit value-laden responses, but when they do, these responses may provide clues to a student's feelings, attitudes, or values. For example, a student might respond to item 1 by writing "boring," "fun," "challenging," "dumb," or any of a variety of other positive or negative remarks. By itself such a response would be of little diagnostic value; taken in combination with responses to other items on history, social studies, or school activities, the entire set of responses might suggest a student's attitude toward learning and perhaps even something about his or her values.

Responses to more detailed stimuli also provide useful clues to what students value. Students can be asked to indicate their feelings about or other reactions to a picture, for instance, or even to suggest what objects or activities should be included in an unfinished picture. Similar responses can be sought using poems. Students can also be presented with unfinished case studies or values situations such as the following and asked to suggest what action the central character *should* take:

5. The student admitted copying test answers from another student when the teacher wasn't looking. The student said he had been ill last night and unable to study much for the test. He needed a good grade to remain eligible to play in the league championships that start tomorrow. The teacher should . . .

When combined with a student's explanation of why a particular action should be taken, a response to such a situation might give evidence of a specific student-held value or attitude.

Other, more limited-response items or techniques may also be used on paper and pencil measures of affect. A semantic differential offers a most useful structured technique for measuring student attitudes and feelings and thus, indirectly, student values. In essence, this technique asks students to indicate from a range of choices how they feel about a topic or statement. Sometimes students are asked to indicate the extent to which they agree or disagree with something by circling or checking a response on a scale like:

Strongly Disagree	Disagree	Undecided	Agree	Strongly Agree
1	2	3	4	5

Laws are to be obeyed.

1	2	3	4	5

The United States has usually dealt fairly with other nations.

1	2	3	4	5

Older people should be shown respect.

1	2	3	4	5

This class has made me think.

1	2	3	4	5

Working in groups has been very helpful in achieving the goals of this course.

Students may be asked to respond on individual scales to any number of statements on a specific instrument. The examples given above illustrate only a few of the types of subjects—including teaching methods and course content—about which student reactions can be elicited. When all the responses on a specific subject are clustered and a score for each tallied (by adding the numbers represented by the student responses, Disagree = 2 and Strongly Agree = 5, for example) a measure of both student attitude and the intensity of this attitude can be obtained.

Another version of this type of scale asks students to indicate their feelings about given topics by responding to a half dozen or more paired adjectives related to each topic. To measure student attitudes toward American imperialism, for example, a number of items like the following might be used:

Annexation of the Philippines

cruel	.	.	.	.	.	kind
bad	.	.	.	.	.	good
foolish	.	.	.	.	.	wise
ugly	.	.	.	.	.	beautiful
undemocratic	.	.	.	.	.	democratic
unfair	.	.	.	.	.	fair

In responding to each pair of adjectives for each topic, students are asked to place a check mark next to the word in the pair they think most accurately expresses their feelings on the subject of the scale (in this instance, annexation of the Philippines) or to put the check at the midpoint of the line if they are undecided or feel either word applies equally well—or poorly. A numerical scale of 3 to 1 or 5 to 1 for positive to negative responses can be used to score the results.

Note that the above example puts all the negative responses on the same side of the scale—the left side. Such a procedure may bias the results in the sense that students may give answers they think the teacher seeks rather than freely expressing their own opinions. Or they may make rapid, unthinking responses by marking all items at the same end of the scale without reading and carefully considering each pair of words. To avoid these pitfalls and to enhance the validity of this measure, positive and negative adjectives may be switched from side to side. In addition, meaningful pairs of responses can be intermixed with irrelevant pairs of adjectives as in this example:

West African Kingdoms Before 1600

kind	.	.	.	.	.	cruel
passive	.	.	.	.	.	active
bad	.	.	.	.	.	good
soft	.	.	.	.	.	hard
foolish	.	.	.	.	.	wise
strong	.	.	.	.	.	weak
excitable	.	.	.	.	.	calm
fast	.	.	.	.	.	slow

In this example, positive and negative adjectives appear randomly on both sides of the scale to encourage students to examine each pair carefully. Such a procedure helps detect indiscriminant checking of responses. And, in evaluating the results for student attitudes related to the topic, only a few of the pairs might be scored (in this case the "kind-cruel," "bad-good," "foolish-wise," and "strong-weak" pairs). The remaining pairs serve merely as distractors to disguise the actual attitudes being measured. Including several kinds of scales, all set in the same sequence, for various aspects of a topic or subject can provide a rather valid measure of student attitudes and feelings. Such a measure can also suggest the intensity of student feelings or attitudes toward a subject.

Other somewhat limited choice items may also be used to identify student attitudes and values. Students can be given lists of items from which they are instructed to select and rank order a specific number in terms of their likes or preferences, in terms of good and bad, or according to any other value-related criterion. Multiple choice items can be used to elicit similar kinds of responses, too. A number of states and educational researchers, for example, in an effort to measure student attitudes and values, have created instruments using questions like these:

6. If the class was taking a test and my good friend asked for an answer to a question, I would

   a) pretend not to hear her.
   b) give her the answer.
   c) say I don't know the answer, although I do know it.
   d) tell her I won't give her the answer.
   e) move my answer sheet so she could see it better.
   f) tell the teacher she asked me for an answer.

7. Laws should be obeyed because

   a) if you don't you might be fined or jailed.
   b) laws protect us from injury and harm.
   c) people expect others to obey the laws they obey.
   d) if we don't obey laws, then our society simply won't work.
   e) laws democratically-made benefit all society as a whole and deserve to be obeyed until changed.

Items such as #6 contain responses that, with considerable inferencing, can be keyed to various stages of Kohlberg's stages of moral reasoning. The responses on item 7 are, in fact, simplified versions of the essential elements of these stages. Such questions have a multitude of uses that include identifying student attitudes and values about honesty, the law, justice, and so on. Yet inferences about exactly what any given response might indicate, especially where students are not allowed or required to explain the reasoning behind their responses, must be made only with extreme caution.

Interviews. Highly structured interviews may also be conducted to elicit value, attitude, or feeling indicators. Such interviews might be built around dilemmas or case studies such as that on cheating presented above. After students have given an initial response, the interviewer then should probe for reasoning behind the initial action suggested. By introducing additional issues into the case (such as the fact that several other students know this student was cheating or that the school has an honor code to which all students including this one had agreed), the evaluator can "test" the student reasoning for consistency and clarity. By recording student responses as literally as possible, one can accumulate excellent data that, when analyzed, may yield valuable clues to student attitudes and values.

Observation. Observation of actual student behavior provides another method of gathering data about student attitudes and values. As noted above, actual behavior is probably the best indicator of affect, if properly interpreted. And a wide range of behaviors may all relate to the same attitude or value. For example, inquiry teaching can foster the development in students of a positive attitude toward learning. Such an attitude is customarily defined as reflecting a like or desire for continued learning in general or at least learning in a particular subject.[12] This attitude may be evidenced in many ways: by voluntarily electing a subsequent course in the same subject area as the initial course; by bringing paper, pencil, or other needed materials to class without constant teacher reminders; by bringing to class unsolicited newspaper clippings about a topic studied previously; by voluntarily making substantive contributions to class discussions; and so on. However, none of these behaviors alone may be assumed to indicate a positive attitude toward learning; any one could signify merely a desire to please a teacher or to earn a few more points toward a higher grade. Nevertheless, observation of these student behaviors over a period of time may well indicate that this student has a positive attitude toward learning in a specific subject area or class.

Cautions in Measuring Affect

Like all evaluation procedures, measures of affect are based on certain assumptions. We often assume, for example, that cognitive classroom tests measure what we say they measure, that they accurately indicate whether or not a student truly understands a concept or has mastered a skill. Yet such a test may really measure the way a student happens to feel at the time he or she took the test, or how sharp his or her eyesight was, or just whether or not the student could read and understand the directions and questions of the instrument. So it is with measures of affect. Such measures are subject to widely varying degrees of interpretation. Whether a particular choice or response or behavior means what we assert or believe it to mean is often open to question. The real meaning of any such response, of course, lies in the intent of the repondent; in many instances this remains unknown to us in spite of our best efforts at instrument design and interpretation.

A second assumption underlying measures of affect is that students respond honestly. Students all too often perceive teacher evaluation in the school setting as essentially a "guess-what-they-want-me-to-say" game; they respond at times in the way they believe they are expected to respond rather than in the way they really feel or believe. Thus, in many instances the attitudes and values sought by the measure remain obscured, and responses may instead reflect a classroom survival value or "please-the-teacher-at-all-costs" type of attitude. Various techniques can be used to guard against these situations, including directions that require students to explain their value-laden responses, a search for patterns of various types of behaviors rather than reliance on single responses or behaviors, and administering measures in contexts that do not bias results. These and other assumptions that underlie efforts to measure values and attitudes are tenuous; they must be constantly kept in mind while interpreting the findings of such measures.

Evaluating the affective outcomes of classroom instruction may range from measuring changes in student attitudes toward learning to evaluating the degree to which students appear to hold or profess the more substantive types of attitudes and values (such as honesty or respect for rules and laws or respect for the rights of others). These evaluations require long-term observation and the use of special instruments and procedures. These measures can also be conducted throughout the school as well as by individual classroom teachers. Indeed, few classroom lessons or even month-long units bring about any specific or lasting changes in student attitudes or values; thus they cannot be evaluated for these types of learning outcomes. Evaluating the affective outcomes of inquiry teaching is at best a long-term, and often a very subjective, effort—but it can be done!

SUMMARY

Evaluation of inquiry teaching may serve many purposes. Helping identify how closely the students approach mastery of course goals is one. Another purpose is to provide data on which teachers can act to improve their abilities to use this teaching strategy. Teachers may gather data for both purposes by measuring student cognitive learning and affect, as well as by securing student appraisals or by recording what actually occurs in their classrooms. The most common evaluation procedures involve the use of teacher-made paper and pencil tests. Because of the continued role such tests play in evaluating student learning as well as in evaluating classroom instruction, careful attention must be devoted to their structure, planning, use, and interpretation. However, analysis of these test results can provide information of use in evaluating one's use of inquiry teaching and in appraising student achievement and building improved student tests. Classroom measures of inquiry learning and teaching do, indeed, serve multiple purposes, and systematic efforts at improving these measures can contribute considerably to improved inquiry teaching in the social studies classroom.

notes

1. Richard W. Burns, "Objectives and Content Validity of Tests," *Educational Technology*, Dec. 15, 1968, pp. 17–18.
2. *New York State Regents Exam: World History—June 28, 1961* (Albany: New York State Board of Regents); p. 5. Reprinted with permission of The New York State Education Department.

3. *Comprehensive Social Studies Examinations—January 1976* (Albany: New York State Board of Regents), p. 5. Reprinted with permission of The New York State Education Department.

4. From *The Carnegie Test for Social Studies Inquiry Skills* (Pittsburgh: Carnegie-Mellon Curriculum Center, 1966). This test was developed as part of a project directed by Professor Edwin Fenton to create a social studies curriculum for able high school students.

5. "Tests and Examinations," in Chester W. Harris, ed., *Encyclopedia of Educational Research* (New York: The Macmillan Company, 1960), 3rd ed., p. 1504.

6. From *The Carnegie Test for Social Studies Inquiry Skills,* op. cit.

7. Horace T. Morse, George H. McCune, Lester Brown, and Ellen Cook, *Selected Items for the Testing of Study Skills and Critical Thinking* (Washington: National Council for the Social Studies, 1971).

8. Copies of these tests may be purchased from the Topical Review Book Company (131 North St., Auburn, N.Y.) and from AMSCO School Publications, Inc. (315 Hudson St., New York, N.Y. 10013).

9. Benjamin Bloom et al., *Taxonomy of Educational Objectives—Handbook I: The Cognitive Domain* (New York: David McKay Co., 1956); David R. Krathwohl et al., *Taxonomy of Educational Objectives—Handbook II: The Affective Domain* (New York: David McKay Co., 1964); Dana Kurfman, "The Evaluation of Effective Thinking," in *Effective Thinking in the Social Studies,* eds. Jean Fair and Fannie R. Shaftel (Washington: National Council for the Social Studies, 1967), pp. 231–253; Byron Massialas and Jack Zevin, *Creative Encounters in the Classroom* (New York: John Wiley & Sons, 1967); Edwin Fenton, *Teaching the New Social Studies in Secondary Schools: An Inductive Approach* (New York: Holt, Rinehart & Winston, 1966), pp. 283–298; and Norris Sanders, *Classroom Questions: What Kinds?* (New York: Harper & Row, 1966).

10. Louis E. Raths, Merrill Harmin, and Sidney B. Simon, *Values and Teaching,* 2nd ed. (Columbus: Charles E. Merrill Publishing Company, 1978), pp. 29–31.

11. Robert L. Ebel, *Essentials of Educational Measurement* (Englewood Cliffs: Prentice-Hall, 1972).

12. Robert F. Mager, *Developing Attitude Toward Learning* (Palo Alto: Fearon Publishers, 1968); William Purkey, *Self-Concept and School Achievement* (Englewood Cliffs: Prentice-Hall, 1970).

15

inquiry teaching
and the
classroom

What happens in the classroom provides the key to successful inquiry teaching. Whatever curriculum building, unit writing, and lesson planning teachers might undertake, whatever tests we might devise or give, whatever the instructional materials or activities we may choose to use, or whatever objectives or goals we might profess, even if based on inquiry—will all be for naught unless we help students actually engage in classroom learning experiences that require their systematic use of the process, skills, and other attributes of inquiry. Teachers and students must also behave in ways that may differ considerably from those to which both are accustomed for inquiry teaching to become a classroom reality.

Inquiry teaching differs significantly from the more conventional expository teaching that characterizes most social studies and other classrooms by focusing on process as well as content. Rather than treat content merely as an end in itself, inquiry teaching uses content as a vehicle to accomplish a wide range of learning goals. It emphasizes concepts and conceptualizing as well as information learning. This teaching strategy is student, not teacher, centered; it requires active student engagement with information (content) rather than passive absorption of that information. Teachers who wish to use inquiry teaching to its fullest potential must be aware of these essential differences and their implications for teaching, both for students and for themselves.

GUIDELINES FOR USING
INQUIRY TEACHING

Inquiry teaching is only one way of teaching. It may be neither desirable nor possible to use it all the time, nor may it be best suited to accomplish all the different objectives we may wish to accomplish in social studies. Inquiry teaching, for example, is obviously not the best way to cover large amounts of content in short periods of time. Yet this strategy may be the most useful way to facilitate retention of information and development of concepts in a relatively short time. Moreover, inquiry teaching seems almost certainly the best way to simultaneously facilitate student development of generalized knowledge, thinking skills, basic learning skills, content learning and selected values, attitudes, and feelings. Brief consideration of the implications of classroom use of this strategy may underscore some of the advantages and limitations of this form of instruction.

Time Requirements

Inquiry teaching takes considerable time. It takes longer to teach a given topic using an inquiry teaching strategy than, for instance, to teach that same topic by the more traditional read-recite-test strategy. But use of inquiry teaching seems to result in better learning—in terms of retention, transfer, and achievement—than do traditional strategies. Awareness of this has important implications for classroom teaching, especially in terms of course coverage, planning, and evaluating the teaching.

Inquiry teaching generally takes more than one class period. More often than not, it requires a series of class periods to complete. One period may be devoted entirely to clarifying a problem or raising questions for investigation. One or two more may be spent in refining hypotheses. Assembling, arranging, and analyzing sufficient evidence to test the validity of the hypotheses may take three, four, or a dozen or more class periods, while drawing meaningful conclusions about the entire investigation may well require several additional periods. Effective inquiry teaching can require considerable time.

Inquiry teaching is simply not well suited to covering with equal emphasis a broad expanse of topics, content, and information. Dictionaries commonly define to cover as "to take in and hide from view." This is exactly what occurs in courses that "cover" topics or content. Students in such courses confront such masses of detail that they customarily learn little of lasting significance. The compulsion in cover-the-text teaching to finish the book and to get through everything usually results in rote learning or learning at the lowest level of cognition—learning that is quickly forgotten. Inquiry teaching, however, does just the opposite. Use of this teaching strategy enables students to get into a topic to a depth sufficient for understanding. Inquiry teaching uncovers rather than covers, and uncovering is the principal task of teaching.

Inquiry teaching is time-consuming in another way, too. Teachers who use this strategy often require considerable planning time, at least until they have mastered its subtleties. Thinking through the sequence of steps that comprise inquiry teaching takes time, as do planning key questions and activities, anticipating student responses and the directions a unit might take, collecting or identifying the information needed in the unit, and planning an appropriate evaluation. Teachers find such planning much easier when working in pairs; they also find that, once the initial planning has been done, revision for reteaching of the same topic requires much less time. And often they are sur- prised that, even when students use the same data in successive classes or years, different types of learning occur, different insights are generated, and different skills may be developed. What may take considerable time in the short run may well save time needed to prepare for classroom teaching in the long run.

The amount of time required for inquiry teaching has implications in terms of content studied as well as for evaluating classroom teaching. Use of inquiry teaching inhibits broad surveys of a wide range of factual information or textbook generalities in a relatively short period of time. But inquiry teaching does not mean that students will come in contact with any less data than will students in expository teaching. Quite the contrary. Frequently, inquiry teaching may use more data in the study of a few topics in depth than will expository surveys of a broader range of topics. For example, a study of political leadership in the United States may be built around an intensive study of only four or five presidents instead of all the presidents. Such a study may well in- volve use of as much factual information as would a more sweeping but also more superficial survey of many more presidents. In such instances the data may be quite different, but it will easily be similar in quantity. Thus, inquiry teaching often means that coverage of many topics must be eliminated in favor of depth studies of fewer topics, that some content that is usually "covered" in many courses must be replaced with new content studied in depth.

Finally, since an inquiry unit or course may continue for many class periods, evaluating classroom teaching is rather difficult although not at all im- possible. It is very difficult to determine on the basis of one class observation or on the perusal of one daily lesson plan whether or not a teacher really is using inquiry teaching. Making such a decision requires familiarity with the entire strategy being used and continued observation over a sequence of learning ex- periences. Seeing one or two techniques in operation is not enough to know what particular strategy is being employed. Rather, one must know how the various techniques interrelate to determine whether students are engaged in in- quiring, memorizing, or whatever. If a teacher uses the same technique day after day, then inquiry teaching is probably not being used. But if a given lesson involves some type of student manipulation of content, inquiry teaching prob- ably is being used.

Inquiry teaching does indeed require more time than most conventional teaching strategies. Yet the benefits in terms of long-range learning seem worthy of this investment. Teachers and administrators, however, need to be aware of this fact in order to prepare properly for and to evaluate accurately use of this strategy in the classroom.

Topics for Inquiry

Crowded course requirements and limited instructional time make it virtually impossible to teach every topic in a history or social studies course through inquiry. This does not mean that one cannot use inquiry teaching, however, for it may be used in any course in at least two ways. We might reduce course content and requirements so that students could continuously engage in in-depth inquiry into a few selected topics instead of trying to engage in a broad superficial survey of many topics; or we could alternate inquiry teaching of some topics with expository presentation of others. However, either alternative raises the same basic question: Of all that we must or could teach in a specific course, what is worth inquiring into?

A number of criteria may be used to identify which of all the possible topics are worth selecting for inquiry teaching. Certainly a topic or body of content about which students express interest or curiosity is more likely to motivate classroom learning than is content which the students view as irrelevant or dull or "over their heads." And, of course, motivation enhances the quality of learning.

Type of subject matter or topics to be studied also provide a guide to identifying subjects for inquiry teaching. Some social studies educators suggest that topics best suited for inquiry teaching are those that represent persistent social or public issues such as political, economic, and social justice; economic security; or the exploitation/conservation of natural resources. Others suggest concentrating on issues of global import such as population, nutrition and food supplies, energy, and world peace. Issues or topics that relate to or imply concerns of personal values or interests may also serve as topics for worthwhile inquiry teaching. So, too, may topics that represent or reflect continuing historical concerns such as the use and abuse of power, social responses to the problem of scarcity, the relationship of the individual to his or her government, and so on. We can use any or all of these subject matter criteria to identify which topics in an American or world history course or in sociology, geography, civics, government, or other social studies courses may be best suited for inquiry teaching.

However, student interest and type of subject matter (as important as these factors are) do not alone prove to be adequate criteria for selecting topics for student inquiry. Declared student interest can be misleading, to say the least. Moreover, inquiry into teacher-selected topics about which students have initially indicated no interest can still pique student interest and generate motivation to the same extent as can the study of topics selected by students. While student interest and motivation contribute to effective inquiry, they can develop during the course of study as well as precede it.

Also, reference to type of subject alone proves to be insufficient for identifying subjects for classroom inquiry. These criteria, like those listed above, reflect certain value assumptions and educational philosophies of curriculum decision-makers more than they do anything intrinsic to content itself. Each criterion implies a specific point of view about what youngsters should know or be able to do within society now and in the future. However, selecting topics for teaching requires consideration of factors beyond the nature of the subject matter, just as it requires consideration of more than the existing degree of student interest. In many instances, these additional factors are even more important than considerations about subject matter alone. In selecting topics and content for inquiry teaching, teachers should consider the following in addition to student interest and subject matter:

1. *The developmental level of the students.* Are the students at the stage of concrete operational thinking as defined by Piaget? Or are they at or close to the stage of formal abstract reasoning? Are students at the lower stages of moral reasoning as defined by Kohlberg, or are they at the conventional stages of reasoning?

    Answers to these questions provide probably the most important criterion for determining what content and topics to use in inquiry teaching. If the content to be used is too abstract, too far removed in time or space from the experience of students, or too impersonal or "other centered," students at the concrete operational level of thinking may not be able to deal with it successfully. If the relationships students are asked to infer are highly abstract, or if the generalizations or concepts they are to develop are too abstract, students capable only of concrete operational thinking will experience considerable difficulty. For best results in inquiry teaching, the data used, the relationships to be made, and the generalized knowledge to be developed should be congruent with the developmental level of the students.

    In other words, students at the concrete operational level of thinking (generally intermediate grade students, but also those typically classified as "slow learners" in the secondary grades as well) should not be expected to engage productively in an inquiry into highly verbal or abstract data about abstract ideas or themes such as the impact of industrialization on social mobility, the relationship of world food supply to world population trends, or the principles expressed in the Declaration of Independence or Constitution. Teachers who wish to teach about such abstract concepts may well have to postpone such instruction until students have developed the abilities to comprehend them; or teachers may need to select data that are relatively observable, manipulable, and close to the experiential background of their students.

    For example, to develop abstractions about human interaction, students at the concrete operational level might use very concrete data about people such as pictures of individuals with their friends, pictures of where people live in relation to where their friends live, or information about the sources of their food, clothes, and other possessions. On the other hand, students moving toward more abstract levels of cognitive development may use more symbolic data about life styles (statistical data about work and travel patterns, maps, sociometric diagrams, and other similar abstract data) to generate inferences about social interaction and other more complex abstractions. Students' cognitive stages of development and levels of reasoning directly affect what they learn as well as how they learn. Topics and materials chosen for inquiry teaching must start where students presently are and move them step by step to the next higher levels. Careful attention to the type of data, the nature of the relationships to be inferred, and the abstractness of generalized knowledge to be developed can ensure that topics chosen for inquiry teaching meet this important criterion.

2. *The function of the topic or content in relation to other topics in the course.* Will study of this content through inquiry move learning forward in terms of student development and course goals? Does this study set up a topic that follows? Does it offer an opportunity to test further by application a skill, concept, or generalization developed earlier?

     Study of any topic by inquiry should move students from a point of relative ignorance to one of broader understanding or competence. It may accomplish this goal by building on a preceding unit, by applying something learned previously, or by setting up a unit that follows. In order to serve well as a topic for inquiry, a topic ought to be part of a larger sequence of learning and not an end in itself.

3. *The extent to which the topic lends itself to the simultaneous pursuit of multiple objectives.* What skills can be reinforced or developed by a study of a given body of content? What concepts, generalizations, and attitudes can be developed or reinforced at the same time? How well does this content serve as a vehicle for accomplishing a number of objectives beyond mere content learning itself?

     Time is precious in all teaching. In order to use limited teaching time wisely and to reap the potential of inquiry teaching, teachers should seek to accomplish several goals simultaneously with whatever content they decide to use. Thus, a topic whose study can facilitate concept development, practice of the skills of analysis, and social interaction skills may prove much more worth teaching by an inquiry strategy than a topic that lends itself essentially to accomplishing only a single learning objective.

4. *Significance of the generalized knowledge, skills, and affective outcomes that can be developed.* Will study of this subject help students develop generalized or conceptual knowledge that has significance beyond the topic itself, that may be used later in the course or in other courses? Will this study present opportunities for the development of higher level analytical skills, rather than merely the skills of memorization?

     Some topics or bodies of content can be used to generate generalizations, concepts, and understandings, to develop cognitive skills, and to achieve affective outcomes that are more valuable than others in their wide use and applicability. Content that will help students, for example, generate concepts that can be applied in the study of other related topics later in the course may well warrant inquiry teaching, while content that at best provides a link between events or periods would not warrant study through inquiry teaching. The significance of the broader insights that can be developed by a study of a specific body of content may outweigh knowledge about that specific content itself.

5. *The extent to which the topic is likely to contribute to achieving the goals of the course.* How well will the content to be used facilitate accomplishment of course goals?

   Although a specific topic may be interesting or fun for the teacher, it may not be worth teaching by inquiry. Any topic or body of content on which we propose to spend considerable time and effort ought to contribute directly to achieving the stated course goals. If the content will, for example, help students move from concrete operational to formal abstract reasoning, if this is the goal of our course, it may be well taught by inquiry. However, if the topic is to serve only introductory, review, or supplemental purposes, it may hardly be worth presenting in an inquiry format.

6. *Availability of appropriate materials for follow-up study.* Do a variety of materials exist for students to use to test the hypotheses generated in class? Are these materials readily accessible? Are they in forms the students can comprehend and use?

   Unless appropriate teaching and learning materials will be available for students to use in testing hypotheses, it will do little good to create inquiry lessons on a given topic. Students must have ready access to a variety of materials at various levels of abstraction, at reading levels they can comprehend, and in durable form if they are to carry an inquiry through to a conclusion in the study of any specific topic. If such materials are not available in the classroom, or resource center, or library, students may have extreme difficulty in completing their study using the basic steps of inquiring.

In sum, one must use a number of criteria to select topics or content for inquiry teaching. Student interest and the nature and social use of the content constitute only two criteria to be considered in making this decision. Teachers must also consider student abilities as well as the potential of the content or topic for enhancing student cognitive and affective development and for achieving a variety of course goals. The availability and quality of learning materials must also be considered. Careful analysis of any potential topic or content in terms of the criteria listed above can help teachers make the most pedagogically sound decisions about where to use inquiry teaching in their courses. Such decisions lie at the heart of effective inquiry teaching and purposeful classroom learning.

Types of Instructional Techniques

Every instructional technique can be useful in inquiry teaching. Oral reports, library research, bulletin board displays, role playing, simulation, and debates can all be used to provide data for inquiry. Even a lecture, or teacher monologue, has a place in inquiry teaching.

Lectures, as all other instructional techniques, may serve a variety of purposes; for one, they are well suited to present information. In inquiry teaching students periodically need information or data to generate and test hypotheses, or against which to apply some newly developed generalizations, or even from which to generate questions for further study. The data may be communicated to students through a variety of media, including lectures. In fact, a lecture may be the best way to put students in touch with data they need but cannot locate on their own; a lecture may be used when we wish students to devote their time to arranging and analyzing data rather than to collecting it; or a lecture might be used to help students refine their skills of separating relevant from irrelevant data or when we wish to model the process of inquiring for them. For, in point of fact, lectures themselves may be organized along the steps of an inquiry strategy if we so choose.

Why we use a particular technique really determines its value in inquiry teaching. One clue to the purpose of a technique is what the students do as a result of its use. What they do with the content of a lecture, for example, determines whether or not this technique serves well as part of an inquiry strategy. If the students merely commit the substance of a lecture to memory and then reiterate it on a later test, an inquiry strategy is not being employed. Or if we lecture day after day, then it is doubtful that inquiry teaching is in operation. But if the students use the data from a lecture to build or test a hypothesis, if they work with the data contained in the lecture, then lectures can play a very legitimate and important role in inquiry teaching.

Certain instructional techniques seem better suited to inquiry teaching than to other strategies. Questioning is probably the most important of these and certainly the most crucial; we generally use questions to guide students through the process of learning by inquiry. Inquiry questions reach far beyond those used by expository teaching in both form and degree of sophistication. Questions in inquiry teaching do not require mere repetition or description of the facts being studied. On the contrary, they emphasize the "why" much more than the "what," the "so what" as well as the "how." As noted in Chapter 6, questioning serves as a major technique in guiding inquiry learning.

In expository teaching, questioning usually serves primarily as a check to see if students can repeat the material from the text, lecture, or class discussion. In inquiry teaching, however, questions such as these represent just the first stage in learning, for we use additional questions of all types to help students move through the entire learning experience.

Some questions are useful in developing hypotheses ("What would happen if . . . ?" or "How do you account for . . . ?"). Building on the responses to these, we can ask additional questions to identify needed evidence ("If this is true, then what do we expect to find?"), to collect evidence ("What does the picture show?"), to clarify or interpret evidence ("What does it mean?"), to categorize or note patterns ("Which of these seem to have something in common?"), and so on. Each kind of question builds on the responses and insights developed to answer the preceding questions and then seeks to probe for new insights and meanings. Thus, in inquiry teaching, questions facilitate learning by guiding one through the process of intellectual inquiry from problem identification to conclusion. Rather than simply seek a recounting of what is already believed to be true, they move students beyond the given material.

How we use questions to guide inquiry will vary, of course. Ideally, the students should be asking the questions. One way to induce student-initiated questions is to confront them with a problematic situation, allow them to develop a problem for investigation, and permit them to proceed, unguided, to seek a resolution that satisfies them. We need ask no questions at all. The entire burden of inquiring can thus be left to the students. Such an approach is highly nondirective and can be quite useful, especially in evaluating how well students have developed the skills of inquiring. Yet this approach can also be quite frustrating to students unaccustomed to learning on their own. Therefore, until students develop frames of reference and concepts that give birth to effective questions, until they become familiar with inquiry itself, teachers need to guide and assist them in learning by asking questions and by stimulating them to ask questions.[1]

Another way we might help students to learn how to engage in inquiry is to allow the students to define a problem for investigation and then to encourage them to ask their own questions. When countered with our questions that require them to engage in various intellectual operations, they can then develop the answers to their original questions. Thus, to a student question such as, "Why do these people select a leader that way?", we could respond by asking, "What reasons can you think of that might explain this?" In this way we can very subtly guide them into the beginning of an inquiry experience.

Another way of organizing questioning is much more direct. Teachers may supply a problematic situation and, after the students have articulated the problem, ask them directly to hypothesize some alternative solutions. Then, by using the types of questions outlined above, we may guide them through the various stages of intellectual inquiry from identifying the kinds of evidence needed to developing meaningful conclusions and even generalizing. Whereas in the previous approach the initiative is left mostly to the students, here it lies almost wholly in the hands of the teacher.

Which approach to use depends on the objectives set for or by the students and their individual skills and backgrounds. If the objective is to test student abilities to use the skills of inquiring, then the nondirective approach may be most useful. If it is to learn how to ask questions and what questions to ask when, then the second approach may be best. Or if the goal is to learn the process of inquiring and to learn some predetermined concept or generalization, the third, more direct approach may be advisable.

Regardless of the approach used, it is important to realize that inquiring proceeds at different rates of speed for different students, depending upon their varying intellectual abilities, their backgrounds of experience, and the data they have available. Questions may come directly from the teacher or the students. These questions may be asked orally or appear in the form of a study guide for use by small groups or individuals engaged in independent study; the guides may be written or typed or on filmstrips, depending on the nature of the materials. For those unacquainted with this way of learning, the questions may be numerous and explicit; for the more experienced, they may be fewer in number and less detailed. But no matter through which media they are communicated, questions must be carefully formulated and presented in a sequence designed to help students proceed through all the various stages of rational inquiry.

The Role of Content

Content, or substantive information in the form of specifics and generalizations, comprises another essential ingredient of inquiry teaching. Inquiry does not occur in a vacuum. It requires something to work with, to inquire into, to think about. A certain amount of content or data are required to generate a problem, arouse curiosity, or create a question in the minds of the students. We may need additional content to generate tentative solutions or answers. Hypothesis testing requires even more content. Data and content are plugged into and used at virtually every stage of inquiry teaching.

The type of content that may be used has no limit. Lists of kings or presidents, information about laws passed during a given period, statistics about a particular topic, or a trial transcript all may be used. Primary and secondary data of any kind and on any subject or from any discipline should be considered. Raw, primary data, a most useful form of data, includes statistics, maps, artifacts, paintings, pictures, diaries, documents, eyewitness accounts, poems, novels, and so on—items unaccompanied by explanations of what they say, what they mean, why they are significant, or how they relate to something else. Textbook accounts, newspaper editorials or features, monographs, interpretive films, reports, and similar secondary materials may also be useful even though they usually represent what someone else believes to be true.

As long as content is treated as data and not final answers, any kind of content or data may be used in inquiry teaching. Secondary accounts may be used to motivate lessons, as sounding boards against which to check the results of student inquiry, as evaluative devices ("In view of our study, how valid is this interpretation?"), as sources of data, or as materials to be analyzed in terms of bias, methodology, and so on. Primary accounts may be used for similar purposes as well as to check the accuracy or authenticity of secondary accounts.

Although the kinds of content that are useful in inquiry teaching do not differ basically from those often used in expository teaching, such content plays a much different role in inquiry teaching. In expository teaching, content tends to be an end in itself. Usually the sole learning objective is remembering it. In inquiry teaching, content does not serve as an end in itself; it is not to be memorized. The learning experience does not aim at absorbing it. Instead, content becomes a vehicle for accomplishing other goals: for clarifying values perhaps, or developing concepts and generalizations, or refining the skills of intellectual inquiry. Content is used, manipulated, pulled apart, and refitted into new patterns in an effort to develop new meanings relevant to the task at hand. Content in inquiry teaching serves as a vehicle for learning something else—as well as an object of learning.

Content may also be used to guide the learning process. The kinds of information students encounter and when they receive the data influence how, as well as what, they learn. So, too, does the way we organize this content. If, for example, students deal only with content that implies an economic basis for imperialism, they will probably develop an economic explanation for this phenomenon. If they are then put in touch with data that refutes or casts doubt on the validity of this explanation, they may ask new questions and search out new kinds of data to investigate. Thus, the way content and data are made available to students and how they are organized may be used to guide learning.

There are a number of reasons to control student access to data in inquiry teaching, at least in its initial stages. One is merely to save time. There is no reason why students should have to find their own data other than to develop the skills of locating relevant information. These skills are only one set of skills necessary to learning. Time must be spent in refining other skills, too. Hence, we should frequently supply students with data they need so that what time is available may be devoted to practicing these other skills. Moreover, great masses of content may overwhelm students unfamiliar with ways to handle data. In this instance, we should provide data to them slowly and in usable amounts. In many cases the kinds of content needed by the students may be inaccessible to them; thus we need to collect it and give it to them. Inquiry involves much more than finding information, and attention must be devoted to developing all facets of this approach to learning rather than just one.

Content may be highly structured or totally unstructured. Data presented to students may be segregated by media, by topic, or by its discipline base. By helping students note similarities and differences, such grouping can direct them in the development of discipline-oriented concepts. While forming such concepts is often desirable, having students sometimes work with completely unorganized content may be just as desirable, for they can use what concepts they are evolving to order the data in their own fashion. Using content arranged in different ways helps students refine the skills of analysis and broaden analytical concepts—important objectives of inquiry teaching.

This is not to say that some content is not worth knowing or that learning content cannot be an objective of inquiry teaching. Students should learn considerable information in the social studies, and experience shows that they can learn it well through inquiry teaching. Because inquiry-oriented learning experiences require students to talk about, mentally manipulate, and even physically work with information or content over and over again, students become so familiar with the content that they know it in the deepest sense of *knowing*. They don't memorize it. It simply becomes a part of their experience because they consciously use and reflect on it. In so doing, however, they learn other things as well.

Learning Materials and Media

Content, as already noted, may be communicated through a variety of media. The written word has been one of the most commonly used media in social studies. Even the materials used in inquiry teaching often consist almost exclusively of collections of documents, other written sources, or excerpts therefrom. This is highly unfortunate and most undesirable.

Many students find social studies courses boring or difficult because of the required excessive amount of reading and the poor quality of most of the writing they must read. Students need to learn how to read, of course. One way to help them accomplish this is to use text or documentary materials, but not exclusively. Students also need to work with other types of media, especially those they will have opportunities to use in their out-of-school lives. As a matter of fact, students can improve reading comprehension while using films and filmstrips as well as by using textbooks. It is vitally important in inquiry teaching that students gain experience in using a wide variety of media other than books and documents.

Lectures, oral reports, guest speakers, debates, songs, newspapers, novels, film loops, sound films, filmstrips, statistics, maps, records, tapes, television programs, and punch cards represent just a few of the nontext media useful in learning. Each of these has special attributes. Maps and aerial photographs, for example, depict spatial distributions and areal relationships better than any other media. Overhead transparencies clarify relationships and sequence. Content should be communicated through whatever media best reveals what is to be shown. And especially in inquiry teaching, the same content ought to be presented via a number of different media (for example, via a map and a chart or graph as well as a photograph) so that students may develop a variety of insights about its significance.

However, inquiry teaching can be employed effectively without access to all or most of the equipment or materials associated with the media described above. Even though many teachers who feel their instructional resources are limited to only a single, standard text claim that inquiry teaching is impossible for them, nothing is farther from the truth. No teacher is limited to a single text, no matter how bleak the situation may appear.

Every classroom teacher, regardless of grade level or school facilities, has a number of potential resources that can serve as media for inquiry teaching. First, there are the public communications media (television, radio, movies, magazines, and newspapers), at least one of which is readily accessible to almost everyone. Second, the students themselves, each possessing a rich and unique background of prior experience, can serve as sources of information. Third, a teacher's own knowledge, talents, and interests can be used to enhance learning in the classroom. Teachers can, for instance, make many of their own materials by taking photographs and slides, using cleared X-ray film on which to draw maps for overlays, and so on. All of these resources can be tapped at various stages in any inquiry teaching experience to identify problems worthy of investigation; to stimulate and suggest hypotheses, alternative plans of attack, and potential consequences of specific decisions; to provide data for testing hypotheses; and to serve as a basis for synthesizing a line of inquiry.

Finally, of course, teachers have textbooks that in themselves prove as useful in inquiry as in expository teaching. Any average textbook, especially if published since 1965, constitutes much more than a collection of words. In addition to the written narrative, texts usually contain all kinds of other learning aids including maps, graphs, charts, cartoons, photographs, timelines, and end-of-chapter word lists and questions. Many texts today, in fact, are simply multimedia packages bound with hard covers. As indicated in Chapter 7, conventional as well as inquiry-oriented textbooks can be used well in inquiry teaching.

Any type of learning material has a use in inquiry teaching. Technical qualities aside, there is no such thing as a bad piece of material for this type of teaching. Some materials, of course, may be inferior or inadequate in the technical sense (the sound may be fuzzy, the paper easily torn, the ink faded, the photographs blurred or too small, and so on). But whether or not the content of a piece of material is good or bad depends not on its accuracy, thoroughness, or bias, but on how we use it. If we assign a piece of material having inaccurate content to be committed unquestioningly to memory, then the way we use it is incorrect. However, this same piece of material might serve a very good purpose if we use it to raise questions, generate hypotheses, evaluate its accuracy, challenge assumptions, analyze author bias, or evaluate student-made conclusions. How we use materials in inquiry teaching and *not* the nature of their content determines their value in learning. There are few, if any, materials that cannot be used effectively in one or more aspects of inquiry teaching.

Student Involvement

Inquiry teaching differs from the more traditional expository teaching in another important way. Inquiry teaching requires the active involvement of the student in the learning experience. Since this type of teaching strategy does not consist solely of passing on to students the results of someone else's wit and wisdom, students cannot remain passive absorbers of information. They must become active seekers. They must find problems to investigate, search for tentative answers, use data to validate hypotheses, synthesize content into new meanings, and apply it in new situations. Inquiry involves making meaning—the job of learners, not teachers. Inquiry teaching helps students make meanings. It requires them to engage in the very process they are learning. Student interaction, with content and with each other, is an important characteristic of inquiry teaching.

Inquiry learning experiences must thus be designed to facilitate both student interaction and thinking. Large-group lectures, whether they include 30 or 300 students, cannot be a mainstay of inquiry teaching. Students must instead spend considerable time in small-group discussion or individual study, research, and investigation. Of course, there are times when large-group sessions may be most useful, as when introducing a new subject for study, or presenting hard-to-find data that students will need, or evaluating the results of a learning experience. But by and large the bulk of class time must be organized to enable students to interact with each other as well as with the teacher, book, film, picture, or other media being used. Students can work in triads or small groups, in committees, or as individuals. In inquiry teaching, students must spend less time in large-group situations than they normally do in traditional social studies instruction and considerable time in small groups or doing independent inquiry.

The implications of group size should be quite clear. Large-group scheduling practices may not be at all conducive to inquiry teaching simply because these practices often lack the flexibility needed to allow for individualized inquiry or grouping or pairing. Instead of structuring teaching by prescribing a certain class size to meet at a certain interval each week, inquiry teaching is best organized on the basis of the kinds of intellectual activities that are involved in learning. Although the general stages are always the same, the time devoted to each depends on the topics under investigation, the students, and the learning objectives. These may vary considerably with each course and teacher.

We should note, however, that inquiry teaching can be as easily undertaken within a class of 30 or 40 students as within a class of 10. Having the students meet regularly in one room enables the teacher to organize them as the situation warrants: they may sit as an entire class to view a film or hear a presentation; individuals may be paired in order to evaluate some data and form hypotheses; students may be arranged in small groups within the room to test certain hypotheses against specific evidence; they may go individually to the library or study center to gather more evidence; and they may reconvene periodically as a class to report, discuss problems, and debate conclusions. Successful inquiry teaching requires that students work together in a variety of combinations designed to enhance their interaction with the data being used. The average classroom of 20, 30, or 40 students offers just the flexibility needed for this arrangement.

Variety

Variety is just as important in inquiry teaching as in any other type of teaching and perhaps more so. Any kind of teaching can become deadly monotonous when following the same pattern without alteration. But inquiry teaching requires considerable intellectual effort—more than expository teaching. Students need variety for at least two reasons: for a change of pace and to develop fully all the skills of inquiry they need to develop. However, variety does not mean just the periodic introduction of a film or a field trip. It means varying the techniques, the materials, and the sequence of steps in the teaching strategy itself while maintaining the integration of all elements in the overall strategy.

A considerable number of different instructional media and techniques can be used throughout any inquiry teaching course or unit. The basic stages of inquiring provide the unifying threads for use of these media, but different techniques may be used in each stage. For example, the first problem in a course might be presented by use of some quotations and pictures. The next problematic situation, however, might be developed by use of newspaper accounts, the next by a role-playing activity, the next by contradictory quotations, the next by a film, and so on. Students may hypothesize in a general class discussion or in small groups. Hypotheses might be tested by all students using all the data or by different groups testing selected aspects of a hypothesis.

Each inquiry experience should be fresh in terms of the media used. By employing a multimedia approach, the teacher can help students refine their skills of using a wider variety of media including those they may expect to find relevant in out-of-school life. When teachers feel it necessary to present data, we may do it one time via film, another time by a record, later by a lecture, and even later by a set of still pictures. Out-of-class assignments may include reading, analyzing maps or charts, studying photographs, and so on. There is nothing more deadening than beginning each unit with the same kind of technique or media, then hypothesizing with the same kind of media and/or technique.

Variety may also be ensured by changing the student arrangement for the various stages of inquiring. If in one unit they hypothesize as a class, in the next they might hypothesize in pairs. If in one unit they hypothesize in the classroom, in another they might do it as a homework assignment. The techniques to use, the media to employ, and the student organization are all quite interrelated. Any combination of these should be determined according to how well it will accomplish the desired objectives and carry through the inquiry process. Since there are many skill, attitude, and knowledge objectives to seek in inquiry teaching, these combinations should vary greatly throughout the overall learning experience.

Varying inquiry teaching does not end here, however. The strategy itself may be varied not only to avoid monotony but also to concentrate on specific sets of skills associated with particular parts of the strategy. Although inquiring normally begins with developing a problem, the students do not have to begin each unit this way. If they do, they will realize before long that if they fail to come up with a problem, they will not have to proceed further—or if they choose a ridiculous problem, they may destroy whatever the teacher has planned—or if they argue long enough, they won't have time for anything else!

To avoid these situations and at the same time to get maximum use out of what little time is available, we may sometimes give the students a problem or present one for study that has concerned many people. Or we can skip this phase of inquiry altogether and introduce the students to a theory or hypothesis advanced by some scholar, for instance, and ask students to determine how well the available data supports it. Such a theory then becomes the problem and makes it unnecessary for students to develop their own. A learning experience might even be launched by looking at evidence someone else has used to verify his/her own hypothesis. In the process of analyzing this, students may not only find new evidence but also refine their skills of working with data and of thinking.

Variety is important for pedagogical as well as psychological reasons. Fresh approaches are more exiciting and interesting. Doing the same old thing with the same media the same way for every learning experience is stifling, to say the least. This is as true for inquiry teaching as it is for any other kind of teaching. Ensuring that this monotony does not occur is an important aspect of inquiry teaching.

THE ROLE OF
THE TEACHER

Classroom teachers play as important a role in inquiry teaching as in any other kind of teaching. Whether or not inquiry occurs in the classroom depends entirely on us. To be successful, we must know what inquiry is and how to go about it, and we must be inquirers ourselves. We must practice what we preach and be able to organize and facilitate learning experiences that require students to engage in inquiry.

The primary function of any teaching is to facilitate learning—to stimulate it, to guide it, and to ensure that it happens. Doing this is a teacher's responsibility. In expository teaching, we generally fulfill this responsibility by telling students what they ought to learn. In inquiry teaching, however, we facilitate learning by the instructional techniques we use and how we arrange them, by the content we select and how we structure it, by the classroom climate we create, and by the role we take in the actual learning experience. How successful inquiry teaching will be depends largely on how we go about carrying out these four major tasks.

Effective inquiry teaching requires us to function essentially as both planners and facilitators of learning. We must first design our unit or course and the individual learning experiences that comprise these units or courses. When necessary, we must also select and prepare the instructional materials for students to use. Then we must translate these from paper to an actual classroom setting by bringing about those behaviors that we have determined will best achieve the established objectives.

Planning for Inquiry Teaching

Advanced planning for inquiry teaching is absolutely essential. The planning stage involves establishing the desired objectives, selecting appropriate content, and then selecting and arranging in sequence the activities that will help the students

1. Define problems for investigation.
2. Hypothesize—develop tentative answers, alternative solutions, or possible plans of attack.
3. Test these hypotheses against evidence.

4. Draw meaningful conclusions about the validity of their hypotheses.
5. Either continue hypothesizing and testing each succeeding hypothesis until a valid "answer" is developed or, having arrived at such a conclusion, apply it to new data.
6. Generalize or conceptualize on the basis of the entire learning experience.

Such planning means conducting what is, in a sense, an imaginary dry run through the contemplated learning experience. In doing so, we must anticipate the kinds of hypotheses that may be offered, identify the data and materials that may be needed to test these, and speculate about the kinds of questions that should be raised. This planning proves absolutely essential to an effective classroom learning experience, for only in this way can we determine the kinds of content and media that will probably be needed or work best in the course of the planned learning experience. Only in this way is it possible to devise the proper questions and to arrange the various learning activities in a sequence that will help the learner move from the initiatory problem to its resolution.

Our main concern in planning as in conducting the actual classroom experience must be how best to guide learning toward our chosen objectives. Several of the tools that we use to guide learning must be developed in this planning stage. These include the questions to be asked and the data or content to be used.

In selecting questions to ask or be asked, we must be aware of the fact that what one learns and how one learns are determined in part by the kinds of questions asked and the order in which they are asked. In planning an inquiry teaching experience, we need to select questions that will require students to hypothesize, to identify the evidence needed to test the hypothesis, and to arrange and analyze this evidence in productive fashion. There are many kinds of questions, but there is only one way to arrange them—so that they stimulate the students to move through the process of using the skills of intellectual inquiry.

The same may be said of content and the media by which it is communicated. What and how one learns is determined in part by the kinds of content used, the order in which it is used, and when it becomes available. By withholding data representing contradictory views on a particular issue or event, we may actually allow students to reach questionable conclusions. By then making these data available, we can lead them to evaluate the results of their inquiry. By presenting only workable amounts of data at a time, we may focus on the development of different skills rather than overwhelm the students with an avalanche of content.

In many instances the kinds of materials needed for a particular learning experience are not available or at least are unavailable in a form commensurate with the abilities of the students. Consequently, we often must prepare some materials ourselves. This is another important part of planning. We may need to collect, redraw, or create maps, prepare transparencies, and type or draw charts. In order to conduct a worthwhile inquiry learning experience, the proper materials must be available, and selecting or making these must be done before launching the actual learning experience.

Making decisions about content, media, and questions—which to use and how to arrange them—constitute the very essence of designing inquiry teaching. Only by carefully advanced and detailed planning can a worthwhile learning experience be created. Such planning is the sine qua non of inquiry teaching.

Conducting the Learning Experience

There are also other ways to guide an inquiry experience. But while these ways may to some degree be planned in advance, they are basically the product of how we operate in our classrooms. This involves the second facet of facilitating learning—conducting the learning experience.

A classroom climate conducive to free and open intellectual inquiry is essential to inquiry teaching. Such a climate opens students to question and discuss, to communicate with each other as well as with the teacher, to direct the learning experience into areas of their interests, and to consider their reasoned views as legitimate as those of anyone else.

Of course, such a climate results partially from the equipment in the classroom and how it is arranged. A room with movable student desks and chairs, with numerous written, audio, and visual references and resources, and with readily available materials offers a fine setting for inquiry teaching. But another factor affects the learning climate—our own behavior as teachers.

We do not create a climate conducive to inquiry by standing behind a lectern at the front of the room or by requiring students to stand when speaking. We create it by designing challenging problems to resolve, by using pairing and grouping techniques that foster student interaction and minimize our intervention and domination, and by enthusiastically joining with the students as an inquirer. We do not create an effective classroom climate by giving answers or by determining the validity of an answer by a show of hands, by requiring students to guess what answer we are looking for, by requiring all students to come up with the same answer, or even by talking in terms of "right answers." A climate conducive to inquiry demands that we redirect questions to the students, ask new questions, and give the students an opportunity to find out for themselves.

An inquiring climate is not created, moreover, by demanding silence throughout the entire class period. It is created by realizing that silence is not always golden and by permitting and even encouraging students to talk among themselves before they venture opinions, hypotheses, and the like. It is not created by repeating the same question in different forms when no response is immediately forthcoming. It is created by allowing time for questions to sink in—for students to think about them and even talk about them. It is brought about by using the lesson plan to get the lesson going, by building on student input, and by referring thereafter to the plan only for the most basic guidance.

We cannot create a classroom climate conducive to inquiry by keeping the students arranged forever in neat little rows. Instead, we should encourage—

indeed, even require—them to move into groups and pairs to engage in some aspect of inquiry. We do not bring it about by requiring silence when viewing some visual materials and then by urging discussion of what everyone thinks they saw or heard, but by showing and reshowing the film or filmstrip and by talking about it while it is being shown. We do not create an inquiry climate by ignoring unanticipated contributions or questions but by treating the contributions of all students with the respect that rational thinking deserves.

Effective inquiry teaching requires considerable awareness of the fact that what we say and do affects how students learn as well as what they learn. Students whose contributions receive a "That's right!" response are in reality receiving an extrinsic reward, when in fact they should be getting these rewards from within—from knowing their contributions are right because the data supports them. Students who get enough "That's wrong!" responses eventually stop contributing altogether. Such a situation is hardly conducive to effective learning.

We must avoid putting students down and thus turning them away from further thinking. We must also avoid ignoring obviously invalid statements, ridiculing them, or responding with an "uh-huh" or "that's interesting" or some other noncommital remark. We may challenge these contributions or ask others to comment on them, but we should never ignore or try to sidestep them. Neither should we write on the board only the ideas we want and ignore any others because, in so doing, we are really indicating to the contributors whether or not we think their ideas count.

Instead, we must honor all results of thinking by accepting them and using them in the learning experience. We should treat all answers as hypotheses, equally valid, subject only to later verification. And we should require evidence. A snap answer of "Charlemagne" to the question, "Who won the battle of Saratoga?" should not be dismissed as inane but rather accepted as a hypothesis and tested by reference to other data. The data should tell if it is invalid—not the teacher.

Above all, we should require students to do the summarizing or concluding. We should avoid ending a class by saying, "Well, today we learned . . . " How do we know what was learned? Only the students can tell, either verbally or by some other observable behavior, what they have learned.

As teachers, we have many roles in conducting inquiry. We must, for one, facilitate communication. We must require students to define their terms and help them say as precisely as possible what they mean. We must see to it that all students get involved and that students talk also to each other rather than only to us. Secondly, we must promote thinking. This requires us to guide the students through the process of inquiry, stopping periodically so that they may summarize what has been established to that point. In so doing, we may have to correct errors of fact or even challenge questionable statements. Sometimes we will have to supply hard-to-get data or steer students to sources of information we know will be useful to them. We may have to act as a devil's advocate by asking questions or injecting data that directly contradicts what the students are saying. We may have to prod or to slow students down. We may have to help unsnarl confusion or ambiguity. And we may have to help the students step back and reflect on what they have been doing. At times we will even have to help the students make connections between what they have learned and what they are now doing.

Successful execution of these tasks requires teachers to be models for inquiry. We must not only know how to inquire, we must do it ourselves and with enthusiasm. We must not in any way be authoritarian or dogmatic. Rather, we must be completely flexible in our teaching techniques. We must permit and encourage challenging questions and creative thinking. We must not insist that what we believe to be true is true but rather accept all views and interpretations for submission to the test of the evidence. And we must do the same for our own views.

We must also continually evaluate what is happening in the course of our planned learning experience. We must learn to know when the students have successfully attained each step in the inquiry process as well as when they have learned what we want them to know. This evaluation may be based on observation as well as on written evidence. Of course, paper and pencil tests may also be administered. Evaluation *must* be an ongoing effort if the inquiry teaching experience is to lead anywhere, for we cannot possibly guide students to a new level of thinking until we know they have attained the preceding level.

Although inquiry teaching often makes some teachers feel insecure, it should not. The security of good inquiry teaching lies as much in knowing how to inquire as it does in knowing any specific body of content. To achieve this security, we must know the process of inquiring, be well organized, be adept at using the skills of inquiry, and have a conceptual framework that leads us to ask a wide variety of useful questions. Security in the classroom lies in knowing what to do next: in knowing that if we just formulated a hypothesis, the next thing to do is identify the kinds of data we need to verify it, or in knowing that if we are working with many kinds of data, we must translate, classify, and interpret them. Knowledge of how to inquire and willingness to engage in inquiry are basic attributes of successful and confident inquiry teachers.

Not all teachers possess these attributes nor can they fill these roles. At least, not all may feel comfortable in so doing. Inquiry teaching requires flexibility, considerable tolerance for ambiguity, a willingness to say, "I don't know," a refusal to give answers, and a knowledge of how to inquire. It also requires considerable knowledge of the content and of the skills being used. It demands an open, creative, enthusiastic person; not all teachers possess these attributes.

THE ROLE
OF THE STUDENT

Just as the teacher's role in inquiry teaching differs from his or her role in the most traditional type of teaching, so too does the role of the student differ. In expository classrooms, students customarily sit rather passively, at best soaking up what the teacher, film, or text says, and writing out answers to questions in the text—answers that can be found somewhere in a given chapter. They know they are to remain quiet throughout the class period. They must copy whatever is written on the board. Their notebooks must be neat and up-to-date. Comparatively little intellectual effort is involved in these activities.

Students as a whole are well aware of how we expect them to act. And they act that way. They normally see themselves essentially as passive receivers to be acted upon by the teachers. They see the active role in learning as one fulfilled by teachers. We do things to and for them. Students get out of the learning experience what we put into it!

In inquiry teaching, however, students get out of the learning experience what *they* put into it. Their role consists of making considerable intellectual effort—of working with information, initiating questions, challenging ideas, thinking. They may even do what they customarily assign to us by telling what they think is so or offering some information they have found. For many students, being confronted with this new set of expectations seems quite difficult at first. As a result, they do not take to this way of teaching until they become accustomed to the freedom and satisfaction it brings. For some, this never happens because they have too long derived satisfaction from being able to regurgitate the answers they think we want. When there are no particular right answers, these students feel lost. They are so programmed into the conventional system that they find it almost impossible to succeed in inquiry learning.

Students often react the same way to inquiry-oriented teachers as they do to inquiry teaching. Students have a very definite image of what a teacher should do: give lectures, assign reading, ask factual questions based on the reading, know all the answers, and test to see if the content has been memorized. All written work is graded. Audio-visual presentations may be "treats" or supplemental; they may be offered but rarely discussed and hardly ever considered essential to the unit under study. Teachers know best and know all. Students expect them to act in a certain way. When they don't, students question their competency or their interest. Many students of all ability levels still want to be told—for psychological security if for no other reason. Being confronted by inquiry teaching may be most upsetting and even frustrating to many students.

Teachers need to be aware of these problems because much of the potential friction or frustration in initiating inquiry teaching can be avoided by treating students the way their new role demands. There is no teller-receiver, adult-child, teacher-client relationship. As Norman Johnson has noted, the student is more than a receiver, more than a child intellectually, more than a client.[2] To assume students are receivers or children or clients assumes they have nothing to contribute to the learning experience. On the contrary, every student can and does give input to any kind of learning experience. They help initiate and direct these experiences, and they do have ideas as to what they ought and want to do.

Students, like all people, will behave exactly as others expect them to behave. An effective inquiry teacher strives to help students develop a positive self-image, to help them realize they can think and succeed on their own. This can be accomplished by creating the kind of classroom climate for inquiry described above, by letting the test for truth be the evidence and the reward be the satisfaction of knowing, "My idea is as good as anyone else's in terms of the evidence." This is an important goal of all education and of inquiry teaching in particular.

WHAT'S THE MATTER WITH INQUIRY TEACHING?

Many teachers do not find inquiry teaching to be a useful or attractive teaching strategy for a variety of reasons. In many instances, their objections or reservations reflect honest questions about the nature and intent of inquiry teaching and thinking. Four commonly raised questions about or objections to inquiry teaching deserve brief comment here.[3]

1. *What about the students who make wrong hypotheses?*

Good for them! Now they can start learning!

A hypothesis, by definition, is an educated guess—a tentative answer. It is in itself neither right nor wrong. Learning starts with a hypothesis but it does not end there. Inquiry teaching does not involve just hypothesis-making. It involves both hypothesis-making and hypothesis-testing. Certainly not all hypotheses test out to be accurate. Many, probably most, do eventually prove inaccurate. The point to remember, however, is that a hypothesis represents not the conclusion of a learning experience but the start of learning. If teachers were to accept student hypotheses as statements of proven fact and stop there, this objection about "wrong hypotheses" might be legitimate. But inquiry teaching requires students to submit their hypotheses to the test of evidence. Even if the original hypothesis turns out invalid, as students conduct their test, they learn new skills, concepts, and information, and they move toward developing a valid answer to their original question. No inquiry can be considered completed until the students have judged the accuracy of their hypotheses against appropriate evidence.

This objection reveals the rightness/wrongness syndrome that prevails in many classrooms and that greatly inhibits effective teaching and learning. Teachers should not allow themselves to be set up, nor should they set themselves up as arbitrary judges of what is correct. The mass of information, complexity of concepts, and subtleties of generalizations in any discipline or subject are simply too great for a single individual to master. Moreover, no one individual (including textbook authors) has access to all the data pertinent to a specific hypothesis or topic. While some hypotheses may prove accurate in the light of available data, no one can ever know how accurate they are because we rarely if ever have all the relevant data. So one cannot usually pronounce things absolutely right or wrong. Inquiry teaching focuses on trying to determine the most accurate answer in terms of the available evidence.

Rather than nip learning in the bud by telling a student his or her hypothesis is wrong, an inquiry teacher can help students test their hypotheses against all relevant information. In doing so, it is the teacher's responsibility to see that the students confront evidence on all sides of the hypotheses, especially when the students' biases seem to lead in a direction unsupported by known evidence. At the same time, however, the teacher must be aware of his or her own biases and be prepared to accept a student hypothesis if supported by the evidence even if the teacher instinctively rejects it as "wrong."

In sum, rightness or wrongness is not the issue. Hypothesis testing does not aim to work toward a single right answer; rather, hypothesis testing aims to narrow the number of potentially correct hypotheses by refuting some and eliminating others. The task of inquiry teaching is to determine the probable accuracy of any hypothesis, and it is the evidence rather than teacher or textbook opinion that provides the final determinant.

2. *Inquiry teaching may work with bright students, but it certainly isn't suited for slow learners.*

Different types of students do respond differently to inquiry teaching, but their responses are shaped more by their previous experiences in school, their learning environments, and the content they are required to use than by their own natural abilities. Inquiry teaching may be used to accomplish worthwhile objectives with teachable students of all ability levels, slow learners included.

Bright students, for instance, often seem reluctant to hypothesize. They usually achieve reputations as "bright" by being good at memorizing and at figuring out what responses teachers are looking for to their questions. They usually answer only when they know they are "right!" But inquiry teaching changes the rules of the classroom for them. No longer are there right answers to memorize. In inquiry teaching, finding evidence to support an answer requires an entirely new approach to learning for students. Some are quite slow to accept this approach. Others never make the adjustment at all.

For slow learners, this situation does not seem to pose a problem. Not having been successful at reading teachers' minds or remembering data in the past, slow learners rarely seem reluctant to hypothesize. If a hypothesis is just a guess, what risk is there in hypothesizing, especially if you've never been right very much anyway? Slow learners often seem eager to hypothesize. They have been doing it all along anyway, and they have little to lose and everything to gain by so doing.

There is another point related to this concern. Bright students often appear to perform better in the entire inquiry process than do slow learners. One reason for this may be the staying power and motivation that the academically oriented students bring to a social studies class. These students are able to sustain a line of inquiry to a conclusion even when the inquiry seems irrelevant. While slow students freely hypothesize, they do not usually demonstrate the will or desire or concentration needed to pursue an inquiry to a logical conclusion. Such a difference should not be interpreted to reflect student ability, however. In most cases it reflects instead what we have asked students to inquire about. For those who live in the here and now, as most slow learners do, the causes of the War of 1812 may not exactly turn them on. For students who think they must please the teacher to get the *A* they need to get into college, having to identify the causes of any war will probably be enough to spark compliance.

While bright students may need encouragement to hypothesize, slower students generally need guidance in carrying a line of inquiry to a conclusion. But both can engage in inquiry.

3. *Inquiry teaching is a fake. It is too teacher-directed and not true inquiry.*

A teacher may dominate any learning situation depending on the learning objectives. But in no case will an effective inquiry teacher be as dominant and directive as a teacher in a conventional expository classroom.

The charge that inquiry is a contrived learning experience that leads students to a predetermined goal applies to textbook teaching better than it does to inquiry teaching. In textbook teaching, the teacher requires students to learn specific statements from a specific source. The teacher insists that each student memorize the assertions presented in the text. Inquiry teaching, however, rejects this indoctrinative approach. Instead, inquiry teaching strives to have students *reach their own conclusions on their own* based on the quality of their evidence and reasoning. Whereas the objective in textbook teaching may well be for a student to know that slavery was a cause of the Civil War, objectives for a similar inquiry unit might be to know a concept of multiple causation and any three important causes of the Civil War. The difference between these approaches is immense.

True inquiry involves independent problem-solving. But true inquiry cannot happen until students know how to inquire. Inquiry teaching attempts to teach students how to engage in inquiry while they simultaneously attempt to achieve other substantive objectives. This requires considerable teacher guidance at first until the students have the skills necessary to go it alone. Furthermore, where teachers themselves are new at inquiry teaching and trying to master its techniques, their role may also be more prominent than later on. However, as teachers and students become more experienced in inquiry, the teacher may gradually slip into the background until students, perhaps as juniors and seniors or towards the end of a course, go off on their own to engage in independent inquiry.

Guided inquiry is no fake. It is a more honest way of teaching than any other approach because it acknowledges the flaws of using a single text as a source of knowledge, a single individual as an arbiter of truth, and a single product as the ultimate goal of learning.

4. *Most students don't know enough to inquire.*

Those who hold this belief assume that before one can inquire one must "know the facts." They assume further that fact learning and inquiry cannot occur simultaneously; in actuality both can and usually do occur at the same time.

It is certainly true that the wider and richer the experience one has and the more information or knowledge one possesses, the more fruitful will be an inquiry into which the person might engage. Yet to delay inquiry until such a storehouse of information has been created ignores the fact that one can accumulate experience by inquiring; indeed, inquiring itself requires students to collect information with which to test hypotheses. Students can learn information as they engage in inquiry learning.

Inquiry teaching and fact learning can go hand in hand. Inquiry cannot occur in a vacuum; one must have some information to inquire about, into, or with. And conversely, learning information to the point of understanding requires more than passive absorption of factual information; it requires processing these facts through thinking into new patterns, insights, and generalizations.

Moreover, any effort to have students learn the facts prior to inquiry assumes that these facts are indeed accurate, that they represent objective reality and are undisputed. It ignores the obvious situation that someone for some reason selected some data for people to learn as if it were true. Inquiry teaching challenges the assumption of the validity of all factual information as given—whether statements of specific facts or generalizations—and puts it to the test of analysis just as it does the interpretations derived from those facts. Inquiry teaching also challenges a further assumption implicit in this reservation: that someone other than the student should determine the validity and appropriateness of the facts to be learned. Such an assumption, if carried out in practice, leads to exposition rather than inquiry; for by the very act of "giving" students only certain factual background, teachers close students from inquiry rather than open them to it, indoctrinating rather than educating them.

CONCLUSION

Inquiry teaching involves student thinking, manipulating, and processing information in order to give it tested meaning. Inquiry teaching certainly is not the only type of instructional strategy that can be used in a classroom. But this teaching strategy more than any other has the potential to involve students deeply in meaningful learning, to excite and encourage active student participation in the classroom, and to help students develop the deeper understandings that characterize knowing. Indeed, inquiry teaching proves most useful where the main objective is conceptual—where the primary purposes are to develop or refine a concept or generalization, to develop a thinking skill, or to analyze or clarify an attitude or value.

To accomplish such goals, some of us may need to develop new views of teaching and learning. We need to view learning as an active endeavor; the teacher as a facilitator rather than as a teller; students as capable, vital, inquisitive individuals; the teaching-learning process as a cooperative student-teacher inquiry into the unknown; and the goals of education as multifaceted rather than as mere fact accumulation. Once educators and students replace the traditional, narrow conception of teaching as giving and of learning as receiving, once we give credit to students for having some interests, concerns, and talents for learning, inquiry teaching can become a reality in social studies classrooms.

Inquiry teaching is not easy, but neither is it mysterious or impossible. It is not an inspirational, "fly-by-the-seat-of-your-pants" teaching approach, either. Rather, inquiry teaching is a very precise way of teaching. With continued practice, evaluation, and reflection this strategy can be used in any social studies classroom where development of student thinking and knowledge are major learning and teaching goals. It is exciting for teacher and student alike. It is productive, and it is fun.

notes

1. See, for example, Francis P. Hunkins, *Involving Students in Questioning* (Boston: Allyn and Bacon, 1976), pp. 100–229.
2. Norman Johnson, "The Problem As I See It," *Carnegie Review*, 18 (February 1969), p. 11.
3. Barry K. Beyer, "What's the Matter with Inquiry Teaching?" in *The Social Studies Journal* (Fall 1973), II:3, pp. 64–71.

Epilogue: what next?

He that cannot reason is a fool
He that will not a bigot
He that dare not a slave[1]

Andrew Carnegie was so impressed when he came across the above quotation that he had it inscribed on a wall of his library, adopting it as a guide for his career. Social studies teachers might well do the same—especially those teachers who seek to help students master the skills of critical thinking. For *critical thinking* means reasoning in action. And teaching students how to reason and to be willing to reason certainly constitute two of the most important goals of social studies teaching today. Using a strategy of inquiry teaching enables teachers to accomplish these challenging goals.

Inquiry teaching is without doubt one of the most stimulating and productive strategies we can use in the social studies classroom. There *is* considerably more to it than first meets the eye. Inquiry teaching is based on sound learning theory. Its strength lies in the fact that inquiry teaching makes learning a cooperative student-teacher quest for knowledge rather than a mere search for right answers. It can and does facilitate, seemingly better than any other type of teaching strategy, learning at all levels of knowledge while it simultaneously helps to develop thinking skills and to clarify values, attitudes, and feelings. Inquiry teaching, furthermore, is a way of teaching students how to learn on their own using the processes of rational thinking. As a strategy for teaching, inquiry teaching appears to have remarkable potential for facilitating significant learning in social studies classrooms at virtually all grade levels.

In the preceding pages we have described a concept of inquiry and a teaching strategy built on this concept. We have developed the dimensions of this strategy slowly. We have also illustrated the various elements of the strategy and demonstrated some ways this strategy may be used at various grade levels to accomplish the wide variety of goals commonly sought in social studies classrooms. Obviously, much more could be written about inquiry teaching. However, the ideas offered here present and exemplify the major aspects of this strategy as well as its significant implications. It has been our intent to explore both the potentials and the limitations of this teaching strategy. By so doing we hope to have stimulated your interest in trying this strategy and to have provided the knowledge that will enable you to use it in your own classroom.

Some Suggestions for Becoming Familiar with Inquiry Teaching

It is extremely difficult to read about someone else's perception of inquiry teaching (or any teaching strategy for that matter) and come away with a command of this strategy. To become proficient at inquiry teaching requires more than just reading about it. Inquiry teaching is not a strategy that can be picked up overnight and used immediately with perfect success. Its mastery requires some time and practice. If you wish to find out more about this teaching strategy and become adept at using it in your classroom, perhaps some of the following suggestions may be useful.

1. Although it has not been the intent in these pages to present a rationale for using inquiry teaching in the social studies classroom, such a rationale has been implicit. A number of excellent books make this rationale explicit. All are extremely well written, provocative, and stimulating. Before moving to initiate or improve inquiry teaching in your present or future classroom, you should read and discuss with your colleagues the following books:

Kellum, David. *The Social Studies—Myths and Realities.* New York: Sheed and Ward, 1969.

> This book is still one of the most exciting, challenging, and provocative books on social studies teaching in print. Kellum deals with numerous traditional aspects of teaching, challenging most of them and raising significant and relevant questions about each. Reflection on his ideas on history, motivation, testing, curriculum, teaching styles, and minority groups will provide a fine basis for a personal rationale for inquiry teaching in social studies.

Postman, Neil, and Weingartner, Charles. *Teaching as a Subversive Activity.* New York: The Delacorte Press, 1969.

> This book remains a classic statement of a rationale for student centered, inquiry teaching. The insights to be gained from these authors about the use (and misuse) of language, the nature of meaning-making, relevant knowledge, motivation, and the like are invaluable for anyone planning to engage in inquiry teaching in social studies at *any* grade level.

Wehlage, Gary, and Anderson, Eugene M. *Social Studies Curriculum in Perspective: A Conceptual Analysis.* Englewood Cliffs: Prentice-Hall, Inc., 1972.

> In this book the authors analyze the basic elements of the social studies curriculum including concepts, generalizations, and explanations. They emphasize the rational nature of curriculum and the opportunities it offers to investigate human motives and values. Their ideas and insights about these topics provide a sound basis for the use of inquiry in the social studies.

2. Examine and analyze with others of like mind some of the many monographs on inquiry teaching and learning, including the following:

Hunt, Maurice, and Metcalf, Lawrence. *Teaching High School Social Studies.* 2nd ed. New York: Harper & Row, Publishers, 1968.

> A classic social studies "methods" text on teaching for reflective thinking, this book devotes pages 65–274 to the teaching of concepts, generalizations, and value analysis. Attention is also given to motivation, discussion, and evaluation techniques.

Massialas, Byron G., and Cox, C. Benjamin. *Inquiry in Social Studies.* New York: McGraw-Hill Book Co., 1966.

> This volume is a scholarly analysis of the nature and use of inquiry in the social studies classroom. It focuses especially on the theoretical rationale for inquiry as well as on participation techniques, evaluation procedures, and materials.

3. Analyze—and/or try in your classroom—some sample, ready-made inquiry-teaching lessons:

Association of American Geographers and the American Sociological Association, *Experiences in Inquiry: HSGP and SRSS.* Boston: Allyn and Bacon, Inc., 1974.

> This volume contains instructors' guides and student materials for 12 model inquiry activities from the High School Geography Project and the Sociological Resources for the Social Studies project, two major innovative curriculum projects of the past decade. The detailed instructor guides provide excellent insights into the use of inquiry teaching. An excellent section on evaluation concludes this volume.

Kownslar, Allan O., ed. *Teaching American History: The Quest for Relevancy.* Washington: The National Council for the Social Studies, 1974.

> The use of inquiry in American history serves as the focus for this 44th yearbook of the NCSS. Essays by social studies teachers, researchers, and educators complement practical sample lessons designed to illustrate the various ways inquiry can be used to help students develop concepts, build a sense of empathy, and deal with stereotypes. Techniques for relating history to current or future social issues are also included.

Ryan, Frank L. *Exemplars for the New Social Studies: Instructing in the Elementary School.* Englewood Cliffs: Prentice-Hall, Inc., 1971.

> Ryan illustrates a variety of approaches for teaching elementary school social studies with lessons from various social studies curriculum projects. The book contains chapters on inquiry strategies, decision-making, questioning, simulation, evaluation, and other techniques useful in inquiry teaching. Sample lessons can be taught in the reader's classroom.

4. Study carefully some books on the nature of thinking skills and some ways to elicit and refine these skills and to implement inquiry in the social studies classroom:

Dana G. Kurfman, ed. *Developing Decision-Making Skills.* 47th Yearbook. Washington: National Council for the Social Studies, 1977.

The authors of the chapters in this volume describe the nature of basic skills related to decision-making and give suggestions for teaching these skills in social studies. Especially useful are chapters on the process of decision-making, thinking skills, questioning, map and graph reading, reading skills, and evaluation techniques.

Fair, Jean, and Shaftel, Fannie R., eds. *Effective Thinking in the Social Studies.* 37th Yearbook. Washington: National Council for the Social Studies, 1967.

The most relevant segments of this volume are the chapters by Charlotte Crabtree on reflective thinking, Millard Clements on inquiry as related to various disciplines, and Hilda Taba on thinking. Dana Kurfman's chapter on evaluating thinking is excellent.

Raths, Louis, et al. *Teaching for Thinking: Theory and Application.* Columbus, Ohio: Charles E. Merrill, 1967.

This book describes a theory of instruction for teaching children how to think. It also provides numerous examples of lessons and learning experiences that teachers may use to help students learn how to observe, summarize, compare, classify, and interpret data.

Sanders, Norris. *Classroom Questions: What Kinds?* New York: Harper & Row, Publishers, 1966.

This is an outline of questions organized according to types that may be used to elicit student thinking—translating data, interpreting data, analysis, synthesis, and evaluation. Reference to this volume will prove quite useful in designing inquiry-teaching lessons and evaluative devices.

5. Read again some books that describe inquiry teaching and various ways to organize and conduct this teaching strategy to get additional insights into ways of using this strategy:

Gilliom, Eugene. *Practical Methods for the Social Studies.* Belmont, Cal.: Wadsworth Publishing Company, 1977.

A number of authors combine to present in this book a variety of methods for implementing inquiry in the social studies classroom. The case study approach, values inquiry, and the use of simulations, quantitative data, and community studies are presented in detail. The book also includes chapters on media and other resources and on test construction and evaluation.

Massialas, Byron G.; Sprague, Nancy F., and Hurst, Joseph B. *Social Issues Through Inquiry.* Englewood Cliffs: Prentice-Hall, Inc., 1975.

This book offers practical guidelines for applying an inquiry strategy to the study of social problems and issues in social studies. It describes specific applications of this strategy to a variety of current issues and also relates techniques of and research on classroom observation to the use of this strategy. The authors describe in detail methods for classroom analysis of inquiry teaching.

6. Reading and analyzing, however, are not sufficient preparation for successful inquiry teaching. It must be practiced too. One may begin by teaching lessons and using materials already designed for inquiry teaching. A number of these sample lessons may be found in the books listed under number 3 above. The lesson you choose may be as long or short as you wish to make it.

And you can teach it several times to a different class each time in order to get the bugs out. Ideally, you should make a video tape of your class as the students engage in this lesson and in all experimental lessons that you teach. You can then replay the tape to analyze what occurred. If this is not possible, perhaps you could ask several colleagues to observe your class and to discuss their impressions with you afterward. Better yet, at the conclusion of the lesson you might ask the students to describe their perceptions of what was going on, of what you did, and of what they were doing or supposed to be doing. This type of feedback will be most useful in mastering inquiry teaching.

7. Next, you can design some inquiry lessons of your own using existing materials. You will have to devise inquiry lesson plans on your own by applying what you have learned from your study of this book. You can use the same procedure as suggested in Chapter 13 to secure feedback on the way you implement these lessons.

8. At this point, you should try your hand at designing some inquiry teaching/ learning experiences and materials of your own. First, you should design some simple one, two, or three-day inquiry lessons involving content you know very well. If possible, these should be developed in cooperation with some colleagues, for several heads are immeasurably better than one in creating new teaching approaches. These lessons should then be analyzed by the group and revised until a workable plan emerges.

9. Finally, you must teach your inquiry lessons, perhaps first to a group of your fellow teachers and then to one of your own classes. Each effort should be examined critically by you, your colleagues, and the students. If several teachers can teach the same lesson and each can observe the others doing so, insights of even greater value may be developed. As a result, when you finally undertake inquiry teaching as an instructional strategy in your classroom, you will have every chance of meeting with success.

Careful preparation and practice are quite essential to successful and satisfying inquiry teaching. Because this type of strategy casts both student and teacher in new roles, it can be frustrating and perhaps discouraging at first. If students have never had to think for themselves or to ask questions and not get the answers, then inquiry teaching will be most difficult for them the first few weeks. If you are inexperienced in inquiry teaching—have neither studied nor practiced it—you too may become quickly disillusioned. Such reactions are to be expected. The change to inquiry teaching normally takes time. Perhaps a typical teacher reaction to initiating inquiry teaching best points up this type of situation:

A pox on . . . inquiry . . . teaching. I am working like a dog in an attempt to espouse (this method) and am not really sure that the current results are worth the effort. I am considering going back to my old techniques of having three films and two reprimands each week. It saves on planning time.

Seriously, I am getting some commendable results with some outstandingly "stupid" children. The only problem is finding the time to prepare for my lessons and making them come off the way they should. But it's getting better rapidly.

Some Suggestions for Introducing Inquiry Teaching

The way in which inquiry teaching is introduced into a classroom has a great deal to do with its ultimate success or failure. As noted above, part of this introduction involves adequate preparation and preplanning on the part of the teacher. But part also requires the creation and maintenance of a proper—informal, risking, trusting—classroom climate. Another part of this introduction requires that the students know what is happening and what the "rules" of this type of teaching are.

Creating a classroom climate supportive of inquiry teaching involves securing administrative support as well as developing an informal classroom atmosphere conducive to risk-taking and open exchange. For starters,

1. Develop a defensible rationale for using inquiry, one drawn from these pages and the books cited here.
2. Be sure your administrators and supervisors understand and support your efforts.
3. Plan your initial efforts with several colleagues and review with them what you are doing in your classroom.

Furthermore, students must understand the "rules" and procedures upon which effective inquiry learning and teaching are based. They must come to realize that *learning* in this context does not mean trying to second-guess the teacher, nor does it involve "coming up with what the teacher wants." Students must also be aware of the new role an inquiry teacher assumes—that of facilitator and resource rather than teller and source. To help students accommodate easily to the use of inquiry teaching, you might

1. Avoid giving answers; allow, indeed, have students use their texts and other materials to justify *their* answers.
2. Allow time for students to think before responding; don't fire a barrage of questions at them.
3. Focus on questions calling for evidence, relationships, synthesis, and evaluation instead of questions that call merely for giving facts. Encourage student questions.
4. Have the students engage in paired or group activities so they get used to working with each other in pursuit of common goals.

The above suggestions can be implemented slowly and easily in the context of a conventional approach or as one introduces various inquiry-related lessons or learning activities. For example, one might ease students into inquiry teaching and learning by following these steps:

1. Start by using short nonthreatening values clarification activities that require small group interaction and some cognitive risk-taking; use focus grouping techniques to discuss content-related matters, for example. This will help break the ice and create a relaxed, risking classroom climate.
2. Teach the Kiev lesson or a similar inquiry lesson, and then discuss what you did and what the students did and why.
3. Discuss the story *It Was Obvious* so students can identify the basic steps of inquiry.
4. Teach another lesson using your text(s) as the data source and again have the students reflect on the procedures and steps used, comparing these to the Kiev lesson and to the story.
5. Have students help you identify a problem in the next (text) assignment and design an inquiry procedure for dealing with this problem. Then teach this lesson and again reflect on the basic steps used.
6. Finally, intermix subsequent inquiry lessons with more conventional approaches more familiar to students. These inquiry lessons can be as frequent or irregular as you wish.

You may select other ways to initiate inquiry teaching. The point is, start small, and don't overdo the process. Once students learn that openness is valued, that rightness depends on evidence (not authority), and that they in fact really do have something to say, it proves easier for them to use this strategy. Following the steps outlined above, or a similar procedure, will help you make the transition to or introduction of an inquiry teaching strategy in your classroom that much easier—and thus potentially that much more productive.

Inquiry teaching may seem difficult, especially at first. But it is by no means impossible. Inquiry teaching can be precisely organized and executed. When mastered, it is fun and, indeed, worthwhile. No other teaching strategy may be used for as wide a range of objectives as inquiry teaching. This teaching strategy means teaching for conceptual objectives, involving students actively in the learning process, using data as a vehicle instead of merely as an end in itself, and making the classroom an arena for thinking. It seems by far the most exciting and challenging type of teaching available for use in social studies classrooms today. But inquiry teaching requires some study and practice in order to be used successfully. This volume may be a start. The rest is up to you!

notes

1. Quoted by Harold Livesay, *Andrew Carnegie and the Rise of Big Business* (Boston: Little, Brown and Company, 1975), p. 74.

indices

AUTHOR INDEX

398

SUBJECT INDEX

PHOTO AND ART CREDITS

pages	3–4	#1–4, 6, 8 from M.K. Karger, *Ancient Kiev* (Leningrad, 1958), Volume I, Appendix; #5 after an original drawing, by Grant Pedigo.
	11–12	from Ian Grey, *History of Russia* (New York: American Heritage Publishing Company, Inc., 1970).
	147–148, and 154	from *Rise of the American Nation*, Vol. I, by Lewis Paul Todd and Merle Curti, copyright © 1977 by Harcourt Brace Jovanovich.
	156	from The Historical Society of Pennsylvania.
	157	(top) from National Gallery of Art, Washington, D.C.; (bottom) from The Metropolitan Museum of Art, New York.
	201–202	#1 Barry K. Beyer; #2 Anthony Kirk-Greene; #3 Robert R. Griswold; #4 David Hamilton.
	223–224	E. Perry Hicks and Barry K. Beyer, *United States Inquiry Maps* (Pleasantville, N.Y.: Sunburst Communications, Inc., 1973).
	231	#1 after an original drawing, by Grant Pedigo. #2 from M.K. Karger, *Ancient Kiev* (Leningrad, 1958), Volume I, Appendix.